A Southern African Guide to World Religions

A Southern African Guide to ***WORLD RELIGIONS***

edited by
JOHN DE GRUCHY & MARTIN PROZESKY

DAVID PHILIP: Cape Town

First published 1991 by David Philip Publishers (Pty) Ltd, 208 Werdmuller Centre, Claremont 7700, South Africa

ISBN 0 86486 172 9

Printed by Creda Press, Solan Road, Cape Town

Contents

List of Contributors

David Chidester is an Associate Professor in the Department of Religious Studies at the University of Cape Town.

John de Gruchy is Professor of Christian Studies and Head of the Department of Religious Studies at the University of Cape Town.

Jocelyn Hellig is a Senior Lecturer in the Department of Religious Studies at the University of the Witwatersrand, Johannesburg.

Jan Hofmeyr lectures in the Department of Religious Studies at the University of Cape Town.

Patrick Maxwell is a Senior Lecturer in the Department of Religious Studies at the University of Natal, Pietermaritzburg.

Ebrahim Moosa lectures in the Department of Religious Studies at the University of Cape Town.

Thillayvel Naidoo is a Senior Lecturer in the Department of Science of Religion, University of Durban-Westville.

Ronald Nicolson is a Senior Lecturer in the Department of Religious Studies at the University of Natal, Pietermaritzburg.

Martin Prozesky is Professor and currently Head of the Department of Religious Studies at the University of Natal, Pietermaritzburg.

Acknowledgements

The editors wish to thank the authors who kindly agreed to contribute their expertise to the creation of this book. In addition, special thanks are due to Patrick Maxwell for invaluable assistance with the technical aspects of the word-processing involved, to Maureen Yardley of the Department of Religious Studies at the University of Natal in Pietermaritzburg, for her help in various connections while the work of editing was being done, and to Mrs H. Margeot of the Department of Geography at the same university for preparing the maps that appear in this book.

1

Introduction

MARTIN PROZESKY

Just as the modern period has made it possible for us to see the whole earth from space for the first time, so too for twentieth century humanity it has at last become possible to form a global picture of religion, if not in every detail, then at least in essentials. We now know, for example, that signs of a spiritual dimension in human existence go back to very ancient times, at or near the birth of the human species, and for many thousands of years religion of one kind or another has been practised in all known regions of our planet. We also know that while the world today contains many vigorous, living faiths with histories going back thousands of years, there are other religions which once thrived but are now extinct, for example the native religions of Central and South America. And in our contemporary world where powerful secular forces challenge the various religions, five out of six people reportedly continue to regard themselves as religious in some sense. (See Appendix for further details.)

But throughout this immensely long history – unlike today – people have existed largely in isolation from other cultures, and for most of the time the various human communities, separated by distance, language, geography and culture, have known little or nothing of the faiths of their fellow humans. In other words, ours has been a religious planet for virtually its entire human history, but at the same time it has been a planet unaware of its own global religious heritage.

Today the position is different. Very few societies remain without a knowledge of at least some other cultures, and in some regions a richly plural culture has emerged, with people of different world-views and life-styles living in close contact with one another. This new situation has greatly helped religious studies scholars, historians and social scientists to encounter and study religion throughout the earth, so that we at last have a substantially complete picture of our spiritual heritage.

Southern Africa occupies a very special place in the context of the world's religions because of its exceptionally rich diversity of faiths and its unique struggle to find a formula for a just, peaceful and sustainable society for all its people. Mecca, Rome, Benares and Jerusalem – historic centres of some of the great faiths of the world – are geographically thousands of kilometres apart but in southern Africa, especially in the main population centres, they exist side by side. Yet despite that physical closeness, the members of the various religions found in this region remain mostly unaware of the faiths that inspire and enrich the lives of their fellow citizens. The apartheid state has not only tried to segregate people racially; it has also helped to prevent Muslims, Jews, Christians, Hindus and African Traditionalists, besides people of other religions, from knowing and appreciating one another's deepest beliefs.

Thus we see that southern Africa is religiously a microcosm of the whole world, having long been home to a diversity of faiths but with little mutual contact and understanding among members of those faiths. Now that this region and, in a broadly similar way, the whole earth are moving towards a new future, it is essential that such ignorance should give way to knowledge and understanding. The present book has been compiled to help meet that need, especially on the part of students but also for other readers. Within its pages readers will find introductory chapters covering all the main religious traditions of the earth, chapters suitable for people with no previous knowledge of the subject except perhaps in connection with whatever faith they may themselves profess. For southern African readers the book is thus at one and the same time an introduction to the world's religious heritage and a guide to the faith of fellow believers in the same region at a crucial period of social change when foundations are being laid for a new kind of future.

There are many fine books on the subject of the world's main religions, but none of them approaches the subject with the needs of southern African readers paramount while at the same time using the expert knowledge of a team of authors from this region who themselves hold widely differing beliefs within a shared respect for and awareness of the beliefs of others. Thus the book, in its own unique way, is an example of respectful co-operation in a country and a world of spiritual, cultural and philosophical diversity.

CONCERNING CONTENTS

The chapters that follow take readers on a journey of discovery through the world's main spiritual landscapes. The journey begins with primal religions – the religions of traditional, tribal societies, some of which existed only in prehistoric times while others have endured till our own time and continue to exert a significant influence in parts of the world. Thereafter we turn to the religions of the ancient civilisations that emerged from about 5 000 years ago. This sets the scene for the chapters that deal with the spiritual traditions that have arisen since those days and now have the greatest following, beginning with the religions of India. Our global journey then moves onward from India, tracing the story of Buddhism and of Chinese religion, before turning westward to the three Abrahamic faiths. These are the religions that claim spiritual descent from the patriarch Abraham, namely Judaism, Christianity and Islam. In all of these chapters the authors outline the history of the religions in question till modern times and explain the main beliefs and practices of their members.

Within the limits of an introductory book it is of course impossible to cover everything, so we have selected the main religions world-wide which have a sizeable southern African following or are specially relevant here, together with the ancient religions because of their inherent interest and great influence on subsequent developments. Inevitably this has meant that some numerically smaller religions, like Shinto in Japan and the faith of the Parsees, could not be included, but this does not detract from the global picture presented in these pages because all the main religions are covered. What is not told in this book is the story of how these faiths came to be in southern Africa, and neither do we include here the traditional African religions of the area. To have done so would unduly enlarge the book. That material – fascinating and important in its own right – is therefore reserved for a second volume.

THE METHOD FOLLOWED

The writing of this book has been governed by a policy of accuracy, clarity and fairness, so that each religion is described in a way which reflects as faithfully as possible its historical development and present character. The aim is to provide reliable information for those who are unfamiliar with most or even all religions, in a way which does justice to the experience of believers themselves within each tradition. In technical terms, this approach is known as the 'phenomenological method'. It involves two main strategies. Firstly, the enquirers set aside or suspend their personal judgements in order to be able to appreciate the subject on its own terms. This suspension of personal convictions and judgements is called 'bracketing' or *epochē*, from a Greek word of the same meaning. Secondly, the enquirers then attempt to achieve as much empathy with the subject as possible, trying to develop a feeling for the religion in question that is as close as possible to the experience of those who are members of that religion. It follows that there is no attempt in this book to promote any of the religions at the expense of others, or to advocate anything other than a sensitive understanding of them all. The advocacy of religion on one hand and criticism of it on the other are important, complex matters, but they are not the concern of this book.

Within this shared policy, the individual authors have been free to present their subject matter as they deem best, though all of them cover the historical development of the religions in question as well as describing central beliefs and practices. There is thus both a basic uniformity of approach and scope for variation in the chapters that follow. Where appropriate, outline maps, glossaries and other informative devices have been included, and each chapter ends with suggestions for further reading.

As a further result of our desire to approach religion in a way that is fair to them all, this book adopts the scholarly practice of dividing history into two great periods, calling them the period 'Before the Common Era' (BCE) and the 'Common Era' (CE) respectively. The dates accompanying these expressions are the same as those in ordinary use associated with the abbreviations BC and AD. By way of illustration, we say that the exile of the Jews to Babylonia happened in the sixth century BCE, not the sixth century BC, or that Islam arose in the seventh century CE, not the seventh century AD.

WHAT IS 'RELIGION'?

The words 'religion', 'faith' and 'spiritual tradition' are used interchangeably in various parts of the book (including this introduction). Obviously they refer to the movements described in the pages that follow, movements existing all around us as important social and personal realities. But what do those words *mean*? What are scholars in the field of religious studies looking for when they investigate the *religious* heritage of humanity? Much as we might want a neat, agreed definition of this phenomenon, the fact is that none exists. Our religions are immensely rich, varied and complex, and therefore continue to frustrate all attempts to define them satisfactorily. But at the same time we do have some indicators to help the person embarking on a journey of discovery through the spiritual landscapes of planet earth. We also have some helpful suggestions from leading scholars about the typical patterns and structures evident in most or even all religions. These give the enquirer basic models of the religious life and are useful so long as we always remember that religion is a complex, living reality in the world and in people's lives, not a set of working definitions and models which we might use to help us understand important aspects of our subject. With this proviso in mind we can turn now to review some influential ideas about the nature of religion.

A working distinction

A useful point to begin such a review is the distinction between the experiences of religious *people* on one hand and the supposed *object* (or objects) of those experiences on the other. Consider, for example, a group of worshippers at prayer. If we focus on them as *subjects* of religious experience, we can imagine the thoughts and feelings they might be undergoing, such as a sense of their needs and vulnerabilities. We can also notice the bodily position adopted during their prayers, which might be kneeling or standing or with head bowed. If their prayers are said aloud, we could hear the kind of language being used and the tone adopted. Some of these details can be observed but others, being the thoughts and feelings of the individual worshipper, only become accessible to other people when spoken about or written, and then only indirectly. But whether these details form part of an inner world of personal experience or are outwardly observable, all of them belong to what is sometimes called *homo religiosus*, to individual people as the subjects of religion, revealing something of the humanness that comes to expression in the religious life.

This human aspect of religion may be all there is, if the various naturalistic theories of religion are correct. But the first task of the student of religion is not to take sides against the believer by accepting such theories, nor to do the opposite and dismiss those theories from further consideration. The first task is to notice carefully the convictions held by the world's religious believers themselves, and these invariably amount to the belief that there exists independently of the believer some kind of religious reality, such as a personal god, the spirits of our departed ancestors or an all-encompassing invisible power of a non-physical kind, and that our greatest good depends on a proper relationship or favourable contact with those independent religious entities. Returning to our example of the group of people at prayer, and assuming that their prayers are said aloud in a language we understand, we soon discover that those prayers are being addressed to somebody or something which the worshippers in question believe exists quite independently of themselves. For a majority of religious people in regions like southern Africa, this object or focus of faith is held to be one or more spiritual beings, but in the religious world as a whole this is by no means always the case, as will briefly be explained near the end of this introductory chapter.

Whether the spiritual beings or powers believed in by religious people really do exist in their own right, as believers themselves are convinced, or whether they are merely unconscious projections of the human mind (as naturalistic theories suggest), is a vital question in its own right. It does not, however, fall within the scope of the phenomenological history of religion as presented in this book, whose task is to report the rise and development of religious conviction, including the central conviction that there is much more to religion than just the believing subject. Without prejudging anything we can thus draw an initial distinction between the human subjects of religion on one hand, and the presumed objects of their faith on the other – bracketing for the purposes of our enquiries any verdict about the soundness or otherwise of that faith, and bearing in mind always that *as historians* we do not have access to the spiritual beings or powers spoken of by believers, if such spiritual entities indeed exist. What we do have is the testimony of believers telling us about the things they believe they encounter in the course of their religious experiences.

Homo religiosus

With this distinction in mind we can move next to some influential views about the human characteristics of religion, starting with a set of proposed definitions which tries to identify the essence or core of humanity's religious experience. Frederick Streng, for example, suggests that the various religions can be understood as *processes of fundamental human transformation* from some or other deeply undesirable state of affairs to something vastly better. Being spared the wrath of a god or having our sins forgiven are well-known examples. Similar to this is the observation by scholars like John Hick that many religions operate as *structures of deliverance* which free or save people from whatever most deeply shackles and afflicts them. The present author reached a similar conclusion after investigating the nature of religion, portraying the various faiths jointly as structures offering people the greatest and most fundamental well-being.

It is important to notice here the connection between religion and our deepest or most serious problems, because this brings us to a third suggestion about the human side of religion, namely that it involves matters which affect us more profoundly and seriously than anything else, matters which are fundamental to our existence. The theologian Paul Tillich captured this insight by saying that the religious life is about *ultimate concern* – in other words, about that which concerns us most profoundly. The single word which has, however, been most widely used in the religions themselves to name the central human quality of the religious life is the word *faith*. In recent times the North American scholar Wilfred Cantwell Smith, after examining all the great spiritual traditions, has argued that personal faith is a universal human reality present in all those traditions as their core. As for the nature of faith, Smith regards it as an orientation of the self towards something that transcends the self.

A MODERN DEFINITION OF FAITH

Faith 'is an orientation of the personality, to oneself, to one's neighbour, to the universe; a total response; a way of seeing whatever one sees and of handling whatever one handles; a capacity to live at a more than mundane level; to see, to feel, to act in terms of, a transcendent dimension'.

'Faith, then, is a quality of human living. At its best it has taken the form of serenity and courage and loyalty and service: a quiet confidence and joy which enable one to feel at home in the universe, and to find meaning in the world and in one's own life, a meaning that is profound and ultimate, and is stable no matter what may happen to oneself at the level of immediate event.'

Faith 'is a planetary human characteristic. . . . it involves [people's] capacity to perceive, to symbolize, and to live loyally and richly in terms of, a transcendent dimension. . . . '

(From Wilfred Cantwell Smith, *Faith and Belief*, pp.12, 140f)

According to Smith, what we think of as religion has a second component besides the core element of faith. Smith calls this second component the 'cumulative tradition' which we find in all religions, namely their complex sets of beliefs, practices and institutions. In this respect the religions differ greatly from one another, and also undergo gradual change themselves in the course of their histories.

The preceding paragraphs have briefly introduced some influential modern interpretations of the supposedly essential human element in the religious life. A second approach to the same aspect of religion (namely the human characteristics involved) adopts a different tactic by offering us an analysis of the typical components of the religious life. One such is Joachim Wach's distinction between three basic ways in which the religions of the world express themselves, which he calls the *theoretical* aspect (for example, doctrines and beliefs), the *practical* (comprising all the things believers do in connection with their faith, like worshipping or acting according to religious rules of conduct), and the *sociological* aspect, which covers people's membership of and roles within the various forms of religious association, like belonging to a synagogue or leading a meditation group.

It is not difficult to connect these three aspects of religion with certain basic aspects of our make-up as human beings, namely our ability to think and speak; our ability to act; and our need to belong to certain social groups in order to thrive as persons. Thus Wach's model of religion is another way of highlighting the human side of our subject.

Using the same analytic approach, Ninian Smart has proposed that religion involves seven typical 'dimensions'. These dimensions are given different content and emphasis in the various religions, but most or all of them can be discerned in any religious movement. His is therefore a more complex but also a more precise model of the structure of religion, and can to some extent be seen as a refinement of Wach's model.

SMART'S 7-DIMENSIONAL MODEL OF RELIGION

1. *Practical and ritual* – covering activities like prayer, worship and meditation.
2. *Experiential and emotional* – which relates to the personal feelings and states of mind of believers.
3. *Narrative or mythic* – meaning the powerful, sacred stories told in all religions, like stories about the creation of the universe by one or more gods.
4. *Doctrinal and philosophical* – which refers to the more technical, abstract kinds of language used by religious thinkers in many traditions.
5. *Ethical and legal* – covering the moral codes and laws taught by all religions.
6. *Social and institutional* – this dimension relates to the tendency in all religions to create groups, structures and roles for members.
7. *Material* – meaning all the tangible, physical expressions of religion, like temples, robes, ritual equipment and artistic creations.

If we reflect for a moment on the analysis of religion offered by Wach and Smart we will notice that their models make no reference to the spiritual powers and beings so real to believers. This is not because these scholars deny that there are such entities, but because their models deal with the human side of religion. However – as we have already noticed – the fact is that believers themselves are convinced that there is much more to religion than just its human side, rich and fascinating though that is in its own right in the eyes of many people. Accordingly, there are other experts who have tried to capture the essence of religion by referring to that other aspect of the phenomenon, namely the objects towards which religious faith is directed according to the perceptions of believers themselves. We turn now to a brief review of this second main way of approaching the study of religion.

The objects of religious belief

Here too there are a number of influential proposals. One of them, made by various scholars including Wilfred Cantwell Smith, notes that all religions apparently teach their members that independently of all else there exist certain invisible powers or beings which are significantly greater than anything else. Another way to put the point is to say that these invisible powers or beings *transcend* the world of ordinary experience. This gives rise to the view that religions are directed at some or other form of transcendence, for example a creator god or an all-encompassing spiritual power.

Another highly influential proposal is to define religion as a set of varied perceptions of and responses to *the sacred*, a proposal associated with such famous scholars as Emile Durkheim (1858–1917), Rudolf Otto (1869–1937) and Mircea Eliade (1907–86). The terms 'sacred' and 'holy' mean that which is deeply significant and set apart or distinct from ordinary or 'profane' things. Sacredness is linked with religious experiences where there is a profound sense of contact with a mysterious reality evoking (so Rudolf Otto contended) a mixture of awe and fascination. A famous example is the story in the Hebrew Bible of Moses at the burning bush, being told to remove his sandals because the place was 'holy ground' (Exod. 3: 5).

We saw earlier in this discussion that Paul Tillich regarded religious faith as ultimate concern. Corresponding to this personal side of religion, he and many others have asserted, is the *ultimate reality* to which that concern relates. This gives rise to a view of the various religions as different ways of seeing a reality which is held to be ultimate – meaning that it cannot be surpassed in importance, power and worth by anything else.

Within the religions themselves a widely used concept to describe what believers regard as the focus of their faith is the concept of *spirit*, signifying that which is beyond material existence, mysterious, free and powerful, whether thought of as a single, all-powerful deity or in some other way. Perhaps resting on the analogy of the wind and the air, this concept of spirit has long been a central religious symbol, so much so that many of us use expressions like 'the spiritual life' or 'spiritual paths' as synonyms for religion. Thus it has been suggested that religion can usefully be described as any activity which is directed in faith towards some or other form of spiritual reality as the supremely worthy focus of life.

As with the other scholarly suggestions discussed above, namely transcendence, the sacred, or ultimate reality, this one must never obscure for us the fact that it too – as summarised in the previous sentence – is a scholarly tool designed to help us make sense of the vast and varied array of facts coming to us from the religions themselves. Around us in the temples, churches, mosques, synagogues and meditation halls of the world, and in the privacy of personal faith, nobody focuses his or her life on 'Spirit', or on 'Transcendence'. Instead, the focus is very specific – on the individual's ancestral spirits who are addressed by name, on Lord Krishna, the Lord Jesus, or Lord Amidha and so forth. Concepts like the ones we have reviewed are *scholarly* terms which attempt to point out the characteristics shared by all those specific focuses of faith; they are not themselves therefore part of the *religious* vocabulary of the world.

Functions of religion

In their different ways the interpretations of religion summarised above all try to identify what the scholars in question think religion really is. Another approach is to investigate the main *functions or effects of religion* in personal and social life, an approach which has generated some extremely important and much-debated results. This is of special significance in southern Africa because certain influential religious groups assisted the apartheid state by declaring that racial segregation policies were, from their point of view, religiously acceptable, whereas many other believers have strongly opposed those policies.

Functional approaches to religion try to identify the part played by religious conviction and by religious bodies in the lives of individuals and in society at large. Noting the facts that all religions provide their members with a conception of reality (or world-view) and especially with a code of ethics, and that believers typically take their religion very seriously, scholars have drawn attention to the importance of the world's religions in determining and imparting basic *values*. Examples of such values are loyalty and obedience to the authorities, willingness to put other people's needs before one's own, and attitudes towards violence or birth control. Some scholars go a step further than just noting these influences by taking the view that religion is humanity's most important historical source of ethical guidance because of the vast numbers of people affected over very long periods of time, and because of the centrality of the values involved.

Others have been less favourable, while still agreeing that religion significantly influences individuals and societies. An important example is the well-known Marxist contention that religion is 'the opium of the people'. This famous phrase implies that religious belief prevents people from achieving a realistic and accurate consciousness of the way society actually works. Like a pain-killing drug ('opium'), it may give the impression of relieving suffering, but in fact – so the theory goes – does nothing to remedy the economic exploitations that are regarded by Marxists as basic to much human misery. According to this approach, religion – especially in capitalist societies – therefore functions as a way of perpetuating both the alienation between rich and poor and the plight of the working class.

Another functional approach has recently come to the fore. Western female scholars in particular have argued powerfully that much in the religious life functions to the detriment of women by marginalising and excluding them from the centres of spiritual power and creativity. This has resulted in a great deal of work seeking out and trying to overcome what they see as sexist elements in religion, whether in the form of masculinist domination or the exclusion of women's spiritual insights and experience from the shaping of religious traditions. Here too the emphasis is mainly on the actual workings of religion in relation to the struggle for social justice and personal fulfilment, rather than on trying to say what the essential component of religion may be. It has even been proposed that our traditional assumptions about religion are themselves suspect because they arise from mentalities shaped by a narrowly masculinist world-view, rather than from an inclusive outlook in which the experience of women as well as men plays a full part.

As will be clear from the explanations already given about the method of this book, it is not our task in these pages to take sides in these important and controversial, but essentially *critical* interpretations of religion as both enriching and impoverishing. But it is very necessary to be aware of them – and of the challenges they involve – as prominent, modern aspects of the story of religion.

OTHER CLARIFICATIONS

To conclude this introduction, here now are some remaining suggestions to help readers achieve a rich and comprehensive understanding of the world's spiritual heritage. Each religion is unique in its concept of transcendent or sacred reality and in the humanness involved, and no two individual believers are religiously identical, but at the same time many religions reveal certain interesting similarities, however differently they may name them or speak of them in detail, and it is helpful to know about these before beginning our journey into those religions. Many, for example, hold the belief that there exists a multitude of personal, invisible, localised spirits, some of which are present within and impart life and movement to what we would call natural objects – like streams, forests and plants. These spirits are usually held to be more powerful than human beings and to have minds and wills of their own, but are not all-powerful. A belief of this kind appears to have been – and in some cases remains – very widespread indeed, reportedly occurring in most parts of the world though always very specific to the cultures and environments in question. During the nineteenth century the term *animism* came into academic use to signify this kind of religion, and is still often used, though its sometimes disparaging connotations mean that fair-minded enquirers should treat it with considerable care.

The same holds for the next set of religions that requires attention. Investigations also show that there have been cultures which see things rather differently. Instead of (or as well as) a sense of the existence of many individual spiritual beings, these cultures hold the conviction that there exists a pervasive, invisible energy or power which shows itself in all manner of exceptional activity both human and natural, such as a great feat of strength or courage. The term *animatism* has been used to denote this orientation, together with indigenous expressions like the Melanesian term *mana*. Here too care is necessary lest the use of such terms obscures for us the actual nature of the religions concerned and their individual characteristics.

Another set of religions, especially those found in the great civilisations of antiquity, involves belief in a plurality of gods and goddesses – imposing divine beings ruling over specific aspects of nature or human existence like the sea or warfare. Religions with this characteristic have therefore been called *polytheism* by many people, another controversial term which is clarified in chapter 3 of this book. But in today's religions two other ways of perceiving transcendent, sacred reality have become dominant. These are the belief that there is but one personal God who is all-powerful, perfect and infinite; a belief shared by Jews, Christians (though their belief is understood in a Trinitarian manner), Muslims, many Hindus and others. The term *monotheism* is widely used as a covering word for this belief, meaning belief in the reality of one god alone.

On the other hand many believers in religions like Hinduism, Buddhism and in the Chinese religions, as well as some Westerners, hold that the ultimate, transcendent reality is not a personal deity distinct from the universe but a single, all-encompassing, spiritual reality in which all things participate. The words *monism* and *pantheism* have been used as labels for this kind of belief. The former stands for views holding in one way or another that reality is a single, unified whole – in contrast, therefore, with dualistic world-views where reality is said to comprise two distinct orders of existence (for example, the physical and the mental). Pantheism is a narrower term than monism and refers to a set of convictions holding in one way or another that nature and the divine are identical. As with most of the other expressions discussed in this section of the chapter, these two terms do not have universal acceptance and should be used carefully and sensitively.

One of the benefits of such terms, on the other hand, is the way they draw attention to similar characteristics and patterns in the world's religions, so that we are not left with the impression that our various religions are unique to the point of complete difference one from another.

As well as these ways of differentiating between and classifying religions on the basis of what at least some scholars regard as their understanding of transcendent, sacred reality, other typologies (ways of grouping things) are also possible, and in some cases are less controversial. Thus the world's religions can be categorised as extinct or living, or according to their origins. We can thus speak about the religions of India, China and the Near East – three regions which have proved exceptionally fertile in the history of religion. What we have done in this book is to use a combination of geographical and historical factors as the basis of our approach. Thus we have not tried to present the religions as animistic, polytheistic or monotheistic, but have presented them as they have occurred in history and on the earth's surface – an approach which involves much less scholarly interpretation than any other. (See Appendix for tabulations of the main religions.)

Lastly, it may help readers to remember that the religions of the world have arisen in very different cultural contexts and physical environments, and have therefore not all been shaped by the same forces. Two such forces are especially noteworthy, namely the use of writing and the emergence of creative, individual religious leadership. As a result of these developments, the faiths that have developed under their influence tend to have two highly significant features not found elsewhere: sacred books and personal founders. The chapters that follow reveal very clearly the nature and extent of these two characteristics, both by their absence and by their presence. Especially noteworthy at this point is the link between the influence of leading figures in certain religions and the great flowering of religions in the remarkably short period of a century or so before and after 500 BCE. The foundations for some important parts of today's religious life were laid at that time in a surge of spiritual creativity stretching from the China Sea to the Aegean, so that the Swiss philosopher Karl Jaspers (1883–1973) called it the 'axis' of history and spoke of that time of exceptional religious and philosophical creativity as 'the axial age'. But whether we accept his division of human history or not, it remains a valuable reminder of the enormous and long-lasting influence our religions have exerted and continue to exert on human life throughout the earth. Mindful of these points, let us proceed now to the story of those religions.

SELECT BIBLIOGRAPHY

Durkheim, Emile. *The Elementary Forms of the Religious Life*, 2nd ed. London: Allen & Unwin, 1956

Eliade, Mircea. *The Sacred and the Profane: The Nature of Religion*. New York: Harper & Row, 1961

Hick, John. *An Interpretation of Religion*. London: Macmillan, 1989

King, Ursula. *Women and Spirituality: Voices of Protest and Promise*. London: Macmillan Education, 1989

Otto, Rudolf. *The Idea of the Holy*, 2nd ed. London: Oxford University Press, 1950

Prozesky, Martin. *Religion and Ultimate Well-Being: An Explanatory Theory*. London: Macmillan, and New York: St Martin's Press, 1984

Smart, Ninian. *The World's Religions*. Cambridge: Cambridge University Press, 1989

Smith, Wilfred Cantwell. *Faith and Belief*. Princeton: Princeton University Press, 1979

Streng, Frederick J. *Understanding Religious Life*, 2nd ed. Encino, California : Dickenson, 1976

Tillich, Paul. *Ultimate Concern: Tillich in Dialogue*. London: SCM Press, 1965

Wach, Joachim. *The Sociology of Religion*. Chicago: University of Chicago Press, 1944

2

Primal Religions

DAVID CHIDESTER

Human life originated 25 000 years ago as a result of genetic experiments conducted by scientists from a distant planet. Those super-scientists from outer space synthesised human beings in test-tubes and placed them in a laboratory that came to be known as Earth. When that experiment caused controversy back home, however, the scientists abandoned their project in genetic engineering, returned to their own planet, and left the humans to live in a primitive condition.

Human beings, therefore, were the result of a failed experiment. At least, that is how the origin of human life was explained by French journalist Claude Vorilhon, who recently claimed to have learned all this when he was captured by extra-terrestrials and taken to their home planet. Adopting the name Rael, he started a movement dedicated to spreading this message of human origins throughout the world, that human beings were the product of an abandoned experiment performed by scientists from outer space.

In the study of religion, however, we learn that human beings were not the result of alien experiments but of their own experiments with the symbolic forms of myth, ritual, and community that we call religion. In the beginning, religion was (as it continues to be) the most basic human experiment in being human in the world. Religion is a humanising enterprise, providing a vital context in which human beings do not merely live but live meaningful and empowered lives as human beings. Those lives are lived in relation to other human beings, but they are also lived in relation to whatever sacred meanings and powers may be perceived to infuse a genuinely human experience. Through discourse, practice and forms of association, religions generate different ways of being human in a world of sacred meaning and power.

In the discipline of religious studies, religion has been defined in many different ways: it might be defined as beliefs and practices relating to supernatural beings, powers, or forces; it might be defined as beliefs and practices in relation to whatever is held to be sacred or set apart from ordinary life; it might be defined as beliefs and practices in relation to concerns that are perceived as most important or ultimate; or, in very broad definition, religion

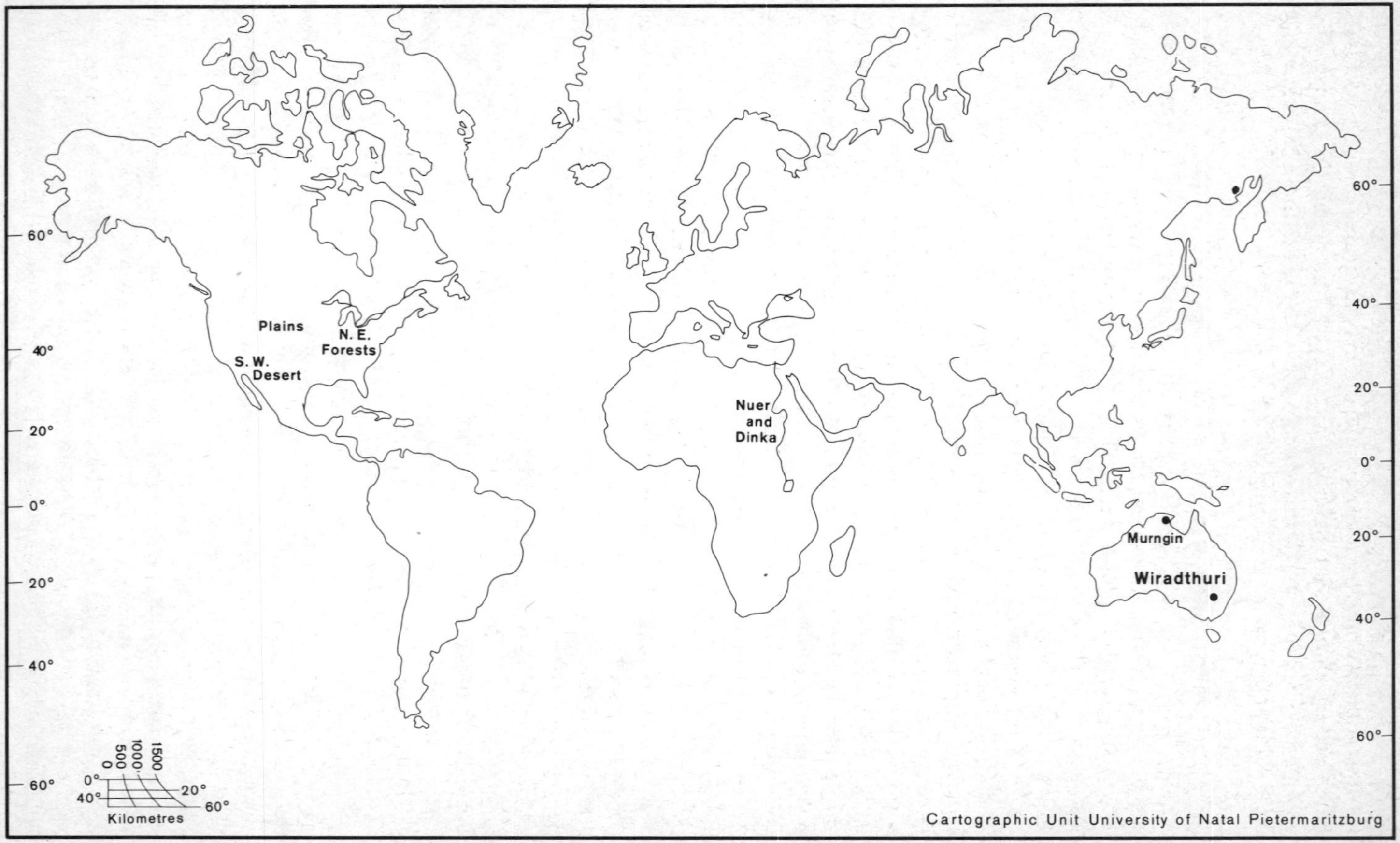

Plains
N. E.
Forests
S. W.
Desert
Nuer
and
Dinka
Murngin
Wiradthuri
60°
40°
20°
0°
20°
40°
60°
1500
1000
500
0
0°
40°
20°
60°
Kilometres
Cartographic Unit University of Natal Pietermaritzburg

might be defined as anything that allows human beings to rise above or go beyond the purely biological functioning of their physical organisms. In this last definition, religion is that activity which makes human beings human. Not aliens from outer space but human beings have conducted those experiments in being human that we observe in the history of religions.

PREHISTORIC AND PRIMITIVE RELIGION

Scholars in the study of religion have sometimes tried to understand religion by reconstructing either its earliest or its simplest manifestations. Nineteenth-century students of religion directed their attention towards what they imagined to be its earliest form – prehistoric religion – or its most elementary, basic, and simple form, which came to be called primitive religion.

Often, the so-called primitive was confused with the prehistoric, as if the small-scale, local religions of island communities, Australia, Africa, and the Americas were fossilised remnants from human prehistory, rather than living contemporaries of the scholars who studied them. Interest in the so-called primitive was often inspired by a quest for the prehistoric origins of humanity. In the study of religion, nineteenth-century scholars thought that the apparently simple religions they called primitive would hold the key to understanding the earliest religious life of humanity.

However, this link between the allegedly primitive and the prehistoric turned out to be problematic. The term 'primitive' had to be abandoned not only because of its negative, pejorative associations, but also because the religions of social groups with relatively simple economies and technologies turned out to be not so simple after all. They produced complex, rich, and meaningful ways of being human just like any other religious way of life. Although this chapter is devoted to those small-scale, local ways of being human that we shall call primal religions, some mention of the limited evidence of prehistoric or archaic religion (as it is also sometimes called) should be made before we begin.

Back to the prehistoric

The earliest evidence for any prehistory of religion is bones. Dating as far back as 100 000 years BCE, burial sites have been found by archaeological excavation all over the world. In those sites, hints of what may have been a religious care and attention in the disposition of the dead are suggested: a child's body was surrounded by a display of ibex horns, an adult male was buried along with flint tools, a woman's skull was adorned with artificial eyes, and in many cases the corpse painted with a red ochre dye before burial. What do these bones and their careful disposition reveal about prehistoric religion?

Prehistoric burials may reveal a symbolic vocabulary in action that was essentially religious. The red ochre with which corpses were painted may have been used to represent blood and therefore may have been a symbol of life. The tools, foods, and other objects buried with the corpse may have been used to represent continued activity after death. In many cases, the positioning of the body may have symbolised religious beliefs in survival after death. Many Stone Age burials arranged the corpse so that it faced towards the east, perhaps indicating a belief in some type of rebirth with the rising sun. More frequently, corpses were placed or tied in a foetal position in the grave. The position of the corpse may have symbolised an expectation of a new birth or it may have been done to bind the corpse in order to prevent the deceased from haunting the living. In any event, these burial practices hint at a symbolic vocabulary surrounding death that suggests they were performed in the context of religion.

Other evidence has led to further conjectures about prehistoric religion. It is possible that prehistoric humans during the old Stone Age (or Palaeolithic period) shaped a symbolic world around the activities of hunting that is reflected in the art of rock paintings. The paintings found on caves in southern France and northern Spain, for example, depict hunters and animals, but also portray what appear to be ritual figures – such as the 'Sorcerer of Trois Frères', which seems to portray either an animal spirit or a sorcerer in animal mask and costume – that may have been part of religious practices for symbolising a perfect hunt.

During the new Stone Age (or Neolithic period), the introduction of small-scale settled agriculture may have encouraged a development of religious symbolism of fertility depicted in female figurines – such as the so-called 'Venus' of Willendorf, Austria – that perhaps represented a mother goddess. Based on such limited evidence, speculations about prehistoric religion have tended to imagine it as beliefs and practices closely tied to the ecologies of hunting or farming within which human communities lived.

Beyond the primitive

When Europeans first encountered remote island, Australian, African, and Native American societies, most of them failed to appreciate the religions that flourished there. Travellers and missionaries often asserted that those people in fact had no religion. For example, the missionary Robert Moffat in southern Africa declared that Satan had erased any impression of religion from the minds of the people he called the Hottentots, Bushmen and Bechuanas in that region. More interested in controlling the wealth of new territories, European colonisers dismissed the traditional culture and religion of people they encountered. For the most part, Europeans did not recognise their humanity, referring to the indigenous inhabitants as savages, natural slaves or subhuman creatures. European scholars of that time called them primitives.

Recent scholarship has tried to move beyond this dismissal of the religion, culture and humanity of the indigenous people of Africa, Australia and the Americas. One way to recover their humanity may be through exploring the meaning and power of primal religion, by reconstructing the religious worlds of the small-scale, local societies previously labelled as primitive.

Primal religious worlds have shared a number of important features in common, features that can be organised in terms of distinctive orientations towards myth, ritual and community. First, with respect to myth and other forms of religious discourse, primal religions are nonliterate, transmitting sacred stories, wisdom and law through the living, immediate medium of oral tradition. Second, with respect to ritual, primal religions are performative, highly ritualised religions, acted out through formalised practices, through dance, prayer, song, chant and other dynamic, participatory forms. Third, with respect to community, primal religions are based in subsistence economies – whether hunting, small-scale agriculture, or some combination – in which economic exchange tends to be cooperative rather than competitive; they invest religious significance in kinship relations, including ancestral relations that remain unbroken by death; and they integrate myth and ritual into a relatively high degree of social cohesion.

Like any other religious world, primal religions involve mythic discourse, ritual practices, and forms of association and interaction that weave together a human community. Therefore, myth, ritual and community in primal religions have ultimately much in common with the contours of other religious worlds. Nevertheless, the characteristic features of primal religions can be elaborated in more detail. This chapter will only indicate some of those features by looking briefly at the primal religions of Africa, Australia and America.

AFRICAN RELIGION

In order to begin outlining some of the features of primal religious myth, ritual, and community, examples will be drawn from two East African religious traditions – the religions of the Nuer and the Dinka. Historically, the Nuer seem to have been a warrior-clan that broke away from the Dinka. As they developed independently, however, their myths and rituals retained much in common. But conflict was also reflected in the religious worlds of the two societies as they worked out their social relations in the medium of religious symbols.

The Nuer and the Dinka were pastoralist, cattle-herding societies, thus the central economic role of cattle radiated throughout their worlds. Not only were meat and milk primary sources of food, but cattle provided almost every aspect of material culture – dung for fuel and building materials, urine for disinfectants, skins for beds, bags, cords and shields, and bones for utensils and tools. In the pastoralist world of the Nuer and Dinka, cattle represented wealth, social prestige and an entire way of life that was embodied in religious myths and rituals.

Myth

The Nuer, Dinka and other East African groups such as the Masai told and retold an important story about the origin of the present human world. In the version of this story told by the Dinka, God and human beings were originally connected by a rope that allowed the first humans – Garang and Abuk – to climb up from the earth to God, the Divinity of the Sky. The original humans were given one grain of millet a day to eat, but that one grain satisfied all their needs. There was no lack, no suffering, no death in that original world in which the sky and earth were joined.

One day, however, the woman – 'because she was greedy' – decided to plant more grain. Raising the long-handled hoe, she accidentally struck the Divinity, who was so offended that he withdrew from the earth to a distant place in the sky. The Divinity sent a small blue bird to cut the rope that linked the earth and sky. From that day, the earth was ruined. Humans had to labour for their food.

Cut off from the Divinity, human beings experienced misfortune, sickness and death. In other words, the present world came into being in the primordial separation of the earth from the Divinity of the Sky.

This story is a myth, an important, compelling narrative of sacred beings, objects or events. Like this story, many myths deal with origins; myths are often *cosmogonic*, or sacred stories about the beginning of the present world. But what does the story mean? No myth is told without interpretation, without the exegetical labour of trying to make sense out of the myth and apply its significance to human life. In this regard any myth may have multiple meanings. It may speak in many voices within the context of different human situations and circumstances.

To put the matter simply, this myth can be seen in three basic ways: firstly as a symbolic code for the interpretation of reality; secondly as a symbolic supplement to the practices of ritual; and thirdly as a symbolic charter for the organisation and interests of a social group. We can take each way of understanding the meaning of myth in turn.

Firstly, myth generates a symbolic code – a shared vocabulary – for the interpetation of the world in which human beings live. Humans do not merely live in worlds; they live in *meaningful* worlds. Myth is one medium through which human beings invest their worlds with meaning. In the case of this Dinka myth, a symbolic code is generated for understanding the nature of the human world: it is separated from the heaven of the Divinity; it requires difficult labour to sustain life; it is riddled with misfortune, illness and death. In this sense, myth provides a symbolic vocabulary for analysing the human condition and particularly for making sense of the experience of suffering in the human world.

Secondly, however, myth provides a verbal supplement to the practices of ritual, a symbolic warrant for actions of worship. The rope that once connected the earth with the sky might have been cut, but ritual provides ways and means of restoring that broken connection. In a symbolic sense, rituals of worship, prayer and sacrifice were seen by the Nuer and Dinka as sacred acts that re-established the rope connecting the human world with the spirit world of the Divinity of the Sky.

Thirdly, myth may provide a symbolic charter for social order. The Dinka creation myth legitimated that society by connecting it with the original human beings; but it also supported subtler interests within Dinka society such as the status of priests who told the myth and supervised the important sacrificial rituals, and the division of labour between men who were responsible for tending cattle and women who were responsible for farming.

A myth may also become a symbolic model for social conflict. In another creation story, myth served as a model for intergroup rivalry between the Nuer and the Dinka. In the version told by the Nuer, God decided to give cattle to human beings. The Divinity summoned Nuer and gave him a cow and a calf. Nuer was to take the cow and give it to Dinka and then return the next morning to receive the calf for himself. But Dinka overheard this conversation.

When Nuer returned the next morning, he asked for his calf. 'Who are you?' God asked. 'I am Nuer,' he responded. Surprised, God exclaimed, 'But who was that who just came to me and said he was Nuer? I already gave him the calf.' Suddenly Nuer realised that he and God had been tricked by Dinka and that he had lost his calf. But God proposed a solution: 'Follow Dinka,' God advised, 'and when you have overtaken him, you may kill him and take his cattle.' The myth concluded that the struggles between the Nuer and the Dinka over cattle began at that time.

However, this myth also provided a symbolic charter for the Nuer that justified their actions in stealing cattle from the Dinka. Since by divine right cattle originally belonged to the Nuer, raiding the Dinka or other groups was not really stealing but an act of restitution that restored cattle to their original owners. As might be expected, the Dinka and the Masai told similar myths which served as symbolic charters for their rightful ownership of cattle and justified their cattle raids.

In addition to justifying cattle raids, these myths also gave a sacred warrant to warriors in those societies. Whereas the myth of the separation of earth from sky supported the activities of priests in restoring the original connection through ritual, the myth of cattle supported the actions of warriors in restoring the original mythic situation of rightful ownership through their cattle-raiding expeditions.

Ritual

Myths in primal religions provide a basic framework for religious thought. More important than what people think, however, is what they do. The active dimension of primal religion is found in practices of ritual.

The ritual life of primal religions appears in those formalised, repeatable practices that are performed in extraordinary, reserved or sacred times and places. Ritual represents a perfect, controlled pattern of action, factoring out all the accidental variables that occur in the ordinary situations and circumstances of daily life. Every movement, every gesture, every element in the ritual drama can be coordinated to create a perfect, controlled pattern of sacred action.

Three basic types of ritual may be distinguished in primal religion. Firstly, rituals of the life-cycle are performed to bridge the transitions that occur during the course of any full human life. The transitions of birth, adolescence, marriage and death all tend to be accompanied by ritual practices which the anthropologist Arnold van Gennep called 'rites of passage'. Such rites move through three characteristic stages – separation from an old status, transition, and reincorporation in a new status. Rites of passage are performed in primal religions to negotiate those often difficult and sometimes dangerous changes in the human life-cycle.

Secondly, rituals of the sacred calendar mark out annual events in the life of a community. Calendrical rituals may celebrate the new year, planting and harvest seasons, the revitalisation of a king, or other important occasions that occur during the year.

Thirdly, rituals of crisis are performed in response to some disruption in the life of a community. That disruption may take the form of illness to which healing rituals respond; it may take the form of drought to which rain-making or other fertility rituals respond; it may take the form of conflict within the community to which witch-finding rituals respond; or it may take the form of conflict with other groups to which the rituals of war and warfare respond. In all these cases, ritual enacts some perfect pattern of sacred action that orders the forces of life and death that otherwise threaten to disrupt a society.

For the Nuer, Dinka, Masai and most other primal religions, the primary form of ritual was animal sacrifice. The ritual killing of animals represented the central religious act. During rituals of passage, ritual events of the calendar or rituals of crisis, these East African pastoral communities killed and offered animals to the Divinity of heaven.

They regarded cattle as the ideal sacrificial victims, the ox in particular representing the most highly valued sacrifice that could be offered. But they also observed principles of symbolic substitution in sacrifice so that sheep, goats, or even, on some occasions, a cucumber might be substituted for an ox in the ritual. Even a pinch of tobacco thrown on the fire as an offering to the Divinity of heaven might be referred to as an 'ox' during a ritual.

All sacrificial victims, therefore, might be symbolised as oxen when they were offered in sacrifice. Frequently offered to fulfil a pledge or a vow to the Divinity, sacrifices were also integrated into every aspect of the ritual life of worship. During life-cycle rituals of birth, adulthood, marriage and death, during the calendrical rituals of spring and autumn marking the opening of the dry and rainy seasons, and during rituals of crisis, particularly in rituals performed in response to illness, witchcraft or warfare, sacrifices were performed.

A formalised, repeatable pattern was observed in the ritual of sacrifice: (1) an ox was brought out to the place of sacrifice and tied there; (2) speeches were made by elders of the community, while libations of milk were poured out; (3) the spirit who was to receive the ox – whether the Divinity, heavenly spirits, or the ancestors – was invoked and the speakers described the reasons why the offering was being made, requesting favours from the spirits in return; (4) the sacrificer placed his hand on the head of the animal to establish a connection and then killed it; (5) the meat was carefully divided according to the social status of those attending the ceremony; and (6) finally, the meat was eaten by the participants, but other parts of the animal might also be used, such as the gall-bladder that might be reserved as a place for spirits – often representing a womb or hut for them to inhabit – and the bile, chyme or other products of the sacrifice might be spread on the bodies of the participants.

Clearly, the animal sacrifice was performed as a religious act of ritual worship. But how should we understand the meaning of sacrifice? Three perspectives on sacrifice might be taken, depending on whether we emphasise the role of *having*, *being*, or *dividing* in the ritual pattern of action.

If we emphasise 'having', we notice that the ritual was focused upon the most valuable commodity that the sacrificer might own. The ox was a valued gift offered to the Divinity or other spirits by the sacrificer, a gift that might be regarded as payment for a state of indebtedness to the divine providers of life. In turn, that payment might be felt to guarantee the further generosity of the

Divinity, the spirits, or the ancestors. *Do ut des* – 'I give so you might give' – is one popular and persistent interpretation of the meaning of sacrifice.

If we emphasise 'being', we might consider the possibility that the sacrificial killing of an ox stood as a ritual substitute for the life of a human being. Symbolic substitution ran throughout the sacrificial practice. Since a cucumber, goat or sheep might be substituted for the most prized victim of sacrifice, the ox, perhaps the ox in some way was a substitution for the being of the human sacrificer, a symbolic offering of a human life to God. Perhaps, when the sacrificer placed his hand on the head of the animal, he indicated not only ownership but also a close identification with the life of the animal that was being offered.

If we emphasise 'dividing', however, we notice that the sacrificial animal was ritually divided in two important ways. It was divided between humans and the spirits, and it was divided among humans in the community. When the sacrifice was divided between humans and spirits, the animal served as a mediator between the human world and the spirit world. In a sense, the humans and the spirits participated in a shared, communal meal during the sacrifice. Sharing a common meal symbolised a connection between the human and spiritual levels of existence. But the dividing of the animal might also symbolise the difference between those two worlds. If the blood, fat and smell of the sacrifice went to the spirits, while the flesh was reserved for humans, then the division of the animal symbolised that even though they shared a common meal the spirits still represented a level of existence that differed from the life lived by human beings.

Finally, the division of the sacrificial animal among the participants was carried out according to a ritualised pattern. The best pieces of meat might be given to those who had the highest status in the community; or they might be given to those with the closest kinship ties to the sacrificer; or the meat might be divided according to other ritual rules that reflected the social relations which existed among the participants. In this way, the systematic division of the animal and the distribution of meat was a regular ritual recreation of the social order of the community.

AUSTRALIAN RELIGION

Over 500 distinct traditional, or aboriginal, groups developed and practised religions in Australia. Many still continue. Some scholars have distinguished between two basic patterns of aboriginal religious life: the inland desert religions that were primarily concerned with fertility, reproduction and life, and the woodland and coastal religions that were mainly concerned with death and rituals that would safely conduct spirits of the deceased back to the underground world from which they had originally come. Whatever their differences, however, Australian religions shared much in common: the power of clan totems, the importance of totemic ancestors, the ritual initiations of children into adulthood, the central role of religious specialists, and the crucial function of funeral rituals in restoring human spirits to the world of the dead.

Behind Australian beliefs and practices, however, stood one basic feature – the Dreamtime. As the primary resource of Australian myth and ritual, the

Dreamtime did not refer to the illusion of dreams but to the spiritual basis of reality. The Dreamtime was the origin of life and the place of return at death. It was that reservoir of spiritual meaning and power which ritual tapped. The Dreamtime animated an entire way of life in Australian religions. In the next three sub-sections the main aspects of this central aboriginal religious reality are explained.

Source of life

In the beginning the ancestors roamed the land, exploring, camping, making love and fighting, and through their exploits they shaped the world. They fashioned the landscape – the rocks, caves, hills, trees, rivers and waterholes, the plants and animals of each region – as they wandered around. When the ancestors finally disappeared, they left their eternal traces in the landscape, merging into the things they had shaped. The ancestors remained present in those sacred traces which they left behind from that time of beginnings, the sacred time of the Dreamtime.

The Dreamtime represented the source of life in Australian religions in at least four different senses. Firstly, the Dreamtime was that sacred time of beginnings in which the immortal ancestor heroes shaped the entire world. Their activities were remembered and retold in mythic narratives about their adventures. Not only providing an orientation towards a time of beginnings, those myths of the original ancestors and their exploits gave a sense of spatial orientation in the Australian world by identifying significant places in the environment with the creative work of the ancestors.

Secondly, the Dreamtime was the power of the ancestors that remained present in the traces they had left. The spiritual power of the ancestors was alive in specific sites, but it was also present in certain plants, animals and sacred objects and most obviously present in the totems that identified Australian clans. Whether that totem of family, lineage and clan was a kangaroo, crayfish, whale, wild duck or some other symbolic emblem, it represented the presence of the totemic ancestor in the lives of his descendants. Therefore, the Dreamtime was not a lost time of origins stretching back on a horizontal line to the beginning; the Dreamtime was both then and now, a time of beginnings, but also a sacred time in the present in which people could contact the power of their ancestors through the traces and totems that represented them.

Thirdly, the Dreamtime introduced the ways of life to human beings. In the Dreamtime the ancestors established the laws for moral and social life, as a path for human beings to follow. In addition, the ancestors gave human beings the sacred ritual practices and ritual objects through which they could stay in contact with the Dreamtime. During rituals, clan members could re-enact the adventures of their ancestors. But participants did not merely imitate their ancestors; they *became* those ancestors. In ritual, they became absorbed by the power and the presence of the Dreamtime.

Fourthly, the Dreamtime was the ongoing source of human life because most Australians believed that children were born with spirits that came from the Dreamtime. Spirit children lived there with the ancestors until they were born in human form. In traditional belief, a man might have a dream, or a vision, or notice some strange movement in the desert that would alert him to the presence of a spirit child. He would then point out the woman who was to be the child's mother. Besides giving the father credit for procreation, the notion of spirit children affirmed the Australian belief that all human beings came from the Dreamtime.

Although all human beings originated in the sacred Dreamtime, Australian religions distinguished between different roles for males and females. Males entered the world in the care of women and in the company of other children. Eventually, however, the male child would be separated from that world of women and children to be initiated into adulthood. As a fully initiated adult male, he could participate in the rituals and ceremonies that contracted the power of the Dreamtime. Through ritual, a man became identified with his totem in life, becoming a sacred being like the ancestors. At death, a man was expected to return to the ancestral source of his clan's sacred totem in the Dreamtime. Women were also believed to have emerged from the spirit world and to return there at death, but they were not acknowledged as having made any spiritual progress during their lives that would invest them with authority in the community. That adult authority for males was acknowledged through rituals of initiation.

Initiation

The mysteries of the Dreamtime were introduced to human beings through initiation. As a life-cycle rite of passage from childhood to adulthood, initiation rituals have appeared in many primal religions. Initiation played an important role in Australian religions.

Some time between age 6 and 13, a boy would be separated from the status of women and children to be initiated into the world of men. In a characteristic initiation ritual of the Wiradthuri of New South Wales, boys of a certain age group were separated from their mothers, other women and the children of the community. Women and children were told that the boys had been taken by a powerful giant named Dhuramoolan, a snake-like monster with a voice of thunder. Removed to a secret place, the boys were given instruction in the myths and laws of their community. During that time, each boy had a tooth extracted. At night, the men hid outside the secret camp, making a frightening roaring noise with a bullroarer, a board attached to two leather thongs swung overhead to sound like the voice of the monster Dhuramoolan.

On the last night, the men told the boys that the monster was coming to burn them and eat them. With their heads covered, the boys felt fire approaching them and the thundering sound growing louder. Suddenly, their headcovers were pulled back to reveal the secret source of the thundering sound, the bullroarer. Returning to the rest of the community after this ordeal, the boys were received as if they had returned from the dead. They were now ready to assume new roles as male adults, but also as living representatives of the power of their totemic ancestors in the community.

Initiation was an ordeal that symbolised entry into adulthood. Almost always it involved some form of physical mutilation – most often circumcision or subincision of the penis – that carved a shared symbol of this new status into the body of the adult. But initiation was also a symbolic death, often expressly treated as a ritual killing, a kind of human sacrifice, from which the boys emerged reborn as men. When a man became a father, he was shown more powerful totems that would introduce him to a higher status. At about age thirty-five, he was shown secret totems and raised to the status of an elder in the community. These rituals marked changes in the male life-cycle that progressively initiated a man into the sacred role as representative of the totemic ancestors. Through these initiations, he became increasingly spiritualised until, at death, he returned to the ancestral world of the spirits in the Dreamtime.

Mysteries of life and death

Some men became specialists in the mysteries of the Dreamtime by being initiated as shamans. Appearing frequently as an important religious figure in prehistoric and primal religions, the shaman was an expert in techniques of ecstasy. As a technical term, *ecstasy* means to be out of the body, out of place, out of the world. Through a variety of techniques, shamans developed powers of vision and healing by going into trance states. They claimed to have the ability to journey to the spirit world. In Australian religions, the shaman was also initiated into these powers through an ordeal that symbolised death and rebirth.

That initiation was a ceremony conducted by old, experienced shamans who had served their community as medicine men. Tired from a long day of hunting, the initiate was settled down at night by a grave, with small fires around him smoking from the forbidden animal fat that had been placed on them. He was told by an elder shaman that while he slept the spirits would visit him, kill him by removing his internal organs, replace them with magical rock crystals, and give him the power to become a shaman. The next morning – if he survived this ordeal – the initiate discussed whatever dreams he might have had and received a personal totem to assist him in his work and protect him from danger. Under the guidance of the elder shamans, he began assisting in their ritual and magical procedures.

The special totem a shaman received in the initiation – perhaps a snake, or the Rainbow Serpent – would guide him on his journeys out of the body through the Dreamtime. The shaman might journey down to the underworld where he could meet other snakes that would give him magical powers by rubbing against him. Then he might ascend to the sky, to the place of the supreme god, in order to gain powers over illness and even death. As a specialist in the knowledge and power of the Dreamtime, the shaman played an important role in the life of Australian religious communities. His journeys in and out of the Dreamtime represented a special ability, but in a sense it also duplicated the journey that each soul was believed to make from the spirit world and back over the course of a lifetime. The extraordinary experiences of the shaman confirmed and gave content to the journey that was taken by each soul back to the Dreamtime.

Many Australian religions assumed that human beings had two souls. The Murngin people of the northern coast, for example, believed that each person had two distinct spirits during life. One was a soul that was associated with the body, a show soul, called a *mokoi*, that was of little value during life and lingered around in the world after death. But the *mokoi* was not the true identity of the person. The genuine essence of a person was the *warro*, or totemic spirit, which came from the ancestral waterhole. The *warro* originally emerged from that well of the totemic ancestors as a spirit child; it developed through a lifetime of initiations into the power of the totems; and, ultimately, that soul returned to the well of the ancestors at death. For the Murngin, each individual had a spiritual essence that came from and returned to the well of the ancestors. Personal survival of death, therefore, was identified with the living power of those totemic ancestors to which all souls returned to be reabsorbed in the Dreamtime.

AMERICAN RELIGION

Flourishing for centuries in the forests of the eastern seaboard and the Pacific Northwest, in the deserts of the Southwest, or on the plains of the Midwest, native North American people developed religious ways of life based on a close relationship with their natural environments. Religious beliefs and practices showed respect and reverence for the earth and the plant and animal life which the earth sustained. Native American religions were also closely related to the ecologies – whether hunting or agricultural ecologies – in which they emerged as meaningful and powerful ways of being human.

In spite of significant differences, Native American religions shared a number of common features. Perhaps the most important feature was a highly developed sensitivity to the dynamics of sacred power that was understood to be diffused throughout the world, infused in human life, and manifested in specific people, places and objects. That sacred power was known by many different names – the Algonkian called it *manitou*, the Iroquois *orenda*, the Sioux *wakantanka* – but in each case it defined a spiritual resource that could be drawn upon by human beings. The chief, the shaman, the priest or the healer might have been expert in focusing and using that power, but sacred power was felt to be available to everyone. Although Native American religions often included beliefs in a creator god, high god, or supreme being, their primary concern was with those persons, places and practices that were focal points for sacred power.

A second common feature in Native American religions was attention to sacred space. In Native American religious beliefs and practices, sacred space was environmental. Specific places in the natural environment – mountains, valleys, rivers, lakes and so on – were understood to be imbued with sacred significance in the religious life of Native Americans. European invaders and colonisers in North America tended to perceive sacred space as architectural. From their perspective, the natural environment only became sacred when some intentional design and construction was imposed upon it. Native Americans, however, found sacred patterns of meaning and power in the natural contours of their environment.

In addition, burial sites were important locations of sacred space in Native American religions. They represented a connection between the living and the dead, as the power and presence of the ancestors were understood to continue in the land and particularly in specific sacred sites that were set apart for burials.

A third common feature was the elaboration of ceremonial ritual in Native American religions. Ritual dramas were celebrated with dancing, singing, chanting, praying and other dynamic practices. Ceremonials often acted out events in the important myths that provided Native Americans with a symbolic code for understanding their world.

However, ceremonials were enacted not merely to understand the world but also to change it. Rituals in hunting communities were performed to ensure success in the hunt; rituals in agricultural communities were performed to invoke rain and to achieve fertility and abundant harvests; but even though ceremonials were often focused upon food, sustenance and the survival of the community, they also served to revitalise the world by placing human beings in contact with sacred power.

Forests

In the hunting societies of the north-eastern American forests, religion revolved around animal ceremonies. Often directed toward a supreme being who was master of the game, these ceremonies empowered hunters and paid homage to animals and animal spirits which gave their lives so that human beings might live.

Because hunting societies were fairly mobile, no permanent places of worship were built. Communion with the masters of the game and animal spirits might occur anywhere. Hunters paid close attention to their dreams for signs of help from guardian spirits or animal spirits. Shamans were particularly important in gaining access to the spiritual world – often located beyond the horizon or in the sky – by going into trance to contact the spirits. Periodically, the community enacted the ceremonial of the Dream Dance in which rhythmic drumming and dancing invoked the power of the animal spirits and guaranteed success in the hunt.

Spiritual communication with the animal world, therefore, was understood as essential to the ongoing sustenance of a human way of life that was based primarily on hunting. The life of hunting required mobility, isolation and self-sufficiency to ensure survival. For most of the year, small family groups moved through the forest in search of food. During those times, religious life was sustained by dreams, prayers and visions in which hunters contacted and communicated with spiritual beings such as the Sun, the Thunderbirds and the Masters of the Animals.

Only during summer, when sufficient food was available, did the hunting families gather together in larger groups to enact ceremonials such as the Dream Dance. The most spectacular ceremonial performed by the hunters of the north-eastern American forests was enacted every eight to twelve years – the great Feast of the Dead.

The hunters of the North American forests showed some ambivalence about the dead. On one hand, the dead were often invoked as spiritual helpers in the hunt. Food and tobacco would be thrown on the fire as offerings to the spirits of the dead. Prayers might be directed toward deceased relatives so that they would intercede with the animal spirits and the masters of the animals. Often, the dead were thought to serve as personal guardian spirits, giving hunters power and success in their pursuit of animals.

On the other hand, however, the hunters told myths about death and the after-life that suggested a radical separation between the world of the living and of the dead. For example, the Ojibway of north-eastern America expected that after death the soul would be just as conscious as when alive. As the soul travelled along the road to the Land of the Dead, it would come upon a giant strawberry. If the soul ate the strawberry, it would for ever be unable to return to the land of the living.

After eating the giant strawberry, the soul would continue on its journey. Suddenly, however, the soul would be grabbed from behind by the Skeleton-Woman of the Land of the Dead. The Skeleton-Woman would crack open its skull, take out its brains, and replace them with moss. After that shocking experience, the soul would lose all interest in the world of the living. No longer a conscious, thinking being, that soul would continue on to the Land of the Dead where it would be for ever separated from the human community.

The great Feast of the Dead seemed to resolve some of this ambivalence about the relation between the living and the dead. This ceremonial event paid respect and reverence to deceased ancestors by honouring their bones; but it also marked the final incorporation of the souls of those deceased ancestors in the Land of the Dead.

At the time of the great feast, each family dug up the bones of its relatives, cleaned the bones of any remaining flesh, and dressed them in new clothes, beads and flowers. These cleaned, dried bones were referred to as the 'souls' of the deceased relatives. For three days the bones were kept in the home of each family while feasts were held and gifts were distributed.

Deserts

The Pueblo Indians who lived in the deserts of the American southwest – the Zuni, Hopi, Tewa and Navaho – developed stable societies that were based on settled agriculture and complex religious ceremonials. Rituals were synchronised with the seasons and the cycles of planting and harvesting in the agricultural ecology of the desert. Since successful farming in a desert environment depended crucially upon rain, many ceremonies were devoted to the spirits that controlled the rain, clouds and thunderstorms. Native Americans of the south-western deserts held beliefs in supreme beings such as the Sun Father and the Moon Mother. But Pueblo Indian ceremonials invoked the rain spirits who were most directly responsible for the survival of human beings in their desert world.

In Pueblo myth, human beings originally emerged into the world from under the ground. A Zuni emergence myth, for example, related how the first humans were trapped in a dark underworld. Carrying sacred bundles and prayer sticks for making rain fall and seed grow, the humans climbed up through the soot world, the sulphur-smell world, the fog world and the feather-wing world, until finally they arrived in the bright, sunlit world. After many ordeals, the human beings found the centre of the world and settled there to grow corn and live in peace.

During that journey, however, death had entered the world. While crossing a river, many women could not hold onto their children and lost them in the water. To their surprise, however, the people later heard the drowned children singing and dancing from the depths of a lake. Although they did not return to the world of the living, those children sent help to the human beings from the depths of that sacred lake through the life-giving rain clouds.

These children of the emergence myth had become rain spirits, spiritual beings the Zuni referred to as *koko* and the Hopi called *kachina*. Thunderbirds, animal deities, star deities, the Sun Father and the Moon Mother and all the dead who were able to get to that sacred lake comprised a supernatural world of rain spirits that could be contacted by human beings through ceremonials.

Depicted in vivid masks and elaborate costumes, the rain spirits were invoked to bring power, health, long life, fertility, and – most important – the much-needed rain in that desert region. The ceremonials often lasted many days, combining private observances in the home with public rituals. Dancers impersonated the rain spirits in ritual dramas that involved the entire community. Prayers, songs, and chants honoured the rain spirits and enlisted their aid in bringing prosperity to the agricultural life of the Pueblo Indians.

The practical objective of those ceremonials was to enlist the aid of the rain spirits in the material survival of the human community. But the ceremonials also enacted a spiritual ideal of Pueblo religion – an ideal called 'harmony' or 'beauty' – by creating a special arena of sacred order and rhythm in the world. Rain rituals revitalised the harmony, beauty and life of the world.

Other rituals, however, also established that ideal of harmonious and beautiful well-being for individuals, families and villages in Pueblo religion. These were rituals of healing. They diagnosed and treated illness; but they also symbolically acted out a perfect pattern of harmony through ritual. Pueblo healing rituals can be illustrated briefly by examples from the practices of the Navaho and Tewa of the south-western American deserts.

Navaho healers used techniques to discover the cause of illness. The healer ran his hands around the patient's body with a trembling, vibrating motion; or the healer gazed into the sky at a particular constellation of stars, praying and chanting until the secret of the illness was revealed; or the healer listened to the patient's body until sounds or voices disclosed the nature of the illness. In each case, however, the cause of the illness was some disruption of the natural balance of elements that were understood to sustain health and well-being. Treatment followed this diagnosis: the patient was treated through techniques designed to restore the harmony which had been disrupted.

The healing ceremony lasted from two to nine nights, depending on the nature of the illness. During that time, the healer sang over the patient to restore harmony through the medium of music. Other healing techniques were also used: herbal medicines, sweat and emetic treatments, purifying baths and hair washings, fumigation with pungent and fragrant herbs, and the visual aid of sand paintings. But all these techniques were coordinated around a basic format of ritual singing to restore the patient to a state of harmony, beauty and health.

The Tewa formed healing societies known as the Bears. The Tewa thought that bears were natural healers because they were able to pull foreign objects out of their flesh and apply healing dressings of mud to their wounds. The Bear societies among the Tewa were responsible for the diagnosis and treatment of illness. Most commonly, their diagnosis of the cause of illness was witchcraft or evil spirits.

While the Navaho used ritual singing to restore harmony, the Tewa used healing techniques designed to counteract such evil contact. The Bears touched the patient's body to feel the sickness; they massaged the body forcefully and applied herbs; they went into trance to discern evil objects that had invaded the patient and sucked rags, stones, sticks or other intrusive objects out of the body. Doing battle against evil spirits, the healers of the Tewa Bear societies chanted 'Be a man' or 'Be a woman' over the patient in their efforts to counteract the dehumanising forces that had disrupted the natural harmony of the human body.

Regularly, the Bears supervised healing ceremonies for the entire community, preventive rituals of healing that were designed to protect the group from contact with evil forces. Putting on special bear paws that covered their arms, the healers moved around the group touching, hitting and slapping everyone. As in many primal religious healing rituals, the Tewa Bear society rituals were ultimately directed towards the community as a whole. They supported a sense of social harmony and well-being by dramatically driving away evil influences that might otherwise have disrupted the community. Like rain ceremonials, healing rituals enacted the Pueblo ideal of harmony for the individual, the community and the world.

Plains

The harmony of Native American religion – like the religious worlds of Australian, African and other primal religions – was violently disrupted with the advent of European invaders and colonisers. In North America, the expansion of the United States crushed Native American religious worlds in the name of Christianity, civilization and racial superiority. The Board of Indian Commissioners made US government policy explicit in 1871: 'The Anglo-Saxon Race will not allow the car of civilisation to stop long at any line of latitude or longitude on our broad domain. If the Indian in his wildness plants himself on the track, he must inevitably be crushed by it.' But a government policy based on the dispossession, removal and extermination of Native Americans was evident throughout American history until well into this century.

Like other primal religions under pressures of conquest and dispossession, Native American religions provided spiritual resources enabling followers to respond to the crisis of a cultural contact that left so many dead or displaced in a strange world. One example of a Native American response to this cultural destruction can be found in the Ghost Dance religion that swept through the plains region of North America toward the end of the nineteenth century.

The Ghost Dance was a religious movement that provided ritual contact with deceased ancestors and a mythic promise that soon the dead would rise, the land would be restored, and the traditional ways of life would be revived. This religious movement was initiated by the Paiute prophet Wovoka, who claimed to have experienced a shaman-like death and rebirth; he journeyed to the heavens, saw and spoke with the dead, and learned that a great catastrophe was about to destroy all the Europeans. Native Americans, however, would survive that destruction and live with their ancestors in a renewed world. Finally, Wovoka received instruction in a ritual dance that he was to teach to the people so that they could perform it while they waited for the dead to return to life.

The Ghost Dance had much in common with the traditional Sun Dance of the Native American religion of the plains region. During the Sun Dance, people from all over the region gathered for ritual dancing, competitive games, exercises in self-torture, tests of endurance and vision quests. The Sun Dance acted out a ritual empowerment for hunters and warriors.

Although the Ghost Dance shared many of the features of the Sun Dance, it was performed by hunters who had lost their buffalo, and by warriors who had lost their land, to European conquerors. The Ghost Dance, therefore, was a ceremonial of revitalisation and redemption. Participants sang, chanted, stripped naked, fell into trance and beheld visions of their ancestors who would soon restore all that had been lost. The Ghost Dance drew upon traditional Native American ritual resources to create a sense of hope in a hopeless situation.

Inspired by the Ghost Dance, Chief Short Bull mobilised the Sioux for battle against the US army. Before going into battle, Short Bull told his warriors that his deceased father had shown him a vision. He saw a tree sprout where they gathered, the dead rise, and the buffalo return to restore their sacred way of life. Because the Ghost Dance would give them power, their holy shirts would make them invincible to bullets, and their sacred songs would make the earth open and swallow the white soldiers; the Sioux were assured of victory in their final battle against the US army. Tragically, the actual battle at Wounded Knee in 1890 resulted in a massacre of the Sioux.

Wovoka disavowed the military purposes to which his message had been put by the Sioux. But the Ghost Dance religion did represent a type of ritual work designed to overthrow white oppression and to recover the spirit of independence, integrity and power represented by the lost world of Native American primal religion.

The Ghost Dance religion of the Plains Indians stands as only one example of revitalisation movements throughout the world that have sought to draw upon the traditional resources of primal religion in modern situations of social crisis. Cargo cults of Melanesia, the Vailala movement of Papua New Guinea, the Maji Maji revolt against German colonial rule in Tanzania, the Xhosa cattle-killing in southern Africa – these, and many other movements, have channelled primal religious resources (often, in addition, appropriating Christian symbols) into a confrontation with the modern world.

When they have provided spiritual resources for people suffering under colonial, imperial or other forms of foreign domination and deprivation, primal religions have generated ways of being human that draw together old traditions and new innovations under extreme conditions of dehumanisation. Revitalisation movements have not merely been introversive retreats to a lost traditional world; they have also represented new strategies for working out meaning and power – new ways of being human – within a dehumanising environment. In these efforts to work out new ways of being human under dehumanising conditions, primal religion has appeared as both the oldest and the newest of the religions of the world.

SELECT BIBLIOGRAPHY

Definitions of religion:

(1) *Religion as relation to the supernatural*: E. B. Tylor, *Primitive Culture*, 2 vols. 6th ed. (New York: G. P. Putnam's, 1920), and Melford Spiro, 'Religion: Problems of Definition and Explanation,' in Michael Banton (ed.), *Anthropological Approaches to the Study of Religion* (London: Tavistock, 1966): 85–126;

(2) *Religion as relation to the sacred:* Emile Durkheim, *The Elementary Forms of the Religious Life,* (trans.) Joseph Ward Swain (New York: Free Press, 1965; orig. ed. 1912), and Mircea Eliade, *The Sacred and the Profane*, (trans.) Willard R. Trask (New York: Harper and Row, 1961);

(3) *Religion as ultimate concern:* Paul Tillich, *Theology of Culture* (New York: Columbia University Press, 1963), Robert Bellah, 'Religious Evolution', *American Sociological Review* 29 (1964): 358–74, and Robert D. Baird, *Category Formation in the History of Religions* (The Hague: Mouton, 1971);

(4) *Religion as transcendent and humanising*: Thomas Luckmann, *The Invisible Religion: The Problem of Religion in Modern Society* (New York: Macmillan, 1967), and David Chidester, *Patterns of Action: Religion and Ethics in a Comparative Perspective* (Belmont, CA: Wadsworth, 1987).

Prehistoric religion: E. O. James, *Prehistoric Religion* (London: Thames & Hudson, 1957); Johannes Maringer, *The Gods of Prehistoric Man* (New York: Alfred A. Knopf, 1960).

Primal religion: David Chidester, 'Primal Transcendence', *Patterns of Transcendence: Religion, Death and Dying* (Belmont, CA: Wadsworth, 1989): 47–86; W. Richard Comstock, *The Study of Religion and Primitive Religions* (New York: Harper and Row, 1971); E. E. Evans Pritchard, *Theories of Primitive Religion* (Oxford: Clarendon Press, 1965); Sam D. Gill, *Beyond 'The Primitive': The Religions of Nonliterate Peoples* (Englewood Cliffs, NJ: Prentice-Hall, 1982); Paul Radin, *Primitive Religion: Its Nature and Origin* (New York: Viking Press, 1937).

Myth: Joseph Campbell, *Masks of God: Primitive Mythology* (New York: Viking Press, 1959); William G. Doty (ed.), *Mythography: The Study of Myths and Rituals* (Alabama: University of Alabama Press, 1986); Alan Dundee, *Sacred Narrative: Readings in the Theory of Myth* (Berkeley: University of California Press, 1984); G. S. Kirk, *Myth : Its Meaning and Function in Ancient and Other Cultures* (Berkeley: University of California Press, 1970).

Ritual: Lauri Honko, 'Theories Concerning the Ritual Process : An Orientation', *Science of Religion: Studies in Methodology* (ed.) Lauri Honko (The Hague: Mouton, 1979): 369–89; Roy A. Rappaport, 'The Obvious Aspects of Ritual', *Ecology, Meaning and*

Religion (Richmond, CA: North Atlantic Books, 1979): 173–221; Jonathan Z. Smith, 'The Bare Facts of Ritual', *Imagining Religion: From Babylon to Jonestown* (Chicago: University of Chicago Press, 1982); Victor Turner, *The Ritual Process: Structure and Anti-Structure* (Ithaca, NY: Cornell University Press, 1969); Arnold Van Gennep, *Rites of Passage*, (trans.) Monika B. Vizedom and Gabrielle L. Caffee (Chicago: University of Chicago Press, 1960).

Nuer and Dinka religion: E. E. Evans-Pritchard, *Nuer Religion* (Oxford: Clarendon Press, 1956); Godfrey Lienhardt, *Divinity and Experience: The Religion of the Dinka* (Oxford: Clarendon Press, 1961); Bruce Lincoln, *Priests, Warriors and Cattle: A Study in the Ecology of Religions* (Berkeley: University of California Press, 1981): 13–48.

African religions: Benjamin C. Ray, *African Religions: Symbol, Ritual and Community* (Englewood Cliffs, NJ: Prentice-Hall, 1976); Dominique Zahan, *The Religion, Spirituality and Thought of Traditional Africa*, (trans.) Kate Ezra and Lawrence M. Martin (Chicago: University of Chicago Press, 1979); Evan M. Zuesse, *Ritual Cosmos: The Sanctification of Life in African Religions* (Athens, OH: Ohio University Press, 1979).

Australian religions: Max Charlesworth, Howard Morphy, Diane Bell & Kenneth Maddock (eds.), *Religion in Aboriginal Australia: An Anthology* (St. Lucia: University of Queensland Press, 1984); Mircea Eliade, *Australian Religions: An Introduction* (Ithaca, NY: Cornell University Press, 1973).

American religions: David Chidester, 'Native Americans', *Patterns of Power: Religion and Politics in American Culture* (Englewood Cliffs, NJ : Prentice-Hall, 1988): 110–38; Sam D. Gill, *Native American Religions: An Introduction* (Belmont, CA: Wadsworth, 1982); Ake Hultkrantz, *The Religions of the American Indians*, (trans.) Monica Setterwall (Berkeley: University of California Press, 1979).

Revitalisation movements: Kennelm Burridge, *New Heaven, New Earth: A Study of Millenarian Activities* (New York: Schocken Books, 1967); Bryan R. Wilson, *Magic and the Millennium: A Sociological Study of Religious Movements of Protest Among Tribal and Third-World Peoples* (New York: Harper and Row, 1973); Peter Worsley, *The Trumpet Shall Sound: A Study of 'Cargo' Cults in Melanesia* (London: Macgibbon and Kee, 1957).

3

Ancient Religions

RONALD NICOLSON

Whereas primal religion is the religion of small clans and tribes living close to nature, in this chapter we discuss religions of ancient civilisations with their cities and their well-developed cultures. We might call these religions *polytheisms*, although that is of course a modern term which covers a broad category of religions ancient and modern. In a polytheisitic religion there is more than one god. It is important to remember, however, that the category of polytheism is a modern one, and that none of the ancient religions would have used this term or described themselves in this way. There is no such religion as polytheism; there are religions in which more than one god is worshipped.

Since many people believe in the existence of many gods but only worship one (this is sometimes called henotheism), or believe in one god who takes many forms or names or aspects, the distinction between polytheism and monotheism (worship of only one god) is a blurred one. The term polytheism is sometimes used judgementally of other religions by monotheistic religions which disapprove of polytheism, but this chapter makes no such qualitative judgement. It endeavours, rather, to explain the ideas behind a religion with more than one god.

We are only concerned in this chapter with the polytheism of ancient religions. We discuss the various characteristics of these religions generally, and include a more detailed description of ancient Egyptian religion in particular as an example. There were other well-developed ancient polytheisms in Greece and Rome, in Scandinavia, Germany and the Celtic world, in the Vedic period in India (discussed in chapter 4), in China, Japan, Mesoamerica and South America. None of these, except Vedic religion within Hinduism, has survived as a major world religion and the European ones have disappeared altogether.

Although it survives in folk religion, therefore, polytheism is mostly found in religions of the past. We might then ask if there is any point in studying this form of religion, since modern religions seem to agree that monotheism or monism are more logical and more consistent with modern knowledge and experience. It would be unwise, however, to make a judgement of this kind.

Whatever may be true of Hindu and Buddhist philosophy, it is a fact that many ordinary Hindu and Buddhist worshippers do operate within something like a polytheistic view of reality. For centuries, also, some forms of popular Christianity have looked remarkably polytheistic, with miracle-working saints whose images are venerated. Perhaps, therefore, a religion which focuses on a number of spiritual beings answers to the experiences and needs of ordinary people in a way that monism or monotheism do not. I shall be suggesting later that in many ways our modern religious world is becoming more like that of the polytheisms of old.

There are a number of different theories about whether polytheism led to monotheism or vice versa; mostly the theories are influenced by the prior conviction that Christianity is a 'better' religion than polytheism. Some, like James G. Frazer, have argued that belief in nature spirits of the woods and springs evolved into polytheism, which in turn evolved into monotheism – to further evolve, some would add, into scientific atheism. Others like Wilhelm Schmidt have argued that an original monotheism, such as Adam and Eve would have enjoyed, degenerated into polytheism, until a new revelation such as the Bible or Qur'an called people back to monotheism. In fact there is no real evidence for either theory. Both theories are the products of certain assumptions, for instance that religions evolve from lower to higher forms, that monotheism is better than polytheism, or that there was an original state of human righteousness. If we suspend judgements and assumptions of this kind, then it will be clear that modern converts from African primal religion to Christianity or Islam seem to have jumped straight from primal religion, of the kind described in the previous chapter, to monotheism without going through any intermediary stage of polytheism. There is no evidence that all of Hinduism is generally evolving into monotheism despite some exceptions to this.

Nor is it true to the evidence to say that monotheism is more suitable for sophisticated, literate cultures than polytheism, or to suggest that as humans become more civilised they naturally gravitate to monotheistic religious belief. Some of the great polytheisms of the past – Greek, Mesopotamian, Chinese – existed in civilisations that were a great deal more sophisticated, literate and cultured than early Jewish monotheism or mediaeval Christianity.

The polytheistic religion of the ancient civilisations cannot therefore be dismissed as being more primitive and less sophisticated than monotheism. It was, however, different from monotheism, not only with regard to the number of gods worshipped, but also with regard to the nature of those gods, the nature of their relationships with creation and with humans, and indeed with regard to the view which polytheism took of the world and of life as a whole. Depending on one's view of reality, polytheism may be more congenial to some world-views and cultures than to others.

Because polytheism lies for the most part in the past and in what are now dead religions, most of us know very little about it, and indeed there is not much literature on the subject in general, though the myths of particular polytheisms are described in many books. Traces of these past beliefs are, however, easier to find than we might think. We have all seen pictures of pyramids, of Greek and

ANCIENT EGYPTIAN RELIGION

Egypt is a hot, desert land, dominated by the relentless sun. There is little or no rain, but through the uninhabitable desert runs the Nile, which each year rises in flood bringing water and fertile soil. Those living on the Nile banks were secure and happy, usually protected by the desert and the sea from foreign invaders, their life running in dependable cycles. The one vulnerability of the land was that Egypt was very long, stretching about 1 600 kilometres, making contact between Lower and Upper Egypt difficult to maintain.

There were four major emphases in Egyptian religion, most of which arose logically from these circumstances.

1. The dominance of the universally worshipped Sun God.

2. The worship of local gods centred around particular temples.

3. An emphasis on a seasonal rising and dying god, and on life after death where the present pleasant, stable life could continue.

4. An emphasis on the divine status of the Pharaoh or King as the religious and political centre of unity in the land.

Particular gods were worshipped at particular temples: Atum at Heliopolis, Ptah at Memphis, Amun at Thebes. Sometimes these gods were pictured in human form, but Ptah was pictured as a bull. Yet because no god could compete with the Sun God for national recognition, each of these gods whom we have mentioned became associated with the Sun God and became, for example, Re-Atum or Re-Amun. Ptah was often depicted with the sun as a solar disk suspended between his horns. Other gods too became associated with the sun. The falcon-headed Horus became Re-Horakhti; sometimes the sun was associated with the beetle, Re-Khepra. We might wish to say therefore that the Egyptians worshipped only one god, but that was not how the Egyptians saw it, and the one attempt to make Egypt monotheistic under Pharaoh Amenhotep IV, *c.* 1366–1348 BCE (who renamed himself Akhenaton, the Servant of the Sun) was short-lived and probably politically motivated.

Egyptian polytheism was unusual in its emphasis on animal-headed gods like Ptah, Horus, Sobek the crocodile, Thoth the baboon, and Bas the cat. It would be easy to assume that these gods represent vestiges from an earlier primal religion, but there is no evidence that this was so, and indeed human-like gods appear very early in Egyptian religion while animal gods became even more popular in later periods, when even cats and dogs were mummified.

There were many stories about the gods and about creation. These stories do not always seem to fit together neatly to modern eyes. Egyptian thought followed a different kind of logic, what one writer has called 'many valued logic'[1]. In one creation story we are told of the creator god who made Shu (associated with air) and Tefnut (associated with moisture). Shu and Tefnut gave birth to Geb (the earth, depicted as male) and Nut (the sky, depicted as female), and Geb and Nut gave birth to the sun. But in another story the sun, Ra, is the creator god who gives birth to himself and to all other gods. We are told that Ra was angry with humans and sent his eye (the sun) to the earth in the form of the cow-headed Hathor to punish humans. But Hathor so enjoyed the slaughter that she would not stop, until the gods sent down beer coloured red to look like blood to cover the earth, and Hathor became drunk and was overpowered.

In one of the most famous stories, Geb and Nut give birth to Osiris, Isis, Seth and Nephthys. In turn, Osiris and his sister/wife Isis give birth to Horus. Seth is jealous and kills Osiris. The grieving Isis finds his body and brings him home. But Seth steals the body, cutting it into pieces and scattering the pieces throughout Egypt. Isis searches for the pieces, and buries them in each place she finds them (possibly a mythological account of the temples for Osiris in various places). Osiris returns from the Other World in the West (where the sun sets), and bids his son Horus to avenge him. After many battles with Seth, and assisted by Thoth, and after appearances before the council of gods, Horus is successful and becomes Pharaoh.

The reigning Pharaoh was thus associated with Horus, and the dead Pharaoh with Osiris. In a sense, therefore, the Pharaoh never changed; he was always Horus, and would be reborn as Osiris. Each year in the dry season Isis searched for Osiris – and each year in the return of the Nile floods she found him. Osiris became associated not only with the dead Pharaoh but with all the spirits of the departed, as well as with the spring harvest and the cycles of the moon. The worship of Osiris, Isis and Horus was taken over by the Greeks and Romans and spread even into Europe.

The belief in life after death led to a highly developed funerary system, at least for the wealthy. The dead bodies were mummified, that is, chemically preserved from corruption, and buried with household items which they might need in the life to come.

Roman temples and statuary. The old religions have left their mark in the names of our months – Januarius and Mars, or Julius and Augustus – to remind us that the Roman emperors were also often deified. The names of our days reflect the Germanic polytheism of the old Europeans: Sun-day, Moon-day, Woden's-day, Thor's-day, Freya's-day. We may know some of the stories told about gods in the Greek or Scandinavian myths – Zeus and the swan, Persephone's descent to Hades, and the story of Baldur the Beautiful.

Polytheism took many different forms in different places. The number of gods might be many or few. Gods might be associated with many different aspects of nature and of human activity. There might be a storm god, a rain god, a sun god. Particular cities might have gods associated with them, like Athens and Pallas Athene, Ephesus and Diana, Babylon and Marduk. There might be a god for warriors, a god for hunters, a god of the harvest.

There are, however, some features which are broadly true of polytheism in general. The gods were normally seen as being very similar to humans. That is, they were *anthropomorphic*, from *anthropos* and *morphe*, Greek words meaning a human form. (Of course, this is sometimes true of monotheistic religion too, for example God walking in the Garden of Eden.) Even the Egyptian animal-headed gods behaved in a human fashion. I have used the word 'god' throughout this chapter in preference to deity; but of course the gods of polytheism could be male or female. Female gods (or goddesses) were by no means always conceived of as being merely the wife of a more important god, and often had a considerable importance in their own right. Nor were female gods always sweet and gentle. Although many goddesses were mother figures, as well as giving life they also gave death (such as Hathor in Egyptian religion) and were often regarded with a mixture of love and terror. Some goddesses like Isis were major figures in the old polytheisms. Unlike the major monotheisms, therefore, in which the god is always conceived of in male terms and spoken of in male language ('he', 'his', etc.), polytheism found room for both male and female concepts of the godhead, a fact which has not escaped the notice of modern feminists.

The gods in these ancient religions acted in very human ways. They married, they had children – and thus they had beginnings, unlike the monotheistic God. They quarrelled, they lied, they cheated, they seduced human men and women. Although they might also be kind and protective they were by no means always benevolent to humans, nor could they be relied on for consistency or faithfulness. The major differences between gods and humans were that the gods were more powerful and were usually immortal. Even in this, however, there were exceptions. A god might die and be raised again, like Osiris in Egypt and Tammuz in Assyria. Dying and rising gods were very important in the understanding of the cycle of the seasons. Sometimes, although rarely, a god might die and not be raised again. In the Germanic myth Baldur is killed through the trickery of the wicked god Loki, and indeed all the gods of Valhalla were to die with the *Götterdämmerung* (twilight of the gods) and the destruction of Valhalla.

The relationship between humans and gods in polytheism was rather different from that which is conceived of in monotheism. For one thing, the gods, while much more powerful than humans, were not all-powerful or omnipotent, for one god could often undo what another god did, and even the High God, if there was one, could be outwitted by other gods and occasionally by astute humans. The gods were not all-knowing or omnipresent, qualities which tend to be associated with the deity of monotheistic religion. Nor were the gods necessarily good. The 'good' existed independently of the gods. The gods became very involved in human affairs, took part in human wars, and might even have love affairs with humans. Humans therefore needed to pray to the gods, or sometimes bribe the gods, in order to secure their help. But they could not rely on the gods, who might act capriciously or kindly as the mood took them. Humans would often need to try to 'second-guess' the gods. By consulting signs in the sky or in the behaviour of birds or animals or the shape of the entrails of a slain beast, it might be possible for a human to find out what it was that the gods were planning to do, and adjust his or her plans accordingly.

Humans therefore were not totally at the mercy of the gods. They might play off one god against another. Humans were also understood to have the power to share with the gods in the shaping of their own destiny. Indeed, by participating in worship and sacrifice, and in fertility rites and agricultural rituals, humans shared with the gods in maintaining the rhythm of life. In a polytheistic world-view there was often greater scope for humans to play their part because the gods were seen in a less absolute way than they were in monotheism.

A feature of many of the ancient religions we are considering in this chapter is that over a period of time the gods might coalesce into other gods. A god previously worshipped under one name might become identified with another previously different god. For example in Egyptian religion the god Ptah, worshipped in Memphis, became known instead as Apis, and eventually became associated with the god Osiris – as well as being simultaneously associated with the sun god Ra. This may seem confusing to modern Western logic, but polytheism was less concerned with a unitary logical system than modern Western thought has tended to be.

In other cases a god worshipped in one era became neglected and forgotten in later periods. Geb and Nut in Egyptian religion were believed to be the father and mother of all the gods, but in fact were not widely worshipped in the accounts we have of Egyptian religion, with very little attention being paid to them.

It is possible that this process may partly be explained by socio-political events, although not all scholars would agree with this. We might guess that a group of people was initially what some scholars would call polydaemonist (polydaemonists believe in many spiritual entities without necessarily conceiving of them as gods), but as the perception of human importance grew, so the impersonal spirits and the animal totemistic deities became the anthropomorphic gods that we have already described. As within a culture humans began to see themselves as special within nature, more in control of their own world, and as the sense of human dignity and importance grew, so the gods were no longer perceived as spirits or as living within trees or rivers, but were seen as human beings writ large. Perhaps, as a people ceased to be merely concerned with agriculture, so the people's sense of identity with nature became lessened. A greater human distantiation from nature meant that the gods, too, became more distant from nature and humans more distant from the gods. In due course small groups were absorbed into larger units, even into nations. They took their god or gods with them into the new federation, but these gods became part of a larger group of gods brought by other people into the federation. It is common to find in polytheism that the gods were arranged into a sort of hierarchy or *pantheon*, with a chief god who frequently had a chief wife and a number of children, and other gods ranged in varying degrees of importance. Thus in ancient Greek religion we find Zeus and his wife Hera and their children. Sometimes instead of being arranged in a family, the gods were arranged in a group, often a triad. Thus in Mesopotamian religion we find An, Enlil and Ea grouped together, or Sin, Shamash and Ishtar. The triad, or the family, did not exclude the existence, however, of other gods who were usually of lesser importance.

The place of the gods in the pantheon might well have been determined by the relative importance of the merging peoples as nations began to form. Thus the fact that Horus is a good god in Egyptian mythology and Seth, his uncle, is a bad god, may indicate that the group which initially had Horus as their totem overcame and dominated a rival group who worshipped Seth. But in due course other nations, with other gods, might invade and possess the land. Although the invaders brought their own gods with them, the older gods were still worshipped, but there was a rearrangement of the pantheon. Previously important gods of the original inhabitants diminished in status, or became merged with one of the newer gods. Enlil, previously mentioned as a Mesopotamian god, was very similar to, and eventually became identified with, the Babylonian Marduk, as the Babylonian empire replaced the Assyrian in the Mesopotamian basin, and Marduk emerged as the chief god.

In many cases, therefore (if the theory is correct), a polytheistic religion seems to have developed out of primal religion, and then to have become increasingly systematised, the gods sometimes being effectively reduced in number, arranged in hierarchies, then rearranged again as circumstances changed. This was not, of course, a conscious process but one which took place gradually and imperceptibly over a long period of time. The myths reflecting the people's religion would have been told and retold in the oral tradition, changing gradually over the years. By the time the culture became literate the polytheism would have become more stable. Since we only have the later, and written, forms of the story available to us, we must perforce reconstruct the original stories and beliefs by guesswork.

Why did polytheism prosper in places like Egypt or India for so long? Because ideas about the function of religion differ from scholar to scholar there could be a number of answers to the question of why some cultures are polytheistic and others monotheistic. It seems clear that polytheistic belief helped resolve a number of issues. It enabled peasant farming communities to explain and, to an extent, control the rhythm of the seasons. Stories of dying and rising gods mirror the 'death' of nature in the dry season and the rebirth of the crops in the wet. There were the myths, for example, of the Egyptian god Osiris being killed by the evil god Seth. Osiris' wife Isis sought his body and brought it back to life. In this and other similar myths in other religions, the worshippers were enabled, by their annual ritual re-enactment of the myth, to feel that they were somehow sharing in bringing back the spring rains and new growth. If the rains were late, they perhaps felt they could do something about it. Similarly, sacrifices to the storm gods would, in their minds, have helped ward off the violence of the weather. For a people dependent on the earth, the rain, and the climate for survival, polytheism and its associated rituals seemed to provide a degree of control over fate.

Many polytheistic religions emphasised a sacred kingship. The king was seen as being closely associated with the gods. In Egypt, the Pharaoh was identified with the god Horus and, when dead, with the god Osiris; in Babylon the king was closely associated with Marduk. Thus the power and prestige of the king was bolstered by being made sacred. As we have mentioned, in Roman religion the Caesar was often seen as a god. Thus, in a wide-ranging empire many diverse peoples could be united around the worship of the emperor. At the same time, since in a polytheism there is no need to deny the existence and power of other gods too, a place was allowed for the city gods and tribal gods of the people of the empire, and local community identity was not suppressed. In the occasional worship of the king on state occasions there was a unity, and in the everyday worship of the community's particular gods there was a permissible diversity. This caused great problems, however, when the Roman empire included first Jews and then Christians amongst its subjects. Jews and Christians refused to worship Caesar even as a matter of form, and were seen therefore as a threat to the unity and security of the empire. Indeed, since a powerful monotheism does not easily allow for religious freedom, they *were* a potential threat to that unity.

Outwardly there might appear to be little difference between polytheism and monotheism. The patterns of worship are mostly very similar: both often had priests, both sometimes worshipped by means of the offering of food and animals and in rare cases human sacrifices too. Both might have temples in which these religious activities took place.

But polytheism and monotheism perceive the relationship between the worshipper and the god(s) somewhat differently, and have quite different views on the nature of reality. In monotheism there is one creator god, who alone gives purpose and meaning to life. Everything in creation is thus dependent on him. The universe is a single, directional whole because God made it, God determines what happens in it, God directs its history. History in monotheism is therefore teleological, that is, it is moving towards an end which God has planned and which God directs.

In polytheism there was no one creator god. Sometimes an ancient 'ancestor' of the gods might be understood to have been the Creator, but usually such a creator god was not conceived of as being currently active or real. The gods themselves were created. There were thus multiple forces operating in the universe, not always in harmony. The existence of accidents and suffering was therefore not such a puzzle in a polytheistic world.

Nor was there a single set of values. Polytheism, like monotheism, might include moral laws and commandments, but these did not usually derive from a single creator god. Often the moral system existed independently of the gods.

In a polytheistic world, therefore, there are many values, which do not necessarily have to tie up into a logical whole. When they looked at their world, it seemed to the people of polytheistic cultures that life was like that: a mixture of different kinds of good and evil, a balance of different forces pulling in different directions. History did not seem to be moving towards some purposeful climax, but to be circular or repetitive, like the seasons of the year.

In an agricultural society, the gods controlling the forces of nature took precedence. In an urban society the gods were often allied instead to cities; and, in an urban society, as human labour diversified, so the gods became associated with these diverse activities. Whereas in an agricultural society everybody is a farmer with much the same needs and religious perspective, in a city there is a division of labour. Some are rulers, some are artisans, some scholars or merchants or soldiers. For each of these activities there was often a corresponding deity, each with his or her place in the scheme of things. Gender roles tend to be more distinct in urban life as well; a peasant and his wife must both tend the land, but men and women were not equally rulers, soldiers or merchants in the ancient world. Gods and goddesses therefore reflected this diversity of gender roles. The development of the pantheon or hierarchy of gods established an order and system in this diverse and plural world. But it was not always as absolute or logical or unified as in a monotheism – because life didn't seem to them to reflect absolute order.

Like monotheism, polytheism too expressed itself by means of 'myths'. Myths are stories about the gods, stories which appear to be set in time and space but are not really. The myths are powerful, poetic, symbolic ways of talking about how and why things are the way they are. Although sometimes the myths were based on past historical events – the Homeric stories about the Trojan War, for instance – they were never really understood to be historical events in the same way that Jews regarded the account of the exodus from Egypt, or Christians the stories about the life and death of Jesus, or Muslims the description of Muhammad receiving the Qur'an. No one in the ancient world tried to put a date to the seduction of Leda by Zeus, or Persephone's descent to the underworld.

Why did ancient polytheisms die? Not because of any deficiencies as a personal religion. But they no longer fitted a changing world environment. It suited the post-Constantinian Roman empire to use Christianity as a central rallying point. The ancient religions of the Roman empire lacked a sense of linear history. The Greek and Roman philosophers became increasingly scornful about the lack of historical sense in polytheistic religion, and about its moral ambiguities. Increasingly, it seems, people were looking for a single explanatory system for the universe, in order to interact with and control it more effectively. People wanted a single moral system which would be of universal validity. They wanted to find a predictable order in life, which polytheism by its nature could not supply. The development of science really requires this. What is more, people's concept of salvation increasingly changed from deliverance from the natural evils that confront a farming community, or human enemies, and turned to a more spiritual hope for life beyond death. Arguably, monotheism seemed to provide better for that hope. 'Christianity could outbid the old religion with teachings that were simpler, more consistent, and more authoritative than any which pagan authorities could supply. Christianity was based on revelation. It upheld a morality based on divine teaching . . . It formed a community that existed independently of the Roman State . . . When the political framework of the empire collapsed, the Church continued to provide a sense of continuity, while its bishops offered authoritative moral instruction and encouragement.'[2]

LUCRETIUS ON THE GODS

The Roman poet and philosopher Lucretius lived just before the time of Jesus. He attacked what he regarded as the superstition of polytheism. He believed that the gods existed, composed of very fine atoms, living in the spaces between the worlds in tranquillity and peace, far removed from the troubles of this world. The gods therefore were not creators. The serious flaws evident in the world made it irrational to believe that the gods had created it or that they governed it. The gods did not interfere with human lives, nor did they require our worship or our sacrifices, nor could they help us. Superstitious religion, in Lucretius' mind, created fear, unhappiness and cruelty. Polytheism had ceased to be a living religion for Lucretius with his early quasi-scientific views about atoms.

Perhaps, though, in our modern world, we have begun to come closer to polytheism again. Modern physicists are not so certain that the universe functions according to a single set of scientific laws. In our diverse modern cities no single religious view is universally accepted. We are not as sure as our forefathers that moral rules can be clearly demarcated. In all sorts of ways the modern West, at least, has become a very pluralistic society. Merlin Stone has argued, from a feminist point of view, that polytheism has the advantage of allowing both male and female characteristics to be seen as part of what is divine. It is unlikely, perhaps, that we shall ever become fully fledged polytheists again; but perhaps we are better able to understand their world-view than previous generations were.

NOTES

1. Erik Hornung, *Concepts of God in Ancient Egypt*. London: Routledge and Kegan Paul, 1982, p. 239.

2. J. H. W. C. Liebeschuetz, *Continuity and Change in Roman Religion*. London: Oxford University Press, 1979.

SELECT BIBLIOGRAPHY

David, A. Rosalie. *The Ancient Egyptians*. London: Routledge and Kegan Paul, 1982

Eliade, Mircea. *The Encyclopedia of World Mythology*. New York: Macmillan, 1985. Articles on 'Polytheism', 'Egyptian religion', 'Greek religion' and 'Mesopotamian religions'

Ellwood, Robert S., Jr. *Many Peoples, Many Faiths*, 2nd edition. Englewood Cliffs, N.J.: Prentice-Hall, 1982

Encyclopedia of World Mythology. London: Peerage Books, 1975

Hornung, Erik. *Concepts of God in Ancient Egypt*. London: Routledge and Kegan Paul, 1982

Morford, Mark P. O. & Lenardon, Robert J. *Classical Mythology*. New York: Longman, 1971

Shorter, Alan W. *The Egyptian Gods*. London: Routledge and Kegan Paul, 1937, reprinted 1978

Stone, Merlin. *The Paradise Papers: The Suppression of Women's Rites*. London: Virago, 1979

4

The Religions of India

PATRICK MAXWELL AND THILLAYVEL NAIDOO

HINDUISM

The greater part of this chapter is devoted to the Hindu tradition. Towards the end, however, there are also shorter treatments of two other religions that arose in India, namely Jainism and Sikhism. Chapter 5 of this book contains a separate account of Buddhism, which also arose in India but which has evolved its present character mostly outside the land of its birth.

The Hindu religious tradition is rooted in a cultural heritage that counts its age in millennia. Its earliest sources are the scriptures known as the Vedas, which form the foundation also for its unique legacy of philosophical ideas. The ancient and very appropriate name for what Westerners call Hinduism is *Sanatana Dharma*, the Eternal Way or Eternal Tradition. The English word Hinduism, which came into existence less than two hundred years ago, is based on the older term Hindu, which itself was merely an adaptation of one of the Persian names for India. Over 90 per cent of the world's Hindus live in India, and over 75 per cent of these live in villages rather than urban contexts. Hinduism does of course exist outside India; it was an important element in the cultures of south-east Asia until at least the mediaeval period and it still maintains a significant foothold on the Indonesian island of Bali. In recent times Hinduism has established a presence in the West, the most well-known, if not perhaps the most important example being the colourful Hare Krishna movement.

Hinduism can be distinguished from many other religious traditions in at least two ways. Firstly, unlike most other religions with very large followings, the Hindu tradition has no historical founder. Secondly, it has a tolerant and inclusive outlook, especially in the realm of doctrines and ideas. It caters for a very wide range of religious and spiritual inclinations. It has no universal creed, no single core of theological ideas and no uniformly authoritative sacred text. Hinduism is also for the most part an unusually hospitable tradition; it has absorbed many originally quite distinct cultural and religious sub-traditions over the centuries. The main tradition has usually tended to reconcile various options rather than firmly choose one to the exclusion of the others.

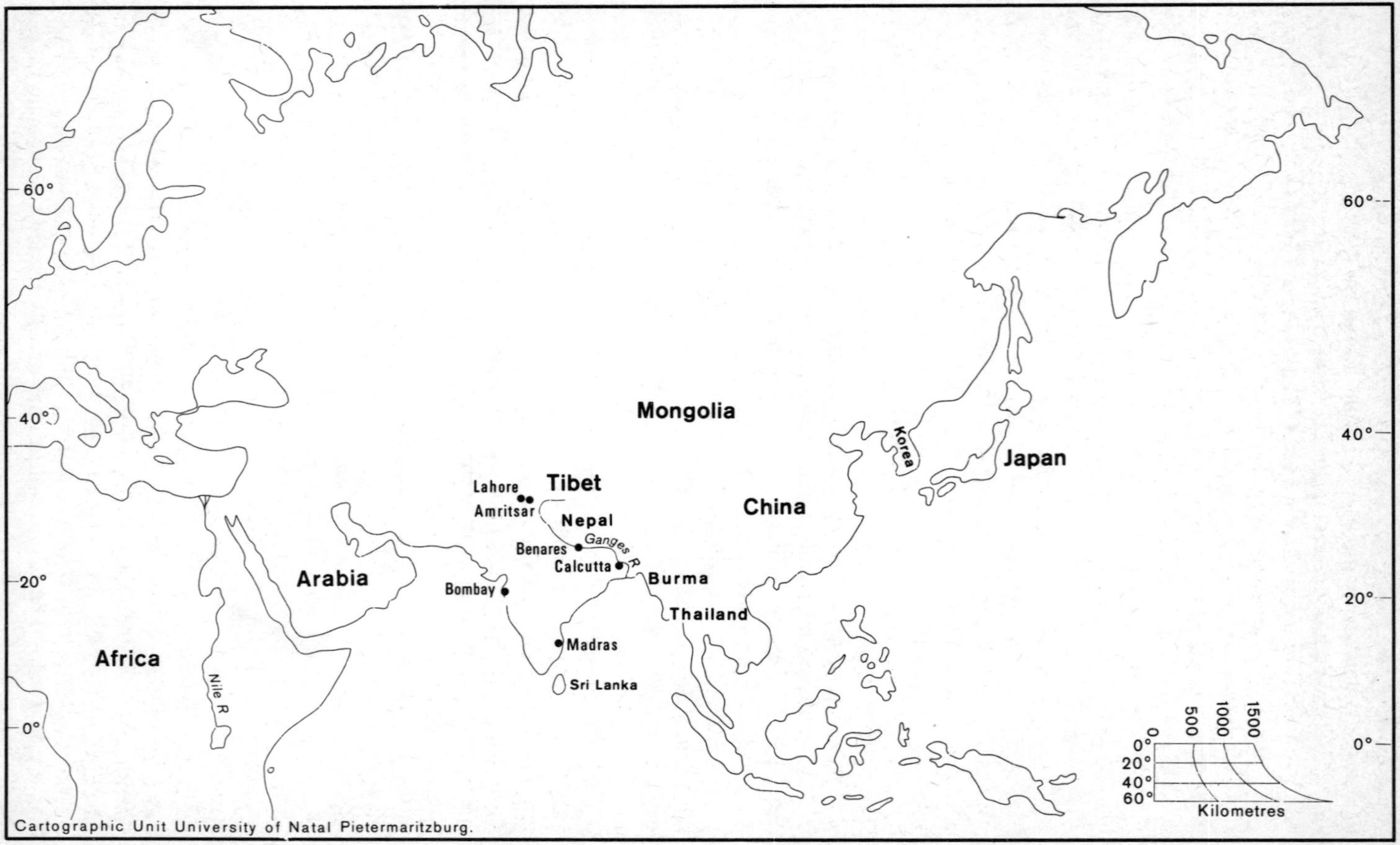
60°
40°
20°
0°
Mongolia
Tibet
Lahore
Amritsar
Nepal
Benares
Ganges R
Calcutta
Burma
Thailand
China
Korea
Japan
Arabia
Bombay
Madras
Sri Lanka
Africa
Nile R
0°
20°
40°
60°
0
500
1000
1500
Kilometres
Cartographic Unit University of Natal Pietermaritzburg.

It is this very diversity and complexity that make an adequate and economical definition of Hinduism almost impossible. Some have recommended that we regard the somewhat artificial umbrella term 'Hinduism' as denoting a loose federation of religious traditions rather than a single religion. The vast Hindu synthesis has generated and embraced mainstream as well as folk and minority strands, popular as well as philosophical dimensions, theistic as well as atheistic theologies, and ritualistic as well as contemplative practices. Is it possible to identify any features which *all* Hindus hold in common? Perhaps not; but the following four themes would certainly be accepted by most who identify with the tradition. (1) Belief in the interminable process of repeated reincarnation, which is governed by *karma*, the universal and impersonal law of cause and effect. (2) The conviction that, in the last analysis, there is one Ultimate Divine Reality who is the spiritual goal of all creaturely existence. This is worth emphasising, especially as this chapter will introduce many Hindu 'deities' and 'divine manifestations', which may create the impression that Hinduism is essentially polytheistic. (3) The perception that the only way to break free from the chain of reincarnations is to come to terms experientially with the Divine Reality. (4) Acceptance of the fact that the scriptures known as the Vedas carry formal religious authority and the recognition that the *Bhagavadgita* (Song of the Lord) is one of the best-loved and most universal of the Hindu scriptures.

Unlike many Western contexts, which have in recent centuries witnessed a significant tension between the disciplines of philosophy and religion, Indian tradition in general and the Hindu tradition in particular tend to conceive of religion and philosophy as together serving as guides along the path that leads to higher wisdom.

HISTORICAL DEVELOPMENT OF HINDUISM

Hindu religious literature and often also those later figures who studied and reflected on the literature, have long displayed an enigmatic indifference to history and to the attitude which regards historicity as crucial to religion. The gathering of scholarly information on the historical development of the Hindu faith has also been made difficult by the characteristic Hindu emphasis that religious truth often seems to transcend and even render unnecessary considerations of biographical and chronological detail. The attempt therefore to identify specific periods of Hindu religious history has succeeded only to the extent that broad and tentative classifications become possible. One such classification follows.

The Indus Valley civilisation

The Indus Valley in the north-west of historic India was the scene of a flourishing civilisation during the period approximately 3000–1500 BCE. It is difficult to reconstruct Indus Valley religion, not least because the script has not yet been deciphered; but archaeologists who investigated the relevant cities, notably Mohenjo-daro and Harappa, have unearthed seals, figurines and other objects which indicate that the culture of the Indus Valley people may have been focused on dimensions such as the mother goddess, phallic symbolism, water ablutions, and certain ascetic practices akin to Indian yoga. Most fascinating of all the discoveries are depictions of a horned figure with phallic characteristics who is seated in a cross-legged posture; in one case he is surrounded by certain animals. Many scholars have regarded the above themes and motifs as anticipations of some of the emphases of later Hinduism, with the enigmatic seated figure being seen as an anticipation of the Hindu god Shiva, a complex deity who is regarded, among other things, as Prince of Yogis as well as Lord of Beasts.

The Vedic age

The Vedic age of India (sometimes called the age of Vedism or Brahmanism or both) saw the flourishing of religious beliefs and practices based on the Vedas, which were the scriptures of people known as Aryans, a word meaning 'noble ones'. The Vedas were transmitted orally for many centuries before being eventually committed to writing. The 'proto-Sanskrit' language of the Aryans has an interesting relationship with other Indo-European languages and cultures such as Persian, Greek, German and English.

Sanskrit term		*Other Indo-European*
Aryan	(ethnic/national designation)	Iran, Eire
Dyaus	(the name of a god)	Zeus (Greek)
Varuna	(the name of a god)	Ouranos (Greek)
Mitra	(the name of a god)	Mithra (Persian)
Agni	(the name of a god)	Ignis (Latin)
Veda	(knowledge)	Oida (Greek)

The conventional scholarly view holds that the Vedic age began at some stage during the second millennium BCE when, soon after the decline of the Indus Valley civilisation, the semi-nomadic Aryans invaded India from the north-west, then gradually spread eastwards across northern India. The Vedic age came to an end in about the fifth century BCE, soon after the emergence of scriptures known as the Upanishads. Given the orthodox Hindu conviction that the Vedas are eternal, however, all scholarly attempts to relate them to particular periods of ancient Indian history are doomed to be controversial. Many Hindus believe that the Vedic age began long before the second millennium BCE, and some even maintain that the Aryans were the immemorial people of India rather than relatively recent invaders into the country.

The classical period

The classical period lasted roughly one thousand years, from about 500 BCE to about 500 CE. This period witnessed the consolidation of both Vedic and non-Vedic traditions into the so-called Hindu synthesis. Important scriptures which are thought to have emerged during this period include the *Laws of Manu* (one of the so-called Dharma-shastras or law manuals), the two Epics (the

Ramayana and the *Mahabharata*), the *Bhagavadgita*, the *Sutras* of the classical philosophical schools, and the early Puranas, notably the Vishnu Purana. The religious phenomenon of *bhakti* (loving devotion to a personal God) was probably in existence in early classical times. By the end of the classical period, the theological and iconographic characteristics of the gods had crystallised, and Hindu temples containing *murtis* or images of various deities were becoming a familiar sight.

Although the term Hinduism can be used comprehensively to include even the Indus Valley period, many scholars see the history of 'Hinduism proper' as beginning with the classical emergence of the *Laws of Manu* and the Epics.

The medieval period

The medieval period stretches from about the sixth century CE to about the middle of the eighteenth century. Important scriptures which were compiled during this period include the later Puranas, of which the most celebrated is the Bhagavata Purana, one of the fundamental holy texts of the modern Hare Krishnas. The medieval period saw the flourishing of the developed theistic *bhakti* movements and also the work of the great Vedantic philosophers Shankara, Ramanuja and Madhva.

It is worth emphasising that some Hindu teachers and authors regard many of the Hindu scriptures just mentioned as having their origins long before 500 BCE.

The modern period

The modern phase of Hinduism began with the establishment of British power in India and was characterised by the establishment of several Hindu and neo-Hindu reform movements. Because of their importance, these are described in some detail below in the final section of this discussion of Hinduism.

THE PRIMARY HINDU SCRIPTURES

Hindu scriptures are conventionally classified as either *shruti* ('what is heard'), which are the primary but not necessarily the most used scriptures, or *smriti* ('what is remembered'), comprising the secondary sources of religious knowledge and practice. It is very difficult to establish the dates of composition of the various *shruti* and *smriti* texts, although most scholars would place almost all of them somewhere between 1500 BCE and 1500 CE. All the *shruti* scriptures and most of the important *smriti* scriptures were written in Sanskrit, the classical language of India.

Shruti comprises the Vedas, the earliest scriptures of the Hindu tradition, while *smriti* encompasses scriptures which are later than, and subordinate in authority to, the Vedas. *Smriti* scriptures are believed to be the compositions of enlightened teachers who, in some instances, are known by name. They draw inspiration from the Vedas, which, in theory if not in practice, they acknowledge to be the final arbiter on religious matters. *Smriti* scriptures, which are discussed in a later section, include the *Laws of Manu*, the two Epics, the *Bhagavadgita*, the classical philosophical *Sutras*, and the Puranas.

Hindus regard the Vedas (sometimes the singular form 'Veda' is used) as *shruti* because they contain revealed truths believed to have been spiritually discovered or discerned by the ancient *rishis* or seers who heard directly the eternal, sacred sounds. The Vedas are not regarded as the compositions of any human mind; they contain spiritual truths said to be *nitya* (eternal) and *apaurusheya* (not of humans, not of personal authorship). The word 'Veda' means knowledge: it is linguistically related to the Greek word *oida*, the German word *wissen* and the English word *wit*.

There are four Vedas: the Rig-Veda, which is the earliest and most important, the Sama-Veda, the Yajur-Veda and the Atharva-Veda. Each of these is divided into four strata, namely Samhita (or Mantra), Brahmana, Aranyaka and Upanishad. Samhita and Brahmana make up the ritual portion (*karma kanda*) and Aranyaka and Upanishad make up the knowledge portion (*jnana kanda*).

The Samhitas contain the following: (1) hymns in praise of various deities (Rig-Veda Samhita); (2) priestly chants or melodies for use with certain sacrifices (Sama-Veda Samhita); much of the content of this Samhita is taken from the Rig-Veda Samhita; (3) sacrificial and ritual procedures (Yajur-Veda Samhita); (4) spells, charms, and speculations (Atharva-Veda Samhita). If the first three Samhitas are biased towards a priestly view of things, the fourth, the Atharva-Veda, served largely as the Veda of the masses.

The Brahmanas are prose texts which were produced probably in the earlier part of the first millennium BCE. They contain elaborate details about the priestly rituals as well as philosophical speculations concerning the nature, methods and meaning of sacrifice. An important preoccupation of the Brahmanas is the drawing up of endless correlations or correspondences between the macro-sphere (the universe at large) and the micro-sphere (for example, the various ritual elements such as chants, recitations, implements, sacrificial locations and ingredients).

The Aranyakas ('Forest books') interpret the various rituals and ceremonials by spiritualising them and expounding their symbolisms, and the Upanishads form the concluding portion of the Vedas. Theoretically, the Upanishads each fall under one or other of the four Vedas, but in practice they are studied as a distinct body of literature. They contain speculations about philosophy and mystical realisations, and it is the Upanishads that are often credited with forming the foundational truths of Hinduism, especially its philosophical dimensions.

What is often confusing to the student of Hinduism is that the term 'Vedas' is ambiguous. Sometimes (as used above) it refers to the whole body of *shruti*, that is, it includes the four Samhitas, the Brahmanas, the Aranyakas and the Upanishads. However, 'Vedas' is quite commonly used to denote the four Samhitas alone. Thus when contemporary Arya Samaj Hindus issue their rallying-cry, 'Back to the Vedas!', they have primarily the four Samhitas in mind.

What follows constitutes a summary of the religion of two of the most interesting and important sections of the Vedas, namely the Rig-Veda Samhita and the Upanishads.

The Rig-Veda Samhita

The Samhita of the Rig-Veda (which we shall now refer to simply as the Rig-Veda) consists of 1 028 hymns, organised into ten books. Books one and ten probably represent a later religious phase than books two to eight, and book nine is devoted to the god Soma. The picture of Rigvedic religion given below is largely a Western scholarly reconstruction. Some modern Hindus, especially those who identify with the Arya Samaj, would disagree with aspects of this account. (The Arya Samaj maintains that the Samhitas uniformly teach themes such as explicit monotheism and reincarnation, among other things.) Vedic religion was basically aniconic; in other words, there were no images or visual representations of the gods. This stands in contrast to the explicit iconolatry (image-veneration) of much of later Hinduism.

God and the gods

The Rig-Veda contains the names of many divine manifestations who were worshipped. Some of these are personifications of natural powers while others are more abstract divinities, but there is no systematic or organised pantheon of deities. Scholarly controversy exists over the extent to which Vedic theology was monotheistic, polytheistic or kathenotheistic (kathenotheism means giving your full attention to one deity at a time). One widely held view is that a gradual development took place from polytheism to monotheism; certainly monotheism is expounded in book one of the Rig-Veda, which is one of its latest strata: 'They call it Indra, Mitra, Varuna, Agni . . . the Real is one, though wise men give it various names . . . ' (Rig-Veda 1.164.46).

Some of the more important and powerful gods in the Rig-Veda are as follows. Indra is the popular god of weather and war, who vanquished the demon of chaos or drought and helps the Aryans in their earthly struggles. Varuna is the upholder of *rita*, that is, cosmic and moral order, who can forgive the penitent and liberate people from ritual and moral sin. Agni, the god of fire, the god of the priests and the priest of the gods, is second in importance only to Indra. As fire, Agni officiates at every sacrifice. His office is strongly mediatorial; he conveys the people's offerings to the gods and mediates divine blessings to human beings. Soma is the divinisation of the *soma* plant, whose hallucinogenic and immortalising juices were extracted and used in the *soma* offerings.

Other deities include Mitra, god of loyalty and promise-keeping, Savitri and Surya (sun gods), the Maruts (storm gods who ride with Indra), Vayu the wind god, Vishnu, a benevolent, all-pervasive deity, and Rudra, the unpredictable father of the Maruts. Some of the Rigvedic goddesses are Prithivi (earth goddess), Aditi, goddess of boundless space, and Ushas, goddess of the dawn. Later Rigvedic gods include Prajapati (Lord of creatures), Vishvakarman (Maker of all things), Brihaspati (Lord of sacred utterance) and Yama (Ruler of the dead). Vedic deities are characterised by varying degrees of anthropomorphism. One of the best examples of this is the god Indra, who fights, boasts about his deeds and is a little too fond of drinking the sacred *soma* juice.

The central Vedic ritual was the *yajna*, or sacrifice. In the Rigvedic fire-sacrifices, the supplicant praises and serves the gods, and hopes that they will grant the requested benefits and blessings (health, long life, happiness, offspring) in return. As time went on, sacrifice began to be conceived in a more coercive way: if the priests performed the sacrifices correctly, the gods would have no option but to carry out their divine functions. This theme is put clearly in the Yajur-Veda: 'even the gods must do the will of the priests if the priests perform the sacrifice correctly'. The very maintenance of the universe was thought to depend on the correctly performed sacrificial rituals. Sacrificial offerings include grains, *ghee* (clarified butter), milk, *soma*, and occasionally animals such as goats, bulls and rams.

A robust, world-affirming atmosphere prevails in Rigvedic religion, in contrast to the distinctly pessimistic outlook of, say, the later Maitri Upanishad. Minimal attention is paid to the hereafter, but in the later strata of the Rig-Veda the after-life seems to be conceived of in terms of alternative destinies: paradise for the righteous and the abyss for the wicked. Furthermore, the Rig-Veda appears to accept a significant distinction between the human body and the inner, immaterial spirit.

The Rigvedic verse 3.62.10 states: 'We meditate on the lovely light of the god Savitri; may he illumine our minds.' This soon developed into one of the most important and universal Hindu religious affirmations, known as the *Gayatri Mantra*.

Other emphases, found especially in book ten of the Rig-Veda, include speculation about cosmic origins in some famous hymns. Rig-Veda 10.90 sees creation as the result of a great primeval sacrifice, in which the cosmic giant Purusha is dismembered; Rig-Veda 10.121 portrays the creator as a cosmic Golden Embryo, whereas Rig-Veda 10.129 registers an agnostic note about cosmic origins. Furthermore, the Aryans had a patriarchal social structure which was based on a threefold class distinction. Soon after their arrival in India they appear to have added a fourth level below the existing three. This fourth level consisted of the darker-skinned indigenous people of India, whom the Aryans tended to despise. The resulting fourfold division is given explicit religious justification in Rig-Veda 10.90.12. These four *varnas* or social classes became entrenched within historic Hinduism as the brahmin priests and teachers; the warriors; the farmers and tradesmen; and the *sudras* or serfs. Lastly, significant correlations are drawn between the macro-dimension of reality which concerns the universe at large and the micro-dimension of reality which concerns the particular and the individual. This important theme is elaborated in the Brahmanas and Upanishads and has significantly influenced subsequent Hinduism. Two examples of this are the idea of the Hindu temple as a microcosm of the universe and the teaching in Tantric (esoteric, magical) Hinduism that the human body mirrors the whole cosmos.

Rudra, a wild, unpredictable god who is paradoxically associated with both disease and healing, and Vishnu, a benevolent god with vague solar associations, appear in the Rig-Veda but do not rank with the great deities. Later, however, under the names Shiva and Vishnu, these two were to become the great deities of classical and medieval Hinduism.

The following terms, which were all in use by the beginning of the Upanishadic period, are easy to confuse: brahmin (or brahman), which means an Aryan or Vedic priest; Brahmanas, meaning scriptures with a priestly and ritual emphasis; Brahma, a creator god, akin to Prajapati; and *brahman*, a term which first meant 'sacred utterance', though by the time of the Atharva-Veda and the Brahmanas it had come to mean 'sacred power' – not only the power behind the sacrifice, but the power underlying all things; in other words, the universal cosmic principle which is so important in the Upanishads.

The Upanishads

There are many Upanishads in the Hindu tradition, but the principal ones were probably produced between the eighth and fourth centuries BCE. The Upanishads presuppose the Vedas but go beyond their teachings. They significantly develop certain late Vedic and Brahmanic emphases, for example the idea that behind the manifest multiplicity of existence lies one, changeless, immortal, universal Divine Reality, and the conviction that there is an intimate and inextricable relationship between the macro-sphere and the micro-sphere.

It has been said that the Upanishads exhibit a movement toward unity (there is *one* divine reality); a movement toward subjectivity or inwardness (the divine reality is *within* you); and a movement toward spirituality (the emphasis is on *inner realisation* rather than external rituals). One meaning of the word 'Upanishad' conjures up the picture of a student sitting with a spiritual teacher. The Upanishads can be referred to as 'Vedanta', meaning 'the end of the Vedas', but in this chapter we shall use the term Vedanta only for certain post-Upanishadic philosophical developments, to be discussed later. Upanishadic teaching spans a broad spectrum, from monism on one hand to theism or at least near-theism on the other. Later Hindu thinkers tended to smooth out or to underplay the tensions and doctrinal varieties within the Upanishads. The historian of religion, however, tries to do justice to both the monistic and the theistic tendencies within Upanishadic theology, as can be seen in the following account of the main teachings of the Upanishads.

Brahman–atman

The Upanishads teach a close association or equation between *brahman*, the absolute, changeless, ultimate, sustaining principle of the universe, and *atman*, the immortal human self in its deepest essence; between reality in its objective mode and reality in its subjective mode; between the macrocosm and the microcosm. The Upanishads do not possess a uniform conception of *brahman*; the idea oscillates between *brahman* as the indescribable One which is beyond the changing multiplicities of the universe (the exclusive Absolute), and *brahman* as the all-pervading, all-encompassing Ground which includes all those things that it undergirds and manifests (the inclusive Absolute). It is best to avoid translating *brahman* and *atman* into English words that are already loaded with Western connotations, such as God and the soul. Instead, one should use terms such as Ultimate Divine Reality and pure consciousness. Moreover, the *atman* must be distinguished from all the merely transient dimensions of the human being such as the bodily, the mental and the psychological.

UPANISHADIC PASSAGES CONCERNING BRAHMAN–ATMAN

This Self – what can one say of it but 'No, no!' It is impalpable . . . indestructible . . . free from attachment . . . (Brihadaranyaka 4.2.4)

Unthinkable is He, unformed, profound, concealed, faultless, compact, impenetrably deep, devoid of attributes . . . beginningless and endless . . . He is called AUM, effulgent, unsleeping, ageless, deathless . . . indwelling all, imperishable, pure, purified, resplendent . . . (Maitri 7.1–7) (AUM is the ultimate sacred sound in Hinduism.)

What is called *brahman*, that is what this space outside a man is; and what that space outside a man is, that is what this space within a man is . . . (Chandogya 3.12.7–8)

. . . he is my Self within the heart, smaller than a grain of rice or a barley-corn . . . this is my Self within my heart, greater than the earth . . . greater than all these worlds . . . This my Self within the heart is that *brahman*. (Chandogya 3.14.4–5)

This finest essence, the whole universe has it as its Self: That is the Real: That is the Self: That you are (*tat twam asi*) . . . (Chandogya 6.8.7)

This Self that indwells all things is within you. (Brihadaranyaka 3.4.1)

Karma and reincarnation

It is not clear exactly when these two doctrines appeared in the emerging Hindu tradition. By the sixth century BCE, both doctrines had certainly established a foothold. Many Western scholars believe that there is no clear evidence of the theme of reincarnation prior to Upanishadic times, but certain Hindus, notably the Arya Samaj, insist that the Samhitas explicitly teach this theme. Reincarnation can be defined as the notion that the essential 'I' continues to endure throughout many successive lifetimes. Reincarnation can take place in human or subhuman form. *Samsara* is the term used to denote the beginningless and endless process or cycle of repeated reincarnations. In the later Upanishads, especially Maitri, there is a mood of profound pessimism about the endless cycle of *samsara*.

Karma can be defined as a sort of impersonal principle or eternal spiritual law which automatically ensures that our basic situation or disposition in this lifetime is in moral and spiritual accordance with how we have lived during previous lifetimes. *Karma* does not entail fatalism or determinism; although what people are now is certainly determined by their past, they nevertheless are significantly free to shape their own future from this point onwards. While Hinduism did not lay as much emphasis on the motives behind human actions as did Buddhism, Hindu tradition recognises that it is the willed, motivated act that typically reaps an appropriate karmic legacy.

The doctrines of *karma* and *samsara* give a plausible explanation of the apparent injustices and evident inequalities of human existence by implying that if the basic circumstances of our present lifetime are negative or unhappy, we alone are fundamentally responsible for this. Once the doctrines of *karma* and reincarnation had won acceptance, they were used to explain and support the socio-religious phenomenon of the four social classes of India.

UPANISHADIC PASSAGES CONCERNING KARMA AND SAMSARA

As a man acts, as he behaves, so does he become. Whoso does good, becomes good: whoso does evil, becomes evil. (Brihadaranyaka 4.4.5)

. . . they are born again here in different places in a form which accords with their former deeds and knowledge – as worms or moths, fish or birds, tigers or lions, boars or rhinoceros, or as men . . . (Kaushitaki 1.2)

Those whose conduct on earth has given pleasure, can hope to enter a pleasant womb, that is, the womb of a brahmin, or a woman of the princely class, or a woman of the peasant class; but those whose conduct on earth has been foul can expect to enter a foul and stinking womb, that is, the womb of a bitch or a pig or an outcast. (Chandogya 5.10.7)

Moksha

The word *moksha* comes from a linguistic root meaning 'to free'. *Moksha* in Hinduism can therefore be translated 'liberation'. In the Upanishads the actual term *moksha* is not used very often, but the concept is crucial for Upanishadic thought in particular and for subsequent Hindu thought in general.

From what does *moksha* liberate? Basically, from karmic and samsaric bondage. *Moksha* is the ultimate spiritual goal of Hinduism, and Hindus over the centuries have developed a number of paths which they believe will lead to this supreme goal. Three main paths eventually emerged: the path of *karma* (appropriately performed works and actions); the path of *jnana* (inner existential knowledge); and the path of *bhakti* (loving devotion to a personal God). In the Upanishads specifically, the goal of *moksha* is usually conceived of in terms of liberation from ignorance, finitude, karmic accumulation and samsaric bondage, to a state of union with *brahman* (*brahman*-realisation). The dominant Upanishadic path to *moksha* is the path of *jnana*, the way of inner, existential knowledge, which is far more profound than merely intellectual or factual knowledge. This inner knowledge includes a deep, transforming realisation of the intimate relation that exists between *brahman* and *atman*.

In the Upanishads, yoga is one of the practical means or tools which can be used with benefit while treading the path to liberation. Yoga is a type of meditational practice which helps to cultivate *jnana*, or inner existential knowledge. The ultimate purpose of Upanishadic yoga is to help bring about union with *brahman*. By contrast, the ultimate purpose of the classical Yoga school is total isolation of the Self from nature, from God and from other selves, rather than any kind of union.

UPANISHADIC PASSAGES CONCERNING MOKSHA

. . . sages, resolute and pure of heart, by practising self-surrender, make the wisdom of the Veda's end their goal; and so at their last hour, transcending death, are all delivered in the *brahman*-worlds . . . As rivers flowing downwards find their home in the ocean, leaving name and form behind, so does the man who knows, from name and form released, draw near to the divine Person who is beyond the beyond. Whoever really knows that all-highest *brahman*, really becomes *brahman*. (Mundaka 3.2.6–9)

Now we come to the man without desire . . . Being very *brahman*, to *brahman* does he go . . . When all desires which shelter in the heart detach themselves, then does a mortal man become immortal: to *brahman* he wins through. (Brihadaranyaka 4.4.6–7)

This my Self within the heart is that *brahman*. When I depart from hence I shall merge into it. He who believes this will never doubt. (Chandogya 3.14.5)

. . . his reward is this: his fetters are cut away, he . . . desires nothing; he has stridden on to a joy unlimited that can never pass away: therein he abiding stands . . . let a man remain without will, without conceptions, without individual self-consciousness: this is the sign of his spiritual liberation. This is the path that leads to *brahman* . . . (Maitri 6.30)

The 'theistic' Upanishads

So far, emphasis has been laid mostly on those Upanishads with a basically monistic view of things. A different outlook, however, is apparent in a number of other Upanishads. These refer to a Person or Lord (Purusha, Isha) who is usually thought to be related to the impersonal *brahman* yet is higher than *brahman*. Shvetashvatara is perhaps the best example of a theistic Upanishad. Because the Supreme Person in this Upanishad is the god Shiva, Shvetashvatara is sometimes known as the Shaivite *Gita*. (A Shaivite is a worshipper of Shiva.) There is evidence that this Upanishad influenced later Shaivite movements. In it, clear distinctions are drawn on one hand between the Personal Lord, who is called both Shiva and Rudra and who is also referred to as Purusha (Person), Bhagavat (Lord), Ishvara (Lord), and All-Maker, and, on the other hand, the many immortal selves, understood as the enduring essence of any creature. Furthermore, these eternal selves are also distinguished from *prakriti*, which is material nature.

Shvetashvatara accepts the category of *brahman* (impersonal cosmic reality) but does not give it religious prominence. The Personal Lord is conceived as being higher than *brahman*. For this Upanishad, the problem is that each self, because of ignorance, has become bound up with, and is therefore in bondage to, *prakriti* or the material universe. The remedy is for each self to come to know God, and this means achieving a close relationship with the Personal Lord as resident within but eternally distinct from the individual self.

Here follow some relevant passages from Shvetashvatara Upanishad.

He is the One who, spreading wide his net, rules with his sovereign powers . . . For One is Rudra . . . over against his creatures stands he, protector; all worlds he emanated, all worlds will he roll up at the end of time . . . He, of gods the source and origin, all-sovereign Rudra . . . (3.1–4)

In the heart of every being he makes his home, all things pervading, Bhagavat . . . a mighty Lord indeed is He, the Person; he speeds existence on its course . . . (3.11–12)

By knowing Shiva, the Benign . . . by knowing God, the one Encompasser of all, a man is from all fetters freed . . . Of him [i.e. God] there is no likeness, Great Glory is his name. His form cannot be glimpsed, none may see him with the eye: whoso should know him with heart and mind as dwelling in the heart, becomes immortal! (4.16–20)

Of lords, supreme great Lord; of gods, the highest God; of kings, the highest King – utterly beyond! So should we know him, God, Lord of the worlds, adorable! . . . Like unto him is none, none greater than he is known . . . No one begat him, no one is his lord. (6.7–9)

The Upanishadic conception of the material universe

The Upanishads do not explain in any detail how our material universe came to be in its present organised condition, but relevant themes do portray the universe in terms of emanation from ultimate reality like sparks from a fire or like a web from a spider; in terms, also, of development from a primordial egg, and as the result of a cosmic act of incest or dismemberment.

FOUNDATIONAL THEMES IN HINDUISM

Some of Hinduism's basic themes are Vedic in origin, the clearest example being the four *varnas* or classes, while others crystallised only after, or independently from, the Vedic–Upanishadic religious complex. We shall mention here six of the most important themes in the Hindu tradition. Some, like the first, have already been explained in the previous section and will therefore simply be briefly indicated in this section; others require fuller discussion.

Brahman–atman, karma and samsara, and moksha

These important Upanishadic themes, which have been introduced in the previous section, were expounded and elaborated during the centuries after the rise of the Upanishads. Three main types of *karma* were distinguished: *karma* that has already brought forth its effects, *karma* that still lies accumulated, and *karma* that is gathered in this life.

The three gunas of prakriti

The three *gunas*, which are prominent in but not exclusive to the philosophical school known as Shamkhya, are the basic elements or fundamental constituents of existence. Everything that makes up *prakriti* (material nature) is constructed of different combinations of these three *gunas*, which are *sattva*, meaning brightness and goodness, *rajas*, which signifies energy and passion, and *tamas*, meaning darkness and dullness. When the universe is in a latent or undeveloped state the *gunas* are in equilibrium; but when (like ours) the universe is in a developed form, then the *gunas* are in a state of dynamic imbalance.

The four goals of life

Hinduism recognises four valid goals in life. They are *dharma*, which means social, moral and ritual obligations, discussed in more detail immediately below; *artha*, signifying economic and political activity, a matter which is dealt with in a classical Hindu text called the *Arthashastra*; next is *kama*, sexual desire and activity, dealt with in the well-known *Kama Sutra* by Vatsyayana (about 400 CE); and fourthly, *moksha*, final liberation from *karma* and *samsara* – this is the highest and final goal of all life. There is a potential tension in historic Hinduism between *dharma* and *moksha*, and various attempts have been made to lessen or resolve this tension, most notably by the *Bhagavadgita*.

Dharma

The Sanskrit word *dharma* cannot easily be turned into English. It can embrace conceptions such as tradition, religion, truth, duty, moral obligation, social obligation and legal prescription. Morever, different types of *dharma* can be distinguished. The two most important have to do with the realm of human obligation, comprehensively conceived. They are *sadharana-dharma*, which includes the basic obligations of human beings generally, irrespective of class, education and stage of life, for example telling the truth, living a pure life, showing forgiveness, exercising self-control, practising goodwill and generosity, and not injuring other beings. The second type is called *varnashrama-dharma*, and means carrying out one's *dharma* in accordance with one's *varna* (social class) and in accordance with one's *ashrama* (stage of life). Let us look a little more closely at *varnashrama-dharma*.

Varna-dharma

As we have seen, there are four basic social classes acknowledged by traditional Hinduism, each having its range of obligations and, except for the *sudras*, its set of rights: brahmins (priests and custodians of spiritual culture), *kshatriyas* (warriors), *vaishyas* (farmers and merchants) and *sudras*, who performed the more menial tasks. This fourfold division was religiously sanctioned as early as the Samhita texts. The three higher classes are 'twice-born' and may study the Vedas, a privilege which is forbidden to the *sudras*, who traditionally may not even hear these sacred disclosures. Only the brahmins may actually teach the Vedas. Relating the four classes and the three *gunas*, brahmins are regarded as *sattva*-oriented, *kshatriyas* as *rajas*-oriented, *vaishyas* are oriented to both *rajas* and *tamas*, and *sudras* are *tamas*-oriented.

Ashrama-dharma

From classical times four successive stages of life were recognised, with each stage requiring different duties and patterns of behaviour. The first one is *brahmacarya*, the stage of the unmarried student. It begins with *upanayana* (initiation), and the student traditionally sits for a number of years at the feet of a Vedic teacher. Next comes *grihastha*, the stage of the married householder and worker. The goals of *artha*, *kama* and *dharma* are very appropriate during this stage. One of the householder's special duties is to perform the five daily obligations which are described below in the section on Hindu practices and rituals. The third stage of life is called *vanaprastha*, a transitional stage during which one lives in seclusion as a hermit, perhaps in a forest hut, with or without one's wife. This stage has become virtually obsolete. The fourth stage is *samnyasa*, the stage of the *samnyasin* or solitary, wandering ascetic, a seeker after *moksha* who has renounced all mundane ties, and is now beyond the demands of class, ritual duty and family obligation.

In practice, many individuals did not go through all four stages. There were *samnyasins*, for example, who experienced only stages one and four. None the less, the theory of the four stages goes some way toward catering for both the world-affirming and world-denying tendencies found in Hinduism.

Hindu conceptions of the universe and time

With a few exceptions, Hindus through the ages have believed that matter is eternal; there is no such thing as creation from nothing. However, this eternal material substratum can fluctuate endlessly between a state of passive disorganisation and a state of dynamic organisation. By classical times Hindus had come to take for granted the four *yugas* or ages: the *krita-yuga*, the *treta-yuga*, the *dvapara-yuga*, and the *kali-yuga*. Each *yuga* is successively shorter and more decadent than the previous one. The *kali-yuga* which we are in at present began, it is said, in 3102 BCE. The four *yugas* together form a *mahayuga* (lasting 4,320,000 years), and one thousand *mahayugas* together form a day of Brahma (lasting 4,320 million years). Samsaric reality is made up of an endless cycle of days of Brahma and nights of Brahma. God sleeps at night and generates another universe anew at the start of a new day. For most Hindus, the time process includes many auspicious or favourable and many inauspicious periods. Astrological considerations help to pinpoint these.

The three paths to moksha

The three paths to *moksha* – the way of works, the way of inner knowledge, and the way of loving devotion to God – run like a dominant thread through classical and medieval Hinduism, but they are best discussed after the *Bhagavadgita* has been introduced in a section below.

CONCEPTIONS OF DEITY IN POST-UPANISHADIC HINDUISM

By the beginning of the Common Era, Vishnu and Shiva, originally minor Vedic deities, had become the two great gods of Hinduism. The other deities had fallen into the background, but they did not disappear. The names of most of them (including Indra, Agni, Surya, Prajapati or Brahma) appear in scriptures called the Epics and Puranas. From the late centuries BCE onwards some Hindus have perceived the one Divine Reality in threefold form as the so-called *trimurti* (triple form of deity), namely Brahma the Creator, Vishnu the Preserver and Shiva the Destroyer, but this neat and somewhat artificial formulation has never been as popular or as widespread as some introductory books on Hinduism suggest. In the last analysis, most Hindus believed in *one* Supreme Divine Principle. By early classical times (the late centuries BCE), this one Supreme Divine Reality had become personalised as either the great God Vishnu or the great God Shiva.

In classical times, both Vishnu and Shiva were believed to have had female consorts, with Lakshmi, divine patron of bounty and prosperity, being the consort of Vishnu, and the many-faceted Uma or Durga the consort of Shiva. The consort was regarded as the dynamic personification of the *shakti* (power or energy) of the male god. By the sixth–eighth centuries CE, some Hindus within the Shiva tradition had chosen to elevate the divine female as consort into the divine female as great goddess; the goddess now enjoyed the rank of Supreme Being in her own right.

To worshippers of Vishnu or Shiva or the Goddess, their chosen god is not merely a partial aspect of Deity. A Vishnu worshipper would regard Vishnu as the great all-encompassing God who himself creates, preserves and destroys; and similarly for worshippers of Shiva or Shakti. Most Hindus in fact worship such an *ishta-devata*, a 'chosen deity'. The god Brahma never attracted significant cultic attention, as did Vishnu and Shiva; yet Brahma's consort Sarasvati (goddess of wisdom and learning) grew in stature over the centuries and became a popular focus of devotion.

Vishnu

The origins of Vishnu (Hari) can be traced back to the benevolent Vishnu of the Vedic Samhitas as well as to non-Vedic contexts, specifically the so-called Narayana and Vasudeva cults of India. The synthesis between Vishnu and the Narayana–Vasudeva elements probably took place before the time of the *Gita*. Narayana and Vasudeva have become important alternative names for Vishnu. Vishnu is a generally benevolent deity, and his cosmic pervasiveness is widely emphasised. This is mythologically represented by his famous 'three (cosmic) strides'. Vishnu is blue, like the infinite sky. He has four arms, and his hands hold a discus (*chakra*), conch shell, lotus, and mace, which denote respectively the weapon for conquering evil and ignorance, water and the primeval creation sound, the unfolding universe, and the power of knowledge. Vishnu's vehicle is Garuda, who is half man, half bird. When Vishnu is active, he rides on Garuda. Otherwise he sleeps on the serpent Shesha, or Ananta, on the ocean. From Vishnu's navel a lotus is born; from this lotus, the creator (Brahma) emerges – and creation gets under way all over again.

An *avatara* (incarnation) is a form or manifestation in which Vishnu appears in order to carry out some saving exploit. In the words of the *Gita*: 'For whenever the law of righteousness withers away, and lawlessness raises its head then do I generate Myself on earth . . . I come into being, age after age' (4.7–8). Vishnu's incarnations will be discussed in detail later. The two most important are the virtuous Rama, the hero of the *Ramayana*, and the resourceful and benevolent Krishna, whose name means 'the dark one', and who features in the Great Epic (the *Mahabharata*), the *Gita*, the Vishnu Purana, the Bhagavata Purana and in other scriptures. Krishna is thought by some scholars to have been originally a human hero, a historical figure of the Yadava tribe. Vishnu's consort is Lakshmi, who is sometimes called Shri.

Shiva

Shiva's other names include Pashupati (Lord of beasts), Mahadeva (Great God), Hara (Remover), and Shankar (Peace-giver). The great god Shiva is the legacy of the Rudra of the Samhitas, and probably also of certain Indus Valley emphases, specifically the enigmatic cross-legged figure referred to in the historical outline of Hinduism earlier in this chapter. Shiva is a complex God, a God of opposites. He is 'the erotic ascetic', the god of the *lingam* (stone pillar), which symbolises biological, psychological and cosmic creativity in general, and fertility and phallic aspects in particular. Yet he is also the god of ascetics, the great Yogi, the possessor of the yogic Third Eye, who meditates in the Himalayas with ashes on his body. An important symbol of Shiva is the trident, which has been said to represent the three *gunas* of *prakriti*, or perhaps the three divine functions of creation, preservation and destruction. Shiva in his form as Nataraja is the Lord of the 'Cosmic Dance', who dances out both the creation and the destruction of the cosmos.

Shiva's consort has both benevolent and fierce aspects: Uma, Parvati (daughter of the Mountain) and Gauri represent his gentle and light side; while Durga (the inaccessible) and Kali (the black one) symbolise the fierce, powerful and dark aspects.

The Goddess (Shakti)

Hinduism has been more hospitable than most religions to the female aspects of deity. The remote origins of the Hindu Goddess are probably to be found in Indus Valley religion and in some of the indigenous Indian cults. Veneration of local or folk manifestations of female divinity (especially those associated with fertility, disease and weather) have probably always been an important part of village Hinduism. It was not until early medieval times that the Goddess (Shakti, Mahadevi) appeared as a focus of worship in her own right as Supreme Deity. 'Shaktism' is a convenient name for the religion of the Great Goddess (or the Divine Mother), the one who herself, out of her limitless cosmic energy, produced Vishnu, Shiva, the lesser divinities and the universe itself.

Shaktism shares a common doctrinal and philosophical stance with Shaivism. Both of them consider the Ultimate Reality to be Shiva–Shakti, but in the Goddess tradition Shakti is regarded as the dynamic moving principle of reality, while Shiva is regarded as its static foundation. The cult of the Mother is strong in south India and in Bengal. What complicates any discussion of Shaktism is that it is bound up with the obscure and complex phenomenon of Tantrism (Tantra), a form of Indian religion which constitutes something of a 'short-cut' to liberation. Tantra involves special initiations, intricate visualisations, symbolisms and rituals, and occult or magical practices, and it lays emphasis on powerful, inner energies and forces which can be tapped and realised by the aspirant, whose body is nothing less than a microcosm of the whole dynamic universe.

We have been looking at the major manifestations of Deity in classical and medieval times, belonging to the so-called great tradition of Hinduism. It should not be forgotten, however, that the Hindu umbrella has also been hospitable to folk traditions or 'little' traditions, which emphasise deities whose origins are often non-Vedic, and who are indigenous to Indian village life.

The little traditions have also included a whole host of lesser entities which can serve as the objects of religious interest. Spirits and ancestors, ghosts, and even animals, snakes, birds, trees and plants have been the focus of veneration and sometimes fear over the centuries.

IMPORTANT SMRITI SCRIPTURES

Smriti scriptures, while technically subordinate to *shruti*, are often more accessible in the sense that they bring out latent meanings of *shruti* texts or convey *shruti* teachings in a more comprehensible form. The main *smriti* scriptures are described in the following paragraphs.

Dharma-shastras (law books)

The Dharma-shastras are believed to have been produced by traditional transmitters of *dharma* (law, morals, tradition) like Manu, Yajnavalkya and others. The most important of these is the *Laws of Manu* (200 BCE–100 CE), which is probably the earliest of the legal shastras. It contains twelve books.

There are many Manus in Hindu tradition and legend; it is the first Manu, Manu Svayambhu (primal man), who is credited with the compilation of the *Laws of Manu*. The compilation was intended to serve as a consolidation of previous Brahmanic religion, but it may also have been produced as a counter-thrust to Indian religious innovations such as Buddhism. *The Laws of Manu* regards the valid sources of *dharma* to be the scriptures (both *shruti* and *smriti*), the behaviour of good people, and individual conscience. Themes discussed in the *Laws of Manu* include creation, the four goals of life, *dharma* appropriate to the four classes and *dharma* appropriate to the four stages of life, the four *yugas*, *karma* and *samsara*, the *samskaras* or life-cycle rituals, the five daily offerings, the duties of a king, the role and duties of women, sins and penances (e.g. for adultery), rules of purity, and laws about food, theft, assault, gambling, debt, purchase and sale, and inheritance. Meat-eating is not prohibited in the *Laws of Manu* and the killing of a cow is regarded as only a minor offence. This stands in contrast to the explicit cow-veneration of later Hinduism. The *Laws of Manu* is very much a brahmin-oriented work; brahmins are given an exalted status as lords of creation.

The Epics: The Ramayana and the Mahabharata

These two Epics are historical and mythological records of actions and exploits, both religious and secular, of memorable men and women. They contain stories, adventures, dialogues and practical illustrations of *dharma* and piety. The Epics were and are popular with the common people. They are useful guides to behaviour, emphasising virtues and exposing vices. Epic literature often relates religious truths to the arenas of daily life.

The two epics are the *Ramayana*, traditionally composed by Valmiki, which relates the story of the heroic couple Rama and Sita, and the *Mahabharata*, also called the Great Epic, which is traditionally the work of Vyasa. The main story of the *Mahabharata* deals extensively with the various feuds of two extended families, the Kauravas and the Pandavas. Both epics have a north Indian setting.

Also contained in the Great Epic is the famous *Bhagavadgita*, the Song of the Lord. The *Gita* issues a call to dispassionate action, a command to unselfish duty in the face of moral conflicts. It contains the teachings of Krishna, who is presented as a manifestation of God incarnate, a God who invites people to worship him in a spirit of *bhakti* or loving devotion. The *Bhagavadgita*, widely acknowledged to be the crown of the *smriti* writings, is the best known and probably the most loved of all the Hindu scriptures.

By the first century BCE, both Epics were mostly complete; by the third century CE, they were probably in their finished form. The Epics do not discuss the construction of temples nor do they show great interest in the worship of images; these matters are dealt with in the Puranas. The cult of images probably developed during the period when the epics were crystallising. The Epics contain accounts of some of Vishnu's incarnations, although the Sanskrit term for incarnation, *avatara*, does not occur in the Epics or the *Gita* in this technical sense. Incarnations of Vishnu who appear in the Epics include the boar, the man-lion, the dwarf, and Rama-with-the-axe. Rama is portrayed as an important incarnation of Vishnu only in the later parts of the *Ramayana*. Similarly, Krishna is portrayed as an important incarnation of Vishnu only in the later parts of the *Mahabharata*.

The *Ramayana* contains seven books (kandas) of unequal length. Valmiki is the traditional author of books two to six. Books one and seven were produced later, and it is only in these two books that Rama is clearly presented as an incarnation of Vishnu.

Here now is a selective outline of the *Ramayana*. The wives of king Dasaratha of Ayodhya bear four sons named Rama, Bharata, Lakshmana and Shatrughana. Vishnu has manifested himself more fully in Rama than in the other sons. The boys grow up. Rama wins Sita, daughter of king Janaka, as his bride. One of king Dasaratha's wives, queen Kaikeyi, holds him to a promise which he made to her earlier, that he would grant her two boons. She asks two things of him: Rama must be banished to the forest for fourteen years and her son Bharata must be installed as Dasaratha's heir-apparent. The king grants these boons. Rama accepts exile, along with Sita and Lakshmana; but Bharata is not willing to accept the throne in his own right. The king dies of grief because of Rama's exile.

During his exile, Rama has many adventures, but throughout everything he lives according to *dharma*. After some years, Sita is abducted by the powerful Ravana, ruler of the Rakshasas (titans, ogres). He takes her to his island domain, known as Lanka. Ravana asks Sita to become his consort, but she refuses. Rama searches for Sita in vain; then he is told about Sugriva, leader of the monkeys, who could be of help to him. Rama proceeds to Sugriva's kingdom. Sugriva's minister, Hanuman, interviews Rama. Rama tells the tale of Sita's abduction. Sugriva meets Rama and promises to help him, and Rama does Sugriva a good turn by killing the troublesome Bali. Sugriva assembles his troops and sends them out to look for Sita. Hanuman finds out that she is being kept at Lanka. Hanuman crosses the sea in spectacular fashion, arrives in Lanka, and explores the city and its palace. He sees Sita and her guard of female titans. Sita again rejects Ravana's advances. Hanuman talks to Sita, but she does not want to return with him. Hanuman destroys part of the city, allows himself to be taken captive, addresses Ravana, escapes, sets fire to the city, and returns home. He tells Rama what has happened.

Rama, Sugriva, Hanuman, Lakshmana and the rest reach the seashore. In Lanka, Ravana prepares for war. Rama's army crosses the sea to Lanka, and various battles take place. Rama and Ravana fight against each other a number of times, and eventually Ravana is killed and Lanka conquered. Rama and Sita meet, but because of rumours questioning Sita's purity, Rama feels obliged to repudiate her. Sita demonstrates her purity by successfully undergoing the fire ordeal, and she is restored to Rama. Rama, Sita, Lakshmana and the others return home. Rama begins his reign at Ayodhya, and receives homage.

The happiness of Rama and Sita is spoiled by persistent questions regarding Sita's purity. Following Rama's instructions, Lakshmana takes Sita to a hermitage and leaves her there. After some time, Rama sends for her and she is brought back home. Her virtue is proclaimed. Sita descends into the earth (which is her real mother), and Rama laments for her. Rama ascends to heaven: '. . . the supremely virtuous Rama . . . entered Vishnu's abode . . . Thereupon Immortals began to worship that God who had returned to his form as Vishnu . . . '.

The *Ramayana* portrays Rama and Sita as the ideal man and woman, husband and wife. Sita is pure, kind and loving; Rama is a paradigm of *dharma* – '*dharma* made flesh and blood'. Rama is pious, brave, truthful, unselfish; he honours his father by willingly going into exile, and he proves to be a model of kingship. Lakshmana symbolises brotherly loyalty and affection, while Hanuman represents the faithful friend and helper.

The *Mahabharata* or Great Epic contains about 90 000 verses, divided into eighteen sections or *parvans*. Sometimes this work is paid the compliment of being called the fifth Veda. Mythologically, this is not inappropriate, as Vyasa, the traditional author of the Great Epic, is the sage whom Hindu legend credits with the division of the once-unitary Veda into four parts. The Great Epic, which is much longer than the *Ramayana*, consists of a detailed account of the origins, causes, progress and aftermath of a prolonged struggle between two great families, the Kauravas and the Pandavas. Besides this main narrative, there are innumerable discourses and sub-narratives that provide examples of the ways in which moral principles are applied in practical situations.

Vishnu is more prominent than Shiva in the Great Epic; yet when Shiva does appear, he tends to overshadow Vishnu. Most of the well-known myths about Shiva can be found somewhere in this vast epic. It is worth emphasising that the

Krishna of the *Mahabharata* is portrayed as an adult. The later pre-occupation with the childhood and youth of Krishna and with the exploits of Krishna Gopala (herder of the cows) is largely a puranic phenomenon.

Yudhishthira, the Pandava king in the Great Epic, is portrayed as a wise king and a true practitioner of *dharma*, despite his weakness for gambling. He is characterised as steadfast, self-restrained, patient, hospitable, truthful, generous, brave, just, serene and fearless. In his discussion of Mahatma Gandhi, R. C. Zaehner sums up Gandhi's life and achievements by paying him the compliment: 'Yudhishthira returns.'

The Bhagavadgita

Technically speaking, the *Bhagavadgita* constitutes a very small part of section six of the Great Epic. The exact relationship between the *Gita* and the Great Epic is unclear and controversial: perhaps the former was composed separately and then subsequently inserted into the Epic. It is difficult to date the *Gita* with any precision. Conventional scholarship tends to place its composition somewhere in the late centuries BCE, but some Hindu teachers, however, date it much earlier.

Although in fact part of *smriti*, not *shruti*, the *Gita* is Hinduism's most famous and most influential scripture. It is set just before the great war (told in detail in the *Mahabharata*) between the Kauravas and the Pandavas, and consists of an extended dialogue between the Pandava warrior Arjuna and his charioteer Krishna, who is a manifestation of the god Vishnu in human form. The *Gita* is India's first literary source for *bhakti*, or loving devotion to a personal God. Also important in the *Gita* is the theme of *nishkama-karma*, or action without attachment. This theme was not obviously present in Hinduism prior to the *Gita*. The expression *nishkama-karma* has been translated into English in many ways: 'selfless endeavour', 'action without the expectation of reward', 'action which renounces the fruits of action', 'desireless action', 'disinterested action', and so forth.

The *Gita* opens with the two great armies gathered for battle. Arjuna the warrior is depressed at the thought of having to kill his relatives. Krishna argues that Arjuna should fight for at least two reasons, firstly because one's eternal, undying self survives even if a person is killed; the self moves on to rebirth in another body. 'As a man casts off his worn-out clothes and takes on other new ones in their place, so does the embodied self cast off his worn-out bodies and enters others new', says the *Gita* (2.22). Thus Arjuna will not be able to kill what is most enduring in the people against whom he fights. Secondly, it is Arjuna's class duty as a *kshatriya* to fight. Krishna puts forward the principle that whatever work Arjuna does, including his fighting, he should do in the spirit of *nishkama-karma*. 'Work alone is thy proper business . . . let not your motive be the fruit of work' (2.47).

Krishna then speaks about two of the three classical paths to, or ways of, attaining liberation: *jnana-marga*, the way of contemplation (or renunciation of action), and *karma-marga*, the way of works. Arjuna must not make the mistake of assuming that the former way is superior. The wise thing to do is to engage in work or action, for one can hardly avoid doing so in this world, but to do this in a way that renounces desire and attachment. In short, what needs renouncing is not human activity in society, but the selfishness that accompanies most of this activity. The discipline of yoga helps to lessen the grip of desire and promote equanimity.

While it leaves a valid place for *jnana-marga* and *karma-marga*, the *Gita* devotes a significant proportion of its eighteen chapters to the third path that leads to liberation, namely *bhakti-marga*, the way of devotion, the way that is open to all. Various divine attributes of the Lord (who is more ultimate than the impersonal *brahman*) are announced in the *Gita*, especially in its middle chapters. In chapter 18, the last chapter of the *Gita*, God's love for human beings is clearly affirmed. Some interpreters claim that in the *Gita* Vishnu is the Lord God, and Krishna is one of his incarnations; other interpreters see the *Gita* as portraying Krishna as the ultimate Divine Reality who has chosen to visit the earthly realm in person.

One of the most memorable sections of the *Gita* is chapter 11, in which Arjuna is given divine insight into the universal, divine form of Lord Krishna. Arjuna humbly confesses his adoration in the face of God's great glory and majesty.

We have presented the *Gita* as a mainly *bhakti*-oriented document, a viewpoint defended by many Hindu and non-Hindu scholars. It is only fair to point out, however, that there are some who interpret it as a scripture whose main concern is to set forth the path of *jnana* or inner spiritual knowledge.

The Puranas

The Puranas ('ancient stories') are popular with the common people. They form great storehouses of mythological, semi-historical, theistic, devotional and sometimes even philosophical Hinduism, and contain extensive accounts of the exploits of gods and goddesses, divine incarnations and religious heroes. The most popular Purana is the Bhagavata Purana, which chronicles the advent of various *avataras* (incarnations) of God. These range from animal manifestations such as the boar and the tortoise, to the advent of the incomparable Lord Krishna himself. Hindu tradition recognises eighteen major Puranas, and eighteen secondary Puranas. We are concerned here only with the major Puranas.

The Vishnu Purana (fifth century CE) is the most well-known of the early Puranas and consists of six books, most of which deal with the conventional puranic topics, namely the endless cycle of creation, destruction and re-creation, genealogies of gods and patriarchs, the history of the Manus, and the history of solar and lunar dynasties.

It is in book five of the Vishnu Purana that we find the famous account of Krishna's birth and early life, including his loving relationships with the *gopis* (or cowgirls) as Krishna Gopala (cow-keeper), the mischievous flute-player who is at once a member of a cowherd's family and the possessor of divine powers who triumphs over evil forces, including demons and serpents. The Vishnu Purana also contains accounts of other *avataras* of Vishnu such as the tortoise, the boar, the man-lion and Kalki. In this text, Vishnu is the Supreme Being – Creator, Preserver and Destroyer. Other divinities (even Shiva and Brahma) are regarded as the 'energies' of the supreme Vishnu.

Of all the Puranas, the Bhagavata Purana (ninth or tenth century CE) is the most celebrated. It combines the epic and puranic accounts of Krishna into a grand synthesis. The Bhagavata Purana is one of the central scriptures of the contemporary Hare Krishna movement.

We turn next to Vishnu's *avataras* (descents or incarnations) as set forth in the puranic tradition. The word *avatara* implies a descent of the divine. In the early Puranas one encounters the idea, already taught in the Epics and the *Gita*, that Vishnu has various *avataras*, but in those Puranas they vary in both number and identity. It is the later Puranas that contain more systematic accounts of the various *avataras*. Ten *avataras* of Vishnu is the most common puranic pattern. Each is a partial manifestation of Vishnu, with Krishna being a fuller disclosure of the divine than any of the others.

The work of the various *avataras* involves one or more of the following: the maintenance or restoration of cosmic order, the upholding of *dharma* according to one's class and one's stage of life, and the bringing of divine grace.

The basic mission of each of the ten *avataras* was as follows. (1) During the flood, the fish protected Manu by securing the ship or ark to its horn by means of a rope. (2) In order to get the elixir of immortality, the gods churned the ocean of milk. The churning-pole (a mountain) churned so violently that the earth was threatened. The tortoise therefore supported the end of the churning-pole on his back, and saved the day. (3) The overburdened earth was cast into the cosmic waters by the demon Hiranyaksha. The boar rescued the earth, lifting it out with his tusks and placing it safely upon the waters. (4) A cruel demon, Hiranyakashipu, tormented his pious son who was a devotee of Vishnu. The man-lion (a creature with the face of a lion and the body of a man) tore the evil father apart. (5) The dwarf obtained a promise from Bali, a demon king, that he (the dwarf) could rule over as much ground as could be covered in three strides. The dwarf, after only two great strides, traversed the universe, leaving the nether regions to Bali. (6) Rama-with-the-axe, a violent brahmin warrior, decisively defeated the *kshatriya* class in order to prevent them from dominating the brahmins. (7) Rama is the divine incarnation who is the hero of the *Ramayana*. (8) Krishna is the central figure of the *Gita* and the Bhagavata Purana. Krishna is widely acknowledged as the fullest incarnation of Vishnu. (9) The Buddha taught Buddhist *dharma* in order to corrupt the demons and lead them astray from the path of Hinduism. (10) Kalki will come at the end of the present age, riding a white horse and carrying a sword. He will destroy the barbarians (non-Hindus) and will regenerate the righteous.

The Sutras of the classical philosophical schools

The classical schools of philosophy produced an important class of philosophical texts or *Sutras*. There are six 'orthodox' schools or systems of philosophy in the Hindu tradition and each of these is represented by at least one important classical text, usually written by a systematiser of the school's teachings. Details about the schools and the *Sutras* are given in the section below dealing with Hindu philosophy.

The Tantras

The Tantric writings are mostly in Sanskrit and were produced from about the seventh century CE onwards.

Vernacular literatures

To the category of vernacular literatures belong texts composed in the respective regional languages of India: Hindi, Marathi, Gujarati, Bengali, Tamil and Telugu. Good examples of Hindi religious literature are the poems of Mira Bai and Surdas, and the Hindi translation of the *Ramayana* epic which was carried out by Tulsidas. The *Tirukkural*, a book of ethics, is popular among the Tamil people.

THE THREE PATHS TO MOKSHA

We have seen that the three margas or paths to *moksha* – final liberation – are discussed in the *Gita*. *Karma-marga* is the way of desireless action, involving the disinterested carrying out of social and ritual obligations. *Jnana-marga* is the way of inner existential knowledge, which overcomes the fundamental problem of avidya or ignorance. *Bhakti-marga* is the way of loving devotion to a personal God. From at least the time of the *Gita*, these three ways of salvation became part of the fabric of classical and medieval Hinduism, with the various sub-traditions often valuing one particular path over another. Most Hindus have conceived *moksha* in terms of some sort of reconciliation with the ultimate Divine Reality, but there is disagreement about the actual condition of the final liberated state. Does one merge into the Divine, like a drop of water returning to the sea, or does one keep one's individuality and enjoy eternal communion (but not union) with the Divine? Many Hindus who favour the *jnana* path tend to hold the former view, while those who tread the path of *bhakti* incline to the latter view. Not all Hindus were (or are) consciously *moksha*-oriented. Many would be content to strive for improved circumstances in this life or a better rebirth in the next life.

SOME HINDU PRACTICES AND RITUALS

There are many categories of Hindu rituals or cultic practices: Vedic rituals, post-Vedic rituals such as the *puja* rituals, life-cycle rituals (the *samskaras*), domestic rituals, temple rituals, obligatory rituals like *sandhya*, optional rituals, daily rituals, seasonal rituals, and others. We classify them as follows.

Vedic sacrifice (yajna)

The *karma kanda* portions of the Vedas, the Samhitas and the Brahmanas, contain the various chants, formulae and ritual actions to be used by the priests in the various sacrificial offerings. Vedic *yajnas* or sacrifices involve offerings to the deities of various substances like ghee and grains, which are consumed in the sacred fire. Vedic sacrifices are ceremonies aimed at praising, appeasing or coercing deities so that they in turn might bestow blessings and other benefits on the cosmos in general and the worshippers in particular. One of the most frequently performed of the Vedic sacrifices was the *agnihotra*, a rite involving three sacred fires and in which offerings were made every day at sunrise and sunset.

Samskaras, or life-cycle rituals

The *samskaras* are life-cycle rituals (what anthropologists call rites of passage) marking the significant landmarks of a person's life. These are performed mostly in the home context, although initiation and the death rituals can be carried out at one or other of Hinduism's sacred places. Between twelve and forty *samskaras* were specified in classical times, and the most important of these are the ceremonies marking birth, the naming of the child, the child's leaving the house for the first time, shaving the child's head, initiation (by which a boy between the ages of 8 and 24 becomes twice-born and is entitled to study the Vedas and perform Vedic rituals), marriage (which is a bond between families and not merely individuals), and lastly funerals.

Ceremonies for ancestors

The *samskara* rites performed at funerals must be carefully distinguished from the *shradda* rituals. The latter begin soon after death and involve ritual procedures whose main purpose is to ensure that the deceased is properly 'processed', and that the potentially troublesome ghost does not return to bother the living. Subsequent *shradda* observances, which involve offerings made from rice and milk, are performed at regular intervals in order to remember and honour the dead person who by now has the status of a respectable ancestor.

The five daily offerings

The householder who has undergone Vedic initiation has five cardinal obligations. According to one ancient version, he has obligations firstly to the gods, offering them fire oblations with ghee; next to the seers, in the form of studying and reciting the Vedas; then to the ancestors, by performing the appropriate *shradda* offerings; then an obligation to feed animals; and fifthly, obligations to humanity, especially to offer hospitality and food to the poor. The *havan* or *homa* ritual, which is a fire offering still performed today by many Hindus, is an important legacy of the first of the five daily obligations. Both the *samskaras* and the *havan* ritual enjoy a special place in the religious life of contemporary Hindus who belong to the Arya Samaj, a reformed Hindu organisation which was established in 1875.

Puja rituals

Puja rituals are post-Vedic and probably incorporate various indigenous Indian ritual elements; none the less they have become pervasive in Hinduism. *Puja* involves worship of a deity through ritual service to its representative image or *murti* in an atmosphere of devotion (*bhakti*). Especially popular in *puja* contexts are the deities Shiva, Vishnu and Krishna. *Puja* can be performed at home, in which case the householder may officiate; at the conventional public temple, with the priest (who may or may not be a *brahmin*) playing a significant part in the *puja* rituals; or at a village shrine dedicated to a folk divinity – this sort of *puja* may involve trance or possession and bloody offerings of goats or fowls; and during festivals. Another important category of *puja*, especially in recent times, is the practice of congregational hymn-singing, known as *kirtana*.

Notice the contrast between post-Vedic *puja* and Vedic *yajna*: *yajna* involves Vedic fire offerings to a distant god, whereas *puja* involves offerings and service to a god who is present through his or her visible image or symbol. *Puja* probably became prominent at some stage during the classical period, around the time when *bhakti* and images were becoming religiously important.

Temple puja

One can distinguish between regular (daily) *puja* performed by the temple priest, and occasional or optional *puja*, in which persons visit the temple to carry out *puja* with the priest's help. Daily *puja* may involve all or some of the following attendances, by means of which the god is treated like a royal guest, through his or her ritually consecrated image.

1. The god is invited to be present.
2. The god is offered a seat.
3. Greetings are given to the god.
4. Water is offered for the symbolic washing of the god's feet, face, teeth, and body.
5. Water is offered for sipping.
6. A water-and-honey drink is offered.
7. The image is adorned with cloth and ornaments.
8. Perfumes and ointments are applied to the image.
9. The image is offered flowers, or receives a garland.
10. Incense is burned.
11. A burning lamp is waved before the image.
12. Foods are offered, like rice, fruit, ghee, and betel leaf, and are then eaten as *prasada* by the worshippers.
13. Bowing or prostration takes place before the image.
14. The god is offered a farewell salutation.

Occasional *puja* is dependent on a variety of religious motives on the part of the devotees: to ask the god for a blessing, whether spiritual or material, to offer thanks or to fulfil a vow that was made earlier. Vows form a significant part of traditional Hindu worship, including goddess worship. Circumambulation of the temple in a clockwise direction may be performed by the worshipper as an act of devotion. Sometimes the god's image may also be carried in procession around the temple, especially on festival occasions.

Darshan is a very important ingredient of *puja*. *Darshan* (seeing or insight) is the process of receiving good spiritual 'vibrations' by being in the presence of the object of veneration.

The relationship between the god and the *murti* is subject to different emphases. To some Hindus, the image of stone or metal is the representative personal form of the god, and may even be referred to as a 'deity'; to others, the image is no more than a symbolic reminder of the god.

Practices relating to sacred places and sacred times

Hindu pilgrimages are not a recent innovation; as early as the Great Epic, pilgrimage is treated as an established religious practice. Pilgrimages can be made to local, regional and national (all-Indian) sites, and can be carried out for a variety of motives: absolution, healing, salvation, merit, blessing, propitiation, and the consigning of a dead relative's ashes to the sacred waters of the Ganges River. The Ganges is so important that it was personified as the goddess Ganga from classical times onward. Most places of Hindu pilgrimage are on rivers, notably the holy city of Varanasi (Benares) on the Ganges. But they can also be at the sea or on mountains. Sometimes holy places have a close link with episodes from Hindu mythology. For example, a Vaishnavite may visit Mathura where Krishna was born, or Vrindavan where Krishna lived as a cowherd.

The Hindu religious calendars list a large number of festivals, some of which are seasonal, and some of which are associated with legends told about favourite gods or goddesses. Hindu festivals can be regarded as combinations of religious ceremonies, processions, cultural activities, prayers, offerings, eating and drinking. They serve many functions, from the averting of evil influences through purification to social and personal re-affirmation. There are many festivals specific to certain regions. The India-wide festivals include Divali (October/November), the Festival of Lights where light symbolises the victory of good over evil, and Holi in the spring (February/March), a colourful occasion during which traditional roles can be reversed. Other popular festivals include Janmashtami, the celebration of Krishna's birthday, and Maha-Shivaratri, the Night of Shiva, which includes fasting for Shiva.

For many Hindus, popular ritualistic worship is not to be regarded as the great end of all religious endeavour. As the Shiva Purana says, the performance of ritual and pilgrimage to holy places is an elementary step in worship; next is worship through symbols and images, which are no more than reminders of the Supreme; then comes meditation and contemplation; and finally the highest state is natural realisation of God's presence.

Other practices

A well-known Hindu practice is cow-protection. Since at least the late classical period, the cow has been protected and respected. The cow is sacred in her own right; there is no cow-goddess or cow-deity, though some maintain that cow-veneration has been given added impetus through the popular theme of the divine Krishna as playful cowherd. The products of the cow (milk, curd, butter, urine, dung) are all regarded as purifying elements.

The practice of yoga could have been discussed in this section of the chapter, but we have preferred to deal with it elsewhere.

SOCIAL LIFE AND SOCIAL STRUCTURES

The home, and the joint or extended family centred around it, have always been an integral part of Hindu religious life. It is through the family that most Hindus learn about, and experience, Hindu practices and teachings. The performance of *samskaras* and *puja*, and the observance of certain festivals like Divali, the Festival of Lights, all have an important link with the home. The problems of pollution, stemming from menstruation, excretion, birth, death and so forth, and the remedies of purification are learnt largely in a domestic context. Each Hindu home has some sort of religious shrine, but this can vary from a special room to a few simple pictures of a favourite deity. One of the most important daily domestic rituals is *sandhya*, which involves devotions at least in the morning and the evening. Traditionally the daily rituals have been performed by male members of the household. However, in recent times women have more and more become responsible for basic domestic worship.

The ancient Hindu conception of four great social classes into which society can be divided has already been referred to. The idea of class (*varna* in Sanskrit) should be distinguished from the phenomenon of caste (*jati* in Sanskrit). While there have been only four great classes, there eventually emerged over two thousand castes, including goldsmiths, blacksmiths, musicians, carpenters, weavers, oil-pressers, potters, barbers and many others. Caste is hereditary; one belongs to a caste group by being born into it. A caste is a group of people linked by the following characteristics: endogamy (marriage can occur only within the group); commensality (one should eat only with those who belong to the group); a common traditional occupation; and common ancestry, though in practice this is a legendary rather than a real criterion.

Castes are ranked hierarchically, with priests at the top end and the 'untouchables' who perform tasks like handling excrement and dead animals at the bottom end. The Indian constitution expressly condemns untouchability, but the problems stemming from centuries of caste life have not yet been eradicated. Hindus believe that functions such as birth, death, eating, excretion and menstruation are characterised by ritual pollution. Caste life therefore has to pay careful attention to the network of regulations concerning the avoidance of pollution and the maintenance of purity. Many Hindus believe that castes gradually grew out of the system of the four *varnas*, that the castes were largely the result of an extensive elaboration of the *varnas*. However, most scholars regard this suggestion as still unproven.

THE BHAKTI MOVEMENTS

Bhakti can be defined as loving devotion to a personal God. The *bhakti* traditions tend to think of God as having many eternal attributes rather than being attributeless (as in certain strands of philosophical Hinduism). The *bhakti* relationship between the worshipper and the gracious God can vary in quality and intensity, from the servant-master model, through that of child-parent and friend-friend to the model of lover-beloved. The higher reaches of *bhakti* transcend the *puja* rituals with which the devotees of lower *bhakti* are often preoccupied. The *Bhagavadgita* is the first literary source for *bhakti*. The *Gita*'s 'love-*bhakti*' has been contrasted with the later 'love-and-eroticism *bhakti*' of some of the Puranas. Many scholars believe that indigenous southern Indian religion influenced the development of Hindu *bhakti*, and also *puja*. Many of the *bhakti* movements and figures discussed below tended to minimise the traditional emphasis on class and caste.

The distinguishing features of *bhakti* groups within Hinduism are their precise modes of worship, their reference to God by particular names, and certain theological or philosophical emphases. Within Vaishnavism, contrast the philosophical dualism of Madhva's followers with the philosophical non-dualism of the disciples of Vallabha. Within Shaivism, contrast the pluralism of Shaiva Siddhanta with the monism of Kashmir Shaivism.

The terms sect, movement and tradition are not used uniformly in discussions of the history of Hinduism. A distinction should be drawn between the broad *bhakti* movements or traditions (such as Shaivism and Vaishnavism) and the more specific sects which emerged within any given tradition (within Vaishnavism one encounters, for instance, sects based on the work of Ramanuja, Madhva, and others). In the *bhakti* traditions the guru, or Hindu spiritual teacher, often has a place of great importance. It is through the gurus of a specific sect that the sect's adherents learn the appropriate practices and beliefs, and are able to appreciate the contribution made by its founder. An excellent example of modern Hindu *bhakti* is the reformed Vaishnavite phenomenon of Hare Krishna. It is also worth emphasising that while sects form an important part of the Hindu tradition, there are Hindus who do not belong to any of the sectarian traditions. In the discussion that follows only Vaishnavite and Shaivite *bhakti* will be discussed, though *bhakti* is not confined to these traditions.

Some examples of the Vaishnavite bhakti tradition

The Alvars (sages or saints) were Tamil Vaishnavites, drawn from all classes of society, who flourished during the seventh to the ninth centuries CE in south India. They stressed the importance of *bhakti* on the part of the devotee, and also the grace of God (that is, Vishnu, also called Mal, Perumal or Narayana). Krishna represented for them the most important *avatara* of the divine, and was presented as the mischievous flute-player who teases and loves the *gopis*. The Alvars highlighted the *gopis'* emotions of rapture, lovesickness and the agony of separation, and even physical symptoms such as sweating and swooning. They believed that God could manifest himself on earth in three modes: firstly, in the form of *avataras* such as Krishna, the fish, the boar, the dwarf and Rama; next in the various statues in south Indian temples; and thirdly in the hearts of the devotees. A further point to note is that the Bhagavata Purana was influenced by the religious life and work of the Alvars.

The Shri Vaishnavas were founded by the *acharya* (spiritual teacher) Nathamuni (824–924 CE). Their *bhakti* was less ecstatic and emotional than that of the Alvars, and laid emphasis on surrender to the God of grace. One of the most well-known *acharyas* was Ramanuja (d. 1137). His basic philosophy and theology was known as *vishisht-advaita*, meaning qualified non-dualism, a view which asserts that there are significant distinctions between the personal God, the many individual selves, and material nature. Furthermore, he helped to make *bhakti* more respectable philosophically than it had been hitherto. His work emphasised neither ecstatic devotion nor the theme of 'Krishna and the *gopis*'.

Chaitanya (d. 1533), the Krishnaite reformer, has turned out to be an important precursor of the modern Hare Krishna movement. The patron saint of Bengali Vaishnavism, he was an important *bhakti* revivalist, and spent much of his life at Puri in Orissa where he worshipped Krishna. His *bhakti* was intensely emotional in character. Chaitanya probably did not claim *avatara* status for himself, but after his death his followers came to believe he was an important incarnation of God – 'the Golden Avatar'. Three aspects of his religion have influenced the contemporary Hare Krishna movement. They are his view of Krishna as God and not merely as an incarnation of God; the encouragement he gave to public chanting of the sacred name of Krishna, as well as to singing and dancing in the streets; and thirdly, his view of human beings as somehow different-yet-not-different from their divine source.

Two very important Krishna-centred Vaishnavite texts are the Bhagavata Purana and Jayadeva's *Gitagovinda* (Song of the Cowherd). The former, especially Book Ten, is a classic *bhakti* text. It includes many famous episodes from the life of Krishna, among them the infant Krishna killing the demoness Putana, Krishna's mother looking inside the child's mouth and seeing the whole universe, Krishna subduing the serpent Kaliya, and Krishna stealing the clothes of the village girls. The Bhagavata Purana also contains explicit accounts of Krishna's relations with the *gopis*. The passionate love which the *gopis* enjoy with Krishna/Govinda is believed to symbolise the devotee's *bhakti*-love for God. In this Purana, Krishna has a favourite *gopi*, but she is not named. Her name, Radha, is given in later works such as the *Gitagovinda*.

Jayadeva, author of the *Gitagovinda*, was a Bengali *bhakta* and poet. The *Gitagovinda*, which begins with an invocation to the ten *avataras* of Vishnu, tells of the love, separation and eventual reunion of Krishna and Radha. Krishna's relationship with Radha is portrayed as analogous to God's relationship with the devoted soul. Jayadeva tended to regard Krishna as God, rather than merely as a divine incarnation; consequently, the name of Krishna's brother Balarama stands in Jayadeva's list of ten *avataras* in place of Krishna's name.

Tulsidas (1532–1623) produced a celebrated Hindi version of the *Ramayana* in about 1574. In this work, all the characters of the *Ramayana* are devotees of the god Rama, and even the evil Ravana is ultimately saved. Tulsidas' *bhakti*, centred on the figure of Rama, was more restrained than Krishna-*bhakti*, and emphasised the wonder of God's grace.

Some examples of the Shaivite bhakti tradition

The Nayanars were south Indian Tamil Shaivites who flourished during the seventh–ninth centuries CE. They stressed the fickleness, unworthiness and even sinfulness of humanity, and encouraged devotion to the gracious god Shiva.

Shaiva Siddhanta was a medieval religious and philosophical movement in south India which was influenced by the Nayanars. Shaiva Siddhanta theology was theistic in character. Clear distinctions were drawn between *pati*, *pasu* and *pasa*. *Pati* is the absolute, incomparable Supreme God, who is Creator, Sustainer and Destroyer, transcendent as Shiva and immanent as Shakti and surpasses all human attempts to conceptualise him; whereas *pasu* signifies a plurality of eternal selves and *pasa* means a fetter – referring to the material and finite aspects of reality. The world is real and eternal, but owes its existence to God as boiling water in a pot owes its condition to the fire burning beneath.

The guru is regarded by Shaiva Siddhanta as a sort of 'bodily manifestation' of Shiva. By Shiva's grace, selves can be freed from their bondage to *pasa* and *karma* until eventually they achieve eternal communion with Shiva, but never total absorption into him.

HINDU PHILOSOPHY

India's philosophical enterprises have always formed an integral part of her religious inquiries. Inquiries into the nature, purpose and goal of existence have always linked these two approaches to the truth. Indian philosophical schools (*darshanas*) are classified into two groups: orthodox – those schools that accept, formally at any rate, the authority of the Vedas; and heterodox – those schools that do not acknowledge Vedic authority, for example the Materialists, Jains and Buddhists. The six orthodox *darshanas*, which were consolidated during the classical period, are the Nyaya, Vaisheshika, Shamkhya, Yoga, Mimamsa and Vedanta schools. Two of the six orthodox *darshanas* are significantly rooted in the Vedic *shruti* tradition, namely Mimamsa, which looks back to the Samhitas and Brahmanas, and Vedanta, which looks back to the Upanishads. The other four *darshanas*, though claiming formal loyalty to the Vedas, are in fact significantly independent of them.

Apart from non-dualistic Vedanta, the *darshanas* were characterised by a realist view of the world, according to which the world really exists, independently of mind; and belief in a plurality of selves. Apart from Mimamsa, the *darshanas* accepted the Hindu doctrine of successive creations and destructions of the universe.

We shall be concerned only with three of the six orthodox *darshanas*.

Three Hindu darshanas

1. Shamkhya

Shamkhya is an atheistic philosophy of dualism, which teaches that there are two eternal categories of reality, *prakriti* (matter or nature, which is in perpetual flux) and *purusha* (spirit, which is eternal and unchanging). Some Shamkhya themes can be found, though less explicitly, in parts of the Upanishads and in the *Gita*. The basic constituents of eternal *prakriti* are the three *gunas*, goodness, passion and dullness respectively. When *prakriti* is in a quiescent or unmanifest state, the three *gunas* are in equilibrium, but when *prakriti* unfolds and becomes manifest, the result is a developed universe like ours, with everything in it made up of myriads of combinations of *gunas*. This cycle of universal quiescence and manifestation goes on endlessly. *Purusha*, on the other hand, is pure, eternal, changeless spirit, which exists in plurality; there are thus many eternal *purushas* or selves. These selves somehow become associated with the realm of manifested *prakriti*, and they forget the eternal, crucial distinction that essentially exists between themselves and the *prakriti* with which they have become entangled.

It should be stressed that dimensions of the human being such as consciousness, mind, ego and the five senses belong to the *prakriti* category and not the category of eternal *purusha*.

The various individual *purushas* need to become aware of their plight through greater discrimination, and need to be liberated from the bonds of *prakriti*. From the profound realisation of the eternal *purusha-prakriti* distinction comes final liberation itself, which consists in the total isolation of each *purusha* not only from the samsaric world of *prakriti*, but also from all other selves.

2. Yoga

It is helpful to distinguish between yoga as a meditative technique, which is not confined to Hinduism, and Yoga as one of the classical schools of Hindu philosophy. Our concern here is only with the latter. The traditional text of the Yoga school of philosophy is Patanjali's *Yoga Sutra*. Controversy exists over the relationship between Shamkhya and Yoga. One scholarly view maintains that the Yoga school, not having its own distinctive philosophy, used the philosophical framework of Shamkhya. The other view argues that the school of Patanjali developed its own distinctive philosophical teaching, which must be carefully distinguished from that of Shamkhya. We shall proceed on the assumption that the former position is true.

Yoga differs from Shamkhya in at least two ways. It emphasises the practice of yoga as a technique which can benefit one who is treading the path to liberation, and it accepts Ishvara (the Lord) as an object of human devotion. Ishvara is basically a *purusha* who has never been affected by *prakriti* or by *karma*; he serves as an inspirer and helper of the yogis.

Patanjali's *Yoga Sutra* discusses eight basic stages of yoga:

1. Restraint or self-control: keeping the commandments of non-harmfulness, truthfulness, not stealing, chastity, non-acquisitiveness.
2. Observance of purity, contentment, austerity, study of the scriptures, devotion to Ishvara.
3. Appropriate posture; the most usual is to sit cross-legged.
4. Control of *prana* (breath or life-force).
5. Sense-restraint: withdrawal of the senses from their objects in the world.
6. One-pointedness of concentration.
7. Contemplation and meditation.
8. *Samadhi*, or that stage of total yogic 'absorption' which is a stepping-stone to the final goal.

This yoga system is sometimes called *raja-yoga*. The ultimate goal of existence for the classical Yoga school, the state of final liberation, is the isolation of each *purusha* from everything else, even from Ishvara himself. This is to be contrasted with the popular later views that saw union with God as the ultimate goal of all yoga.

3. Vedanta

Vedanta, which can be translated as 'the end of the Veda', is an appropriate name for this *darshana*, as its teaching arises out of the Upanishads, which mark the culmination of *shruti* speculation. In the Upanishads the unity of all existence is summed up in the reality of *brahman*, the one Absolute, the one Being. Everything emanates from *brahman*, rests in *brahman* and returns to *brahman* when it is dissolved. The traditional text of classical Vedanta is Badarayana's *Vedanta Sutra* (also called the *Brahma Sutra*), which begins with the words: 'Desire to know *brahman* . . .' This *Sutra* is a cryptic and enigmatic work, and forms a sort of interpretive summary of Upanishadic teaching. It contains attempted refutations of Shamkhya and other philosophies. The *Vedanta Sutra* is capable of yielding many different philosophical and theological interpretations. Subsequent Vedantic thought ranges from mystical monism to devotional realistic pluralism. Vedantists through the centuries have singled out the Upanishads, the *Gita* and the *Vedanta Sutra* as their threefold scriptural foundation and have written important commentaries on these works.

In the medieval period, three Vedantist figures, who were all southern Indians, stand out: Shankara (788–820), Ramanuja (d. 1137), and Madhva (d. 1319). Their theological orientations are known, respectively, as *advaita* (non-dualism), *vishisht-advaita* (qualified non-dualism) and *dvaita* (dualism). The differences between these three positions have to do partly with the ways in which they view the relation between ultimate reality, the self and matter.

For Shankara, *brahman* is the single non-dual reality, and the so-called self or *atman* is not different from *brahman*. Shankara taught the doctrine of *maya*, a term that is used elsewhere in Hinduism with different connotations. *Maya* denotes the illusory existence of the world of multiplicity, which is falsely superimposed upon the one *brahman* by the power of ignorance. People superimpose false ideas of plurality upon the *brahman*-reality as a person might falsely superimpose the idea of a snake on what is in reality a piece of rope viewed in a dim light. Shankara operated with a doctrine of two levels of truth: from the standpoint of higher truth, only the non-dual *brahman* exists. This *brahman* is without qualities or attributes. From the standpoint of lower truth, however, the familiar world enjoys a sort of derivative reality, and God can be conceived of as a personal deity to whom devotion may be given. Final liberation consists basically in the profound realisation that 'I' am indeed no different from the eternal, non-dual *brahman*. Unlike Ramanuja and Madhva, Shankara taught that this liberation is attainable before 'my' physical death.

For Ramanuja, matter and the selves are real as is the personal God, though the first two are certainly dependent on God. Ramanuja sees a clear analogy between God and the world on one hand, and the human self and the human body on the other. Just as the human self is intimately related to the body yet is distinct from it, so God is intimately related to the world, yet he can be distinguished from it. Ramanuja's teaching endowed *bhakti* with a certain amount of philosophical respectability.

Madhva drew five clear distinctions within reality: the personal God is distinct from individual selves; God is distinct from matter; one individual self is distinct from another; individual selves are distinct from matter; when matter is divided, then its parts are distinct from one another. For both Ramanuja and Madhva, there remains an eternal distinction between the liberated self and the Divine, though the two exist forever in a relationship of intimacy. Madhva, alone among Hindus, taught that some evil souls will remain for ever separated from God and from the liberation he offers.

The celebrated Vedanta tradition has left its mark not only on modern Hindu figures such as Vivekananda, Ramana Maharshi, and Radhakrishnan, but also on the neo-Vedanta of the West, which has been expounded by Aldous Huxley, Christopher Isherwood and Bede Griffiths, who has lived in India for many years. This Western neo-Vedanta subscribes to the following themes: (1) The world of consciousness and matter is the manifestation of an ineffable, transpersonal Divine Reality within which all lesser realities have their being. (2) Humans possess a double nature – a phenomenal self or ego and an eternal self or spirit. The latter is a spark of divinity; the human self is of the same nature as the Divine Reality. (3) Human beings are capable not merely of knowing about the Divine Reality; they can also realise its existence in a direct, immediate, intuitive way. This intuitive knowledge unites the known with the knower. The basic purpose or goal of human life is to achieve this inner God-consciousness.

MODERN HINDUISM

From 1803, the ailing Mogul empire in India was placed under 'British protection'. As a result of the Indian Revolt of 1857–8, formerly called the Indian Mutiny, the British crown assumed full power over India and the impact of the West was to be increasingly felt in India. The era of the British Raj (1858–1947) had begun. The Raj would see the emergence of the Indian national movement as well as the appearance of the many manifestations of reformed Hinduism.

Some of the more important modern Hindu movements and figures are Rammohan Roy (1772–1833), who founded the Brahmo Samaj in 1828; Dayananda Sarasvati (1824–83), the founder in 1875 of the Arya Samaj; Ramakrishna (1834–86) and his disciple Swami Vivekananda (1863–1902), who helped to introduce Hinduism to the West; Mahatma Gandhi (1869–1948); Shri Aurobindo Ghose (1872–1950), the philosopher and teacher of Integral Yoga, of which the ultimate aim is union with the Divine; Ramana Maharshi (1879–1950), the sage of the holy hill Arunachala in south India; Sarvepalli Radhakrishnan (1888–1975), Vedanta philosopher and theologian; Paramahansa Yogananda (1893–1952), whose life-story is told in the famous book *Autobiography of a Yogi*; Swami Sivananda (1887–1963), who founded the Divine Life Society in 1936; Swami Chinmayananda (b. 1916), a significant teacher of modern Vedanta; transcendental meditation and the Maharishi Mahesh Yogi (b. 1918); the International Society for Krishna Consciousness (popularly known as Hare Krishna), founded in America in 1966 by His Divine Grace A. C. Bhaktivedanta, Swami Prabhupada, who died in 1977 – this is the modern Hindu group which lays most emphasis on a personal God, a God who is the recipient of loving devotion from his worshippers, who chant his holy names; and finally Sathya Sai Baba (b. 1926), the charismatic, miracle-working god-man and world-teacher. It is impossible to discuss all these figures and movements. We shall consider only the first four.

1. Rammohan Roy is often described as the father of modern Hinduism. He was well educated and his conception of neo-Upanishadic, reformed Hinduism was influenced by Islam, Christianity and Western culture. He believed in a lofty monotheism, and taught that worship of the one true, eternal God does not require ritual religion, image worship or popular superstitions. He wanted the caste system to be stripped of its cruder aspects. Roy's interest in social reform is illustrated by his criticisms of child-marriage and by his part in the agitation that led to the abolition in 1829 of *suttee* (more correctly, *sati*), the practice of widows burning themselves to death on the funeral pyres of their husbands.

In 1828 Roy founded the Brahmo Samaj to promote the theistic-unitarian religion in which he believed. This somewhat intellectualist movement never gained a large popular following, appealing mostly to educated Hindus of a broadly liberal persuasion. Well-known figures who were influential in the Brahmo Samaj include Debendranath Tagore (father of the famous Rabindranath) and Keshab Chandra Sen. The latter was more radical than Roy or Tagore in the sense that he wished to repudiate caste, but more conservative in that he and his fellows looked more kindly on the visible and tangible representations of deity in popular Hinduism, and on the Indian tradition's legendary heritage. In 1866 the Brahmo Samaj divided into two groups, one led by Tagore and the other led by Sen. In 1878, Sen's group, the Brahmo Samaj of India, experienced a further split. Sen was more influenced by Christianity and the figure of Jesus than were the other main Brahmo Samaj figures.

2. A reformer of Hinduism who was quite unimpressed by the legacy of British rule in India and by the presuppositions of Westernisation was Dayananda Sarasvati, who became convinced that the four Vedic Samhitas are the infallible and authoritative sources of truth. 'Back to the Vedas!' was his rallying-cry. In his view Hindus should follow pure Vedic monotheism, and not be led astray by image worship, the notion of divine incarnation, or various accretions to Vedic Hinduism such as ancestor veneration, caste, pilgrimages and astrology. The true God is formless and can never take on form of any kind. Sincere worship of God and adherence to the way of right living will yield final liberation, a state in which the self attains true communion with God but is never fully absorbed into God, as some in the Hindu tradition have taught. Dayananda encouraged social reform, protesting against child marriage, the unhappy plight of widows and the fact that women were educationally deprived. He was a supporter of Indian nationalism and argued for the promotion of Hindi as a national language.

Dayananda founded the Arya Samaj in Bombay in 1875 in order to promote Vedic religious and social ideals. The Arya Samaj has always had a significant missionary orientation, and seeks to bring Hindus who have been proselytised by Islam or Christianity back to a fruitful understanding of their Vedic heritage. Both the Brahmo Samaj and the Arya Samaj (as well as other later reform movements) instituted congregational religious worship, which, apart from rare exceptions, was something of an innovation in the Hindu tradition.

3. Ramakrishna, born Gadadhar Chatterji, was one of the most notable mystics of modern India. In 1855 he became priest at a temple of Kali near Calcutta. He was devoted to the Divine Mother in the form of Kali and frequently experienced *samadhi*, the high ecstatic state of yogic-mystical realisation. Ramakrishna lived for a while as a Muslim (from 1866), and for a while as a Christian (from 1874). In the late 1870s he began his semi-public ministry, preaching a modified version of Advaita Vedanta. He emphasised the divinity within every human being, and taught that the different living religions form different paths to the same spiritual goal of God-realisation, which involves profound, intuitive self-knowledge of the inner divine Ground. In short, God is in every person and in every religion. Ramakrishna regarded both the experience of *brahman*, the formless Absolute and the experience of the personal God or Goddess 'with form' as valid modes of religious life. After Ramakrishna's death in 1886 some followers came to regard him as an incarnation of the Divine.

Ramakrishna met Naren, who would become his spiritual heir and who later took the name of Vivekananda, in 1881. Vivekananda became a committed disciple of Ramakrishna and after his teacher's death he travelled extensively in India, while in 1893 he represented the 'universal religion' of Hinduism at the World Parliament of Religions in Chicago. Some years after his return to India, Vivekananda founded the Ramakrishna Mission, a monastic order with a neo-Vedantic religious orientation and significant social, educational and humanitarian concerns. Its standpoint is that every human being is worth caring about, for every human being bears the spark of divinity within. Swami Vivekananda followed, and skilfully expounded, the basic teachings of Ramakrishna. However, one difference of emphasis is worth noting. Whereas Ramakrishna regarded the personal Divine and the transpersonal Absolute as two equally valuable aspects of the same reality, Vivekananda's Vedantic teaching suggested that the infinite, transpersonal Absolute represents a higher stage of religious endeavour than the more limited experience of Deity as personal.

4. Mahatma Gandhi, born Mohandas Karamchand Gandhi in 1869, remains one of India's most famous spiritual figures. Gandhi's Indian background had both Hindu and Jain roots, and he was also influenced by the ethics of Jesus and by literary figures like Tolstoy, Ruskin and Thoreau. From Jainism Gandhi learned that all religious aspiration is inevitably incomplete, provisional and partial; no one standpoint has a monopoly on truth; and that in a world of violence, the way forward lies in the practice of *ahimsa*, non-violence towards all living creatures. Gandhi's support for cow-protection represents just one example of this principle. He taught that when *ahimsa*, which he believed was one of the main themes of the *Gita*, is applied in a social context, the result is a powerful spiritual and practical weapon: the way of *satyagraha*, truth-force, holding fast to the truth. *Satyagraha* seeks to bring about social and political justice by the exercise of persuasion and love, though it may involve the tactics of non-cooperation and civil disobedience; here Gandhi was influenced by Thoreau. These tactics Gandhi learned to practice during his long stay in South

Africa from 1893 to 1914, and he continued to implement them during his later years in India when he became involved in the Congress movement.

Gandhi also taught *sarvodaya*, the well-being of all, a concept which informed his concern for the untouchables, whom he referred to as *Harijans* or children of God. Gandhi seemed to transcend or perhaps resolve some of the dichotomies of much conventional religion. A major example of this was his refusal to draw significant distinctions between spirituality and social involvement: religious transformation and socio-political betterment are inseparable aspirations of one who is committed to God; and what is commitment to God but commitment to follow the truth? His example had clear political implications but went beyond the merely political. He taught that India would have to conquer herself morally and religiously before she could win through to genuine political freedom. He was assassinated in 1948 by a representative of right-wing Hindu orthodoxy.

As a conclusion for this discussion of Hinduism, we reproduce an insightful passage from J. L. Brockington's book *The Sacred Thread*, in which he underlines the ability of the Hindu tradition to keep alive a creative tension between tradition and adaptation: 'Hinduism does not reject the old in favour of the new but blends the two, expressing new dilemmas in traditional language and accommodating fresh insights to established viewpoints. The ability to adapt itself to changing circumstances has been a mark of Hinduism throughout its history, and the unifying factor bringing together its many diverse threads lies in their common history within this unique weaving together of tradition and innovation. Hinduism is ever the same, yet different.' (Brockington, 1981: 209)

★ ★ ★

JAINISM

There are over two million Jains in India today. They follow the path trodden by the Indian ascetic Vardhamana, although they believe that their tradition is much older than Vardhamana's time. Vardhamana, who probably lived during the sixth century BCE, is recognised as the historical founder, or rather consolidator, of Jainism. He and his 23 legendary predecessors are known as Tirthankaras (ford-makers), those who have built a liberating ford across the great river of rebirth.

At about the age of 30, Vardhamana renounced his settled life, gave away his possessions, plucked out his hair, and set out to seek liberation as a wandering ascetic. He achieved enlightenment after twelve years, then spent many more teaching his message of liberation. His austere life was characterised by hardship. Vardhamana was in his seventies when he eventually gained ultimate liberation from *karma* and reincarnation. In recognition of his spiritual achievements, he is accorded the titles Mahavira (Great Hero) and Jina (Victorious One). Jains lay great emphasis on Mahavira's practice of *ahimsa*, which means non-harmfulness to all living creatures, and they believe that

Mahavira began to practice this cardinal Jain virtue when he was in his mother's womb. (Mahatma Gandhi's teaching on *ahimsa* was influenced by Jainism.)

Mahavira's teaching drew a clear distinction between the two basic categories of *jiva*, the many eternal, immaterial, individual selves, which are found in every living entity, and *ajiva*, which comprises everything that is not *jiva*, including the world of material nature. Mahavira interpreted reality atheistically; there is no place for the great Hindu gods in his scheme of things.

The *jiva* is prevented from realising liberation because it has become weighed down by *karma*, which in Jainism is conceived as a kind of rarefied matter. Passions and desires serve merely to reinforce the state of bondage in which the *jiva* finds itself. The only way out of this predicament is to adopt the Jain way of life; asceticism and *ahimsa* are the means to eliminating present *karma* and preventing the accumulation of future *karma*. Once the *jiva* has been cleansed from its weighty karmic load it is free to rise to the realm of final liberation, which is located at the very top of the universe. There the self remains in tranquillity for all eternity, the possessor of infinite perception, infinite knowledge, infinite power, and infinite bliss.

All Jains are members of the *sangha*, or Jain congregation, which is composed of monks, nuns, laymen and laywomen. Both monastic and lay Jains take solemn vows that guide their spiritual lives. The vows of the Jain layperson are milder than those of the monastic Jains, of which there are five:

1. *Ahimsa*, abstaining from harmfulness to all living creatures, including insects. This obviously entails a strict vegetarianism. According to Jain tradition, Mahavira himself is supposed to have strained his drinking water in case he swallowed living things, and gently swept insects from his path with a small broom.
2. Abstaining from false speech.
3. Abstaining from taking what is not given (i.e. no stealing).
4. Abstaining from unchastity.
5. Abstaining from all attachments.

At some stage during the first century BCE, two branches or denominations of Jainism emerged: the Digambaras (sky-clad, those who remain naked, clad only with the sky) and the Svetambaras (white-clad, those who wear a minimum of white clothing). While these two divisions of Jainism are in broad agreement about the main teachings and practices of the Jain tradition, they differ over the question of what exactly constitutes the canon of Jain scripture. The Svetambara canon, which is the more accessible of the two, comprises about 45 scriptural texts.

An interesting philosophical belief held by the Jains which had some influence on Gandhi was the doctrine of non-onesidedness: no one perspective gives a person the whole truth about things; no statement is either absolutely true or absolutely false.

Later Jainism adopted a number of religious innovations, such as temple-building and image-veneration, which proved especially popular with lay-people. A reform movement, whose adherents are known as the Sthanakvasins, was established in the fifteenth century in opposition to such innovations.

Because of their doctrine of *ahimsa* the Jains have never been allowed to practise farming, but nothing in their teaching forbids them to engage in commerce, banking or education, in which fields they have shown their aptitude.

* * *

SIKHISM

Sikhism is one of the youngest of the world religions. It has often been said that Sikhism is the result of a mixture of Islam and Hinduism. Certainly its clear monotheism reminds one of the Islamic stress on the unity of God, but it has in fact been significantly influenced by Hinduism, especially its Vaishnavite strand. *Karma* and reincarnation are two important themes which Sikhism took over from Hinduism generally. There are about ten million Sikhs in India, and perhaps a million in other parts of the world. The majority of Sikhs, and most of the Sikh holy places, are in that part of India known as the Punjab.

Certain late medieval reformers within Hinduism (who are sometimes referred to as the *sants*) came to regard many traditional Hindu rituals and practices as hindrances to religious faith. Among these *sants* was Kabir (1440–1518), whose background was that of Vaishnava Hinduism. Kabir rejected caste, and saw little point in Hindu image-worship. He called himself the child of both Ram, the Hindu god Rama, and of Allah, the god of the Muslims.

Nanak (1469–1539), who was probably influenced by Kabir, was one of the most famous *sants*. Nanak founded the religious tradition which later became the religion of Sikhism. (The word *sikh* means disciple.) Nanak had a transforming religious experience at about the age of 30. While bathing in a river, he encountered God, who commissioned him to communicate divine truth to the world. When Nanak eventually emerged, he announced: 'There is no Hindu and no Muslim . . . I shall follow God's path. God is neither Hindu nor Muslim and the path which I follow is God's.' After a long period of wandering, Nanak settled down at Kartarpur, a village near Lahore. Before his death he appointed a disciple, Angad, as his successor.

Nanak was a strict monotheist. The one God (the True Name, the True Guru) is sovereign, eternal, inexpressible, formless and transcendent, yet he is also personal, gracious and immanent. He is the Creator of the world, which is real but transient and derivative in comparison with God's reality. God has no *avataras* (incarnations), but his word of revelation is communicated to the world by the guru – Nanak and his successors. The guru serves as a reliable guide on the path of God's truth. Human beings can attain liberation through their devotion to God and their meditation on the Divine Name both in private and in a context of congregational worship. Liberation involves freedom from the cycle of reincarnation and a merging of our limited light into the light of God. While treading the path to liberation, asceticism and external rituals are far less important than the cultivation of an appropriate inward spirituality and the service of one's fellow human beings. Image worship, pilgrimage and caste have no place in Nanak's religion, which envisaged a casteless brotherhood or sisterhood of human beings. Nanak's religion has a high regard for family life.

After Nanak's death, nine gurus succeeded him. The office became in time hereditary. The completion of a special place of worship at Amritsar (where today the Golden Temple stands) and the compilation of the Adi Granth (the Sikh scriptures) were two important achievements made in the time of the guru Arjan (1563–1606). The sixth guru was Hargobind (1595–1644; guru from 1606), who helped the Sikhs to become more militarily prepared than they had been previously. The last guru, Gobind Singh (1666–1708; guru from 1675), transformed the organisation of Sikhism through his institution of the Khalsa in 1699. The Khalsa was a militant order or brotherhood into which Sikhs were initiated.

With the death of Gobind Singh, the line of gurus and the formative period of Sikhism came to an end. The guru-authority was now believed to rest with the Adi Granth, which has served as both the authoritative spiritual guide of the Sikhs and the focal point of Sikh worship.

During the seventeenth century the Sikhs increased their military and political profile, and came into significant conflict with the Mogul imperial rulers of India, under whom Arjan died as a martyr. The political and military fortunes and tribulations of Sikhism during the eighteenth and nineteenth centuries, including the exploits of the renowned Sikh resistance fighter Maharaja Ranjit Singh, cannot be pursued here. The Sikhs experienced a major upheaval in 1947, when the Punjab was partitioned between the secular state of India and the new Muslim state of Pakistan. Hundreds of thousands of Sikhs were forced to leave Pakistan for India. In 1966, India formally established the state of Punjab, with Punjabi as the official language. This state has a clear Sikh majority.

SELECT BIBLIOGRAPHY

Baird, Robert D., & Bloom, Alfred. *Indian and Far Eastern Religious Traditions*. New York: Harper & Row, 1971

Baird, Robert D. (ed). *Religion in Modern India*. New Delhi: Manohar Publications, 1981

Basham, A. L. *The Wonder That Was India*. London: Sidgwick and Jackson, 1954

Bleeker, C. Jouco & Widengren, Geo (eds). *Historia Religionum, Volume 2: Religions of the Present*. Leiden: Brill, 1971

Bowes, Pratima. *The Hindu Religious Tradition: A Philosophical Approach*. London: Routledge and Kegan Paul, 1977

Brockington, J. L. *The Sacred Thread: Hinduism in Its Continuity and Diversity*. Edinburgh: University Press, 1981

Burghart, Richard (ed). *Hinduism in Great Britain: The Perpetuation of Religion in an Alien Cultural Milieu*. London: Tavistock, 1987

Chatterjee, Margaret. *Gandhi's Religious Thought*. London: Macmillan, 1983

Cole, W. Owen, & Sambhi, P. S. *The Sikhs: Their Religious Beliefs and Practices*. London: Routledge and Kegan Paul, 1978

Cole, W. Owen, & Sambhi, P. S. *Sikhism*. London: Ward Lock, 1973

Dhavamony, M. *Classical Hinduism*. Roma: Universita Gregoriana Editrice, 1982

Eliade, Mircea (ed). *The Encyclopedia of Religion*, 16 volumes. New York: Macmillan, 1987

Ellwood, Robert S. *Many Peoples, Many Faiths: An Introduction to the Religious Life of Humankind*, 2nd edition. Englewood Cliffs: Prentice-Hall, 1982

Hindu Myths, introduced by Wendy Doniger O'Flaherty. Harmondsworth: Penguin, 1975

Hindu Scriptures, translated and edited by R. C. Zaehner. London: Dent, 1966

Hinnells, John R. (ed). *A Handbook of Living Religions*. Harmondsworth: Penguin, 1985

Hinnells, John R. & Sharpe, Eric J. (eds). *Hinduism*. Newcastle-upon-Tyne: Oriel, 1972

Hopkins, Thomas J. *The Hindu Religious Tradition*. Encino, California: Dickenson, 1971

Hutchison, John A. *Paths of Faith*, 3rd edition. New York: McGraw-Hill, 1981

Isherwood, Christopher. *Ramakrishna and His Disciples*. London: Methuen, 1965

Jackson, Robert & Killingley, Dermot. *Approaches to Hinduism*. London: John Murray, 1988

Kennedy, M. T. *The Chaitanya Movement*. New York: Garland, 1981

Kinsley, David R. *Hinduism: A Cultural Perspective*. Englewood Cliffs: Prentice-Hall, 1982

Knott, Kim. *My Sweet Lord: The Hare Krishna Movement*. Wellingborough: Aquarian, 1986

Lott, Eric. *Vedantic Approaches to God*. London: Macmillan, 1980

Mahadevan, T. M. P. *Outlines of Hinduism*. Bombay: Chetana, 1961

Moore, Albert C. *Iconography of Religions: An Introduction*. Philadelphia: Fortress, 1977

Murphet, Howard. *Sai Baba: Man of Miracles*. London: Vrindavanum Books, 1984

Noss, John B. *Man's Religions*, 6th edition. New York: Macmillan, 1980

O'Malley, L. S. S. *Popular Hinduism: The Religion of the Masses*. Cambridge: University Press, 1935

Organ, Troy W. *Hinduism: Its Historical Development*. New York: Barron, 1974

Parrinder, Geoffrey. *Avatar and Incarnation*. London: Faber, 1970

Prabhupada, A. C. Bhaktivedanta Swami. *Bhagavad-Gita As It Is*. Los Angeles: Bhaktivedanta Book Trust, 1983

Radhakrishnan, S. *The Hindu View of Life*. London: Allen and Unwin, 1931

Richards, Glyn (ed). *A Source-Book of Modern Hinduism*. London: Curzon, 1985

The Rig-Veda: An Anthology, selected, translated and annotated by Wendy Doniger O'Flaherty. Harmondsworth: Penguin, 1981

Sivananda, Swami. *All About Hinduism*. Divine Life Society, India, 1988

Smart, Ninian. *Doctrine and Argument in Indian Philosophy*. Atlantic Highlands, N.J.: Humanities, 1964

Stutley, Margaret. *Hinduism: The Eternal Law*. Wellingborough: Aquarian, 1985

Sutherland, Stewart *et al.* (eds). *The World's Religions*. London: Routledge, 1988

Yogananda, Paramahansa. *Autobiography of a Yogi*, 11th edition. Los Angeles: Self-Realization Fellowship, 1979

Zaehner, R. C. *The Bhagavadgita: With a Commentary Based on the Original Sources*. London: O.U.P., 1973

Zaehner, R. C. *Hinduism*. Oxford: University Press, 1966

Zaehner, R. C. (ed). *The Concise Encyclopedia of Living Faiths*, 3rd edition. London: Hutchinson, 1959

5

Buddhism

JAN HOFMEYR

Buddhism is the most successful missionary religion to have originated in India. Since its founding almost 2 500 years ago, it has spread throughout the countries of the Far East, exercising a considerable influence on their religious and cultural histories. More recently, beginning in the early part of this century, it has also established itself in the West as a small but well-organised religious movement.

THE LIFE OF BUDDHA

The founder of Buddhism was a historical person born in about 563 BCE in a village close to the modern Nepalese border. According to tradition, his name was Siddhartha Gautama and his father ruled over a small kingdom in the region. The family were of the Ksatriya class. Legend has it that his birth was viewed as an auspicious occasion. A prediction was made that he would become either a great political leader or a great religious leader.

Buddha's father, wishing his son to become a political leader, tried to shield him from painful experience. Perhaps the father believed that it is when human beings suffer that they tend to become religious. The young Siddhartha is therefore said to have lived his early life in luxurious surroundings. When he ventured out of the palace grounds his father would send people ahead to ensure that the way was cleared of any potentially painful experience. In time, Siddhartha married and had a son.

At the age of 29, Siddhartha is said to have ventured out of the palace grounds secretly, to see the real world. On three successive days, according to tradition, he saw an old man, a sick man, and a dead man. These visions of disease, old age and death troubled him a great deal. Then, on the fourth day, he came across a wandering ascetic. He resolved to follow the example of the ascetic and renounce the ordinary world. That night, when everyone was asleep, Siddhartha crept out of the palace and rode away in search of an ascetic with whom to study. According to tradition, the gods knew that this was a moment of great importance for humankind. They lifted his chariot off the ground so that no-one would hear him leaving. For the next six years he wandered in the region of northern India, seeking teaching from a variety of ascetic leaders, and living an austere and ascetic life himself. In the process he attracted a small group of fellow ascetics who were impressed by his discipline.

Siddhartha was a great ascetic. According to tradition he ate so little that he could eventually feel his spine through his stomach. Then one day he collapsed from starvation and probably would have died had his friends not nursed him carefully back to health. After this experience, Siddhartha decided that the rigorous ascetic path was not the path to enlightenment. He therefore started to eat in moderation. This disappointed his ascetic friends and they left him. Undaunted, Siddhartha continued his own pilgrimage in search of truth. Eventually he arrived at Bodh Gaya. Adopting the lotus position he sat under a bo tree and vowed not to move until he had discovered the truth about life.

According to tradition, Mara, the evil temptress, tried to distract Siddhartha from his task by offering him beautiful maidens and political kingdoms, but Siddhartha resisted all temptation. As he sat, meditating beneath the tree, his concentration deepened until eventually he achieved an insight into the true character of life. The moment of enlightenment is viewed by Buddhists as the greatest moment in human history. Even the gods recognised the importance of the event. Flowers rained down around Buddha in recognition of his enlightenment. Then Mara returned to taunt Buddha with one last temptation. She suggested that no-one would be able to understand his teaching and that it would therefore be futile for him to take the fruits of his enlightenment to ordinary people. Buddha rejected Mara and went in search of his former companions. He found them in the Deer Park near Benares. There he delivered the first sermon and laid the foundation for the Buddhist teachings and way of life.

Buddha spent the remainder of his life wandering across northern India, converting people to Buddhism and establishing Buddhist communities. After some persuasion, he admitted women to the monastic order which he used as the foundation of Buddhist organisation. To people who were not inclined to live a monastic life, Buddha taught an ethical doctrine, encouraging them to lead good lives as a way to achieve better rebirths in future. In this way he gained many lay followers.

Buddha died as a result of food-poisoning at the age of 80 in about 483 BCE. By that time, the movement he had founded was firmly established and well supported by members of the aristocracy and the business class. The religious environment in which he was operating was highly competitive. However, of all the different sects and movements available to people at the time, Buddhism was the one which emerged as having the greatest popular appeal.

THE FIRST TEACHINGS

It is almost impossible to assemble the original teachings of Buddha with any certainty. The earliest texts that we have were written down about 500 years after his death. However, a strong indication of what he may have taught can be gained through textual analysis, and it is on this basis that we shall set out what tradition regards to have been the original teaching of the first sermon. To judge by the record, there were many beliefs current at the time of Buddha which he found no reason to question. He and his followers seem to have taken for granted the belief that spiritual entities exist. He therefore believed in the existence of both gods and devils. Buddha also believed in the doctrine of rebirth and in the law of *karma* (or destiny). However, the heart of Buddhist teaching was laid down when he gave the first sermon. It is in this sermon that we find the four noble truths. Here they are, taken from the Buddhist scriptures:

THE FOUR NOBLE TRUTHS

1. Now this, O monks, is the noble truth of pain: birth is painful, old age is painful, sickness is painful, death is painful, sorrow, lamentation, dejection, and despair are painful. Contact with unpleasant things is painful, not getting what one wishes is painful . . .

2. Now this, O monks, is the noble truth of the cause of pain: that craving which leads to rebirth, combined with pleasure and lust, finding pleasure here and there, namely the craving for passion, the craving for existence, the craving for non-existence.

3. Now this, O monks, is the noble truth of the cessation of pain: the cessation without a remainder of that craving, abandonment, forsaking, release, non-attachment.

4. Now this, O monks, is the noble truth of the way that leads to the cessation of pain: this is the eight-fold path, namely right views, right intention, right speech, right action, right livelihood, right effort, right mindfulness, right concentration . . .

To the Western mind, these truths may seem strange, for they say nothing about reality. Rather, they are an analysis of the character of human experience. And in the Buddhist view, what is fundamentally true of human experience is that it is painful. In Pali, the Buddhist classical language, the word here is *dukkha* and can also be translated as 'frustrating' or 'suffering'. The second noble truth involves the assertion that the cause of pain is 'craving'. Here the Pali word is *tanna* which can also be translated as 'clinging' or 'grasping'. The cure for the pain caused by craving is 'non-attachment' and the way to become non-attached is through the eight-fold path.

In order to understand the rationale behind the Buddhist teaching it is helpful to move on to a second doctrine of the Buddhists, namely that of the three marks of being. In the Buddhist view, our experience of being is marked by three characteristics: *anicca* (impermanence), *anatta* (no soul), *dukkha* (pain). It is when we understand these 'marks' of being that we can begin to understand the logic behind the four noble truths. According to the Buddhist, what is experienced to be fundamentally true of being is that it is impermanent. Nothing lasts. Everything is subject to a constant process of birth and death, creation and decay. There is therefore nothing which, in terms of the way Indians understood the word 'Absolute', qualifies as Absolute. This being so, there is also no soul. In the Buddhist view, therefore, all of the human being is transient.

The reason why life is painful is to be found in the disjunction which arises between what we seek and what we get. In the Buddhist view, people are in a permanent state of seeking, for craving burns like an unquenchable fire in the heart of most ordinary beings. Human experience is therefore permanently characterised by a nagging sense of unfulfilled longing. This nagging psychic pain is what the Buddhists mean by *dukkha*, and in the Buddhist view, it is present even in the midst of pleasure, for craving constantly seeks out new objects, and satisfaction is therefore never complete. The only way to stop this nagging pain is through the elimination of the craving which causes it. This, in turn, demands commitment to the eight-fold path.

The eight-fold path may appear, at first sight, to be something like the Buddhist equivalent of an ethical system. However, there is an important difference between the Buddhist path and other systems, for example the Ten Commandments. The difference is that the Buddhist path constitutes a progression describing the steps to enlightenment. In its detail, there are eight steps. Broadly speaking however, the steps can be grouped into three phases. The first phase is made up of the first two steps and can be thought of as psychological or intellectual. They are right views, which basically means 'being in agreement with Buddha', and right intentions, which means 'being motivated to follow the Buddhist path'. These are entirely rational first steps, for it stands to reason that unless one agrees with Buddha that life is painful, one will not even begin to follow the Buddhist path. The first step is therefore to agree that Buddha was correct when he asserted that life is painful.

The second step also follows, for it is not enough to agree with the Buddhist analysis. One also has to be motivated to do something about it. Thus, once intellectual assent has been gained, a commitment to the Buddhist path is the necessary second step.

The third, fourth, and fifth steps are generally considered to be the ethical component of the Buddhist path. Right speech is to 'abstain from lies and slander, from reviling, and from tattle'. Right action is to 'abstain from taking life, from stealing, and from lechery'. Right livelihood is 'that by which the disciple supports himself, to the exclusion of wrong modes of living'. In other words, it is to choose a career which does not compromise one's Buddhist principles. These three aspects of the path are similar to what we find in religions the world over. In Buddhism, however, the rationale behind these prescriptions is that they are a necessary step in the elimination of desire or 'grasping'. It takes self-control and control of the passions to live according to these ethical standards. By living in accordance with them, it is possible to subject the passions to discipline and control. Once 'grasping' has been subdued sufficiently through ethical practice, one is ready for the last three steps in the eight-fold path. These are right effort, mindfulness, and concentration. They involve intensive meditation and are therefore monastic. Right effort 'is when [the disciple] puts forth endeavour and energy, struggles and strives with all his heart, to stop bad qualities which have not yet arisen from ever arising, to renounce those which have already arisen, to foster good qualities which have not yet arisen . . .' In other words, right effort is the first step in gaining control of the mind. Having gained control of bodily action through the previous steps, one now turns one's attention to consciousness and begins to eliminate the forms of passion in consciousness.

Right mindfulness 'is when realizing what the body is, what feelings are, what the heart is, and what the mental states are, [a disciple] dwells ardent, alert, and mindful, in freedom from the wants and discontents attendant on any of these things'. What is indicated in this passage are the first steps to non-attachment. Clearly, meditation is seen to produce a detached state of mind in which it becomes possible to observe the workings of the body and the mind without being absorbed into them. Thus, the actions of body and mind are seen to pass on while the disciple observes, is alert to them, but is not affected by them.

Right concentration 'is when, divested of lusts and divested of wrong dispositions, [a disciple] develops, and dwells in, the first ecstasy with all its zest and satisfaction, a state bred of aloofness . . . ' It is hard not to read these words without supposing that the last step of the eight-fold path involves mystical experience of some kind. With the craving destroyed, ecstasy results, experience is no longer painful, and non-attachment becomes the mode of life.

The word used by Buddhists to describe the ultimate goal is 'nirvāna'. It is a difficult word to interpret. In India at the time of Buddha, it was widely used to refer to the state of god-realisation which many of the ascetics preached as the ultimate goal – a state in which union with the Absolute is experienced. However, the Buddhists are much less clear. There was, in Buddhism, a fundamental aversion to making ontological or metaphysical statements. Nirvana was not therefore thought of as a special fixed state. It was not a place (as, for example, many Christians think of heaven as a place), nor was it a state of union with the Absolute. However, it was thought of as following the extinction of craving and was thought to involve the cessation of rebirth. Moreover, as the passage above suggests, to have achieved the extinction of craving is a blissful experience.

THE EARLY PERIOD: BUDDHISM IN INDIA

According to tradition, when Buddha died a council of his leading disciples, including those who had achieved nirvana, was held to formalise and codify the teaching. Ananda, one of his most well-known disciples, recounted the Dharma (or formal sermons and teachings) of Buddha. Another disciple, Upali, recounted the monastic rules that had been established to regulate the lives of the Buddhists. The teachings were confirmed by the gathering and written down as the Sutra Pitaka and Vinaya Pitaka respectively. They constitute two of the three components of the Tripitaka (or three-fold canon) of the Buddhists. The third component, the Abhidharma, is also supposed to have been recorded at the first council, but is almost certainly a later addition to the Pitaka.

There are signs from the texts that even in the earliest period there were tensions between various groups of Buddhists. About a hundred years after the first council, a second council was called at Vesali. At this council the tensions became manifest and Buddhism split into two schools, the Mahasanghika and the Sthaviravada. The Mahasanghika were a more 'liberal' school, believing that

Buddhism would need to be adaptable if it wanted to grow. Although they were the smaller of the two groups, they named themselves the 'great community' on the apparent assumption that their ability to adapt would make them more successful. The Sthaviravada were more orthodox. They were the forerunners of the contemporary Theravada school based in Sri Lanka. The records indicate that the early disputes turned around both doctrine and discipline. For example, there were arguments over whether or not new rules could be added to the *pratimoksha* or system of monastic rules. The tradition also developed an early tendency to divinise Buddha. In this early period, the tendency to divinise Buddha became overt when a second group, the Vatsiyaputras, broke away from the Sthaviravada school because of their belief in some form of personal entity, the *pudgala*.

The rise and spread of Buddhism in this early period was strongly linked to political developments. In about 322 BCE, a soldier named Chandragupta Maurya gained control of the state of Magadha and founded the Maurya dynasty. Using this state as a base, he extended his control across India through military victories. Chandragupta advocated the idea of a united India under one king. After his death, his son Bindusara took over and the empire continued to expand. Bindusara was succeeded in 273 BCE by his son Asoka. By that time the Mauryan empire covered most of the Indian sub-continent and also stretched into present-day Afghanistan. Asoka is remembered as one of the ancient world's great rulers and statesmen, but from our point of view his particular importance is that he adopted Buddhism as the state religion for his empire. With Asoka's active support, Buddhism spread throughout India. For many centuries, Buddhist philosophers dominated philosophy at the elite levels of Indian society. The period also saw the gradual emergence of two distinctive sets of doctrines, the Hinayana and the Mahayana schools. The two represent the orthodox and the 'reform' schools of Buddhism respectively. The Mahasangikas who were responsible for the first split are generally regarded as the forerunners of the Mahayana tradition.

The word Hinayana means 'smaller vehicle' and is usually interpreted to mean that the conservative schools are not thought of as being as effective as the reform schools. In the centuries following Buddha's death, the Hinayana Buddhists elaborated on the original teaching in a number of important ways. The most important collation of the newer teachings is the Abhidharma. The Abhidharma contains a detailed exposition of the process of dependent origination. All things are explained as transient, but composed of five permanent elements (or strands) which come together in various ways to make up the variety of transient things.

New doctrines developed to classify Buddhists in terms of their advancement along a path of spirituality. At the top are the *arhats* or monks who have achieved nirvana. Next are the 'non-returners', those who will not be reborn. They are followed by the 'once-returners', meaning those who will be reborn only once; and so on. A lot of effort was also put into the development of the tradition for the laity. The ideas of *karma* and merit were elaborated. Lay Buddhists were advised on how to practise Buddhism in such a way that merit could be accumulated. The historical evidence suggests that, as time passed, people found it increasingly difficult to achieve nirvāna. The Hinayana tradition has lived on in Sri Lanka in the form of Theravada Buddhism.

Mahayana Buddhism, or 'the greater vehicle', grew slowly out of tendencies that had developed in the Hinayana schools. By about 100 BCE the Mahayana schools had become distinctive enough to be recognisable as a major strand of Buddhism in their own right. The core of Mahayana teachings are the Mahayana Sutras, imputed by Mahayana Buddhists to Buddha himself and supposed by them to have been passed on to a select group of his most advanced followers. Among the most famous of these is the Prajnaparamita Sutra ('The perfection of wisdom'). The Mahayana Sutras broke with earlier Buddhist texts in claiming authority, not just as commentaries on the original texts, but as original themselves. The differences between the Mahayana and Hinayana traditions are numerous. From the point of view of popular Buddhist practice, the Mahayana tradition has a far richer mythology and exhibits a clearer tendency to divination and to devotional forms of Buddhism. However, there were also specific doctrinal innovations which had lasting consequences for the development of Buddhism. It is from the Mahayana schools that Buddhists developed the new ideal of the *bodhisattva*. The word *bodhisattva* means 'enlightened being' and the ideal of the *bodhisattva* is counterposed against that of the *arhat*. A *bodhisattva* is one who has postponed final nirvana in order to lead others to nirvana. This the *bodhisattva* is able to do because he no longer needs the merit which results from his actions. Merit therefore becomes available to others, and in this way the *bodhisattva* contributes to the release of all beings. Mahayana Buddhists considered the older ideal of the *arhat* to be a lesser goal. The *arhat* is more concerned with his own release. The *bodhisattva* is concerned with the release of all.

The introduction of the *bodhisattva* ideal marks a decisive break from original Buddhism in that it implies the possibility of people achieving nirvana, not through their own effort, but with the help of others. This is new, for early Buddhism stressed the importance of individual effort and the responsibility of the person for his or her own release. One of the most popular *bodhisattvas* was Amitabha who, it was believed, had healing powers. The *bodhisattvas* added impetus to the tendency for Buddhism to develop devotional elements.

MADHYAMIKA BUDDHISM: THE DOCTRINE OF EMPTINESS

One of the greatest Buddhist philosophers to come out of India was Nagarjuna who lived around 200 CE. He founded the Madhyamika (Middle Way) school of Buddhism.

Nagarjuna adopted the Mahayana view that the path of the Hinayana Buddhists was a lesser path. The Abhidharma he considered to be a lesser teaching, dealing with only a limited perspective on reality. The heart of Madhyamika teaching is the doctrine of *sunyata* or emptiness. In order to understand this concept, we have to understand the doctrine of *svabhava* or own-being, against which it was directed. An 'own-being' is that which defines things in their essence. It is that which makes things what they are. An 'own-being' is that whose 'otherwise being never occurs'; in other words, it never changes.

Most Indian philosophies affirmed the existence of something that could be thought of as 'own-being'. In other words, most philosophical systems confirmed the existence of at least something which was thought of as permanent and unchanging. Even the Hinayana Buddhists thought of the *dharmas* – the constituent elements of which all things are made – as permanent in some sense. Nagarjuna launched an attack on this concept. Using as his starting point the Buddhist belief in 'conditioned co-production', the view that all things are produced in interaction with other things, he argued that nothing existed independently, but that all things were in a constant state of interplay and change in relation to each other. Sustained meditation on this truth, he asserted, led to the direct realisation that all things were transient and that there was therefore nothing which qualified as 'own-being'. Reality, in other words, was empty of essences, it was empty of 'own-being'. The word *sunyata* is usually translated as 'emptiness'. In some texts, this has been taken to mean that Nagarjuna held that nothing exists. However, this is a serious misinterpretation. It is only 'own-being' which does not exist. There is 'a world', but it is in constant flux. Nothing in the world survives from moment to moment. It is like a flame: it has continuity, yet there is no part of it which is permanent. In this sense, then, for all its apparent solidity, the world as we see it is hollow. In its true character, it does not have the solidity and permanence which it seems to have.

The assertion of the emptiness of reality had profound consequences for Nagarjuna's views about thought. He identified one of the root causes of human suffering as the tendency to conceptual thought. Words and concepts are what cause us to 'see' the world as stable or permanent. In reality, however, a word is merely a convenient tag by which we refer to what are passing phenomena. Our mistake is to think of the thing as somehow permanent because we constantly refer to that phenomenon using the word.

In the Madhyamika view, a belief in the propensity of conceptual thought to distort our perception of reality ran very deep. Concepts are based on memory. We derive a concept through our application of past experience to present experience. The concept then becomes a label through which we think of things as identical to their predecessors. But if the world is changing all the time, then concepts are based on linkages between things which do not exist anymore. The memories on which the development of concepts depend, even if perfect, are memories of a reality which no longer exists. Concepts are therefore no more than abstractions from memories of past and no longer existing realities. Yet, our tendency is to be trapped by concepts. When we look at the world, we do so through the concepts and names which we have developed for things over time. In so doing, we distort the present, for we apply ideas developed in the past to the present. It is as if our experience of the world is overshadowed by our memories of it when we see it through the concepts and names we have developed for it. When experience is mediated by concepts, memories of the past distort the perception of the present.

The ideal of the Madhyamika Buddhists was to see reality as it really is, unmediated by conceptual thought. While logical argument could be used to push people in the direction of such perception, mainly through the way it destroyed their current views, in the end meditation is required if a direct experience of the emptiness of things is to be had. This direct experiencing of reality as it unfolds is enlightenment. It is quite a different goal from the one we find in early Buddhism.

One of the questions which we have to ask in relation to Madhyamika Buddhism is this: If it is true that all concepts are faulty, what then of the Madhyamika concepts themselves? Are they not also fundamentally false? Nagarjuna's response was to argue that beliefs and concepts can be graded in terms of the accuracy with which they represent reality. A square circle is quite clearly something which cannot exist. Most beliefs and concepts, however, are not false. They are merely imperfect representations of the present because of their dependence on the past. While they are faulty, therefore, they are less faulty than non-sensical ideas like that of a square circle. The doctrine of 'emptiness' is also a concept, and is also therefore fundamentally flawed. However, of all doctrines, it expresses more closely than any other the true character of reality. Moreover, it points people in the direction of the direct perception of emptiness and is therefore a useful or liberating doctrine. In the end, however, the true character of reality can only be experienced. It cannot be mediated through conceptual thought.

THE DECLINE OF BUDDHISM IN INDIA

The key to Buddhism's early success in India was its popularity among ordinary people as an ethical doctrine and its promotion by Asoka as the state religion of the Mauryan dynasty. Some of the most innovative philosophy from this period was Buddhist in nature. Yet, the advent of Nagarjuna marks the peak of Buddhist influence in India. Starting in the early period of the common era, Buddhism began a steady decline in the land of its birth.

One of the first shocks to Buddhism came with the advent of the Sunga dynasty in north-eastern India. The Sunga rulers encouraged the development of Hinduism at the expense of Buddhism and extended patronage to Hindu religious leaders. The power of Buddhists was curtailed by their removal from positions of influence in the state. In the Kusana and Satavahana dynasties which followed, Buddhism revived again, but by about 500 CE new and more assertive forms of Hinduism were beginning to gain support among the educated elite. Hindu philosophers began to incorporate Buddhist ideas into their own systems, thus making Buddhism superfluous. Among the best-known of these was the philosopher Sankara. His system of Advaita Vedanta is sometimes viewed as a Hindu adaptation of the Madhyamika system of Nagarjuna. The fact that Advaita Vedanta continues to exist to the present day as one of the most successful forms of neo-Hinduism is testimony to the philosophic power of his system.

While Buddhism was losing ground at the philosophical level, it was also losing ground among ordinary people. In its original forms, Buddhism had always been a relatively austere doctrine. It was far less amenable than Hinduism to devotional forms of religion. This problem was exacerbated by the gradual tendency of the Buddhist monastic communities to become isolated from ordinary people. Originally, Buddhism had been founded on a doctrine of no possessions. It was because Buddhists were not supposed to possess anything that they had to beg for food. They were not allowed to own land and therefore could not farm. At the same time, they were not allowed to own things with which goods could be produced, and were not in a position to earn a living. In time, however, the Buddhist communities became quite wealthy. Endowments led to the monasteries owning land and this led, in turn, to the monastic communities becoming self-sufficient. In this way they began to lose contact with ordinary people. Once they had lost contact, they also lost support.

Devotional forms of Hinduism and forms of peasant Indian religion had persisted among ordinary people throughout the time of Buddhist dominance. When Hinduism began to re-assert itself philosophically, it found a large populace of ordinary people, ready and willing to follow. In the end, Brahmanic Hinduism proved to be better integrated at the common and the elite levels than Buddhism. The fundamental structure of Indian society, with its division between castes or classes, was better suited to the Brahmanic religious system. Moreover, Hinduism accommodated with greater ease the devotional and peasant religious forms.

THE SPREAD OF BUDDHISM OUTSIDE INDIA

From the very beginning, Buddhism had a strong missionary orientation. This missionary effort received a considerable boost during the time of Asoka. Probably the most important early success was the transmission of Buddhism to Sri Lanka in about 200 BCE. At that time, Hinayana Buddhism was the dominant tradition. Sri Lankan Buddhism has therefore descended from this tradition. Called Theravada or 'the doctrine of the elders', it is the most important branch of Hinayana Buddhism still in existence.

The heart of the Theravada teaching is contained in the three-fold canon – the Sutra Pitaka, Vinaya Pitaka, and Abhidharma Pitaka. It was the first written collation of Buddhist teaching and was assembled about 500 years after Buddha's death. Since then, the Theravada tradition has been restricted to commentary and analysis of the original canon. While there are many other religious works which play a role in Theravada Buddhism, it is the Tripitaka which constitutes the summation of Buddhist scripture.

Although Theravada Buddhism is one of the more austere forms of Buddhism, emphasising as it does that Buddha was only human and not divine, the Theravada Buddhists invested considerable energy in the compilation of a 'legendary' life-history of Buddha. Buddha's previous lives were described to illuminate the path an enlightened being has to travel. A tradition also developed around accounts of his death. Since early times, a strong commitment to relics of Buddha was present in Buddhism. The Theravada Buddhists used the accounts of his death to trace an historical line of contact which could prove the authenticity of their relics.

Theravada Buddhists resisted the tendency to divinise Buddha which developed almost spontaneously elsewhere. In time, however, they gave in to the need of ordinary people to have some kind of focus for worship. However, this was underscored by a strong sense of the difference between the monks and the laity. Theravada Buddhism has always maintained a distinction between the spiritual development of the monks and that of the laity.

In some ways, Theravada Buddhists are pessimistic about the long-term development of Buddhism. They believe that the original teaching will gradually be weakened through time until, in the end, it disappears. However, the current Buddhist age would be succeeded by a new age when Maitreya, the Buddha-to-be, comes to earth to re-establish Buddhism and create a perfect society.

The spread of Buddhism in this early period continued beyond Sri Lanka and into the countries of Burma and Thailand. As in Sri Lanka, the forms that Buddhism took in these territories were strongly shaped by the Hinayana tradition. However, from about 100 CE, Buddhism moved with increasing strength into China, and in this case, it was the Mahayana traditions which were dominant. The tradition was transmitted along trade routes, battling in the early Han dynasty against the domination of Confucian ideology. In two respects, Buddhism ran strongly counter to the mainstream of Chinese society. Firstly, its tradition of begging was at odds with the Chinese commitment to hard work; and secondly, its monastic disposition did not fit with the importance assigned by the Chinese to family and ancestors. However, Buddhism continued to grow in popularity, peaking in the centuries 600 CE to 900 CE, when it received considerable support from a sympathetic state.

Coincidentally, just as Buddhism was beginning to flourish in China, the Japanese began to adapt elements of Chinese culture for themselves. Buddhism moved across to Japan as part of this process in about 600 CE. There it flourished under the patronage of the ruler Shotuku Taishi. At about the same time, Buddhism was beginning to penetrate the mountain kingdom of Tibet, and by the thirteenth century the Tibetan form of Buddhism was advancing strongly among the Mongolian population of central Asia. In each of the above localities, Buddhism developed distinctive forms which have persisted to the present day.

BUDDHISM IN CHINA: CH'AN AND THE PURE LAND

A variety of Buddhist schools gained a foothold in China. However, in time the more scholastic forms became secondary, being displaced by Ch'an Buddhism and the Pure Land tradition.

Ch'an Buddhism began to emerge with some force during the sixth century CE. According to tradition, the origins of Ch'an can be traced to a rather formidable Indian missionary named Bodhidharma who came across to China in the early part of the common era. He taught a doctrine of the direct transmission of the teaching, without words. Bodhidharma is known as the first patriarch of Ch'an Buddhism in China. According to tradition, he stood in a line of teachers which was traceable back to a favourite follower of Buddha, Ananda. Ch'an Buddhists believe that Buddha once gave a sermon consisting solely of the holding up of a lotus blossom. None of his followers understood this wordless demonstration of the truth except Ananda, who smiled in recognition of what Buddha was trying to communicate. From that time on, Ch'an Buddhists believe that the doctrine has been passed directly from one teacher to another down to the present.

The account of Bodhidharma's activity in China begins with his crossing the Yellow River on a reed. When he arrived at the court of a Chinese emperor who had done much to sponsor Buddhism in China, the emperor asked him how much merit he, the emperor, had gained through his patronage of Buddhism. Bodhidharma replied: 'No merit whatsoever.' Rather taken aback, the emperor then asked Bodhidharma what Buddhism taught. Bodhidharma responded by blowing a single note on his flute. Exasperated, the emperor then asked Bodhidharma who he thought he was. Bodhidharma answered, 'Nobody', and walked out.

This famous encounter between the legendary founder of Ch'an Buddhism and the Chinese emperor illustrates the importance in Ch'an of anecdotal stories that illustrate the Ch'an approach to Buddhism. After his encounter with the emperor, Bodhidharma is supposed to have gone to a cave where he sat and meditated for nine years. He attracted the attention of a Chinese man called Hui-ko who sat outside imploring Bodhidharma to teach him. Bodhidharma completely refused. Eventually, so the legend runs, Hui-ko became so desperate that he cut off his arm and presented it to Bodhidharma as a sign of his seriousness. At that Bodhidharma relented and then followed one of the most famous discourses in Ch'an Buddhism:

> 'What is your problem?'
> 'I have no peace of mind.'
> 'Well show me your mind then, and I will pacify it.'
> 'But when I look for it, I can't find it.'
> 'There!'

According to tradition, Hui-ko became enlightened the moment he realised that there was no mind to show. If there is no mind to show, then where can the trouble be? The anecdote is important from a number of points of view, because it illustrates not only the Ch'an approach to teaching, but also the intensity of commitment which Ch'an Buddhism expects. In this story we see the Ch'an 'question and answer' method at work and also the surprise element. Hui-ko had no way of anticipating that the dialogue would take the surprising turn that it did. Yet, in a matter of three sentences, Bodhidharma completely disarmed Hui-ko of the 'illusion' that his mind could be troubled.

Ch'an Buddhism has been strongly influenced by Taoist ideas, which are more fully described in the next chapter. In particular, the two traditions share a similar understanding of the impermanence of reality. However, Taoism was a more optimistic doctrine than original Buddhism in the sense that it aimed, not at withdrawal from the world, but harmonious participation in it. This greater optimism has rubbed off on Ch'an Buddhism. Ch'an Buddhists aim at *satori* or enlightenment in the midst of everyday reality rather than in isolation. Yet, it remains a tough monastic doctrine whose cultural influence was always wider than the number of its actual adherents. Ch'an Buddhism was adopted by the Japanese in the period 600 CE to 900 CE. In Japan it is known as Zen Buddhism, and it has persisted into modern times as one of the more influential forms of Buddhism.

In the long run, however, the most popular form that Buddhism has taken in China is represented by the Pure Land school. This is a highly devotional form of Buddhism whose roots go back to a cult centring on the *bodhisattva* Amitabha. The cult was established in the fifth century CE and promised its adherents rebirth into the 'pure land' of the Western Paradise. In a sense it was a highly materialistic form of Buddhism, for the 'pure land' was conceived in truly wonderful terms. It offered a perfect life for human beings in which all those things missing in ordinary life would be fulfilled. In the sixth century, the Pure Land school was re-inforced by the introduction of the 'Pure Land Sutras'. These, it was argued, had been handed down from the Indian missionary Bodhiruci who was reputed to have established the Pure Land school.

In time, numerous Pure Land schools developed in both China and Japan. All of them had in common a highly devotional orientation with its focus in Amitabha. The earlier Buddhist goal of reaching nirvana was replaced in these schools by the goal of rebirth into an unearthly paradise. Pure Land Buddhism survives today as one of the more popular forms of devotional religion in Taiwan.

BUDDHISM IN THE WEST: ZEN BUDDHISM

It would probably be fair to say that, of all the schools of Buddhism, the one that has had the greatest impact in the West is Zen Buddhism, the Japanese form of Ch'an Buddhism.

The word *ch'an* means meditation, and Zen Buddhism is therefore meditation Buddhism. Its philosophical origins lie in the teachings of Madhyamika Buddhism on one hand, and Taoism on the other. At the heart of its views about reality is the doctrine of 'emptiness'. As was explained in a previous section of this chapter, this doctrine holds that reality is empty of essences, and is in constant flux. However, reality can be seen for what it is through the practice of meditation. The aim of the Zen Buddhist is to achieve *satori* or enlightenment. The enlightened person sees the world as it is and acts perfectly in the world.

Zen meditation is an exceptionally arduous discipline. It begins with counting the breaths as a way to focus the mind and has a three-fold aim: To develop *joriki* or meditation energy; to achieve *kensho* or enlightenment; and *mujodo no taigen* or to carry perfect mind back into everyday life. Regarding the first aim, it is clear from the accounts of the Zen Buddhists that *zazen* or meditation produces a feeling in consciousness which is best described as meditation energy. It is a kind of power which enables Zen Buddhists to sustain long periods of focused concentration, and arises as a natural consequence of meditation.

The second aim of meditation is the achievement of *kensho* or enlightenment. This is the experience of a moment which signals the final realisation of the truth of Zen Buddhist teaching, namely that the world is both 'empty' and perfect as it is. Zen Buddhists argue that there is no particular state which is the state of enlightenment. This is because the world is subject to constant change and there is therefore nothing which is constant and can be called 'the enlightenment state'. It is human ignorance that clouds this reality. Human habits of thought and action distort reality. Conceptual thought in particular obscures the true nature of reality. When 'the winds of discursive thought' have been stilled, then reality as it unfolds can be experienced directly and immediately for what it is. To 'see' reality in this way, and to live spontaneously in it in a way which is unbound by conventions of thought or action, is to be enlightened. But enlightenment does not imply a changed state of mind. It implies only a mind which has recognised that, if left alone to run by itself, it is perfect.

The final aim of *zazen* is to carry the 'enlightenment mind' into everyday life. In other words, it is to sustain the meditation experience back into the process of everyday life.

In time, two schools of Zen developed, the Rinzai and Soto sects. The first stresses that enlightenment is a sudden and dramatic event. The second stresses that enlightenment comes gradually through sustained meditation. The Rinzai criticise the Soto for not achieving enlightenment because there is no recognisable moment in which enlightenment occurs. The Soto, on the other hand, criticise the Rinzai for failing to provide a base of depth in the enlightenment experience. Among the more famous innovations attributed to the Rinzai school is the *koan*. A *koan* is a riddle which appears to admit of no solution. One of the most famous examples is: What is the sound of one hand clapping? The purpose of the *koan* is to force the person to the realisation that discursive thought is faulty. The *koan* admits of no 'logical' answer because it employs concepts that do not belong together. Yet, the Zen Master forces the person to seek an answer for it. Eventually, when the person has been driven to the realisation that the riddle admits of no logical answer, then conditions are ripe for the person to clear the mind of conceptual thinking and see into the true nature of reality. That then constitutes the moment of enlightenment.

Zen Buddhism has made an institutional home for itself in the United States in recent times. It is an arduous discipline and seldom involves more than a relatively small number of adherents. But its cultural and intellectual influence stretches far beyond the number of its adherents.

BUDDHISM IN TIBET

Buddhism reached Tibet in about 600 CE, and by the tenth and eleventh centuries it was strongly established there and spreading throughout Mongolian lands. As has so often been the case, one of the reasons for its success was the support it received from the state. By the eighth century, taxes in Tibet were being levied to support the work of Buddhist monasteries.

Tibetan Buddhism derives from the Vajrayana schools of Indian Buddhism. Tibetan Buddhists believe that the truth is expressed at many different levels. They are catholic in their approach to scripture and incorporate both Hinayana and Mahayana texts in their sacred canons. In fact, the Tibetans were prolific, adding commentaries and philosophical discourses of their own to the original work of their Indian teachers.

There are two schools of Tibetan Buddhism, the earlier 'red' hats, and the later 'yellow' hats. Both derive from the Vajrayana tradition, but the red hats emphasise the more exotic and esoteric forms of Tibetan Buddhism. The yellow hats are more restrained. Both however espouse a mythology which is extremely rich in its details. They believe in an extensive pantheon of buddhas and *bodhisattvas*, supplemented by a range of male and female deities and demons. In time, the better-known and more influential monks were added to the pantheon. An interest in magical powers is more prevalent in Tibetan Buddhism than in other forms of Buddhism. Tibetan Buddhists incorporate tantric practices into their religion.

The priests of Tibetan Buddhism are called 'lamas'. From early times, they showed an interest in political affairs and at various times throughout the last millennium, there have been periods when Tibet was ruled by the lamas. From about 1500 CE, political processes ensured the gradual ascendancy of the yellow hat school of Tibetan Buddhism. By the 1750s the yellow hats had gained complete control of Tibet and instituted a theocratic Buddhist state ruled over by the Dalai Lama. This was to last until 1951 when the communist Chinese invaded Tibet and the Dalai Lama was forced into exile. Today, the Dalai Lama lives in India, a figure who retains religious authority, but without political power.

BUDDHISM IN MODERN TIMES

The twentieth century has seen all the world's great historical religions come under considerable pressure. The era of European colonial expansion, beginning in the eighteenth century with a vengeance, has confronted all the religious traditions of the East with fundamental new challenges. European forms of government and social organisation have put other cultures of the world under unprecedented stress. Some have risen to the challenge in a way which can only be described as remarkable. Others have crashed. On the whole, the Far Eastern nations have adjusted to the impact of the West in a highly effective way. At the religious level, Christianity, the dominant religious ideology that accompanied colonial expansion, has made very little progress.

Throughout the Asian countries, Buddhists have responded with energy and imagination to the challenges posed by interaction with the West. In response to secular Western culture, Buddhist reforms have emphasised the humanistic and ethical teachings of Buddha. Philosophical Buddhism possesses an intellectual austerity which has fitted it well to meet the challenges of the sceptical modern mind. At heart, Buddhism is not a religion which depends on belief in certain intangible realities. It is more precisely a religion which depends on an analysis of the quality of human experience. To the extent that Buddhists take an ontological view of things, the only doctrine of fundamental importance is the belief in impermanence (*anicca*). In the twentieth century, this belief has fitted increasingly snugly with the views of modern science.

The ethical aspects of Buddhism also provided it with a resource which has enabled it to adapt to the impact of the ethical pressures generated by Western social norms. Buddhist reformers have emphasised its internally democratic nature and also its community orientation. In many of the Far Eastern countries, Buddhist monks have played a leading role in criticising what used to be seen as the exploitative colonial administration of the Western nations. In fact, in many of these nations the emergence of Buddhism into a position of pre-eminence in the twentieth century has a lot to do with the role Buddhists played in resistance to colonial rule. In Sri Lanka and Burma, for example, the nineteenth century was characterised by a rising tide of anti-colonial nationalism. Buddhists were an important element in the promotion and consolidation of this process. As a result they have been able to retain positions of religious pre-eminence and political importance.

In some Asian countries, for example South Korea and Taiwan, Buddhism has survived alongside other traditions rather than gained pre-eminence among them. In these cases, political transformation has not been linked to Buddhism. In fact, in the case of Japan the modern era began with the removal of the special privileges which Buddhists had previously enjoyed. When the Tokugawa shogunate came to an end in 1868, Buddhism failed to hold its position because of its close association with the establishment. In the Meiji restoration it was replaced by Shinto. Until after World War Two when Japan became a secular state, Shinto was the state religion of Japan. Yet Buddhism has continued to be an important part of Japanese cultural life. New forms of Buddhism have emerged which can only be described as popular mass movements. Among the most important of these are the Soka Gakkai and the Reiyukai sects. Their success has been particularly marked among poor people.

One of the most interesting features of the modern era has been the return of Buddhism to the land of its birth, India. This process has involved three distinct elements. The earliest, and probably the least important, began with the creation of small Buddhist societies in the early part of this century. Highly rationalist in orientation, these societies involved intellectuals who had moved away from traditional forms of religion under the impact of Western secular intellectual standards. Buddhism was a philosophy which they found satisfying. A second strand in the re-emergence of Buddhism in India resulted from the movement of refugee Buddhists into India, particularly after the Chinese take-over in Tibet. Since the Chinese take-over, India has become the headquarters of the Tibetan lamaist tradition, and the Dalai Lama lives there and operates his mission from Indian soil.

Perhaps the most important example of Buddhism in modern India is to be found in the state of Maharashtra. There hundreds of thousands of people have been converted to Buddhism under the influence of Dr Ambedkar. In Maharashtra, Buddhism has again become a genuine grassroots movement in India after an absence of some 2 000 years.

An important development in the modern era has been the movement of Buddhism into the West, to which there was a brief allusion above. This process began towards the end of the last century. Initially, the process was based largely on the establishment of Japanese and Chinese immigrant communities, especially in the United States. In Britain and across the continent there were also small groups of European enthusiasts, some of whom had strong links with theosophy. However, the real spread of Buddhism, particularly in the USA, can be said to have begun with the emergence of the youth culture of the 1960s. The most influential forms of Buddhism in the West have been Zen and Lamaism. Zen Buddhism in particular seems to have had an appeal to the Western intellect which many of the other forms of Eastern religion lack.

It is interesting to compare the impact that Zen Buddhism has had in the last twenty years with the impact it had in the 1930s when the first serious attempts were made to convert Western people. One Zen master apparently described the attempt to plant Zen in California as being like the attempt to get a lotus flower to grow by holding it against a rock of granite. Yet, by the 1960s Zen Buddhism was attracting widespread interest, and in the 1970s, California had a governor in Jerry Brown who openly proclaimed his interest in Zen Buddhism.

The most difficult regions for Buddhism in the modern era have been the communist dominated nations. Shortly after the Bolshevik revolution in Russia, the Mongolian People's Republic was established. Buddhists lost their state privileges, and without state patronage, began a struggle to survive. This process was repeated in mainland China after the victory by Mao Tse-tung over his nationalist rivals in 1949. Buddhism was unable to escape the stigma of having been an establishment movement. Buddhists were defrocked and their lands and buildings confiscated. The early pressure on Buddhists intensified during the Cultural Revolution. Buddhist organisation suffered severe setbacks, from which it has only begun to recover since the death of Mao. In North Korea, Cambodia (Kampuchea) and Tibet, Buddhism has suffered similar reverses. In fact, the attack on Buddhism in Tibet by the Chinese has been far more severe than in China itself.

Buddhism, like all the world's religions, faces the future under pressure. Only time will tell whether the new communities established in the West will survive and whether the older communities will continue to adapt in a way which keeps them viable.

SELECT BIBLIOGRAPHY

Conze, E. *Buddhism: Its Essence and Development*. New York, 1959

Conze, E. *Buddhist Thought in India*. London: Allen & Unwin, 1983

Conze, E. (trans). *Buddhist Scriptures*. Harmondsworth: Penguin Classics, 1969

Guenther, H. V. *Buddhist Philosophy in Theory and Practice*. Harmondsworth: Penguin, 1972

Radhakrishnan, S. & Moore, C. A. *A Sourcebook in Indian Philosophy*. Princeton: Princeton University Press, 1973

Watts, A. *The Way of Zen*. Harmondsworth: Penguin, 1982

Zimmer, H. *Myths and Symbols in Indian Arts and Civilization*. Princeton: Princeton University Press, 1972

6

The Religions of China

JAN HOFMEYR

China is the most populous country in the world with over a billion people. It is not the earliest of the world's great civilisation, and writing only came late to China – in about 1600 BCE. But China is the only one of the world's great, ancient civilisations that has retained the status of a world power into the modern era.

Three religious systems have flourished at one time or another in China: Taoism, Confucianism and Buddhism. Each is unique, yet there is a commonality to them by virtue of their being Chinese. All the religious systems of China focus on a common goal: the achievement of harmony. The ideal for human beings is reached when there is harmony between all things. Even Buddhism, imported as it was from India, took on a particularly local character in China.

Although the intellectual life of China has been dominated since about 300 BCE by one or other of the above systems, there have also been other influential religious currents in the history of that land. One in particular, folk religion, has remained a common feature of Chinese religious practice from earliest times right up to the present. Folk religion has persisted through the changing of the dynasties and through the rise to prominence and subsequent decline of each of the major systems of religious thought.

In this chapter we shall focus on two of the three major religious systems, exploring them in relation to an overview of Chinese history. The third of the religions in question, Ch'an Buddhism, was dealt with in detail in the previous chapter on Buddhism.

THE EARLIEST PERIOD: FROM PREHISTORY TO THE HAN

Traditionally, the Chinese begin accounts of their history with the emperors Yao and Shun. Yao and Shun are thought to have lived around 3000 BCE and are regarded as perfect examples of wisdom and authority. They set an ideal example of government and taught their people how best to live. However, in the absence of hard evidence of their existence they remain legendary figures.

Archaeological excavations currently push Chinese history back to at least 6000 BCE, but there is no evidence in this early period for the existence of great states or dynasties. The earliest recognisable state is the Shang dynasty which was established in northern central China in about 1600 BCE.

In this early period China was occupied by tribes organised according to a basic agrarian pattern. Villages were small and consisted of simple mud-brick huts. Animals such as hens and pigs had been domesticated and basic grain crops were grown. Graves in this early period contained tools and ornaments, suggesting a belief in some form of after-life. Bones similar to those found in Shang excavations exist, suggesting a belief in divination. Pottery fragments depict dragons and snakes, two of the most common forms of animal symbolism found in later Chinese religion. If religious practice at this time followed the later pattern, then divination would have been linked to veneration of ancestors or to the powers of nature; and the animal symbolism would have indicated a concern with rainfall and harvests.

In time, the villages grew bigger and many erected fortified defences. There is evidence of ancient pottery factories and markets. Some houses were larger and more elaborate than others, suggesting the beginnings of social differentiation. In these circumstances, the Shang dynasty emerged. The Shang people were clearly stratified socially. Their leaders appear to have come from a warrior class. They were the first people in the region to use writing and to develop a metals technology. Shang writing is a prototype for modern Chinese and is therefore easily interpreted. The basis of their economy was agriculture. However, the ruling elite seems to have devoted most of its time to leisure activities and to making war. The elite operated from large cities, qualitatively different in size and complexity from anything that had existed before. Yet most of the common people continued to live as farmers or traders in small villages.

Most of the evidence for what the Shang people believed and practised is found on the so-called 'oracle bones'. These are the shoulder bones of sheep and deer which have been heated and then cracked; sometimes tortoise shells were used. A statement would be inscribed on one side of the bone with its negation on the other. The bone would then be heated and the pattern of the cracks used to determine which of the statements was true, the original statement or its negation. When finished, the results of the process would be inscribed on the bone. In this way the Shang people looked for answers to their religious and social questions.

The questions for which the Shang sought answers related to harvests, the weather, disease and warfare. In their questioning they appealed to ancestors and to a great variety of natural spirits who, it was supposed, were in a position to help. Sometimes the results of their enquiries would indicate that certain rituals should be performed and offerings made. These could include animal and human sacrifices. As with many ancient religious systems, the Shang people seem to have believed that a properly made offering would oblige the ancestor or spirit to use its power to the benefit of the Shang. The ruler of the Shang state was the centre of religious practice.

One of the spirits to whom requests were often submitted was Shang-ti, 'the Ruler Above'. Shang-ti seems to have been thought of as a ruler of the divine realm, analogous to the ruler of the Shang state. He was the supreme god of the Shang. The concept of Shang-ti is therefore the earliest evidence we have of a belief in a supreme being among the Chinese.

The centrality of the ancestors to the fortunes of the Shang ensured that Shang culture was permeated by a strong bond of continuity between the living and the dead. In fact, it could even be argued that Shang people were more powerful when dead than alive. As ancestors, they were understood to be in a position to ensure good fortune for their descendants. However, they were also in a position to cause calamities if not properly looked after. Shang people therefore lived with a constant sense of the presence of their ancestors and of the power of the ancestors to affect their lives. As many commentators have pointed out, the strength of this bond between the living and the dead created a natural tendency for the culture to be conservative, a tendency which has persisted to the present day.

One of the tribal groups often mentioned in Shang writings was the Chou. They lived to the west, sometimes warring and sometimes trading with the Shang. Eventually, in 1122 BCE, the Chou completely defeated the Shang under the leadership of King Wu. They established the Chou dynasty, a dynasty which was to see the rise of the great philosophers of ancient China. The Chou people adopted many of the beliefs and practices of the Shang people. They adopted Shang writing and continued to venerate the ancestors of the Shang rulers. However, to the adopted elements of Shang culture, the Chou added elements of their own. The emergence of the Chou dynasty therefore saw a new phase in the development of Chinese religious history.

Early Chou society was organised on a feudal basis. Chou emperors ruled over partially independent states governed by nobles. Succession was hereditary. Most of the people were peasant farmers working the lands of the nobles. In return for working the land, the farmers were protected by the nobles and allowed to keep a certain amount of their produce for personal use. There was also a small class of artisans and traders centred around the cities. It was the emperor's responsibility to protect the realm from foreign attack. Emperors were also expected to arbitrate in the event of disputes between the nobles. Finally, they were responsible for the great state rituals, for example that marking the new year. In return for these services, the nobles vowed loyalty to the emperors and brought them gifts once a year.

In contrast to the Shang, the religious beliefs of the Chou are contained in written books. Chief amongst these are the *Shih ching* or Book of Odes, the *Li chi* or Book of Ritual and Protocol, and the *I ching* or Book of Changes. From these sources we discover that the Chou continued with the key religious practices of the Shang, namely the veneration of ancestors and the performance of the rites associated with agriculture. However, to these basic elements they added important new elements. One of these was the concept of T'ien or Heaven. The concept of T'ien was more abstract and less anthropomorphic than that of Shang-ti.

To the Chou, T'ien was superordinate to Shang-ti. The Chou saw their emperor as the 'Son of Heaven', not in a direct sense but in a symbolic sense. They believed that emperors were fitted to rule by their being virtuous. The virtuous emperor receives the 'mandate of Heaven' and in this sense is the 'Son of Heaven'. The Chou argued that the fact that they had defeated the Shang was evidence of the corruption of the Shang. A displeased 'Heaven' had transferred its mandate from the Shang to the Chou.

In the Chou period the development of religious understanding was closely allied with what many would call archaic science. From earliest times, the attempt to harmonise human activity with the patterns of the world had been a focal point of Chinese religious practice. It was this motivation which had led to the tradition of divination. During the period of the Chou this motivation was carried further. The Chinese began a serious attempt to discern the basic structure or pattern beneath the surface phenomena of natural processes. Two sets of ideas played a crucial role in the development of their ideas: Tao, and the yin-yang cycle.

Originally *tao* meant 'way' or 'path'. In time, however, it came to be used of the paths travelled by the objects of the heavens, the stars, planets, sun and moon. Eventually, the entire majestic process of celestial change came to be referred to as the 'way'. This, in turn, led to the word being linked to the many other processes of change associated with astronomical change. The changes of the seasons were read from the stars and used to create the first calendars. These rhythms were then linked to the earthly rhythms of growth and decay, and to the agricultural rhythms of plowing, planting, and harvesting. By this process of association, the word *tao* eventually came to be known as 'the way' in its most fundamental sense, namely the majestic and orderly process through which all of creation revolves. The 'Way of Heaven' was then 'the way of the creative process'.

In order to account for the nature of particular processes of change, the Chou elaborated on the concepts of the *yin* and the *yang*. *Yin* is 'cool, dark, passive'; *yang* is 'open, warm, aggressive'. *Yin* is the night, *yang* the day; *yin* is the winter, *yang* the summer; *yin* is female, *yang* male. Through the interaction of the *yin* and the *yang*, all things are created and all processes of change regulated. The most important early attempt to set out the concepts of *yin* and *yang* in a systematic way was the *I ching*, the Book of Changes, used mostly for purposes of divination.

In time, the authority of the central Chou domain was weakened as the various states grew in power and influence. By the eighth century BCE the emperor had very little control. Then in 771 BCE the capital city was attacked and the emperor assassinated. The remnants of the Chou royal family fled to the east where they established a much smaller feudal state. China entered a long period of turmoil as first one state and then another became predominant. Alliances were formed between the states until, by 300 BCE, only seven large states were left. One of these, the Ch'in, took over the royal domain in 256 BCE, thus bringing the Chou dynasty to a formal end. By 221 BCE the leader of the Ch'in had conquered the remaining states and inaugurated the Ch'in dynasty.

The Ch'in dynasty was shortlived. By 202 BCE it had been replaced by the Han. Yet, in that short time it made a lasting impression, for it was with the Ch'in dynasty that the geographical shape of China as we know it today was established. In fact, the name 'China' comes from the Ch'in. The Ch'in dynasty was also important for having faced the formidable problem of trying to unite the disparate elements of which China was composed. The Ch'in emperor had a rather radical approach to this problem. He decreed the destruction of all books on the basis that the only way to unite the people would be to have them all sharing the same ideology. He attempted the first systematisation of Chinese law and embarked on massive public works programmes. It is to the Ch'in emperor that we owe the great wall of China.

The first Ch'in emperor died in 205 BCE and was succeeded by his son, a weak and ineffectual person. In the hands of his son, the kingdom did not last long. Civil war broke out and by 202 BCE a new unifier of the realm had emerged. He was Liu Bong, a former peasant and general in the Ch'in army. Liu Bong established the Han dynasty. It was during this crucial dynasty that the basic pattern of Chinese civilisation was laid out and formalised.

The Chou dynasty had lasted for nine hundred years. The last four hundred of these were spent in constant turmoil and political disorder. Yet the Chou dynasty saw the emergence of the great philosophies of China. It was also the formative period for the classical religious and philosophical literature of China. If the Han dynasty was the one in which Chinese civilisation took formal shape, then the Chou dynasty was the one in which the seeds of this were sown. We must now attend to the greatest of the ancient Chinese philosophers to emerge during the Chou dynasty, Confucius and the largely legendary Lao-tzu.

THE PHILOSOPHY OF CONFUCIUS

K'ung-tzu, as he is known by the Chinese, was born in 551 BCE in the state of Lu. According to tradition he was the son of a poor nobleman. As was customary for the nobility, K'ung-tzu entered the public service. He eventually rose to the position of Minister of Justice in his home state. However, he did not last long. He seems to have had trouble because of his tendency to criticise the government. Eventually he left the state of Lu under circumstances which are difficult to reconstruct. According to the orthodox tradition, he left out of disillusionment. However, if one reads between the lines it seems that he may have had to leave in a hurry and that he was therefore in trouble when he left.

K'ung-tzu spent the next thirteen years of his life seeking employment as an adviser on government at the court of various nobles. His efforts never met with more than temporary success. However, he had by this time developed a considerable reputation for learning and wisdom. Gradually a group of young scholars assembled around K'ung-tzu. At the age of 70 he returned to his home city and set up a school. He spent the last three years of his life teaching the young about his ideas on government and social relations.

In certain respects, K'ung-tzu led a normal life. He was married and one of his grandsons became one of his greatest students. He died in 479 BCE. He based his own studies on what came to be called 'the five classics': *Shih ching*, *Li chi*,

I ching, *Shu ching* (Book of History), and the *Ch'un-ch'iu* (Spring and Autumn Annals). In fact, he is said to have edited them, giving them their final form. However, while K'ung-tzu devoted himself to these books, his own teachings are recorded in the so-called *Lun-yu* or *Analects*. Our main source for his ideas will be the *Analects*.

The Analects

By his own account, K'ung-tzu 'set his heart' on learning at the age of 15 (Bk 2.4). In fact, the *Analects* opens with the following rhetorical question: 'Is it not a pleasure to learn and to repeat or practice from time to time what has been learned?' (Bk 1.1) For K'ung-tzu, however, learning was not independent of teaching. And the basic source for both was tradition. K'ung-tzu claimed to be no more than a 'transmitter' of tradition: 'I transmit but do not create. I believe in and love the ancients' (Bk 7.1).

Yet, he was also a great innovator; and one of the first innovations was his attitude to the popular religious practices of his time:

> Chi-lu asked about serving the spiritual beings.
> K'ung-tzu said, 'If we are not able to serve man, how can we serve the spiritual beings?'
> 'I venture to ask about death.'
> K'ung-tzu said, 'If we do not yet know about life, how can we know about death?' (Bk 11.11)

These lines hardly need any explanation. K'ung-tzu is not rejecting conventional religious practice. However, it is clear that his priorities lay closer to ordinary life than to what people thought of as the religious. And he was also clearly more concerned that people learn to relate to each other properly than that they devote energy to discovering how to relate to the gods. This view is reinforced in another *Analect*:

> Fan Tzu asked about wisdom.
> K'ung-tzu said, 'Devote yourself earnestly to the duties due to men, and respect spiritual beings but keep them at a distance. This may be called wisdom.' (Bk 6.20)

K'ung-tzu is not denying the existence of the spirits. But he is suggesting that social responsibilities come first. The main task K'ung-tzu set himself, therefore, was to establish proper relations in society.

The social system advocated by K'ung-tzu was set in the context of a hierarchical understanding of society. Social order was understood to depend on the maintenance of certain key social relations. In the *Li chi*, one of the main texts for Confucian teaching, we find the following description of these relations: 'The father is merciful, the son filial; the elder brother is good, the younger brother submissive; the husband is upright, the wife complaisant; the adult is kind, the child obedient.'

There were other classifications of the key relations. In particular, some systems included that between ruler and ruled as one of the key relations. In all cases, the basis of the relations was hierarchical. One member is dominant and the other submissive. The dominant member of the relationship owes benevolence to the submissive one. The submissive one, in turn, owes obedience to the dominant one. There was nothing egalitarian in this system. K'ung-tzu clearly believed, as did most Chinese, that people are equipped differently to handle different sets of reponsibilities. Some are fitted to command, others to obey. On the whole, men were understood to be above women, elders above the young, and rulers above the ruled.

Of the key relations, K'ung-tzu selected that of the father and the son for special attention. In a world in which most social activity outside the home involved men, this must have seemed natural. From this special relation we get the concept of 'filial piety'. Its importance for social order can be seen in the following passage, taken from the *Analects*, Bk 1.2:

> Yu-tzu said, 'Few of those who are filial sons and respectful brothers will show disrespect to superiors, and there has never been a man who is not respectful to superiors and yet creates disorder.'

In other words, the respect which is learnt in the relations of dominance between father and son, and elder and younger brother, is the basis for the respect for authority on which social order depends.

When it comes to the specifics of what filial piety involves, the *Analects* are frustratingly inexplicit. Consider, for example, the following passage:

> Meng yi tzu asked about filial piety. K'ung-tzu said, 'Never disobey.' Fan Chi said, 'What does that mean?' K'ung-tzu said, 'When parents are alive, serve them according to the rules of propriety. When they die, bury them according to the rules of propriety and sacrifice to them according to the rules of propriety.' (Bk 2.5)

In reading this passage it would seem that the key to the content of 'filial piety' is the 'rules of propriety'. This brings us to one of the most crucial concepts in the thought of K'ung-tzu, *li*. *Li* can be translated in a variety of ways. It is ritual, custom, good manners, and propriety. By the time of K'ung-tzu, a book on ritual practice had already started to take shape called the *Li chi*, the Book of Ritual and Protocol. For K'ung-tzu the concept of propriety (or *li*) was a general one; it represented the entire corpus of traditional practices, both formal and informal, upon which the regulation of Chinese social life depended. People were understood to be good if their lives were in accordance with propriety (*li*), a well-ordered state was one organised in accordance with propriety (*li*).

The relation between father and son, even though central, was only one among the relations on which social order depended. The key to all relations was *li*. This signals the centrality assigned to tradition by K'ung-tzu. Many people have mistaken the importance assigned by him to tradition for a stultifying conservatism. However, it is clear from the *Analects* that K'ung-tzu was not conservative in the narrow sense of the word. In *Analects* Bk 2.15 we find the following:

> K'ung-tzu said, 'He who loves learning but does not think is lost; he who thinks but does not learn is in danger.'

Now, the Chinese concept of thinking is very different from the Western one. In the West we tend to associate thinking with a rational activity, one whose locus is the intellect and which therefore excludes feeling to a certain extent. For the Chinese, however, thinking was primarily a holistic activity, a single blending of feeling and intellect. Thinking, in a sense, was held to involve the 'harmonisation of feeling' rather than, as it tends to be seen in the West, the 'rationalisation of ideas'.

In the passage above we see that the 'harmonisation of feeling' was an essential aspect of the response to tradition for K'ung-tzu. To learn was not merely to know, nor even to be clever in the manipulation of ideas. It was more deeply to have responded to tradition in a personal way. It was to have internalised the evocative impact of tradition by harmonising the feelings that resulted from the impact. Learning could only be counted as having occurred if it resulted in such internalisation and, consequently, in a change of character. But the nature of that change had to be guided by thinking, that is, by 'harmonisation', otherwise the person would be lost. In other words, unless what had been learnt had been internalised in a creative way, tradition would not provide a guide to action. By the same token, thinking could not do without learning. According to K'ung-tzu, 'he who thinks but does not learn is in danger'. So we see that, while tradition, if it was to have value, had to be harmonised in accordance with its personal impact, uninformed thinking, or the 'harmonisation of feeling' without tradition, was dangerous. Personal feeling in the raw could not be trusted to provide a proper foundation for action or for the development of character.

K'ung-tzu set very high standards. In our discussion we have seen that he did not value mere book learning very highly. Yet he also did not seem to think that many people would be equipped to follow the high standards he set. Most people must be led. In his view, 'the common people may be made to follow it [the Way] but may not be made to understand it' (Bk 13.6). People therefore need a person of superior character or virtue to act as an example.

This brings us to the concept of the 'superior man'. The 'superior man' is a man of humanity (*jen*):

> K'ung-tzu said, 'The superior man regards humaneness as the substance of everything. He practises it according to the principles of propriety. He brings it forth in modesty. And he carries it forward in faithfulness. He is indeed a superior man.' (Bk 15.17)

The way to become superior was through a rigorous and disciplined programme of self-cultivation. As the passage above indicates, this involved the study and the practice of *li*, meaning good manners, custom, ritual. But as we have also seen, it was not enough simply to conform to the 'rules of propriety'. *Li* had to be internalised so that it became inextricably bound to individual character. The end result of such a process would be a perfect sense of proportion, a perfect composure and sense of balance in both attitude and behaviour, and a complete self-control. The result was 'the man of humanity', or *jen*. So, K'ung-tzu says: 'To master oneself and return to propriety is humanity' (Bk 12.1).

We see, in this view, that humaneness was a quality which K'ung-tzu believed to be embodied in *li*, tradition and custom. However, we have also observed that it was creative, for it was up to each person to internalise tradition in a unique and creative way. When pressed to give an explicit guide to action, an explicit maxim expressive of *jen*, K'ung-tzu came up with his own equivalent of the 'golden rule'. 'Do not do to others what you do not want them to do to you' (Bk 12.2).

This looks so much like the other religions of the world that we might be led to believe that the ethical bases of the world's religions are the same. However, this would be a grave mistake, for K'ung-tzu's rule is cast within the context of his non-egalitarian approach to society. The framework within which the rule functions here is that of a society in which relations of obedience and authority were natural. Thus, doing the right thing in any situation does not involve simply not doing to others what you would not want them to do to you. Rather, it involves calculating what the appropriate thing to do is given the status of the person concerned. Thus, doing the right thing involves putting yourself into their shoes and asking what they might rightfully expect from you within the framework of hierarchical social relations. Further, *li* is the guide.

K'ung-tzu did not believe that many people were capable of attaining the levels of superiority which he set as the standard. However, we can get a feeling of his intentions from his own description of himself. He says: 'At seventy I could follow my heart's desire without transgressing moral principles' (Bk 2.4).

We turn finally to the question of government. In a real sense, K'ung-tzu's life was a failure in at least one respect: he never achieved the levels of influence he sought on government. Yet the reform of government was one of the main tasks he set himself. This was in a context of considerable turmoil in the political affairs of China. What then were his ideas with respect to government? The best place to begin is the following long passage from the *Analects* Bk 13.3, in which K'ung-tzu articulates one of his most important ideas, the 'rectification of names':

> Tzu-lu said, 'The ruler of Wei is waiting for you to serve in his administration. What will be your first measure?'
> K'ung-tzu said, 'It will certainly concern the rectification of names . . . If names are not rectified, then language will not be in accord with truth. If language is not in accord with truth, then things cannot be done. If things cannot be done, then ceremonies and music will not flourish. If ceremonies and music do not flourish, then punishment will not be just. If punishments are not just, then the people will not know how to move hand or foot . . . '

The best place to begin an analysis of this passage is with a consideration of the link between ceremony, music and justice. To K'ung-tzu, the link was harmony, the harmony implicit in the order of ceremony, the order of traditional music, and the order of justice. Again, it is not far from the order implicit in *li*. Clearly, therefore, for K'ung-tzu justice and its application depended on the sense of harmony which could best be learnt from music and ceremony. Justice was therefore something which could not be based merely on a study of law.

The consequences of a failure to apply justice are spoken of in terms of confusion among the people. What seems to be intended here is a warning about the social consequences of arbitrary justice: when justice is inconsistent in its application, order breaks down because people do not know what to do. Now, if social order depends on proper justice, and proper justice depends on the development of a sense of harmony through the performance of ceremony and music, then it is essential that ceremony and music be performed. But for this to happen, it must be possible to describe how to do them. This in turn requires that words have precise meaning – 'names', to use K'ung-tzu's terminology, 'must be in accord with truth'. The 'rectification of names' is then a programme to define the meaning of words, to give them precision. K'ung-tzu seems to have been battling against a situation in which *li* (tradition, custom, good manners) had broken down. As a result, the behaviour appropriate to a 'name', such as father or king, was no longer clear. This is why, for K'ung-tzu, the rectification of names was an essential element in the reconstruction of social relations. Words had to be given a proper meaning, social roles had to be clearly defined, language had to be in accord with truth. With names rectified it would be possible for 'the ruler' to be a ruler, for everybody, including the ruler, would know what was expected of him. And so for all other social roles and social situations.

The ideal ruler was one who was himself rectified:

> Chi Ch'ang Tzu asked K'ung-tzu about government. K'ung-tzu replied, 'To govern is to rectify. If you lead the people by being rectified yourself, who will dare not to be rectified?' (Bk 12.17)

This verse brings the concept of the 'superior man' to that of government – the ideal ruler is one who has perfected himself as a ruler; that is, one who, through a process of disciplined self-cultivation, has internalised the *li* appropriate to his social station. K'ung-tzu believed that a ruler of this kind would have tremendous moral authority, so much so that government of the kind to which we are accustomed would hardly be necessary. He said: 'If a ruler sets himself right, he will be followed without his command. If he does not set himself right, even his commands will be disobeyed' (Bk 13.6). By contrast, government based on decree was not good:

> K'ung-tzu said: 'Lead the people with governmental measures and regulate them by law and punishment, and they will avoid wrongdoing but will have no sense of honour and shame. Lead them with virtue and regulate them by the rules of propriety, and they will have a sense of shame and, moreover, set themselves right.' (Bk 2.3)

In other words, it is possible to obtain obedience through punishment. But it is far better to set a social tone by the power of virtuous example that leads the people themselves to conform to *li*, the rules of propriety.

K'ung-tzu is often portrayed as narrowly conservative. However, in his context he was revolutionary. Through the way in which he conceptualised *li*, he brought great implicit order to the complex set of relatively loosely formulated formal and informal traditions of his time. Further, while he accepted the hierarchical stratification of society, he broke fundamentally with tradition by introducing the idea of formal training for government. Moreover, for K'ung-tzu, everybody was to be given an opportunity to develop the skills appropriate to government. K'ung-tzu was therefore the first person in the cultural history of the world to advocate equality of opportunity and education for all, irrespective of social rank. As we shall see, his system had such power that it eventually became the basis of social organisation in the Far East for many centuries.

THE TEACHING OF LAO-TZU

Lao-tzu is a legendary figure in Chinese history. The Chinese themselves have long argued about who he was, and the tendency of Western scholars is to believe that he never existed. However, even if Lao-tzu never existed, the book with which he is credited does. It is the *Tao-te-ching* (Book of the Power or Virtue, of the Way) and it has had a lasting influence on Chinese philosophical and religious thought.

The *Tao-te-ching* can be dated to about the fifth century BCE. It is, in other words, contemporaneous with K'ung-Tzu. It is one of the shortest religious classics ever written, containing no more than 81 verses. The verses are of no particular length or order and the style varies between the profoundly poetic on one hand, and the flippant or jocular on the other. The best place to begin is with the opening lines:

> The Tao that can be told of is not the eternal Tao;
> The name that can be named is not the eternal name.
> The nameless is the origin of Heaven and Earth;
> The named is the mother of things. (Verse 1)

The *Tao-te-ching* opens by giving a standard warning found in most of the world's great religions, namely that the root of the world cannot be named – it is beyond description. The choice of the word *tao* to refer to it is a pragmatic one based on necessity. 'Tao' is best translated as 'way' (or in this case 'cosmic process'), suggesting that the root of the world is not a being, but a process. The last line of the quotation suggests that our understanding of this process as being a world full of differentiated things instead of the single, harmonious process that it is, is due to the act of naming.

The nameless – that is, the indescribable Tao – is the origin of Heaven and Earth; it is the creative source of the world. As such it is the power driving the creative process. The way in which creation flows through its activity is set out in verse 42:

> Tao produces the One.
> The One produced the two.
> The two produced the three.
> And the three produced the ten thousand things.
> The ten thousand things carry the *yin* and
> embrace the *yang*, and through the blending
> of material force they achieve harmony.

This must rate as one of the briefest accounts of the creative process to be found anywhere in the history of the world's religions. The words 'ten thousand things' are a standard formula used by the Chinese to denote everything. As far as they were concerned, ten thousand things was enough. In this passage we see that the ten thousand things are rooted in the interaction of *yang* and *yin*, the positive and negative or active and passive forces. The result of this interaction is 'harmony', that is, the process as a whole is harmonious; and harmony results from the 'blending of material force'. The word for 'material force' is *chi* or 'life essence'. If we return now to the opening lines, 'the two' are best thought of as the *yin* and the *yang*. All things come from their interaction. Biological processes of reproduction are the most obvious examples of this process and provide a useful analogy for how the whole process is supposed to work. When two people marry they form a new unit, a 'third'. That unit is what makes children. In the same way, all the myriad interactions of the *yin* and the *yang* form units (or 'thirds') which produce everything. If the two are the *yin* and the *yang*, what is the One? We get an idea about this from verse 40:

> All things in the world come from being.
> And being comes from non-being.

The One is being. It is the manifest, observable stuff of creation. It consists of two basic elements, the *yin* and the *yang*, which in turn make everything. But underlying it is non-being. This leads us to one of the great differences between Taoist thought and what we find in other religions of the world. In Taoism, that which is prior and upon which everything is based is not, as we usually find, some form of 'absolute being'. Rather, that which is prior is best described as 'non-being'. The best way to think of the Taoist view here is to imagine the world as a vast empty space. It is because the Tao's character is vast and empty (rather than cluttered up and full of stuff) that it can be described as soundless and formless non-being. The world process (Tao) is like a vast, spacious bowl in which things arise and interact, almost spontaneously. As spaciousness, the Tao is undifferentiated, but the two together – that is, the space on one hand, and the collection of the ten thousand things interacting on the other – are the one world process.

In spite of the early warning against trying to describe the Tao, there are many verses in the *Tao-te-ching* in which it is described. One of the most important is verse 34:

> The Great Tao flows everywhere.
> It may go left or right.

> All things depend on it for life, and it does not turn away from them
> . . .
> It clothes and feeds all things but does not claim to be master over them.

Two features of the Tao stand out in this passage – its aimlessness and its benevolence. The lines may be interpreted literally to mean simply that because Tao is everything, everywhere the Tao goes is by definition everywhere there is to go. However, in another translation, that of Fung Yu-lan, Tao is described as 'drifting about'. Tao, in other words, proceeds without plan or pattern. It has no specific purpose in mind (as for example is thought to be the case with the supreme being of Judaism, Christianity, and Islam). Nor is it attempting to maintain a rigidly set order or pattern of creation (as in Hinduism). Rather, it is a dynamic unplanned process which may go 'this way or that'.

If the Tao is aimless, how does the world maintain its coherence? And what possible meaning can there be for human life? We can begin to answer these questions by returning to verse 42:

> Reversion is the action of the Tao.
> Weakness is the function of the Tao.

Tao acts by reversion. The background to this crucial idea is the concept of the interaction of the *yin* and *yang*. The word 'reversion' is here used to describe the oscillation between the two poles of the *yin* and the *yang*. In this view, the Tao acts by oscillating between certain limits – it is not unlike the Western idea that many social processes involve something like the swing of a pendulum. So we see that, in the view of the *Tao-te-ching*, all processes involve a rhythmic, pendular swaying between the two extremes. This is why we find so many of the following kinds of line in the *Tao-te-ching*:

> Calamity is that upon which happiness depends;
> Happiness is that in which calamity is latent.
> Who knows when the limit will be reached? (Verse 58)

In a straightforward way, these lines can be interpreted as implying that if we did not have the one side of the pole, we would be incapable of knowing the other. Our sense of the difference between 'calamity' and 'happiness' depends on the existence of the two poles. However, the Taoist view is deeper than this, for what is being argued is that the occurrence of one is dependent on the occurrence of the other. The process of life oscillates inevitably between the two extremes. Happiness can only be had once there has been calamity. Similarly, calamity inevitably follows happiness. In the words of the *Tao-te-ching*, 'calamity is latent' in happiness. Finally, in this connection, notice that while we can be sure that life and the world will follow this process of oscillation, we cannot know 'when the limit will be reached'; in other words, we are unable to tell where the turning-point is.

We have seen that the Tao is everything. Mostly it is empty, but the ten thousand things arise as part of its effortless creative action. It is dynamic, yet runs according to no pattern that can be described. It is not 'going anywhere', yet it is not chaotic. It is spontaneous, aimless, and yet harmonious. How are human beings supposed to live in a world seen in this way? Here is what the *Tao-te-ching* has to say:

> When man is born, he is tender and weak.
> At death, he is stiff and hard.
> All things, the grass as well as the trees, are tender and supple when alive.
> When dead, they are withered and dried.
> Therefore, the stiff and the hard are companions of death.
> The tender and weak are companions of life. (Verse 76)

The implication of these verses is clear: in a world which is dynamic and subject to constant flux, the best way to live is to be flexible. The Tao moves without plan or pattern – it does not know where it is going to next. In order to be in harmony with it therefore, a person must be prepared to bend. In a world characterised by the implacable tidal motions of the Tao, any attempt to fix reality and stem the tide is ultimately doomed. Not only are the tender and weak 'companions of life', they are better fitted to survive.

In another famous metaphor, the *Tao-te-ching* compares the superior person with water. 'The best man is like water . . . it benefits all things and does not compete with them' (Verse 8). Yet water has enormous power: there is nothing softer and weaker than water, yet there is nothing better for attacking hard things (Verse 78). From this we get the following dictum:

> To yield is to be preserved whole.
> To be bent is to become straight. (Verse 22)

Three ideas summarise the Taoist approach to life: *wu-wei*, *wu-hsin*, and *tzu-jan*. Loosely translated these mean: no action, no mind, and spontaneity. Specifically they indicate that the best way to live life is to do nothing which invites a counter-action, to empty the mind, and to be spontaneous or natural. We get out of step with the Tao, according to the *Tao-te-ching*, when we attempt to change the course of things. We know that this is happening when what we do meets resistance or when our mind fights against the way things are. The best course is to allow life to take its course. If this seems an overly negative approach to life it must be remembered that the basic view of reality is one of harmony and benevolence. Life, in the Taoist view, can be its own reward when lived in accordance with the way things naturally are. To be spontaneous and yielding is to be the way the Tao itself is. It is to allow yourself to be driven by the power which drives the Tao itself.

We come now to government. The *Tao-te-ching* was written at a time of political turmoil in China. It reflects a disillusionment with the state of government at the time, describing the courts as extravagant and their activity as 'robbery'. Here is how the *Tao-te-ching* describes the forms of government:

> The best [rulers] are those whose existence is [merely] known by the people.

> The next best are those who are loved and praised.
> The next are those who are feared.
> And the next are those who are despised . . .
> [The great rulers] accomplish their task; they complete their work.
> Nevertheless their people say that they simply follow Nature [*tzu-jan*].
> (Verse 17)

The best kind of government is one whose governing touch is so light that people are hardly aware of being governed. It is one which leaves people feeling as though they are free and ungoverned. It encourages people to behave naturally and spontaneously since, in the Taoist view, this is the best way to be. It is because light government is the best government that a government which is loved and praised only comes second. For a people to love a government they must be aware of its activity as a government. This is not as good as a government whose touch is so light that it is not felt. Third comes a government which is feared. This is better than a government which is despised. In other words, it is better to have order, even if the order is based on fear, than to have the kind of disorder that arises when government has no authority.

Underlying the Taoist view on government is an almost mystical belief in the inherent virtue of nature and therefore of the natural (unregulated) person. It is further underpinned by a thread which the Taoist philosophers shared with K'ung-tzu, namely a faith in the power of government by virtuous example:

> Therefore the sage says:
> 'I take no action and the people themselves are transformed.
> I love tranquillity and the people of themselves become correct.
> I engage in no activity and the people of themselves become prosperous.
> I have no desires and the people of themselves become simple.' (Verse 57)

However, where the Taoist philosophers differed from K'ung-tzu was in their understanding of virtue. For Confucius, virtue was something which resulted from the diligent application of *li* or ritual form to the raw material of nature. For the Taoist, nature untampered with was virtue itself.

RELIGION IN CHINA: FROM THE HAN TO THE NINETEENTH CENTURY

The emergence of the Han dynasty saw the first peaceful systematisation of Chinese culture in the history of the region. A uniform system of weights and measures was instituted and the writing standardised. The first university was established and a system of education for government based on the Confucian classics was introduced. Out of this developed a new class of government bureaucrats, educated along Confucian lines. The Han dynasty therefore saw the triumph of Confucian ideas as the source for ordering social relations.

Apart from the regularisation of social relations that resulted from Han rule, Confucianism had other important effects. A key element of Confucian thought had always been the performance of ritual for the sake of ritual form. In other words, ritual was highly valued by the Confucians as a way to teach people to develop a sense of order and proportion. This ideal was realised in Han times through the promotion of state rituals emphasising the place of the emperor as the mediator between heaven and earth. Rituals were also introduced to honour K'ung-tzu during this period. State officials presided at these rituals, not, as is usually the case, a specialist priestly class. In fact, in the early period of the Han dynasty there was no priestly class. The emperor occupied the centre of social order and ruled by the 'mandate of heaven'. Chinese history was re-interpreted as a succession of governments whose success or failure depended on the extent to which their rule was virtuous. Government in accordance with the mandate would be reflected in prosperity and social order. Disorder and collapse were understood to arise when the ruler no longer satisfied the mandate.

Under the Confucianism of Han rule, Taoism continued to develop and flourish. In particular, Taoist alchemy and the solitary practices of Taoist hermits seeking immortality, became popular. It is to this era that we owe the popularity of the Chinese belief in the immortals. The immortals were understood to be a group of beings who had achieved immortality through the practice of alchemy and meditation. They were, in other words, the proof of the possibility of immortality taught by the Taoists.

The period of Han rule was one of great stability for the Chinese. Foreign trade flourished as far afield as the Roman empire. Eventually, however, the weight of pressure from nomadic peoples on the borders of China began to exact a toll on the Han. This, coupled with the internal divisions which had begun to develop, eventually led to the collapse of the dynasty in 220 CE. With the passing of the Han rulers, China entered a four-hundred-year period of civil war similar to that which had characterised the last centuries of the Chou dynasty. But the imprint of the Han was to prove lasting. The importance of the Han dynasty can be gauged by the fact that, even today, the Chinese refer to themselves as the 'people of the Han'.

The relative chaos that followed the collapse of the Han created opportunities for alternatives to Confucianism. In the absence of the strong, centralised religious and ideological control which was in place during the Han dynasty, Taoism gradually transformed itself into a full-blown religious sect. It was the first religious movement organised on a sectarian basis that China had known. It cut across social classes and ran independently of government institutions. At the centre of the sect was a concern with health and immortality. A professional priestly class whose main functions were to dispense medicine and to perform rituals, developed. In addition to medicine, they believed in mobilising unseen spiritual powers for healing. The two functions were not seen to be separate. For example, medicine had to be made in a way that tapped into the unseen powers, otherwise it would not be effective. Alongside the social functioning of the sect, a vigorous meditative tradition continued to develop, aiming at the achievement of long life and immortality.

In 581 CE China was reunited again under the Sui. In 618 CE the Sui were followed by the T'ang. The T'ang dynasty lasted for close to 300 years. The

T'ang improved on the system of civil administration introduced by the Han. In the early period the dynasty was characterised by considerable tolerance of cultural and religious diversity. Buddhism, which had entered China during the closing phases of the Han dynasty, dominated the intellectual life of the early T'ang. The classics of both the Taoists and the Buddhists were added to the official state curriculum for scholars studying for government service. Extensive trade relations developed with the West and both Christianity and Islam entered China.

The most important religious development in the period of the T'ang was the emergence of Ch'an (in Japan, 'Zen') Buddhism. The impact of Ch'an Buddhist ideas on the artistic and cultural life of China was considerable and lasting. Ch'an Buddhist ideas were closely interwoven with Taoist ideas, particularly the understanding of the cosmos as 'empty' and subject to ceaseless change. This helped to give Buddhism a character with which the Chinese could identify, and which, in turn, made it easier for them to accept a further element of the Buddhist tradition, namely its monasticism. Under Chinese influence, Buddhism developed a unique new character which continues to be embodied today in the teachings of Zen Buddhism.

Towards the end of the T'ang dynasty, a reaction against foreign influences set in and Buddhists in particular were subjected to considerable persecution. Confucianism began to reassert itself and once again became the only subject for state scholarship. This situation was to last until the period of Mongolian rule from 1260–1368 CE. Mongolian rule was replaced by the Ming dynasty, which again instituted the Confucian system of state examinations and reinstated Confucianism as the state religion. This situation was to last until the modern era. By this time Confucianism had itself taken on many elements of the other religious systems, namely Taoism and Ch'an Buddhism. Buddhism especially had an influence on what scholars have come to call 'neo-Confucianism'. Throughout this period, popular religious practice at the levels of the village and the family continued in a form not much different from that of the earliest times. Taoist and Buddhist spiritual entities were added, but the form itself remained more or less constant.

CONCLUDING REMARKS: THE MODERN PERIOD

For centuries there had been interaction between the nations of Europe and the Chinese. However, from the nineteenth century onward the influence of the demands made by Western traders began to exercise a truly disruptive influence on the fabric of Chinese society. The Confucian-dominated administration of China fought and lost battles against the British, French, Russians, Germans and Japanese. Gradually they lost their grip on the nation. One of the most important challenges to the regime was the religiously inspired T'ai-p'ing rebellion of 1850 to 1864. The T'ai-p'ing was a synthesis of elements of Christian and Chinese belief. Motivated by peasant discontent with the central administration, its followers sought to overthrow the Chinese government and establish, in its place, a utopian egalitarian society. The war resulted in 20 million people dying.

In many ways, the egalitarian and peasant-based thrust of the T'ai-p'ing rebellion reached its ultimate conclusion when the Communist Party took power from the nationalist forces of Chiang Kai-shek in 1949. Instead of 'gods' or abstract concepts of the Tao, Mao placed the equally abstract concept of 'the people' and especially the peasants. The concept of the 'Son of Heaven', used of the rulers of the past, was replaced with the concept of the 'Son of the People'. In other words, while 'the way' was to be found in the inherent wisdom of the people, it was the ruler who interpreted that will for the people. In many ways, the communist rebellion was a massive reaction against the highly stratified and centuries-old society which the Confucians had instituted. The communists were severely anti-elitist. Communist rule in China has been punctuated by periods of considerable social upheaval usually initiated by the leadership and aimed at any signs of an emergent elitism. In the Cultural Revolution, intellectuals and artists in particular came under severe and prolonged attack.

Where will China end? How is the religious history of China likely to continue? It is difficult for any Westerner not to notice the influence that Confucian ideas still have on the pattern of social life in the Far East. Yet of the fact that Chinese religious history has entered a decisive new phase in the modern era there can be no doubt. We can know as little about where it is going as we know about where our own traditions are going.

SELECT BIBLIOGRAPHY

Chan, W. T. *A Sourcebook in Chinese Philosophy*. Princeton: Princeton University Press, 1963

Creel, H. C. *Chinese Thought from Confucius to Mao tse-tung*. New York: New American Library, 1953

Fung, Y. L. *The History of Chinese Philosophy*, vol. 1. (trans. D. Bodde). Princeton: Princeton University Press, 1952

Graham, A. C. *Chuang tzu: The Inner Chapters*. London: Unwin, 1986

Lau, D. C. (trans). *Confucius: The Analects*. London: Penguin Classics, 1979

Reps, P. A. *Zen Flesh, Zen Bones*. Harmondsworth: Penguin, 1978

Ronan, C. *The Cambridge Illustrated History of the World's Science*. Cambridge: Cambridge University Press, 1984

Schwartz, B. I. *The World of Thought in Ancient China*. Cambridge, Mass.: Harvard University Press, 1985

Sullivan, M. *The Arts of China*. Berkeley: University of California Press, 1984

Watts, A. *The Way of Zen*. Harmondsworth: Penguin, 1982

7

Judaism

JOCELYN HELLIG

Judaism is one of the major religions of the world, yet it does not conform in every respect to what we normally associate with religion. To be Jewish is not a matter of having a central belief or individual commitment of faith. It is intimately associated with a particular way of life which is lived and expressed within a community context. Primarily, to be Jewish is to be aware of God as having chosen a particular people to play a role in the history of the world. It involves a sense of belonging to that group of people, which, on one hand, is a natural community, the 'seed of Abraham', and which, on the other hand, shares the collective memory of a common historic experience. Ethnicity and religious calling are intricately interconnected.

The most important event in the history of the people Israel is the exodus from Egypt (*c.* 1250 BCE). Not only is this the pivotal point of all Jewish history, but it is also the core revelatory event of Judaism as a holy way of life. The exodus from Egypt must always be viewed as a complex of events in which Jewish people believe that God called a particular people, a small, insignificant and undeserving slave-people, out of a state of bondage and led them to a land which he had promised to give their forefathers, Abraham, Isaac and Jacob. God sealed the wondrous act that he had performed on their behalf by entering into a covenant with them. Since God had heard their cry and responded to their suffering, they were under obligation to him to observe the rules of the covenant. Israel was thus given a special mission in the world. A people had been formed, born of God's mercy. They were never permitted to forget the circumstances of their birth as a people and were commanded: 'You shall be holy; for I the Lord your God am holy' (Lev. 19: 2). Holiness implied a dual obligation for the Jews: they were required to maintain awareness of the God-given quality of everything in the universe and to express their gratitude to God by extending to all of humankind the same quality of love and mercy which had been bestowed upon them. 'The stranger who sojourns with you shall be to you as the native among you, and you shall love him as yourself; for you were strangers in the land of Egypt' (Lev. 19: 34).

Jewish people believe that by God's choosing of the people Israel, they became a separate people, a people destined 'to dwell alone' and 'not be reckoned among the nations' (Num. 23: 6), a people called to be 'a kingdom of priests and a holy nation' (Exod. 19: 6). To be chosen to live by a covenant is not a matter of mere privilege, but a state of responsibility, the neglect of which would mean judgement by the harshest of standards: 'You only have I known of all the families of the earth; therefore I will punish you for all your iniquities' (Amos 3: 2).

Central to Judaism are thus the concepts of peoplehood and of holiness. What God demands of this small people and what happens to them is of significance in the destiny of the entire world. While their chosenness has a distinctly particularistic element to it, it also has a universalistic thrust. The God of the Jews is also the God of the entire universe. This is evidenced by the fact that in the same line in which God calls the Jews to be his own possession among all peoples, he also states: 'For all the earth is mine' (Exod. 19: 5). His choosing of the people Israel is a mystery and Jews claim no special privilege, except the gift of the Torah. So central is the doctrine of chosenness to Judaism that Arthur Hertzberg was prompted to state: 'The essence of Judaism is the affirmation that the Jews are the chosen people; all else is commentary.'

Judaism's entire understanding of the world is based on its convictions about God. Awareness of the power and mercy of God lies at the base of all Jewish belief and practice. His oneness and uniqueness are expressed in the central conviction, the *Shema*: 'Hear O Israel, the Lord our God, the Lord is One' (Deut. 6: 4). As one of the oldest religions in the world, Judaism's chief contribution to the world has been monotheism. However, while the belief that there is only one God has been of great significance not only to Judaism, but to the entire Western world, it is not so much the numerical significance but the *nature* of God which is of ultimate importance.

God is seen as one, the only deity worthy of worship. He is good and created a world which he himself judged to be good (Gen. 1: 31). Theism implies a God who is concerned with his creation and one with whom humankind can enter into a relationship. As a result of this concern, God reveals his will, either through prophets or through historic events. God is the ruler and controller of history, making his will known in and through history. Judaism's conception of history is linear. Beginning with creation, God intervenes in the world through revelation and will consummate history at the end of days.

THE HISTORY OF JUDAISM

Ancient Judaism

The biblical period

Judaism is rooted in history. It is, therefore, not possible to separate its major tenets from its history. Jewish consciousness goes back to the exodus and beyond, to Creation itself. According to the Bible, God created the world in six days and on the seventh day he rested from his labour, hallowing the seventh day. Because Judaism sees the created world as good, the material world is neither insignificant nor something to be shunned. This informs one of the major emphases in Judaism, the hallowing of the everyday act. Judaism, rather than seeking salvation, promotes a way of life in which each and every action is elevated above the mere physical level and is imbued with holiness.

The earliest historical period of Judaism is the period of the patriarchs, who wandered in the ancient Near East during the early centuries of the second millennium BCE. Their movements are recorded in Genesis, whose broad historicity has been authenticated by archaeology. Substantial migrations were taking place in the ancient Near East at that time and some of these migrations are represented in the stories about the individual patriarchs and their families. Genesis, in describing their movements, reveals a migration to Egypt under Abraham and a later settlement there under Joseph. While the presence of the Hebrews was originally welcomed in the land of Egypt, a king arose who 'knew not Joseph' (Exod. 1: 8), and oppression of the people began.

According to Genesis, God had called upon the patriarch Abraham to leave his country and everything which was familiar to him, in order to go to a land which God would show him (Gen. 12). Abraham was promised that God would make of him 'a great nation', that he would be blessed and his name made great. Abraham acted upon faith, since the promises were only fulfilled later, in the exodus, the event from which the history of the Jews as a people begins. It is thus only in the light of the exodus that previous promises to the patriarchs are fulfilled, according to Jewish belief, and that the patriarchal accounts make sense. Equally, it is from the exodus that all subsequent prophecy is held to take its orientation.

The covenant demands active loyalty. Through it, Judaism became a religion not of faith, but of the realising deed. The kernel of the covenant obligations is encapsulated in the Decalogue or Ten Commandments in which God made his relationship with his people clear: 'I am the Lord your God, who brought you out of the land of Egypt, out of the house of bondage' (Exod. 20: 2). Having made explicit his act in history on their behalf, God then spelt out the terms by which they were to show their indebtedness to him. The Commandments deal with both their relationship to God and their obligations towards their fellow human beings. Judaism's body of laws determines the way the Jew is to walk his or her way through life, and is known as *halakhah*. Observance is based on freedom of the human will and on choice. 'I call heaven and earth to witness against you this day, that I have set before you life and death, blessing and curse; therefore choose life' (Deut. 30: 19).

Closely associated with the exodus is the concept of reward and punishment. If the people were faithful to their covenant obligations, they would live safely in the land which God had given them. Disobedience would result in exile from that land. Righteousness, as it is perceived in Judaism, demands a perfect balance between the relationship of humanity to God (the vertical relationship) and the relationship between one human being and another (the horizontal relationship), the latter also including the relationship of humanity to the world of nature. An over-emphasis on either one of these, at the expense of the other, would disturb the balance and result in idolatry. God does not want homage and prayer from humanity unless that devotion is accompanied by social justice. Thus it was that the prophet Amos, as God's spokesman, could state:

> I hate, I despise your feasts,
> and I take no delight in your solemn assemblies.
> Even though you offer me your burnt offerings,
> I will not accept them . . .
> Take away from me the noise of your songs;
> to the melody of your harps I will not listen.
> But let justice roll down like water,
> and righteousness like an ever-flowing stream. (Amos 5: 21–4)

Amos is not against the practice of the cult itself, but he rails against a cult which is not accompanied by social justice. Conversely, a relationship with humanity and the world, which takes no cognisance of the God-given nature of the world and its creatures, can result in the deification of science and technology, thus cancelling out humanity's ability both to perceive God in the world and to treat the world with concern and respect.

Moses is regarded as the first and greatest of the prophets in Judaism, since it was he who first spoke the message of God to the entire people and it was he who brought them the Torah, the basis of all Jewish belief and action. Shortly thereafter, they entered the promised land, conquering it and then settling in it. With the Jews' transformation from a nomadic to an agricultural existence, they encountered the mystery of fertility and were tempted to turn to the Canaanite fertility gods. The role of the prophets who succeeded Moses was to focus the people's attention on the covenant and, if they had strayed from it as they so often did, to call for their return, their *teshuvah*, or repentance.

Historically, the punishment of the Jewish people took the form of exile from their land. During the centuries when they had possession of their land, they established a monarchy, and, under King David, established Jerusalem as their capital city. The Davidic line was to assume importance in relation to the messianic expectation which developed later in Judaism. The messiah was to be a scion of the house of David. The Temple was built in Jerusalem by Solomon, and because the Temple was the place of God's presence among his people, Jerusalem became the holiest city for Judaism. After the death of King Solomon, the united empire, which had been established by David, became divided under two monarchies, the northern kingdom of Israel and the southern kingdom of Judah. The northern kingdom was destroyed by the Assyrians in 722 BCE. Most of its population was deported, and other people were settled in the land. The scattered population of Israel became known as the 'lost ten tribes of Israel'.

The first major exile from Judah occurred in 586 BCE, when the Jewish leadership was exiled to Babylon under Nebuchadnezzar, and a poor, leaderless remnant was left behind. Although the exiles' life in Babylon was tolerable, it was only with exile from their land that they came to a full realisation of the extent of their loss: 'By the waters of Babylon, there we sat down and wept, when we remembered Zion' (Ps. 137: 1). In the face of defeat and exile, many questioned God's sovereignty. It was at this time that the prophet Deutero-Isaiah (author of chapters 40 onwards in the Book of Isaiah) spoke his message. Opening his prophecy with the words, '"Comfort, comfort, my people," says your God' (Is. 40: 1), he assured them that God had not forgotten them. Israel was still his people and he was still their God. The exile had been foretold by the prophets and the event had vindicated their dire warnings. Far from putting God's faithfulness into question, the exile should have affirmed his justice. However, God's punishment is never the last word. Judgement is followed by restoration. Thus, Deutero-Isaiah reinterpreted their suffering, giving it its ultimate meaning in the figure of the suffering servant. The suffering servant was none other than the small people Israel who were suffering vicariously on behalf of all of humankind and who would ultimately lead the whole world to the knowledge of the Lord.

Purified through their suffering, they were to be taken back to their land. There was to be a new exodus in which all obstacles would be removed (Isa. 40: 4). Indeed, such a return took place when King Cyrus of Persia conquered Babylon. Cyrus, designated as God's 'anointed' (Isa. 45: 1), was seen as an instrument of divine redemption. In the first year of his reign, 538 BCE, he issued an edict which permitted the Jews to return to their land. Their Temple was to be rebuilt at the expense of the royal treasury. Although this benevolence was a remarkable, new development, and the project seemed optimistic, very few Jews undertook the long and hazardous journey back to Judah. Thus, from the time of the exile to Babylon, a diaspora (dispersion) of the Jewish people has existed, and from that time until today, a substantial sector of the Jewish community has continued to live in the diaspora.

During the period of the exile, when the Jews were separated from their promised land, old patterns of faith were re-emphasised in order to enable the people to retain their identity and keep their religion alive. Increased emphasis was placed on sabbath observance, circumcision and observance of the dietary laws. Although none of these was new, their growing prominence encouraged the separation of the Jewish people from their neighbours so that they would be less subject to the temptation to assimilate into the surrounding culture and religion. One of the important institutions which probably arose during the exile is the synagogue. While its origin cannot be accurately dated, the circumstances for its development were right. Because Jews were now separated from their cultic centre in Jerusalem, prayer took the place of sacrifice. While sacrifice could only be offered in the Temple, prayer could be offered anywhere.

Another important development during the exilic period was the institution of a new form of teaching of the Torah. This can be dated back to Ezra, who during the period of the restoration, read the Torah publicly in Jerusalem, and gave an accompanying oral interpretation of it. This was a form of exegesis or commentary on the Torah which made the written text both more explicit and more adaptive to the particular time and circumstance of the people. It was to grow into the oral Torah, or Talmud, which is the primary medium through which Jews understand the contents of the Bible and through which they interpret the laws that govern every aspect of their lives.

As Judaism developed these new thrusts, a new era of Judaism was inaugurated. It is at this point that Christian scholars perceive a caesura or transition in Judaism. They designate the religious expression of the pre-exilic period as 'Israelite religion', and label that of the post-exilic religious expression as 'Judaism'. While the division is a convenient and tempting one, it is, from the Jewish perspective, entirely inaccurate. For Jews there is no separation at all. They see the various periods of their history as part of the same continuum, their religious self-consciousness going back to the exodus and beyond.

The Hellenistic period

The Hellenistic period began with the sweeping conquests of Alexander the Great in 331 BCE. The resulting encounters of the people Israel with other civilisations, both in and outside of their land, played an important part in the development of Judaism. Its response to successive conquering powers – such as the Persians, the Greeks and the Romans – demonstrates the capacity of Judaism to maintain its own identity and to enrich itself and the surrounding civilisations, without becoming lost in them. The Hellenistic period marked the amalgamation of Greek and Jewish culture. Representative of this development was the philosopher Philo of Alexandria (*c.* 25 BCE–40 CE), who proved to be more influential in Christian than Jewish thought.

One response to Hellenism was the formation of sects in Judaism, the Pharisees, the Sadducees and the Essenes, all of whom were active at the time of the inception of Christianity. Of these, it was to be the Pharisees who would mould Judaism and determine its course. The primary characteristic of the Pharisees was their acceptance of the validity of the oral Torah. They were modern and adaptive in their methods of interpretation and, thereby, sought to make the Torah the inheritance of the entire people of Israel. Because they were commoners, their teachings had a great deal of appeal to the Jewish masses. They were the only sect to retain influence after the catastrophic exile of 70 CE, their teaching growing into what came to be known as 'Rabbinic Judaism'.

The patterns of religious practice established during the exile and elaborated by the Pharisees enabled Judaism to survive the far longer exile which was to begin in 70 CE. This tragic event transformed the Jews from a people who had their own land and could make their own political decisions into a landless, powerless people. For almost two thousand years, they were destined to wander over the face of the earth as the often unwanted guests of host nations. Lacking power over their own destiny, they were at the mercy of these nations. Unable to make decisions of any real political moment, their primary mode of encounter with the world became that of compliance. Judaism was forced to adapt to a situation of powerlessness.

One of the primary functions of Rabbinic Judaism was to reconstruct the ravaged community and to endow Jewish life with meaning. The disaster which had befallen the Jewish people was interpreted, in the traditional biblical way, as God's just punishment of a disobedient and erring people. Subsequent catastrophe also tended to be interpreted as divine punishment. This was to become a dismal constant throughout the many years of diasporan powerlessness.

By the time of the destruction of Jerusalem, Christianity had arisen. Initially, it was a Jewish messianic sect, but with its spread to the gentile world it was progressively 'de-Judaised'. The Christians adopted the Hebrew Bible as the 'Old Testament'. However, a serious point of cleavage between the two communities resulted from the different way in which they interpreted the promises in the Hebrew Bible. From a Christian perspective, the Jews had interpreted their scriptures incorrectly. For example, nascent Christianity, while also viewing the disaster of 70 CE as a manifestation of divine punishment, had a very different view about the nature of the crime. For Jews the crime could never have been anything other than infidelity to the covenant. In Christian eyes, on the other hand, the fall of Jerusalem appeared to confirm the truth of the new religion. Not only were the Jews seen as having been unfaithful to the covenant, but they were perceived as having been punished for their rejection of Jesus as the Messiah and, even more seriously, for the crime of deicide. The basis of conflict between the two religious communities had been laid.

The Talmudic period

Scholarly activity continued in Palestine where the Mishnah (teaching) was developed. From the time of the exile to Babylon, there had been a significant number of Jews there. Babylon was soon to take over as the main centre of Jewish scholarship. Using the Mishnah as their basis, two groups of Jewish scholars, one in Palestine and one in Babylon, each produced a Gemara (completion). Together, the Mishnah and Gemara make up the Talmud. Most of the main features of Judaism were articulated in the Talmud. Torah observance, as interpreted by the Talmud, became the centre of Jewish life. The oral Torah, as later written down in the Talmud, thus became the prism through which the written Torah (Hebrew Bible) was read and understood.

Medieval Judaism

Christianity became the official religion of the Roman empire in the early fourth century CE, and with the consolidation of Christian influence in the fifth century, there was a great deal of restriction and persecution of the Jewish people by the Christian church. The advent of Islam in the seventh century brought new forces to bear on the Jewish people. The early Middle Ages marked the Geonic period of Judaism (based in Babylonia) in which the Talmud was clarified and elaborated by means of codification and through the *Responsa* literature.

In the eleventh century, the centre of gravity of Jewish activity moved westwards, to North Africa, Spain, and to a lesser extent, to north-western Europe. There had been a remarkable flowering of Islamic culture in the first few centuries after its inception. One of the most important features of Islamic civilisation was its capacity to adopt and adapt the cultural achievements of the civilisations which it conquered. This applied particularly to the fruits of classical civilisation and is especially apparent with regard to Greek philosophy. Jewish scholars achieved great intellectual heights under Islamic rule and Muslim Spain subsequently took over as the centre of the Jewish intellectual world. There was a mutual development of intellectual activity and Jews played an important part in the transmission of classical civilisation to the world. While it was in Muslim Spain that the Jewish Golden Age gained its impetus, it was in the time of Christian reconquest that the Jewish Golden Age in Spain achieved its full flowering, the greatest Jewish scholar to emerge being Moses Maimonides (1135–1204). He represented the peak of Jewish philosophical activity. Other great philosophers of this age were Solomon ibn Gabirol and Jehuda Halevi.

The expulsion of the Jews from Spain in 1492, as the immediate outcome of the reconquest of Spain by Christianity, resulted in a scattering of the centres of Jewish activity. Uprooted Jews settled predominantly in the Ottoman empire, in Constantinople and Salonica. Others moved to different parts of the Mediterranean basin and, later, to Hamburg, Amsterdam and London. Expulsion of the Jews from France and central Europe forced them to migrate further east. Eastern Europe was thus to be home to most of the subsequent major developments in Judaism. The Spanish Jews had become known as Sephardim, while the Jews in Eastern Europe were known as Ashkenazim.

In the wake of the expulsion and the intense degree of Jewish suffering which ensued, mysticism received a new impetus. The Cabbalah or Jewish mystical tradition, though old, was augmented and reinterpreted and gained wide currency. The most influential interpreter of Jewish mysticism was the sixteenth-century scholar Isaac Luria (1534–72), who established a school of mysticism in Safed, Palestine. His doctrines were later to assume an important place in the movement known as Hasidism. It is in the context of Jewish mysticism's emphasis on the messianic expectation that we should understand the advent of messianic pretenders, the most noteworthy being Shabbetai Zvi (1626–76).

Fine schools of talmudic scholarship were established in Russia, Poland and Lithuania. However, in response to some of the casuistry which had developed in rabbinic law, and in the wake of the antinomianism of the Shabbatean movement of the late seventeenth century, the Hasidic movement was founded in Poland in the eighteenth century by Israel Baal Shem Tov (1700–60). He placed great stress on the spirit of the Torah rather than on the letter of the law. In addition to his prescription of joyous prayer accompanied by song and dance, this had tremendous appeal for unschooled people. The new movement's permissiveness with regard to observance and study of Torah, its emotionalism, and its emphasis on a charismatic leader (*tzaddik*), created a perception that Hasidism was a complete departure from normative Judaism. The Hasidim were excommunicated as heretics by the mainstream of the Jewish establishment. It was only later, some years after the work of Shneour Zalman of Lyady, who combined intellectual pursuit and Torah observance with Hasidic joyousness, that Hasidism was accepted into the matrix of orthodox Judaism as Habad Hasidism. Its main centre – originally in Lubavitch in north-west Russia

– has moved to Brooklyn, New York, where the Lubavitcher Rebbe is the charismatic leader of the sect.

Modern Judaism

The French Revolution in 1789 marked the beginning of the modern period of Jewish history. Political emancipation of most European countries was achieved in the period between this event and the Russian Revolution of 1917. This was also the period of the Enlightenment (*Haskalah*), when Jews were exposed to the conflicting currents of European culture. As a consequence of these forces, religion began gradually to lose its hold. The rise of nationalism led to a great deal of ambiguity with regard to Jewish nationhood or peoplehood. As social and religious walls of separation began to collapse, some Jews began to question the need to remain a separate, identifiable minority and wanted to merge with the surrounding society. It is in this spirit that Reform Judaism emerged. Its central feature was the rejection of the authority of the oral Torah. It challenged the binding nature of the *halakhah*, both biblical and talmudic, espousing the view that revelation is an ongoing or progressive process, and that patterns of faith and worship applicable in earlier times are not necessarily binding in the modern era. Since the oral Torah is the very foundation of rabbinic Judaism, vehement opposition was inevitable. As a reaction to the secular Enlightenment of the nineteenth century, there was a revival in orthodoxy itself and the *musar* (ethico-pietistic) movements arose in the talmudic schools in Europe. A most important development in Judaism was the neo-Orthodox movement founded in Germany by Samson Raphael Hirsch (1808–88). This drew together religious observance and secular knowledge. Orthodox practice was combined with a wholehearted entry into the civic, cultural and even national life of the host country.

The years 1881 to 1914 marked the massive movement of Jews from Europe to America, which became the major centre of Jewish life. Reform Judaism had failed to arrest complete assimilation of Jews into the surrounding culture and religion, and its success in Europe was therefore limited. In the pluralistic society of the United States, on the other hand, it proved to be remarkably successful and the locus of Reform Judaism moved from its land of origin, Germany, to America. Reform Judaism placed emphasis on the potential goodness and intellectual capacity of humankind. Encouraging Jews to merge with the host nations, it did not see the need for a Jewish homeland in Israel, and was, in its early phases of development, anti-Zionist. Despite its universalism and adaptations to modernity, there were many who did not want to go to the extremes that Reform demanded but who, on the other hand, did not want to be bound in every detail by Orthodox practice. A compromise was reached through the establishment of Conservative Judaism. This is an American movement, which accepts the *halakhah*, but does not regard it as binding in all its aspects. It thus gives weight to tradition but simultaneously accommodates to modernity. Reconstructionism, established by Mordecai Kaplan (1881–1983), is another modern American movement. It emphasises peoplehood within the matrix of Judaism as a civilisation, but denies the doctrine of chosenness or the idea that the Jewish people have a special divinely ordained mission in the world.

In the second half of the nineteenth century, the Zionist movement arose. While there were several forms of Zionism, the motivation underlying all was a return of the Jewish people to the land of Israel. There were socialist Zionists who opposed the strictly religious view and felt that a return to Israel would enable them to implement their ideas of social justice. There were cultural Zionists who, more than mere nationalist rebirth, wished to see a cultural revival of the Jewish people. Political Zionism was born of a generally less optimistic assessment of the willingness of the gentile world to absorb the Jews as equal citizens. Its founder, Theodor Herzl (1860–1904), believed that the establishment of an independent Jewish homeland in Palestine was the only way that anti-Semitism could be countered. With the Balfour Declaration of 1917, in which the British government viewed with favour the establishment of a Jewish homeland in Palestine, the dream of Zionism had been converted into the possibility of a practical reality. After a difficult struggle, Israel was declared an independent Jewish state on 14 May 1948.

Jews had entered the twentieth century, embracing its ethos of modernity. Ironically, it was in this most 'enlightened' and modern of centuries that the Holocaust, the most barbarous crime against the Jewish people, was enacted. Six million Jews, almost the entire Jewish population of Europe, were destroyed by the Nazi regime during World War Two. The Holocaust made a number of issues clear to Jews. Firstly, Jews were, at all times, subject to anti-Semitism, which, when taken to extremes, could result in their destruction. Since the Holocaust was the culmination of Jewish political powerlessness, it was essential to establish Israel as the homeland of the Jewish people. Not merely a place of refuge and a haven for Jews, it also had to be an independent Jewish state. Only a restoration of political power could return the Jewish people to history. From 70 CE to 1948 Jews were not participants in history, but merely its objects. Lastly, because the optimism of Reform Judaism had not been supported by history, from this point it became pro-Zionist.

The twentieth century has witnessed both the greatest tragedy to befall the Jewish people, the Holocaust, and the re-establishment of the state of Israel. No modern Jewish thought or theology can be undertaken in isolation from these two events as both have had a profound bearing on Jewish life both in and outside of Israel. The Jewish community has been convulsed by these two events, and it is still too soon to perceive in which direction Judaism will develop in response to them. On one side of the spectrum, there has been a development of 'secular' Judaism, particularly in Israel. There has also been a massive defection from Judaism, particularly in America, evidenced by large-scale intermarriage. On the other side of the spectrum, there is currently a world-wide return to Orthodox practice.

HOLY WRITINGS

The Tenakh or Hebrew Bible

Judaism's holy book is known as the *Tenakh*. This name is an acronym made up of the first letters of the three sections which make up the Hebrew Bible, the Torah (the Five Books of Moses or Pentateuch), the Nevi'im (Prophets) and the Ketuvim (Assorted writings). The term 'Old Testament' is not one which is favoured by Jews because it implies that their holy scriptures have been superseded, and this, for Jewish self-understanding, is not the case.

Torah

The holiest section of the Jewish scriptures is the Torah, which, in Orthodox belief, was revealed to Moses on Mount Sinai as God's immutable word. Because of its holiness, it is faithfully transmitted from generation to generation and is written by hand on a parchment scroll by a qualified scribe. It must contain no errors, omissions or additions. The Torah is God's instruction to the Jewish people, the basis of their covenant obligation. Although it contains many laws, ritual, civil and ethical, the translation 'Law' is inadequate and it is more accurately translated as 'Instruction' or 'Teaching'.

The Five Books of the Torah are written in Hebrew and are named after the first important word in the text and not according to basic theme, as they are in the English translations. Thus, Genesis, Exodus, Leviticus, Numbers and Deuteronomy are known respectively as *Bereshit, Shemot, Vayikra, Ba-midbar* and *Devarim*. While they are not history books, the entire message which they contain is imbedded in an historical context, recording God's dealings with his people Israel.

The Torah is chanted aloud in Hebrew, directly from the parchment scroll. This occurs in the synagogue during the morning service every sabbath and on Mondays and Thursdays. Since there are no vowel indications or chanting instructions in the Torah scroll, the reader must be well versed for the task. A different but specified portion (*sidrah* or *parashah*) is allotted to each week, the content of the portion becoming the guiding motto for the whole week. The name of the *parasha* is also taken from the first significant word in the Hebrew text. The entire Torah is read, portion by portion, during the course of a year. Upon its completion, it is re-started with great rejoicing at the festival of Simchat Torah, which takes place in late September or October each year.

Nevi'im (Prophets)

The second section of the Hebrew Bible, Nevi'im, contains the prophetic writings. As the Hebrew term *Tenakh* makes explicit, in the Hebrew Bible the classical prophets are placed in a central position, unlike the Christian translations in which the classical prophets are placed at the end of the 'Old Testament'. The former prophets are Joshua, Judges, I and II Samuel, and I and II Kings. The latter prophets are Isaiah, Jeremiah, Ezekiel and the twelve 'minor' prophets who include Amos, Hosea, Joel, Zechariah and others. The book of

Daniel is not included in the prophetic section, but can be found among the Ketuvim.

Sections from the prophets are chanted in the synagogue after the Torah reading. The prophetic passage is known as the *Haftarah* (Completion). It is read from a printed book. Not being read sequentially, the prophetic portions have been specially selected. This is not a random process but has been determined in such a way that the prophetic passage either harmonises with the meaning of the Torah passage, or fits in with the Jewish calendar. Thus, on the three sabbaths preceding *Tisha be'Av* (the anniversary of the destruction of both Temples), Jeremiah 1 and 2 and Isaiah 1 are read, these being prophecies of God's wrath. On the seven sabbaths thereafter, prophecies of divine consolation, taken from Deutero-Isaiah, are read.

Ketuvim (Selected writings)

The third and last section of the *Tenakh*, Ketuvim, is of great significance in Jewish worship. Psalms (Tehillim) assume particular importance in the Jewish liturgy, for while almost all other sections of the *Tenakh* deal with God's actions on behalf of his people, the Psalms reflect the human response. The Psalms give expression to a variety of human responses to the divine, such as adoration, jubilation, supplication, longing, questioning, and hope. Different psalms are allocated to each day of the week and to each festival. They form an integral part of the Jewish liturgy. A group of Psalms (113–118), the *Hallel* (Praise), is read on sabbaths and festivals. Other groups of psalms are recited in the synagogue in times of personal or national crises such as severe illness of a member of the community, drought, or war. The five *Megillot*, or scrolls, are read on various festivals and fasts in Judaism. The Song of Songs is read on Pesach (Passover), the Book of Ruth on Shavuot (Pentecost or Weeks), Ecclesiastes on Succoth (Tabernacles), the Book of Esther on Purim (Lots) and Lamentations on Tisha be'Av (the ninth day of the month of Av).

The Talmud

The Talmud is made up of the Mishnah and the Gemara, and constitutes the oral Torah, *Torah she-be-al peh*. Orthodox Judaism insists that both the written and oral Torah were revealed to Moses on Mount Sinai. In addition to the written Torah, Moses received an explanation of the precepts and the method by which the text was to be interpreted. Orthodoxy, therefore, does not see the oral Torah as divinely inspired, but as part of the original revelation. Reform Judaism, on the other hand, asserts that the oral Torah was formulated by human beings in response to historical conditions. It disputes the Orthodox claim that the oral Torah is immutable. Rejecting the injunctions which it regards as 'obsolete', Reform Judaism stresses the ethical commandments and the universalistic aspect of Judaism. Conservative Judaism also holds that the oral Law is conditioned by history, but steers a middle course, maintaining fidelity to its role and force within Jewish tradition.

The Mishnah

The Mishnah is the second great literary work in Judaism. The rabbis of the Mishnah period are known as the *Tannaim* (teachers). The rabbinic mode of interpreting the *Tenakh* was through the *midrash*. Deriving from the word 'to search out', 'to investigate' or 'to expound', *midrash* seeks to discover the underlying meaning of the Torah. It becomes a guide towards living and is of two types, *halakhic midrash* and *aggadic midrash*. The former contains the legal material, as expounded from the Torah, and is binding. The latter contains homiletic, narrative material which encases the legal material in a wider context of ethical intention and meaning. *Aggadah*, which is not binding, serves to draw out of the text the maximum moral instruction, keeping the ethical ideals of the law alive and meaningful and setting the tone for its observance. A great deal of *aggadic midrash* (on the Pentateuch and the five *Megillot*), can be found in what became a separate collection, known as *Midrash Rabbah* (the Great Midrash).

Using the midrashic method, a succession of rabbis worked on the Mishnah from the late first century CE. It was probably completed in its present form in about 200 CE by Rabbi Judah Ha-nasi. The Mishnah is written in Hebrew and is a compendium of law which elaborates the laws in the Torah in six sections or orders (*sedarim*), each one being made up of tractates. There are 63 tractates in all.

The Gemara

The completed Mishnah formed the basis of a great deal of further elaboration of the laws governing Jewish life. The rabbis who worked on it, the *Amoraim* (speakers), produced the Gemara (Completion). Together, the Mishnah and Gemara make up the Talmud (Study). The mode of procedure was to quote a passage of the Mishnah for wide-ranging discussion, which tended to move from one subject to another by means of free association. While the Mishnah was the standard work used, additional material also formed the basis of discussion. There was the *Baraita*, Tannaitic teaching which was not included in the Mishnah but which was made up of isolated statements that also appear later in the Talmud. The *Tosefta* (Aramaic, 'Addition') was also used as a basis for elaboration and was a work of the Tannaim, parallel to the Mishnah and supplementing it.

There are two Talmuds, one elaborated in Babylon, the Talmud Bavli, and the other elaborated in Palestine, the Talmud Yerushalmi. The latter was not written in Jerusalem, as the name would suggest, so the term 'Yerushalmi' is a misnomer. It was as a deliberate repudiation of the Roman designation of Israel as 'Palestine' that the name Talmud Yerushalmi was given. The schools in Babylon, at Sura and Pumbedita, came to be more influential than the schools of Palestine. In each case, the Gemara reflects intricate rabbinic discussion and argumentation in an attempt to reach a true and exact interpretation of biblical commands. However, in the formulation of the laws, there was always an interplay between the demands of everyday life and the binding nature of the holy text. The rabbis were concerned primarily to elucidate the law in areas of practical significance. Because conditions in the two places were different, and the rabbis often cited cases arising out of their actual experience, and because of the weight of custom (*minhag*), the two Talmuds are very different. The Babylonian is about seven times as long as the Palestinian Talmud, containing almost three thousand pages. The Babylonian Talmud was completed in the late fifth century, about a century after the Palestinian Talmud, and is generally regarded as *the* authoritative text for Orthodox Judaism.

Because of the way in which Talmudic literature originated, it is vast and varied. Strictly speaking, neither Talmud is complete, since they both contain long passages of the Mishnah, which are not provided with a Gemara. From the close of the Babylonian Talmud, until the eleventh century, the centre of halakhic development was in Babylonia and was undertaken by the sages there known as *Geonim* (exalted ones). Their work represented the first attempts to codify the vast body of material in the Talmud. The *Geonim* also contributed to the dynamic development of the *halakhah* in the post-talmudic period by means of the *Responsa*. Through questions and answers, the questions often coming from distant places, the rabbis supplied halakhically based answers to a variety of real life problems. The *Responsa* grew into a literature which not only expounds theological problems, but also reveals a great deal about the sociological history of the Jewish people.

Over the centuries, there were several other attempts at codification of the Talmud. One of the most important of these is Maimonides' *Mishneh Torah* (Repetition of the Torah). Another is Joseph Caro's code of laws in the *Shulhan Arukh* (Prepared Table). The latter became an authoritative handbook of Jewish law, but because Caro was a Sephardic Jew, his work reflected Sephardic customs. With the later annotations of a Polish (Ashkenazi) rabbi, Moses Isserles, the *Shulhan Arukh* has become the basic handbook for Orthodox Jews the world over. An important commentary on the *Tenakh* and Talmud emanated from Rashi (abbreviation of Rabbi Shlomo ben Yitzchak, 1040–1105), who founded a rabbinic academy in Troyes, France. His commentary has become an essential and lively part of Jewish education to the present day.

MAIN BELIEFS IN JUDAISM

Several of the central convictions of Judaism have already been covered in this chapter. However, Judaism is not so much a system of faith or credal religion, as it is a way of life which is based on a detailed body of laws. These determine the way in which a person is to walk his or her way through life. It has, therefore, been difficult to formulate a central creed for Judaism. One of the more successful attempts was that of Maimonides in his Thirteen Principles of Faith. They are also sung in abbreviated hymn-form in the Yigdal prayer. The thirteen principles affirm the following:

> God exists and is the creator. He is one, incorporeal, and eternal. Prayer is due to God alone. The words of the prophets are true and Moses is the father of the prophets. The Torah, as it is now in our hands, was given to Moses. The Torah is immutable and the creator will never give another Torah. God is omniscient and knows the thoughts and deeds of

> human beings. He will reward those who observe and punish those who violate the commandments. The messiah, though he tarry, will come. The dead will be resurrected by the creator when he wishes.

This creed, even though it has been accepted into the daily liturgy of the Orthodox Jewish prayer book, has come under attack. Judaism has always emphasised deed rather than faith and since there are 613 *mitzvot* (commandments) which the Jew is required to fulfil, it is questionable whether there is any authenticity in singling out only thirteen. Nevertheless, they do help to indicate some of the central tenets in Judaism and they also serve, as they did in Maimonides' day, to distinguish Jewish from Christian and Muslim belief.

While not having a single authoritative and universally accepted creed, Judaism does have a very definite religious outlook. In the process of living according to Torah obligations, the Jewish people believe that, by imbuing every aspect of life with holiness, they become God's co-workers in perfecting the world. Inseparable from Judaism's holy way of life are the concepts of a holy God and a holy people.

God

For Judaism, God *is*. 'In the beginning God . . .' (Gen. 1: 1) are the opening words of the Bible. Nowhere does the Bible attempt to prove God's existence. God is perceived not in abstract theological terms, but in a close relationship with his people Israel, bringing them out of their bondage in Egypt and demanding of them a particular course of action. He is, therefore, not a nameless cosmic principle, but is known to his people in history as God of the fathers, Abraham, Isaac and Jacob. Despite this intimate closeness, humans, in their frailty and limitedness, can never fully know God. Jewish tradition states this clearly: *lu yadativ hayativ* – 'If I knew him, I would be him.' Thus, when Moses asked to see God's face, he was permitted to see only his back. This indicates that God, while always recognisable, can never be fully seen or grasped.

Judaism's primary assertion about God is that he is one (Deut. 6: 4). Many scholars argue that absolute monotheism was a late development in Judaism. Zwi Werblowsky, in opposition to these views, has asserted that the term 'absolute monotheism', while not being totally adequate, is nevertheless the closest we can come to describing the earliest Jewish understanding of God. While the belief in one God articulated itself more clearly as time went on, it would not have developed in the way it did had absolute monotheism not been implicit from the very beginning.

Oneness has several implications. Of cardinal importance is the fact that one God demands one morality. One universal law of righteousness is, therefore, applicable for all humankind. Monotheism allows for no ambiguity.

There is no dualism in Judaism. God forms light and creates darkness. He makes weal and creates woe (Isa. 45: 7). Judaism came into contact with the Persian religion of Zoroastrianism, which suggested that evil is to be ascribed to a power opposing God. Although this is a metaphysically attractive view, offering a solution to the existence of evil which retains God's goodness by not implicating him in the causes of evil, Judaism did not succumb to dualism. Dualism tends to make an absolute of evil, while Judaism regards evil as contingent on a prior and much more fundamental good. Dualism despairs of the evil side of reality, while, for Judaism, there is nothing that cannot be retrieved for the good. If, as dualism implies, the power for evil is as strong as the power for good, there is no guarantee that good will prevail. Dualism thus falls prey to giving the ultimate triumph to evil.

The one God is also the creator of the universe. He is distinct from creation, and creation itself bears testimony to his greatness: 'The heavens are telling the glory of God; and the firmament proclaims his handiwork' (Ps. 19: 1). The belief that God created the world, which he deemed to be good, and that there are no rival spirits or demons in the world, coupled with the fact that he gave humankind dominion over the rest of creation, led to secularisation or 'this-worldliness'. Human beings were empowered to walk the earth unafraid, harness nature, and thereby develop science and technology.

God is understood as totally transcendent, one so holy and awe-inspiring that his name may not be uttered. The commandment not to utter God's name in vain is taken so seriously by Jews that the name of God, YHWH (the tetragrammaton), is never uttered. The holy name is always circumlocuted. In prayer, the name *Adonai* (My Lord) is used, while for purposes of study, rabbis used a variety of circumlocutions – *Hashem* (the Name), The Holy One Blessed Be He, Heaven, the Power. Yet, despite the remoteness that this suggests, God is also experienced as so loving and close that he has been portrayed by the rabbis[1] in unabashedly anthropomorphic terms. Thus, in the rabbinic imagination, God goes into exile with his people, suffers with them, wears phylacteries with the faithful, and even enters into debate with the rabbis on obscure points of Jewish law. One of the most important supplications in the liturgy is addressed to 'Our Father, Our King', an address which accurately displays the dialectic in the Jewish people's experience of God's closeness and remoteness.

As Milton Steinberg has pointed out, God, when properly served, is ultimately the emancipator of human beings and their societies. He is the power which works within individuals, inspiring them to oppose servitude both in themselves and in others. Jews know, as no other people, of his power to liberate, for the exodus is the classic instance of liberation, the proof that because God exists, every bondage can and will be broken. God is also the saviour of humanity, not so much in the sense of a life after death, but in *this* world. When the term 'salvation' is used in Judaism, it denotes a victory over human limitations and perverseness; a victory over greed, selfishness, hatred, pride, cynicism and any active opposition to and rejection of goodness and truth. Awareness of God and the doing of his will free the human spirit from all impeding restraints and from any tendency towards evil which would corrupt it.

Humanity

There is a distinct polarity in the Jewish understanding of the human being. Humans are frail and weak, their lifespan is short and 'spent with sorrow', while the years pass 'with sighing' (Ps. 31: 10). A person is, on one hand, a 'maggot' and a 'worm' (Job 25: 6), 'crushed before the moth' (Job 4: 19), and on the other, a being 'crowned with glory and honour' (Ps. 8: 5), the peak of God's creation. Human weakness can only be fully appreciated when one takes cognisance of the human capacity for sin. Although Judaism has not developed a doctrine of original sin, it remains fully aware of sin's reality and of humanity's constant temptation to sin. In the Jewish view, sin means the departure from the path of life which God has ordained for the Jew to follow. Jews must observe the *mitzvot* (commandments), which submit the whole of life and every detail therein to holy discipline. Whether eating, dressing or mating, the Jew is always to be reminded of God's sovereignty. Only Jews are bound by the intricate rules of the covenant. They were chosen for the special privilege and obligation of keeping these *mitzvot*. This is not expected of the gentiles, who can lead a righteous life by following the seven Noahide commandments.[2]

Rabbinic Judaism developed the view that each person is born with a good impulse, *yetzer hatov*, and an impulse for evil, *yetzer hara*. By following Torah commandments, which are seen as good because the giver thereof is good, the good impulse is likely to become predominant. Judaism accepts bodily existence as essential to the full life and does not expect suppression of natural urges. The rabbis asserted that if it were not for the evil urge, no man would marry, build a house or have children. By submitting the whole of life to divine command and thereby, to discipline, each person can utilise natural urges to improve human life and the world itself. The direction which a person wishes to take in living his or her life is based on freedom of moral choice, which is clearly underscored by the rabbinic maxim that 'all things are in heaven's hands except the reverence for heaven'. However, if the Jews, as individuals or as a community, fall into error, they are expected to repent of their evil ways and, by active deeds of kindness, prayer and genuine repentance, can achieve complete reconciliation with God, who remains ready to accept the repentant sinner.

The basis of all morality in Jewish understanding is Torah. One of the highest virtues, therefore, is the study of the Torah. This pursuit should be undertaken with humility, patience, and care: 'As wine does not keep in vessels of silver and gold, but only in earthenware, so learning remains wholesome only in the humble.' Judaism cherishes human independence of thought and accepts diversity of opinion. This is reflected in the Mishnah, which both includes divergent opinions and expresses the conviction that words uttered by scholars of opposing opinions are all words of the living God.

To live a truly Jewish life is to subject one's entire life to holy discipline. Nowhere is this more obvious than in the observance of the dietary laws (*kashrut*). The Orthodox Jew gives no rationale, such as health reasons, for their observance. They are God's laws and are observed with unquestioning cheerfulness. The basic laws are biblical, but have been vastly elaborated in the Talmud. Often, an injunction which is obscure in the Torah is given its full meaning in the Talmud. An example of this is the intricate body of laws that has emerged regarding the consumption of milk and meat produce. Three times in the Torah it is simply stated that Jews may not boil a kid in the milk of its mother. The Talmud interprets this as prohibiting any mixture whatsoever of meat and dairy produce. Not only may one not boil a kid in the milk of its mother, but milk and meat produce may not be cooked together, eaten together, or prepared in the same utensils. The *kosher* household must, therefore, have different utensils, crockery and cutlery for 'meat' meals and for 'milk' meals. There are several other biblical prohibitions. With regard to meat, the dietary laws permit for consumption only those four-legged animals which both chew the cud and have cloven hoofs. They prohibit the eating of birds of prey and those animals which 'creep or crawl upon the earth'. Not only must animals be ritually slaughtered (the manner of which is made explicit in the Talmud rather than in the Torah itself), but meat must be soaked and salted to remove all excess blood. Some sections, even of permitted animals, may not be consumed and because of this only the forequarter is eaten. There are no prohibitions on fruit and vegetables.

In the Hebrew Bible, humanity is given dominion over the rest of creation and is free to use the world in order to live life to the full. Jews take seriously the commandment to be fruitful, to multiply and to fill the earth. This results in a positive attitude to human sexuality. Jews are expected to use the benefits offered by this world, but not to abuse them. They thus become God's co-stewards over creation, enjoying life and the world, but precisely because their lives are under the divine charge, this enjoyment of the world can never result in hedonism.

Ethics

Jewish ethics are grounded in the Torah, given clear and unambiguous force in the prophetic books, and elaborated by the rabbis in such a manner as to have become inextricably part of the entire fabric of Jewish life. Thus, they may not be separated from the ritual *mitzvot*. All of God's commandments must be observed, the ritual *mitzvot* serving, not as is so often charged as a replacement for, but as a reminder of the ethical *mitzvot*. The good life in Judaism is lived under the divine command and extends from duties to the self to duties towards the whole of humankind.

Since all human beings are children of God, all are equally entitled to justice and mercy. Humans were created in God's image, and should therefore imitate God in their behaviour, exhibiting the godly traits that are inherent in them. Since God is just and merciful, to live in God's image is to emulate his mercy and justice. Jews can only fulfil this by observing the *mitzvot*. Jews claim no inherent superiority over other people. They merely assert that they have been given a special advantage in receiving the Torah, and it is in the very terms of the Torah that their duties towards all of humankind are commanded.

Except by virtue of character and conduct, no one human being is better than any other. Judaism demands that one cares for the stranger, the orphan and the widow, and that one loves one's neighbour as oneself. So central is the Jew's duty to his fellow human beings that Rabbi Hillel (first century BCE), when asked to encapsulate the whole essence of Judaism while his hearer (a potential convert to Judaism) stood on one foot, formulated the 'golden rule' of Judaism: 'That which is hateful unto you, do not do unto others. Thou shalt love thy neighbour as thyself. This is the whole Torah, all the rest is commentary. Now go and study.'

The Prophets, in whose words the ethical content of the Torah is brought into sharp and unambiguous focus, decried cultic practice that was not accompanied by social justice. They castigated the Jewish people's failure to show concern for the widow and the orphan. They did not condemn possession of wealth, but called for its more equal distribution. Jewish ethics teach that all people have the right to possess things by which to live. The Talmud, therefore, forbids the Jew to encroach in any manner whatsoever on the capacity of any other person to make a living. It demands scrupulous honesty in business transactions and in obligations towards employees. In fact, the highest form of charity is not the mere giving of money to the indigent, but giving in a way which empowers them to make a living with dignity.

Prophecy laid the ground for social protest which, in turn, aims to create a better and more equitable world. Underlying prophecy, as Huston Smith points out, is the twin conviction that the future of any people depends largely on the justice of their social order, and that individuals are responsible both for the condition of society and for the 'tidiness' of their personal lives. Prophecy is grounded on the assumption that the prerequisite for political stability is social justice. Injustice breeds its own demise and, since God demands the highest of standards, he will not forever tolerate exploitation, corruption and mediocrity. It is in the countries that have been influenced by the prophetic vision that there is the greatest potential for the achievement of social justice.

The messianic idea

By doing the will of God and living up to the noblest ideals of Judaism, the Jew reveals God's glory. Through the performance of the *mitzvot*, the Jew hallows God's name, thereby imbuing every aspect of life with divine dignity and beauty. Jews become God's co-workers in the hallowing of the world. There is a dynamic thrust to Jewish practice, both ritual and ethical, which projects forward in the direction of the moral perfection of the world. Jews look towards the day when injustice will be removed from the earth, when men will beat their swords into ploughshares, when the lion will lie down with the lamb, and when there will no longer be war. The idea of a messianic figure is not clearly biblical. When the term *mashiach* (anointed one), is used in the Hebrew Bible, it refers to a king or priest and, on one occasion, it is applied to a gentile, King Cyrus.

The idea of a messianic figure was a later development in Judaism. While Reform Jews expect the coming of the messianic age rather than the coming of a messianic figure, and while there are variations even in the traditional views on the messiah, the generally accepted belief is that the messiah will be a human being, a descendant from the house of David, appointed by God. The messianic redemption will be both particularistic and universal in that the Jewish people will be restored to their homeland from their dispersion and the Temple will be rebuilt. Only thereafter will the entire world be redeemed. The messiah will be armed by God with the power and authority to purge the world, *this* world, of all evil. Through him, God will establish eternal goodness and righteousness on earth:

> They shall not hurt or destroy
> in all my holy mountain;
> for the earth shall be full of the knowledge of the Lord,
> as the waters cover the sea (Isa. 11: 9).

Prayer

Prayer and benedictions are ever-present in the daily life of the Jew since every act is elevated to holiness through the utterance of prayers. Orthodox Jews pray in Hebrew, while in Reform temples a great deal of the service has been translated into the vernacular. The Jewish liturgy is rich and varied. Prayer is not random or individually spontaneous, nor does it need to be, because there are prayers in the liturgy to suit every occasion and to pour out every conceivable emotion. The Jewish prayer book or *siddur* is structured in terms of the fact that there is a predetermined order in which Jews express their devotions to God.

There are three main prayer sessions during the course of the day, *Shacharit*, *Mincha* and *Maariv* (the morning, afternoon and evening prayers respectively). On sabbaths and festivals a fourth prayer session is added after *Shacharit*. This is known as *Mussaf* and is associated with sacrifice in the times when the Temple still stood. Thus, there is an emphasis on the verbal repetition of sacrifice, even though it is not possible to enact sacrifice any longer. On the Day of Atonement, a concluding service called *Ne'ilah* is added.

Although the individual may pray at home, congregational prayer is regarded as more effective, and for certain prayers, such as the *Kaddish* for the dead, a *minyan* or quorum of ten adult males or more must be present. Orthodox Judaism permits only males to make up a *minyan*. In Reform Judaism, women are counted in the quorum. Orthodox Judaism excuses women from the performance of any *mitzvot* which are tied to time, such as the three prayer sessions. This allows them full freedom to bear children and raise their families without unnecessary intrusion of time-bound rituals. In Orthodox synagogues, men and women sit separately. Either they are divided by a screen, or the women sit in a gallery above the men. In Conservative and Reform synagogues, men and women sit together.

Prayers are led by the rabbi or by any adult male who is sufficiently competent to do so and who is of good character. In most prayers, he leads and the congregation responds. A cantor leads the prayers in many synagogues, intoning them in plaintive or joyous traditional melodies. When the cantor has an exceptionally beautiful voice, he may attract a large number of congregants to attend the services, particularly on sabbaths and festivals. The presence of a cantor adorns the service, but is by no means essential.

During the week-day morning prayer session, men wear phylacteries (*tefillin*) and a prayer shawl (*tallit*). The phylacteries, small cube-shaped leather objects, contain biblical verses, among them being the *Shema*. These are hand-written on parchment and are bound on the forehead as 'frontlets between the eyes' and on the left arm opposite the heart. The *tallit* is fringed, the fringes arranged and knotted in such a manner that they add up to 613, to remind the Jew of the 613 *mitzvot* in the Torah.

Men always wear a head-covering for prayers and benedictions, and must always do so when entering a synagogue. Although this is not of biblical but of talmudic origin, the weight of custom has assumed the force of law. Covering the head is a sign of humility and awe before God who is above his creation. While some men only wear a head covering in the synagogue or for prayer, the wearing of the skull-cap (*yarmulke* in Yiddish, *kippah* in Hebrew) has increased markedly with the modern upsurge of traditional Judaism. Only married women need to wear a head-covering in the synagogue.

HOLY TIME

As part of the concept of hallowing life, all activities, even the most mundane, must be subjected to holy discipline. In addition to the everyday act, there are special occasions in the life of every Jew which are celebrated within a ritual and community context. These fall into two categories, the life-cycle rituals of the individual Jew and the holy round of festivals and fasts which are celebrated or commemorated by the entire community.

The life-cycle rituals

Jews, like all members of the world's religions, celebrate the passage through life with appropriate rituals. These 'rites of passage', as they have been called, mark the transitions through the various stages of life, imbuing each transition with holiness.

Birth

Jews place great emphasis on procreation, the Talmud stating that a man without children is as though he were dead. The birth of a child is a joyous occasion. A boy is circumcised on the eighth day of his life provided that he is in good health, failing which, the circumcision is postponed. The circumcision brings him into the covenant of Abraham and is thus known as *brit milah* (the covenant of circumcision). The child is named and welcomed into the community with prayer and rejoicing. The ceremony is performed by a *mohel*, a man well versed in Torah and competent to perform the operation, and is followed by a festive meal. In the case of a girl, the child is named in the synagogue by her father at the Torah reading following her birth. Jews are given Hebrew names by which they are called for all ritual purposes, from birth to death. A son would be called, for example, *Moshe ben Avraham* (Moses, son of Abraham), while a daughter would be named *Rachel bat Avraham* (Rachel, daughter of Abraham). Western names, equivalent in meaning, are usually given for use in the secular world. Jews generally name a child after a close but deceased relative, not only to perpetuate the memory of the relative, but in the hope that his or her qualities will be emulated by the child throughout its life.

Education and bar mitzvah

Education has always been important in Judaism. Children imbibe a great deal of Jewish education in the home. However, since many Jews have secularised, it has become important to send children to Jewish day-schools where they learn Hebrew, Jewish history and tradition, which will enable them to become active members in the community. According to traditional Judaism, a boy should learn Torah at 5, Mishnah at 10, and at the age of 13 is ready to assume religious responsibility as an adult male in the community. The transition to adulthood is marked by the ritual known as *bar mitzvah* (son of the commandment). The central features of this ritual are the reading in the synagogue of a section of the Torah and the *Haftarah*, and the celebration of a feast. By means of the ritual, the boy assumes his religious responsibility within the congregation, becoming solely responsible for his religious deeds, his father being absolved thereof. The *bar mitzvah* ritual is of late origin, only having become a permanent feature of Jewish life since about the fourteenth century. Prior to this, a boy entered adulthood without an obligatory ritual.

It is only in the modern era that girls have marked their entry into adulthood with the *bat mitzvah* (daughter of the commandment) ceremony, which is celebrated at the age of 12. The custom arose in Reform Judaism, which insists that the girl performs the same ritual as does the boy. In Orthodoxy, *bat mitzvah* was introduced later, girls performing a lesser ritual than their male counterparts and usually celebrating the ritual collectively. Because it is not obligatory, many girls enter adulthood without such a celebration. Ideally, *bar mitzvah* marks the beginning of a life of religious discipline and commitment. Ironically, in the modern secular world, it often signals the end of an active Jewish education.

Marriage

Marriage and procreation are highly valued in Judaism, being based on the commandment to be fruitful and multiply. The Talmud, regarding an unmarried man as only half a man, asserts that marriage is essential for the fulfilment of human potential and regards human sexuality positively. Sexual intercourse is encouraged, but since it is an act which must be elevated to holiness, there are laws which limit excesses. It may only be performed in marriage and only at certain times, intercourse with a menstruating woman (*niddah*) being taboo.

The Jewish marriage ceremony is a joyous occasion replete with symbolic rituals. The couple are married under a *huppa* or canopy which symbolises the Jewish home that they will build together. The parents of both bride and groom stand under the canopy and perform their part in the ceremony. The couple is blessed and an oration is given by the officiating rabbi. Twice during the ceremony both bride and groom sip from a goblet of sweet wine which has been sanctified by the officiating cantor. This symbolises the fact that they will share the cup of life with both its joys and its sorrows. The groom gives the bride a plain gold ring which he places on her right forefinger with the words: 'Be thou consecrated unto me, by this ring, under the law of Moses and of Israel.' The *ketubah* (marriage contract) is then read in Aramaic by the rabbi. The *Sheva Berakhot* (seven benedictions) are chanted. The ceremony is concluded by the groom stamping on and shattering a glass. This symbolises the destruction of the Temple and reminds the couple, in their moment of greatest joy, of the reality of Jewish suffering. This moment is accompanied by shouts of *Mazal tov* (Good luck!) from the guests. A festive meal, accompanied by dance and song, follows. Among traditional Jews, the *Sheva Berakhot* are recited each evening for an entire week after the wedding at successive festive meals.

Illness and death

Judaism places stress on the care and cleanliness of the body. The Talmud forbids one to live in a town without a physician. This means that when illness befalls one, one is obliged to seek competent medical treatment. While God is the ultimate healer, the physician is God's co-worker. It is a religious duty to visit the sick and lighten their burden. When death approaches, the sick person should have his or her close friends and relatives nearby and should be encouraged, if possible, to repent of sin and to utter the words, 'Hear O Israel, the Lord our God the Lord is one', as a final affirmation of faith. Even if the person is too ill to recognise anyone, the presence of those who care is important. Their prayer and encouragement give the assurance that one's companions will take one to the gates of eternity and that one does not have to face death alone.

Jews must be buried in a separate, consecrated burial ground. The funeral takes place as soon as possible after death, but not on a sabbath or festival. The corpse is washed, wrapped in a white shroud and placed, without any ornament, in a simple wooden coffin by voluntary Jewish workers of the same sex as the deceased. In some countries, notably Israel, the dead are committed to the earth in the shroud only. Rich and poor are buried in the same manner for, in death as in life, all are equal before God. It is customary to bury males with the prayer shawl (*tallit*) which they wore during their lifetime. The Jewish funeral is a simple but frank ceremony. The male mourners rend their clothes while blessing God, 'the righteous judge', and the coffin is carried by pall-bearers to its final resting-place. After blessings and an oration by the officiating rabbi, the grave is covered with earth, each male present shovelling three spadefuls of earth on the coffin. In Orthodox circles, the friends and relatives of the mourners frequently cover the entire grave with earth, this being the last physical act which can be performed for the dead, and from which one can expect no reward. Cremation is not permitted by Orthodox Judaism.

A stringent mourning period follows. The first meal, the meal of comfort, is supplied by friends lest the mourners, in their grief, forget to nourish themselves. For the first seven days (*shiva*), the mourners are not permitted to undertake any of the normal activities associated with life. They sit on low stools. They may not adorn themselves, wear leather shoes, bathe, shave or indulge in sexual intercourse. They may not even study and are not permitted to leave the house except on the sabbath when they attend the synagogue. For this reason, the congregation comes to the house of mourning where the necessary prayer sessions are performed by a congregation of at least ten adult males, including the mourners, who say a special prayer, the *Kaddish*. This prayer is not for the deceased, but simply affirms the greatness and glory of God.

Mourners are encouraged to give full vent to their grief. Several theories have been given for the stringency of the mourning ritual, some emphasising the psychological, others the sociological benefits. The ritual certainly enables the family and the religious community to face the reality of death and to adjust to the loss of one of its members. This is the closest that the Jew comes to non-life and is the only time that Jewish ritual is not fully life-affirming. The first thirty days (*shloshim*) after the funeral are marked by a return to one's normal working world, but are still days of mourning, music and entertainment being prohibited. For a parent, one must mourn for an entire eleven months, while for a spouse, life returns to normal after thirty days. Every year, on the anniversary of the death, the deceased is remembered in the *Yahrtzeit* ritual. A candle burns for an entire 24-hour period and the *Kaddish* is said by close male relatives in the synagogue.

The Holy Year

Festivals

Tied in with the emphasis on holy discipline is the concept of holy time. The Jewish calendar is punctuated with holiness, the most frequently observed festival or holy day being the sabbath which commences each Friday with the onset of twilight and ends on Saturday night with the emergence of three visible stars in the sky. In commemoration of creation, the Jew hallows the seventh day by ceasing from all forms of creative work and by entering into a spirit of peace and harmony, which is expressed in both a family and community context. As part of the need to define precisely what constitutes work, the rabbis introduced a number of prohibitions. These are all undergirded by the requirement that Jews imitate their God and perform no work which he performed during the six days of creation. Thus, for example, Orthodox Judaism forbids one to switch on a light, for even the creation of an infinitesimal spark would be a desecration of the holiness of the sabbath day.

The observant Jew does not see the sabbath day as being hedged around with restrictive laws, but as a day of spiritual renewal. It is also a day on which the earth itself is allowed to rest from human intrusion. The sabbath is an island of peace in a hectic world, a day of complete rest from all mundane weekly activities. The sabbath is welcomed in the synagogue as a pure and pristine bride each Friday evening with the *Lecha Dodi*: 'Come my beloved to meet the bride.' The image of the Jewish people being married to the sabbath is central to the Jewish consciousness. A *midrash* states that while the other six days of the week were paired, the sabbath stood alone. Complaining to God of her loneliness, she was given the people of Israel as her spouse.

The sabbath is inaugurated when the mother of the home lights the sabbath candles. At the evening meal the father of the house makes a benediction over a goblet of wine, before partaking of plaited loaves of white bread, of which there are always two, commemorating the double gift of manna on every sabbath day during the forty-year period of Jewish wandering in the desert after the exodus. The sabbath benedictions link the creation with the exodus. The affirmation that the world is God-given is thus tied in with the concept that God, the Lord of history, is in control of the destiny of the Jewish people. The end of the sabbath is marked by a short but beautiful ceremony, *Havdalah*, the division of the holy from the profane. As part of the ritual, fragrant spices are smelled in order to console the Jew as the bride departs for another week.

The Jewish calendar is divided into twelve lunar months, which means that the year is shorter than the normal Western calendar year. Because the festivals have a dual meaning, historical and agricultural, they have to fall at the same season each year. The rabbis have thus intercalated a leap month, the month of *Adar*, at predetermined intervals. There are three major festivals in Judaism, the *shalosh regalim*, or pilgrimage festivals. During the time in which the Temple stood, the Jews were expected to visit it in Jerusalem on these festivals with their harvest offerings. All festivals are commemorated for one day longer in the diaspora than they are in Israel, lest there was any miscalculation, in distant places, of the time of onset.

Pesach (Passover) is the festival of spring (taking place from 15 *Nisan*, corresponding to April) and the festival of freedom. It commemorates the exodus from Egypt. Because of God's miraculous intervention, the Jewish people left Egypt in so great a hurry that their bread did not have sufficient time to rise. Jews may therefore eat no food containing leaven during the entire eight days (seven days in Israel) of the Passover. The entire house has to be cleansed of leaven. Jews are commanded to eat *matzah*, unleavened bread, the 'bread of affliction'. Each Jew is to feel as if he or she, personally, had been redeemed from bondage in Egypt. This is achieved at the two *Seder* meals at which the entire *Haggadah* is read at a festive meal which follows a specific order of events. The proceedings of the evening are prefaced by one basic question (divided into four parts): 'Why is this night different from all other nights?' This gives rise to a host of questions and answers concerning the special nature of the miracle. All present are encouraged to ask pertinent questions in order to draw out and elaborate in a variety of ways the meaning of freedom. The initial question is traditionally asked by the youngest member present and is answered by the reading, with joy, song and a spirit of inquiry, of the *Haggadah*. The purpose of the commemoration is not only to relive the miracle, but to convey its meaning from generation to generation. There are several symbolic foods which are eaten as part of the meal, such as bitter herbs, symbolising the bitterness of slavery, and salt water, symbolic of tears.

The festival of Shavuot (Weeks, also known as Pentecost) takes place seven weeks or fifty days after the Passover. It is the festival of first fruits and commemorates the giving of the Torah. Synagogues are decorated with greenery and children bring gaily decorated baskets of fruit, which are later distributed to the poor, to the synagogue. Many Orthodox men stay awake during the entire night to study the Torah. It is customary to eat milk foods on this festival, one of the reasons being that the Jews had just been given the laws of *kashrut*, the dietary laws of Judaism, and they had not yet had time for animals to be slaughtered according to God's commandments.

The festival of Succoth (Tabernacles or Booths) is celebrated for seven days from 15 *Tishri*, corresponding to September–October, and is followed immediately by a one-day festival, Shemini Atzeret. In the diaspora a ninth day is added, Simchat Torah, on which is celebrated the finishing and restarting of the reading of the Torah. In Israel this festival is celebrated together with Shemini Atzeret. Succoth, also known as the 'time of rejoicing', is celebrated by the building of temporary shelters or tabernacles in which Jews take their meals and in which the very traditional sleep. Although the walls of the structure may be permanent, the roof must be temporary and is usually constructed with fresh palm leaves or branches of trees placed on a wooden pergola. The festival commemorates the wandering in the desert and, by exposing one to the elements, emphasises human vulnerability and God's protection. Each synagogue, and several Jewish households, have their own *succah*. They are colourfully decorated with fruits hanging from the roof, with pictures, posters and flowers, which are usually put up by the children of the family. The *succah* is pleasantly shaded and infused with the fragrance of fresh greenery. This is a joyous festival, much enjoyed by all members of the family and the community. Only on the first two days (one in Israel) is work prohibited.

There are several minor festivals in Judaism. Purim, as related in the book of Esther, celebrates the saving of the Jewish people of the Persian empire from destruction by Haman. It is not a religious holiday in that one does not have to refrain from work on this day. The scroll of Esther is read in the synagogue. The participation by children is ensured with the custom of children drowning out the name of Haman – by the use of ratchets, rattles or hooters – every time it is uttered. Young children at Jewish schools or nursery schools dress up in fancy dress. It is customary for adult males to revel and drink until they are unable to discern the difference between 'Blessed be Mordecai' and 'Cursed be Haman'. This is thus known as the Adloyada (Aramaic, 'inability to know') carnival.

Another minor festival is Hanukah, the festival of lights, which takes place during December. It commemorates the re-dedication of the Temple by the Maccabees after Antiochus Epiphanes had plundered it. The Maccabees found enough oil to burn for only one night, but it miraculously burned for eight. An eight-branched candelabrum is used. Starting with the lighting of one candle, on each evening the number is augmented by one, until there are eight candles burning. This is all done with song and celebration. Gifts are given and games, which emphasise the miracle of the spiritual salvation of the Jewish people, are played.

The Days of Awe

Rosh Hashanah is the new year festival which celebrates the anniversary of the creation. Held on the first two days of the month of *Tishri*, it is preceded by the last month of the Jewish calendar, *Elul*, which is dedicated to introspection and repentance. During *Elul*, with the exception of the sabbath, the *shofar* (ram's horn) is sounded every morning after the prayers in the synagogue. In the last week of *Elul*, special prayers of repentance (*selichot*) are said. This culminates in Rosh Hashanah, two joyous, festive days, but also days of divine judgement. It is believed that on Rosh Hashanah one's fortune during the coming year is decreed. Traditional foods, such as apples dipped in honey, are eaten to ensure a sweet year. The *shofar* is sounded several times in the synagogue during the services, as a call to repentance. The traditional greeting on these two days is: 'May you be inscribed and sealed for a good year.' This is based on the belief that the heavenly book, in which each person's deeds are recorded, is open for ten days from Rosh Hashanah to Yom Kippur (the Day of Atonement).

Yom Kippur is the holiest day in the Jewish calendar. On this day, no work may be performed. It is a solemn fast-day on which no food or liquid may pass one's lips. Beginning in the evening and ending on the following evening, it is dedicated to prayer and repentance. On this day, one's fate for the coming year is sealed. Since the three days, two on Rosh Hashanah and one on Yom Kippur, are such important days in the Jewish year, almost all Jews, from the most traditional to the secular, attend the long synagogue services. They are known as the *Yamim Noraim*, the Days of Awe.

Fast days

In addition to the Day of Atonement there are several dawn-to-dusk fast days in Judaism. The day before Purim is the fast of Esther, while the day after Rosh Hashanah is the fast of Gedaliah. The most important of all the lesser fast days is the fast of Tisha be'Av (the ninth day of the month of Av), the day on which both Temples were destroyed. This fast thus commemorates the destruction of both the first and second Temple. Ironically, it is on this day that other catastrophes, such as the expulsion from Spain in 1492, befell the Jewish people. It is the only fast day, apart from Yom Kippur, on which one fasts for a full 24 hours. While it is not a religious holiday on which Jews abstain from work, it is a solemn day of mourning. The Lamentations of Jeremiah are chanted in mournful tone in the darkened synagogue. One may not wear leather shoes and must sit on a low stool. In Jerusalem, pious Jews pray and lament at the Western Wall – the last remnant of the ancient Temple – throughout the night and day of Tisha be'Av.

INSTITUTIONS AND LEADERSHIP

The most basic institution in Judaism is the synagogue. It is the place of gathering for prayer as well as the focal point for community activities. The synagogue is also the 'school' for the promotion of Jewish values, and hence is also known by the German-derived name, *shul* (school). There is often a Hebrew school (*heder*) attached to the synagogue where girls and boys learn Jewish traditions and the Hebrew language in order to equip them to pray in the synagogue. There are frequent *shiurim* or lessons on the Torah for adult men and women. These may be given after the synagogue service on the sabbath morning or on the sabbath afternoon, and there are additional *shiurim* for both men and women on various evenings during the week. The synagogue is the gathering-place of the youth. It is the place in which both the joyous events and the tragedies in the lives of individuals and the community are commemorated.

There are several large and fairly ornate synagogues as well as thousands of small modest synagogues or house-*shuls* throughout the world. Reform Jews call their places of worship Temples. The large synagogues and Temples generally have a cantor and choir to lead the services. The modern trend, particularly within traditionally Orthodox Judaism, is to return to the smaller, more informal house-*shul* or *shtiebl*, in which a member of the congregation or the rabbi leads the service, while the congregation sings in response.

The main functionary in Judaism is the rabbi, the title meaning 'teacher'. A rabbi is not a priest but is one who is well versed in knowledge of the Torah and Talmud and who can lead the community with regard to how they should conduct their lives. He assists the community in relation to marriage, divorce, and counselling on a variety of issues both ritual and ethical. It has become customary in the Western world for the rabbi to give a sermon during sabbath and festival services. Traditionally, the rabbi gave a *derashah*, a learned discourse on the Torah. Many of the more Orthodox synagogues have returned to this practice.

Orthodox Jewish life is governed by a rabbinic court or Beth Din (house of law). The Beth Din is led by rabbinic authorities, *dayanim* (judges), who make judgments on matters such as *kashrut* and on claims or disagreements within the Jewish community. They also control conversions to Judaism and issue bills of divorce. Diaspora Jews generally have secular representative bodies as well. There are philanthropic societies, some of which see to the well-being of Jews, and others which extend their activities to the wider world. An important institution is the *Chevra Kadisha* (holy friends) who, in addition to giving assistance to the living, undertake all Jewish burials and ensure a dignified burial for all Jews, rich or poor. Other institutions, such as the various Jewish Boards of Deputies, safeguard the civil rights of Jews within the wider society.

SYMBOLS OF JUDAISM

There are several symbols for Judaism, one of the most powerful being the burning bush (Exod. 3: 1–10), the bush which was burned by fire but would not be consumed. It is often used as a symbol of the people Israel who, despite the several attempts to destroy them, continue to survive. The most commonly used visual symbol is the *Magen David* or shield of David. Being neither of biblical nor of talmudic origin, its derivation is very obscure. Although it does appear on early Jewish synagogues and gravestones, it was far more commonly used in non-Jewish environments and only became a widely used symbol after the seventeenth century. It was adopted as a symbol by the first Zionist Congress in 1897 and was subsequently incorporated into the flag of Israel. Another commonly used symbol is the seven-branched candelabrum which was used in the Temple.

Some of the other symbols associated with Judaism are the Torah scroll, wrapped in its ornate mantle, the *shofar*, or ram's horn, and the *mezzuzah*. The *mezzuzah* is the small encased hand-written parchment scroll, containing the *Shema*, which is placed on the entry to all Jewish homes and buildings and on the doorposts of every room in the Jewish home. It affirms God's oneness and uniqueness, reminding the Jews of their duty to observe God's commandments when going in and when coming out of their homes, or, more precisely, at every moment of their lives.

NOTES

1. The successive generations of authoritative teachers of Judaism who emerged from the Pharisaic movement and expounded on the law.
2. The Noahide laws are injunctions, traditionally given to Noah, which have been elaborated by the rabbis. Gentiles as well as Jews are bound by these commandments.

SELECT BIBLIOGRAPHY

Bright, John. *A History of Israel*. London: SCM Press, 1964
Cohn-Sherbok, Dan. *The Jewish Heritage*. Oxford: Basil Blackwell, 1988
De Lange, Nicholas. *Judaism*. Oxford: Oxford University Press, 1986
Epstein, Isidore. *Judaism*. Harmondsworth: Penguin Books, 1959
Mendes-Flohr, Paul R. & Reinharz, Jehuda (eds). *The Jew in the Modern World: A Documentary History*. New York: Oxford University Press, 1980
Nigosian, Solomon. *Judaism: The Way of Holiness*. Great Britain: Crucible, 1986
Steinberg, Milton. *Basic Judaism*. New York: Harcourt Brace Jovanovich, 1975
Smith, Huston. *The Religions of Man*. New York: Harper and Row Publishers, 1958
Untermann, Alan. *Jews: Their Religious Beliefs and Practices*. Boston: Routledge and Kegan Paul, 1981
Werblowsky, Zwi. 'Judaism', in C. J. Bleeker & G. Widengren (eds). *Historia Religionum*, vol. 2. Leiden: E. J. Brill, 1971
Zuidema, Willem. *God's Partner: An Encounter with Judaism*. London: SCM Press Limited, 1987

8

Christianity

JOHN W. DE GRUCHY

For the outsider, and often for the insider as well, the Christian religion presents a complex and perplexing set of beliefs, institutions, ceremonies and personalities. As these are often in conflict with each other, it would even appear as if there are several different Christianities. Given the obvious diversity and divisions within the Christian church, such an assumption would not be unwarranted. The same is true, of course, of other world religions, though perhaps not on the same scale. Yet there are clearly things which all Christians share in common and which give them their identity as Christians. All, for example, believe in Jesus Christ as Lord and Saviour even though they may disagree on precisely what such belief entails, and how it should be expressed in word or deed.

In what follows we shall explore those key elements which give Christians their common identity, and examine some of the differences which separate them, suggesting reasons for such divisions. As we do this we shall not only describe the core beliefs, ethical commitments, scriptures, rituals and institutional organisation of Christianity, but also see how these various dimensions of the Christian religion are part of an historical process and, as such, have been shaped by different historical contexts. For whatever else Christianity may be, it is a social movement which has taken root in a wide variety of historical periods and cultural contexts. As a result, however much it may be in continuity with its origins, it has also developed and changed through the centuries, and is still in the process of doing so. Indeed, it is the historical development of Christianity within diverse cultural contexts which, in large measure, explains the diversity and the divisions of which we have spoken.

Thus in order to understand Christian faith and practice, and its embodiment in institutions, rites, and symbols, we need to trace its development and examine its character in its various historical settings. But we also need to begin at the beginning and examine the roots which have both given the movement its core identity and nourished, sustained, and renewed it through the centuries. Although the story is a continuous one, we have divided it into two sections, the first, covering the first thousand years from Jesus of Nazareth to the Great Schism which divided the Eastern church from the Western; the second, covering the second millennium, from the medieval church to the modern period.

THE FIRST THOUSAND YEARS: FROM JESUS OF NAZARETH TO THE GREAT SCHISM

Jesus the Messiah

Christianity has its roots in the story of the people of Israel, much of which is described in the Hebrew scriptures or what Christians call the Old Testament. The first Christians were all Jews living in Palestine in the middle of the first century of what is now commonly accepted as the Christian era (CE). They acknowledged the God of 'Abraham, Isaac and Jacob' as their God, they worshipped in the Temple in Jerusalem, attended services in the synagogues, and they accepted the teachings of Moses and the prophets. What primarily distinguished them from other Jews at the time was their conviction that a certain wandering preacher and teacher, Jesus of Nazareth, who had been crucified by the Roman authorities at the instigation of Jewish religious and civil leaders, was the promised Messiah, God's anointed one or, in the Greek of the New Testament, the Christ.

Jesus, a name derived from the Hebrew word for 'saviour', was born in the town of Bethlehem, not far from Jerusalem, in the province of Judea in Palestine. The precise date of his birth is unknown, though in all probability it was a year or two before the death of King Herod the Great in 4 BCE, during the reign of Caesar Augustus, who ruled over the Roman empire from 27 BCE to 14 CE. Since 63 BCE, when Rome had gained control over Palestine, Roman political and military authority had firmly established itself in the region. Indeed, Herod was appointed king of the Jews by the Romans, and ruled in Jerusalem from 37 BCE until his death as a loyal servant of Rome. Roman rule, in fact, dominated not only the palestine of Jesus' day but the Mediterranean world as a whole, thus providing the political context in which the Christian movement was born and nurtured.

Judaism at the time of Jesus (*c.* 4 BCE–33 CE) was divided into several different groupings each of which had emerged in the centuries following the return of the Jews from exile in Babylon. All of them were concerned about the future of the nation and the restoration of the kingdom of Israel as it had once been under the reign of King David. But they differed quite fundamentally in their understanding of how this should be done, and in how it related to their religious traditions and convictions.

The Sadducees, who were religiously conservative but politically influential, advocated peaceful co-existence with the ruling Roman authorities, who in turn used them to govern the Jewish nation. Through the high priest and the priestly class, the Sadducees controlled the temple and its enormous wealth derived from tithes, taxes and land, and thus were the wealthy elite of the day. The Zealots, by way of contrast, were revolutionaries whose zeal for their religion and the

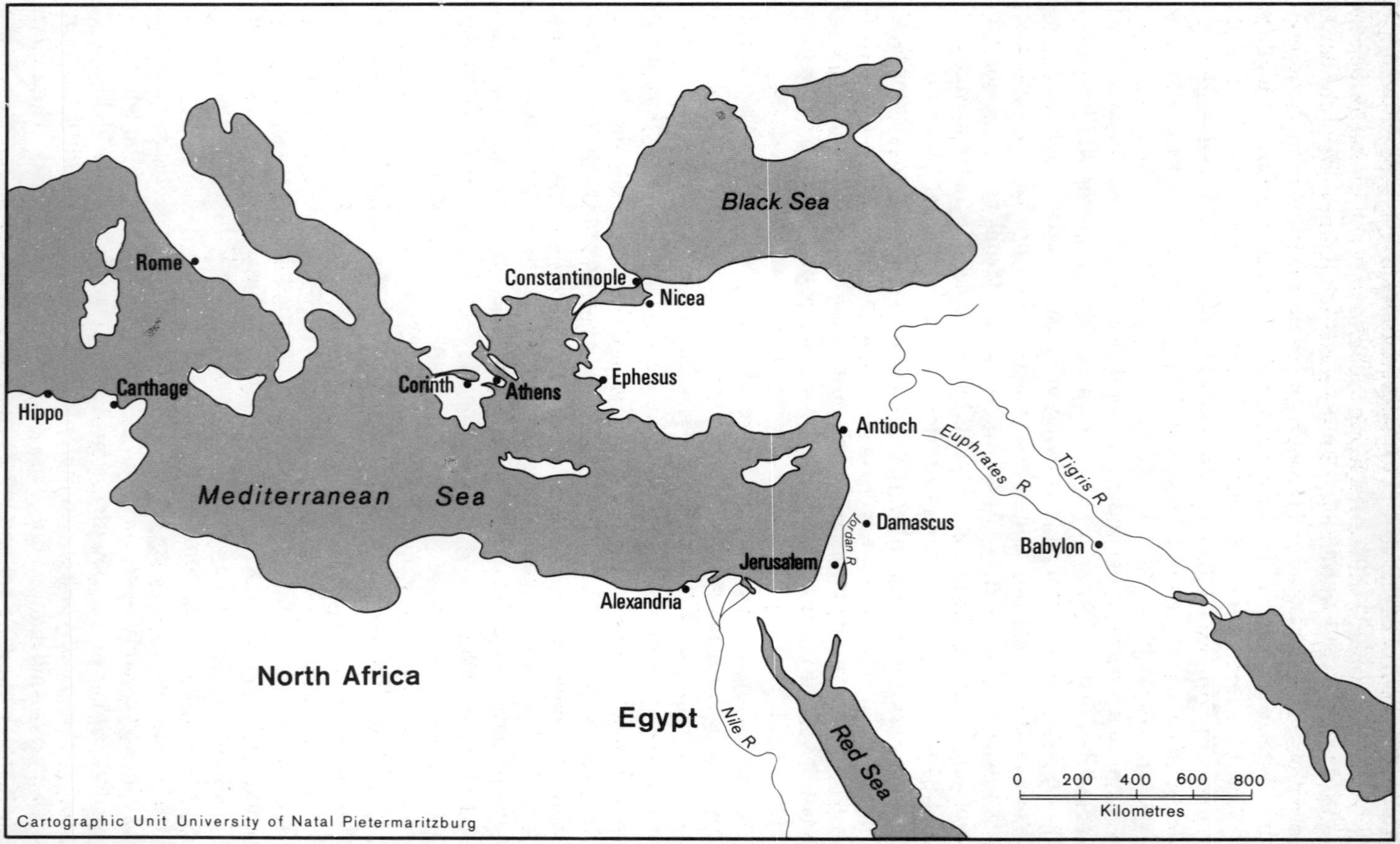
Black Sea
Rome
Constantinople
Nicea
Corinth
Athens
Ephesus
Carthage
Hippo
Antioch
Euphrates R
Tigris R
Mediterranean Sea
Damascus
Jordan R
Babylon
Jerusalem
Alexandria
North Africa
Egypt
Nile R
Red Sea
0 200 400 600 800
Kilometres
Cartographic Unit University of Natal Pietermaritzburg

national freedom of Israel led them to oppose and seek to overthrow Roman rule by violent resistance. The Essenes, living in community at Qumran on the edge of the Dead Sea, had withdrawn from the social and political life of the nation into monastic seclusion where, through prayer and the study of the Scriptures, they prepared themselves for the coming of God's righteous rule or kingdom.

The Pharisees, like the Essenes, were primarily concerned about God's righteous rule and its fulfilment in Israel, but instead of withdrawing into the desert they sought to live in absolute faithfulness to the Torah in the midst of the social and political life of the nation. In doing so they helped to lay solid foundations for Rabbinic Judaism. It was this form of Judaism alone which survived the destruction of Jerusalem by the Romans in 70 CE and the failure of the Bar Kochba revolt against Rome in 132 CE, as well as the subsequent diaspora of the nation. It was also the form of Judaism with which the early Christians were most familiar. Jesus of Nazareth belonged to none of these groups, but his life was lived in relation to them especially after he began his ministry at about the age of 30.

We know very little about Jesus' early life for the only records which we have about him are not biographies but testimonies of faith. These testimonies or gospels (from the Greek *eu-angel*, literally 'good news'), named Matthew, Mark, Luke, and John, comprise almost half the New Testament. They were written between about 65 CE and the end of the first century, though they were based upon earlier oral and written traditions which circulated amongst the early Christian communities or churches. The dates normally given for their final form are: Matthew 90 CE; Mark 70 CE; Luke 80–85 CE; John 90–95 CE.

The gospels contain many of Jesus' sayings and accounts of his deeds, but focus primarily upon the narrative of his birth and especially his death and resurrection from the dead. While Matthew, Mark and Luke, as distinct from John, are similar in structure and content (hence their designation 'synoptic gospels'), each gospel was written in a different setting and addressed to a specific audience. This accounts to a large extent for their diversity of approach and content. Despite their differences, however, they are all united in their proclamation that Jesus of Nazareth was God's chosen Messiah.

According to all four gospels, Jesus' ministry was introduced by the preaching of his cousin John the Baptist, an ascetic prophet, who, though he might have had some contact with the Qumran community, saw his responsibility to prepare the nation of Israel for the coming of God's righteous reign. His message was that the people of Israel should repent (Greek *metanoia*, literally 'change their hearts and minds') and be baptised (a rite of purification practised in Judaism), and thus live in expectation of the coming of the Messiah who would inaugurate the kingdom or reign of God. With the birth of Christianity, baptism would later become the rite whereby converts to Christianity were publicly accepted into the church.

Jesus himself was baptised by John, and so at the outset of his ministry identified with the people in their past sins and their hopes for God's coming kingdom. But Jesus went further, and after John was imprisoned by King Herod for his preaching, took the decisive step of proclaiming that with his own coming, God's rule was at hand. 'The time has come,' he said. 'The kingdom of God is near. Repent and believe the good news!' (Mark 1: 15) The phrase 'kingdom of heaven' which we generally find in Matthew means the same as 'kingdom of God'. Orthodox Jews refused to mention God by name so they often used a substitute, like 'heaven', in place of the sacred name, a custom which Matthew would have respected.

A significant number of gospel sayings indicate that Jesus perceived his primary mission as directed to the people of Israel. Yet it is equally true that Jesus' proclamation of the coming of God's kingdom did not coincide with the nationalistic aspirations of the major groups within Judaism which we have identified. Moreover, Jesus' teaching about the way in which the kingdom would come was significantly different. He did not join the Essenes in the desert in their withdrawal from social life in anticipation of the coming kingdom, nor did he join in the revolutionary struggle with the Zealots, even though Jesus had some sympathy for their cause. Indeed, the Jewish authorities in Jerusalem, the Sanhedrin, suspected him of being another one of a number of messianic pretenders who had arisen to drive the Romans into the sea and establish his own kingdom. Jesus was thus a threat to their politics of co-operation with the Romans and therefore to their own self-interests, not least those derived from the wealth of the Temple. This was a major reason why they eventually sought his death.

The group with which Jesus had most contact was the Pharisees. They were most prominent as teachers of the people and Jesus was, in some respects, a rabbi or teacher like them. Much of Jesus' teaching was similar to theirs, but whereas the Pharisees of his day stressed strict obedience to the Law of Moses or the Torah (the written and oral tradition handed down from the fathers) as the way to remain faithful to the covenant relationship with God and thus enjoy God's blessing, Jesus sought to reinterpret the Torah by going behind the tradition to what he perceived to be its original meaning and intention. He taught with a sense of personal authority; hence, for example, he declared: 'You have heard that it was said to the people long ago, "Do not murder, and anyone who murders will be subject to judgement." But I tell you that anyone who is angry with his brother will be subject to judgement' (Matt. 5: 21). Moreover, while Jesus, according to the gospels, felt a special responsibility towards the Jews, his ministry reached out to include all people irrespective of their nationality or class, something which was perceived by orthodox religious leaders as a threat to the very existence of Judaism.

Jesus not only rejected the strategies of the Sadducees, Essenes, Zealots and Pharisees in establishing God's kingdom, his understanding of the kingdom was also fundamentally different. The message of the kingdom which Jesus proclaimed was not about the restoration of the kingdom of David as a political entity, but the transformation of human society and life as a whole. It was, in fact, the universal vision of the kingdom anticipated by the servant songs of the Book of Isaiah. It is therefore understandable that those whose vision of the kingdom was determined by nationalistic hopes, exclusive to the future of the Jewish people, misunderstood what Jesus taught.

At the same time, the gospels make it very clear that what Jesus proclaimed about the kingdom was received as good news by the common people, especially in Galilee, who often found the strict teaching of the Pharisees more than they could manage to live by, and moreover suffered repression at the hands of the Roman authorities and their Jewish surrogates. Indeed, as Luke tells the story, when Jesus' mother, Mary, was first told about the child she was to give birth to, she burst into song, declaring that God

> has brought down rulers from their thrones but has lifted up the humble. He has filled the hungry with good things but has sent the rich away empty . . . (Luke 1: 52–3)

Jesus understood his own task and mission in similar terms. In his first recorded sermon in his home town of Nazareth, Luke tells us (4: 16–21), Jesus read from the scroll of the prophet Isaiah (61: 1–2):

> The Spirit of the Lord is on me, because he has anointed me to preach good news to the poor. He has sent me to proclaim freedom for prisoners and recovery of sight for the blind, to release the oppressed, to proclaim the year of the Lord's favour.

Having done so, Jesus then identified himself with the prophet's words. 'Today this scripture,' he said, 'is fulfilled in your hearing.' Although these words would have brought joy to the poor, the hungry, the sick, and the oppressed, they also evoked opposition. It was not easy for the people of his home town, and especially their religious leaders, to accept what sounded like blasphemous arrogance. So it is not surprising to read that they were furious, drove him out of the town, and tried to kill him (Luke 4: 28–30). Thus, right from the outset of Jesus' ministry a pattern of conflict was established between him and those who felt threatened by him.

Jesus' preaching and teaching did, however, initially attract the crowds, especially in the villages and towns along the coast of the Sea of Galilee. And it was there that he began to gather around him an inner core of disciples of men and women. Notable amongst these were the fishermen Peter, James, and John, but the circle also included a converted tax-gatherer, Matthew, a few Zealots, and notably several women, one of whom was Mary of Magdala, a former prostitute. Jesus' teaching was directed chiefly to them as they journeyed with him from one village to the next, and as Jesus sought to build them into a community of God's kingdom. Thus much of the teaching was in the form of parables which sought to describe the nature of God's kingdom, how one should anticipate it, how one could enter it, and how one should live accordingly. Of particular importance was Jesus' famous Sermon on the Mount (Matt. 5–7, see also Luke 6: 17–49) which is a composite summary of his teaching on what it means to live as part of God's kingdom, or Jesus' reinterpretation of the Torah.

The gospel stories are full of episodes in which Jesus encounters people who either join him and his disciples, or, for a variety of reasons, turn away from him and reject his message. Jesus had no qualms about meeting and relating to people of all kinds and reputations, whether they were Pharisees, Roman soldiers, despised Samaritans, lepers or harlots, and much of his ministry was spent in healing the sick. In fact, Jesus must have appeared to his contemporaries much like other charismatic rabbis who were well known, especially in Galilee, for their power to heal. For Jesus' healing was not an end in itself, as much as he had compassion for all in need, it was a sign of God's reign. Through his healing of the sick Jesus was proclaiming that God's kingdom was imminent, and that its coming meant the healing of God's people and the establishment of God's purposes of *shalom* (a Hebrew word for the peace or wholeness of God's future reign on earth.)

A very important element in Jesus' teaching concerned the 'Son of Man'. This phrase could simply mean a 'human being', as it often does in Hebrew and Aramaic (the language Jesus spoke), but when used by Jesus it more likely refers to the enigmatic figure we read about in the Book of Daniel (7: 13–14). In Daniel's dream, the 'Son of Man' is God's anointed agent who would come at the end of the ages to fulfil God's purposes and establish God's kingdom. In some of Jesus' key parables he spoke of the 'Son of Man' as one who was yet to come, and scholars therefore disagree on whether or not Jesus had himself in mind. Jesus' identification with the 'Son of Man' is suggested at various places in the gospels, however, and there is no doubt that the early Christian community came to believe that he was God's anointed agent to whom 'all authority, glory and sovereign power' (Dan. 7: 14) had been given, and that he would return at the end of the ages to exercise his rule. Jesus himself, according to the synoptic gospels, believed that the kingdom of God, the coming of the Son of Man, and the hour of judgement for the world, was at hand. Thus his teaching is set in an eschatological framework and sometimes expressed in vividly apocalyptic terms (see Mark 13). ('Eschatology' is a technical term referring to looking at the present age and its order in terms of its anticipated end and the fulfilment of God's reign; 'apocalyptic' is a particular mythical way of describing the end of the present age in terms of cosmic upheavals through which the new age is born.)

Throughout the synoptic gospels there is a tension between the kingdom which the early Christians believed had been ushered in through the death and resurrection of Jesus, and the final manifestation of that kingdom at the end of the ages. In John's gospel the tension is largely overcome. This can be seen in the fact that the fourth gospel generally substitutes the phrase 'eternal life' or 'life in the new age' for the kingdom of God, and by the proclamation that in Jesus such life is both a present and future reality for those who believe in him. None the less, early Christian belief, liturgy and practice were profoundly eschatological and strongly influenced by apocalyptic ideas, as can be seen for example in the final book in the New Testament, the Revelations or Apocalypse according to John.

Central to Jesus' teaching was his understanding of God as a father or, in Aramaic, *Abba*. By using this metaphor for God, Jesus did not intend that his hearers should perceive of God in masculine terms (he also used a feminine metaphor for God, see Matt. 23: 37), but rather in terms of personal relationship. Moreover, Jesus understood his own relationship to God in similar terms. If scholars are divided in their opinion on the relationship between Jesus and the 'Son of Man', there is consensus (at least among Christian scholars) that Jesus was conscious of a very special relationship with God. This is seen in the way in which he referred to God as his *Abba*. There is no doubt that Jesus was a normal human being, not some kind of demi-god who was somehow not fully like the rest of humanity. Jesus got hungry, he grew thirsty and tired, he was tempted, he enjoyed company and times of family celebration, and his death at the end was one of severe pain and agony. But in describing Jesus' relationship to God as his father, the gospels also point to a reality which paradoxically marks Jesus off from the rest of humanity. Of course, it is impossible to plumb the depths of Jesus' own consciousness and psyche, a task which many have tried without success. Nevertheless, his relationship with God as *Abba* has a remarkable uniqueness about it, and one which surfaces at crucial moments in the gospel accounts, supremely during the events which culminate in his death and his final cry from the cross: 'Father, into your hands I commit my spirit' (Luke 23: 26).

Much of the gospel narrative has to do with Jesus' final days in Jerusalem, his dramatic entry into the city, his last supper with his disciples (which became the basis for the later Christian rite of Holy Communion or the Eucharist), his passion (or suffering) and death, and the claim of the first Christians that he had risen from the dead on the third day. The authority of Jesus' life, ministry and teaching was all dependent upon the fact that he suffered death for the sins of his people Israel, and, more especially, that God had raised him from the dead, thus vindicating who he was and what he had done. Jesus' death and resurrection was at the heart of the good news which the early Christian community proclaimed.

Jesus' death (either during the Jewish Passover in 30 or 33 CE) was the result of a combination of forces. The charge which the Jewish authorities in Jerusalem, the Sanhedrin, brought against Jesus was twofold. On the one hand, they charged him with blasphemy, a charge which appealed to orthodox Judaism; on the other hand, they charged that he was seeking to lead a violent insurrection in order to become the king of the Jews, a charge aimed at getting a death penalty conviction by crucifixion from the Roman authorities, who really did not wish to become embroiled in Jewish religious matters.

In his claim to forgive sins, in his teaching about the 'Son of Man', and in his challenge to the traditional teaching of the Pharisees, Jesus had, from the Pharisees' perspective, clearly blasphemed – that is, usurped God's authority and brought discredit to his sacred name. This was an unpardonable sin, and the Pharisees sincerely believed that such blasphemy would bring judgement on Israel. So Jesus had to die as one cursed by God and, as the high priest who condemned him to death declared, 'for the sake of the nation'. But this religious charge of blasphemy, however real, was in many ways a smokescreen for the true reason the authorities sought Jesus' death.

Although Jesus had made it clear that his teaching about the kingdom of God was not to be understood in political terms, even though it had clear social implications, the Jewish authorities and, indeed, the Roman as well were clearly worried about the appeal which Jesus had for many people, especially the more disadvantaged in society. Matters reached a climax when Jesus entered the city of Jerusalem on what is now known as Palm Sunday, and then proceeded to 'cleanse the Temple' (Matt. 21). This prophetic act was a direct challenge to the authority of the Sanhedrin, and a threat to the influence and wealth of the Sadducees and the priestly class. And, in so far as the Romans needed the Sanhedrin and the Sadducees to maintain law and order in society, it was also a threat to Rome. Despite their fundamental misunderstanding of his ministry and purpose, they were correct in perceiving the threat which Jesus presented to their material interests and position in society. They knew they had to get rid of him once and for all. Jesus, as his mother Mary perceived at the time of his birth, had become too much of a threat to the powerful, the mighty and the proud.

The story of Jesus of Nazareth, at one level, ends at the time of his death on the cross. For the first Christians Jesus' resurrection was as much an event in history as was his death, and the gospels take great pains to make this point. But they also indicate that it was an event which transcended history and was, as such, a matter of faith beyond historical proof. The belief that he rose again from the dead was clearly not something shared by all people living in Jerusalem or Israel at the time or else in all probability many more would have become Christians. What distinguished the first Christians from their fellow Jews was precisely the conviction that Jesus had been raised by God from the dead and thus vindicated as Messiah. This is the corner-stone of Christian belief, for without it there would be no church and, Christians believe, no good news about God's kingdom and salvation.

From Jewish sect to universal faith

Although the first Christians were all Jews who believed in Jesus as the Messiah, the Christian movement soon spread beyond the confines of Judaism into the gentile world. This is the major theme of The Acts of the Apostles, written sometime between 80 and 85 CE by Luke, the author of the gospel bearing his name. Acts is, in fact, a continuation of the gospel story, and like the gospels it is not primarily a historical text but a testimony of believers, only in this instance their witness is to the ongoing work of Jesus the Messiah through his Spirit at work in the Christian community.

The story of the primitive church as told in Acts begins with the risen Jesus meeting with his disciples and continuing his teaching about the kingdom of God. Ironically, as the text indicates, the disciples had still not fully understood Jesus' teaching and mission. Nevertheless, before his departure from them, depicted as an ascension into heaven, Jesus commands his disciples to proclaim the good news of the kingdom to all peoples and nations, and promises them the power and authority of God's Spirit to carry out the task.

The gift of the Holy Spirit to the assembled believers on the day of the Jewish feast of Pentecost (the Feast of Weeks celebrating the first fruits of the wheat harvest) marked the birth of the Christian community or church (*ekklesia*, the Greek equivalent of *synagogue*, meaning 'an assembly of people'). From this point on, under the leadership of Jesus' former disciples, notably Peter, now designated apostles ('those who are sent'), the Christian movement began to expand. At the centre of its mission was the apostolic proclamation that Jesus of Nazareth, the one who was crucified by the authorities in Jerusalem, had been raised from the dead by God, and thus had been vindicated by God as the Messiah of Israel. Moreover, they continued, Jesus the Messiah was present through the Holy Spirit, a belief demonstrated by the ability of the apostles to heal the sick in Jesus' name.

The preaching (*kerygma*) of the first apostles and missionaries had a common core and followed a basic pattern which has been summarised as follows:

> The prophecies are fulfilled, and the new Age is inaugurated by the coming of Christ. He was born of the seed of David. He died according to the Scriptures, to deliver us out of the present evil age. He was buried. He rose again on the third day according to the Scriptures. He is exalted at the right hand of God, as Son of God and Lord of the living and the dead. He will come again as Judge and Saviour.[1]

Despite this distinctive and unifying tradition which characterised the preaching of the early church, it is also clear from the New Testament that the apostolic preaching was shaped by different situations and contexts, and that this in turn affected the content of the gospel as well. Indeed, it has been argued that in 'different situations the actual gospel was different, and could be as different as the situations themselves'.[2] The good news concerning Jesus Christ was addressed to diverse situations, which required that the preaching be adapted to meet different human and social needs.

As described by Acts, the early Christian community in Jerusalem grew rapidly. A major reason for this growth was the communal and caring quality of its life. We get a glimpse into this early community in the vivid description given by Luke:

> They devoted themselves to the apostles' teaching and to the fellowship, to the breaking of bread and to prayer. Everyone was filled with awe, and many wonders and miraculous signs were done by the apostles. All believers were together and had everything in common. Selling their possessions and goods, they gave to anyone as he had need. Every day they continued to meet together in the temple courts. They broke bread in their homes and ate together with glad and sincere hearts, praising God and enjoying the favour of all the people. And the Lord added to their number daily those who were being saved. (Acts 2: 42–7)

This passage captures several dimensions of the life of the early Christian church, even though it is somewhat idealised. It refers to the fact that the church regarded the testimony of the apostles concerning Jesus as their guide and authority; they met regularly for fellowship (*koinonia*, or sharing a common life), the 'breaking of bread' (a reference to the Lord's Supper or early Eucharistic worship), and prayer. It is noteworthy that they continued to worship in the Temple, but it is equally important to note that they 'broke bread' in their homes. This indicates that while they still identified with Judaism, the celebration of the supper of the Lord was something which bound them to each other in a unique way. This sense of belonging found expression in their caring for each other, even to the extent of selling their private possessions to ensure that everyone in the community had sufficient for his or her needs. At the same time, the community reached beyond itself as the apostles performed miraculous deeds. The effect of all this was not only winning high regard within the wider community, and attracting many others into its life, but also arousing opposition from the Jewish authorities and, through them, the Roman authorities.

Rapid growth required the development of an organisation which could cope with the demands of an increasing number of people, especially widows and others in need. In order to meet this demand, and to enable the apostles to continue their work of ministry, a team of seven helpers (sometimes regarded as the first 'deacons', from *diakonia* meaning 'service') was chosen to assist in the day-to-day practical affairs of the community. It is noteworthy that all of them have Hellenistic or Greek names, indicating that the primitive church had already begun to include within its membership Greek-speaking (or Hellenistic) Jews.

The growing strength of the church in Jerusalem and beyond inevitably attracted the attention of the Jewish authorities and in turn, the attention of the Roman authorities. Luke is at pains to show, however, that the first Christians were not a threat to the Roman empire. Indeed, Acts is in many ways an apologia for the church, addressed as it was to a Roman benefactor, Theophilus, who may well have been an important government official. At the same time, however, the preaching of the good news concerning Jesus the Messiah brought the apostles and other Christian preachers into conflict with the Jewish civic and religious leaders. Earlier on Peter and John had to make it clear to the Jewish authorities that they would not desist from preaching that Jesus was the Messiah, and that even if they were ordered not to do so they had to 'obey God rather than man' (Acts 5: 29).

Such boldness resulted in the death of the first martyr (*marturion*, literally a witness), Stephen, who had been one of the seven elected to serve the Jerusalem church, but who was clearly a persuasive preacher as well. Stephen's speech before the Sanhedrin (Acts 7: 1–53) is a forthright statement of the conviction that Jesus is the Messiah promised by God to the children of Israel, a promise which is traced back to the call of Abraham. It is equally a powerful declaration that Jesus, like the Hebrew prophets of old, was rejected and murdered by the people of Israel, especially their leaders. Given the content and tone of his speech before the Sanhedrin, it is not surprising that he was stoned to death. It is also not surprising that the church as a whole was persecuted and scattered, a fact which, ironically, led not only to the dispersion of Christians but also to the spreading of their message concerning Jesus the Messiah.

The New Testament is largely silent on the early expansion of the Christian movement into such places as North Africa, but it does tell us a significant amount about its development in Asia Minor and Greece, and thus about its encounter with the Hellenistic culture of the Roman empire. According to Acts, the apostle Peter was the first to discover that God's purpose for the church was not to be confined to Jews. But it was the apostle Paul who really became the missionary to the gentiles, and who played a major role in enabling the church to spread and consolidate throughout the Roman empire. The account of his three famous missionary journeys, his eventual arrest in Jerusalem by the Jewish authorities, and his final journey to Rome to stand trial, take up a considerable part of the Acts of the Apostles.

Thus, while the story of Acts begins in Jerusalem and focuses especially on the ministry of the apostles Peter, James, John, the evangelist Philip, and the martyr Stephen, the principal character for two-thirds of the story is Paul of Tarsus, a converted Pharisee and missionary to the gentiles. Paul's conversion while on a journey to persecute Christians in Damascus was one of the most celebrated events in the early church; it was also an event which had far-reaching consequences for its development. Indeed, some liberal scholars in the nineteenth century argued that Paul distorted the simple message of Jesus about the kingdom of God and began the long process which led to the formulation of Christian dogma and the institutional church as we know it. This hypothesis is not widely held any longer, but it is true that with the ministry of Paul the church took a major leap forward in its movement beyond Judaism into the gentile world. It is also true that Paul played a very influential role in the development of early Christian theology and doctrine.

Much recent scholarship has focused on the social composition of gentile Christianity and, in particular, on the congregations founded by Paul. There can be little doubt that the message of Jesus and the kingdom of God had a special attraction for the disadvantaged and poorer sections of society. This comes out clearly in the synoptic gospels. But as Christianity made inroads into the Greek and Roman worlds, it resembled less and less what we would now call a proletarian movement. Certainly, slaves figure prominently in the Pauline literature, but the picture presented is of urban congregations made up of a cross-section of society, with the exception of those at the very top and even the very bottom of the social ladder. Furthermore, the radical egalitarian teaching of Jesus, echoed by Paul in his letter to the Galatians, and the communalism of the primitive church in Jerusalem, was gradually replaced by the patriarchal and hierarchical values of the Roman world.

Paul's letters to the various churches he founded, or with whom he had close contact, form much of the New Testament outside the gospels. Each of the letters deals with issues and problems which affected the life of the churches. The earliest of these, Paul's first letter to the church in Thessalonika, written about 49 CE, deals for example, with problems resulting from the perceived delay in the return of Jesus, or the *parousia*. Other significant issues were the challenge of Gnosticism (Colossians), divisions caused by charismatic gifts (I Corinthians), the relationship between Christian masters and slaves (Philemon) and, in particular, the relationship between Jews and gentiles in the church (Galatians and Romans). The letter to the Romans is also the fullest expression of Paul's theology as a whole.

Paul's theology is multi-dimensional, ranging from his doctrine of justification by grace through faith and new life in the Spirit, to his understanding of the church as the 'body of Christ', Jesus as the cosmic Lord, and ethics as a response of gratitude to God rather than a set of precepts to be obeyed. Central to all else was his teaching that the death of Jesus Christ on the cross and his resurrection from the dead are the means whereby humankind is saved from sin and its consequences. For Paul, as for primitive and especially gentile Christianity, the basic declaration of Christian faith was the claim that 'Jesus is Lord' (*kurios*). This was the confession of faith required at baptism, and would bring Christians into conflict with the Roman authorities, for whom the emperor had a divine status.

Besides those of Paul, there are other letters and writings which, together with the gospels and Acts, comprise the New Testament. These others letters (including I & II Peter; I, II, & III John; and Hebrews) also address pastoral problems in various congregations or regions. The final book in the New Testament, the Revelation of John (written c. 95 CE), is apocalyptic in character. That is, like the Book of Daniel, it provides a mythical interpretation of history seen from the perspective of God's redemptive purposes. Its intention is to affirm God's ultimate victory over the powers of evil through the death and resurrection of Jesus, and thereby to encourage and enable the church to endure persecution and trial in the present.

Paul's advocacy of the gospel as a message of freedom from the obligation to obey the Jewish dietary and other religious observances eventually won the day, after much struggle over the Judaisers, who wanted Christianity to remain faithful to Jewish legal observances. We get some insight into this struggle from the account of the Jerusalem Council, probably held in 49 CE, described in Acts 15. Indeed, it was only after the destruction of Jerusalem in 70 CE and the failure of the Bar Kochba revolt in 132 CE, together with the diaspora of the Jews and the expulsion of Christians from the synagogues, that the Christian movement finally separated from Judaism and became a distinct religion on its own.

Indeed, Christians who survived interpreted the destruction of Jerusalem as a judgement of God on the blind and vindictive Jewish nation because it had rejected Jesus the Messiah. All the more was this attitude in evidence during the revolt of Bar Kochba. Christians had by that time completely separated themselves from the forces of Jewish nationalism and took no part in the revolt. They particularly rejected the claims to messiahship put forward by the followers of bar Kochba. They rejoiced at his downfall. For his part the Jewish leader regarded the Christians as a dangerous fifth column. So the parting of the ways between Judaism and Christianity became firmly entrenched setting the stage for the centuries of antagonism which were to come.

Orthodoxy and heresy

The rapid and dramatic development of Christianity beyond the confines of Judaism into the complex world of Hellenistic culture had a profound impact upon the church. It was one thing to proclaim to Jews that Jesus of Nazareth was the Messiah who fulfilled the hopes of Israel, it was quite another to interpret what this meant to Greek-speaking gentiles for whom the Hebrew scriptures and the messianic expectations of the Jewish prophets and people were unknown and meaningless. Moreover, Christianity increasingly became a universal religion with a majority of gentile believers, so its leadership soon changed. By the second century, in fact, all the major church leaders and theologians were non-Jews. The problem which they faced was no longer to convince Judaism that Jesus was the Messiah, nor was it to counter the Judaisers who wished to keep the Christian movement as a Jewish sect. The challenge which they faced was translating Christian faith and practice into a very different cultural context and philosophical world-view, while at the same time remaining faithful to the gospel.

The key figures in enabling the church to meet this challenge are usually referred to as the second-century Apologists or, more broadly, the Apostolic Fathers who dominated the shaping of the life and teaching of the church until the fifth century. It was during these first four centuries of the church's existence that the boundaries of Christian orthodoxy (that is, right belief) were established and the church was given its classic episcopal institutional form (dioceses or regions ruled by bishops). This 'primitive catholicism' or what some scholars refer to as the beginnings of the 'great church', emerged in the struggle against wrong belief or heresy (from *haeresis*, a wrong choice), and competing movements and sources of authority which often led to schism or division.

In speaking about heresy, it must be kept in mind that heretics regarded themselves as faithful Christians, and they were by no means less moral or intelligent than those regarded as orthodox. In fact, in their teaching some of those who were rejected as heretics rediscovered elements in early Christianity which had been lost, and the movements they generated sometimes began as a protest against the laxity of dominant groups and clericalism. It must also be kept in mind that sometimes what was initially regarded as true and acceptable was later rejected as false. From the perspective of emergent orthodoxy, however, heresy, however legitimate its protest, was one-sided and destructive of the gospel, and heretics were obstinate and self-willed people who had no apostolic mandate. The designation 'heresy' or 'heretic' thus presupposed the emergence and perspective of a dominant and controlling orthodoxy. A very early heresy was Ebionitism, a movement that sought to keep Christianity Jewish. But as Christianity penetrated the gentile world, the chief heresies that challenged the defenders of orthodoxy were Gnosticism, Montanism and Marcionism.

Gnosticism was a complex phenomenon found throughout the Middle East. Indeed, some influential Gnostics were members of the church itself who were engaged in trying to interpret Christianity to a pagan world in as creative a way as possible. Gnosticism's often brilliant leaders were united in teaching that human redemption is achieved through special knowledge or wisdom (*gnosis*). The material world or matter was regarded as the source of the human predicament, and therefore the Gnostics rejected the God of the Old Testament, the Creator of the world, in favour of the redeemer God of the spirit. Through initiation into the sacred mysteries the elect were enabled to know this saviour God and transcend the bondage of the body and the material world. A consequence of this view was the rejection of the incarnation of Jesus, that is, the belief that Jesus as Son of God became a truly human being 'in the flesh'. Jesus was regarded, rather, as some kind of demi-god similar to the dying-and-rising-again redeemer figures found in the mythology of some Hellenistic mystery cults.

Montanism, named after a self-styled prophet Montanus, was an apocalyptic movement which emerged towards the end of the second century in Asia Minor. Sometime around 156 CE, or perhaps 172 CE (depending on which source we follow), Montanus had prophesied the imminent end of the world, and the coming of the New Jerusalem in Phrygia, near where he lived. Prophets were relatively common in the first few centuries of Christianity, but amongst the leaders of the church there was also a growing wariness of their teaching if it smacked in any way of novelty in faith or practice. For the orthodox, Montanism undermined the historic truth which had been handed down from the apostles through the recognised leadership of the church. By the same token, Montanism was a reaction to the growing institutionalisation of the church, emphasising as it did the freedom of the Spirit and rediscovering the apocalyptic expectations of primitive Christianity. It also promoted an ascetic and rigorous form of Christian discipline which was to attract into its membership none other than Tertullian, the North African father of Latin Christian theology.

Marcionism was a movement which traced its origins to Marcion (died *c.* 160), a dedicated missionary and son of a bishop, who was passionately committed to rejecting everything Jewish in Christianity. This meant a radical separation of the gospel from the Torah, the rejection of the Old Testament and God the Creator, and all apostolic writings which stressed the continuity between Christianity and Judaism. Indeed, for Marcion only the writings of Paul and the gospel according to Luke were regarded as truly Christian. For Marcion, as for Gnosticism, Jesus Christ was not truly human simply because one coming from the true God could not have been born in the flesh of woman.

In their response to Gnosticism, Montanism and Marcionism, the Apologists, notably Clement of Rome (*fl. c.* 96), Ignatius of Antioch (*c.* 35–*c.* 107), Justin Martyr (*c.* 100–*c.* 165), and Irenaeus of Lyons (*c.* 130–*c.* 200), strongly affirmed the unity of God the creator and redeemer, the reality of the incarnation of Jesus Christ, the goodness of creation and the body, the witness of the Spirit to Christ, and the continuity between Christianity and the Old Testament, the law and the gospel, prophecy and its fulfilment in Jesus Christ. In their opposition to heresy, the Apologists and early Church Fathers appealed to a 'rule of faith' which they claimed went back to the apostles themselves; they asserted the continuity of apostolic succession and authority through the acknowledged bishops of the catholic (that is, universal) church; and they made a decisive contribution to the final composition of the New Testament. Although the early Apologists were sometimes not as brilliant as their opponents, and often rather legalistic, they laid some of the key theological and philosophical foundation stones upon which classical Christian doctrine was soon to be built.

The Bible used by the early Christian church was the Greek translation of the Hebrew scriptures known as the Septuagint. It was the Septuagint which was read in worship and from which many of the Old Testament quotations which we find in the New Testament were originally taken. As the gospels, the writings of Paul and other apostles and missionaries began to circulate, these provided a secondary source of scripture. But the question soon arose as to which of these specifically Christian writings should be regarded as authoritative for the life and faith of the church as a whole, and which should be rejected as apocryphal (of doubtful authenticity). This question led to the process which we now call the 'formation of the canon' (*kanon*, rule, measure, standard).

Three considerations were dominant in the writings of the Apologists in determining the canon. Firstly, whether the writing in question had apostolic authority, having been written either by an apostle or by someone in close contact with an apostle; secondly, whether the writing was accepted by the universal church and not just a particular congregation; and thirdly, whether its contents strengthened and built up the church in its faith and practice. By 170 the Muratorian Canon of the church in Rome was widely accepted. It listed much of what is now in the New Testament. There were, however, differences of opinion amongst the churches on some writings and it took until the fourth century to finalise the matter. The canon was formally closed at the Council of Carthage (397 and 419).

The formation of the canon of the New Testament was conterminous with the development of the institutional structures of the church. From earliest times each congregation appears to have had recognised leaders known as elders, presbyters or bishops (*episcopoi*), together with deacons. But gradually the office of presbyter was distinguished from that of bishop. Bishops became representative leaders of several congregations within a particular city or region called a diocese (a term used in the Roman imperial administration).

Within a short space of time several dioceses became prominent, notably Antioch, Alexandria, Byzantium, Carthage and Rome. Each of these tended to become a focus of different emphases and even interpretations of the Christian faith, and sometimes there was theological and political conflict between them. In due course, the church in Rome, on the grounds that its first bishop was the apostle Peter, but also because of its location at the centre of the empire, achieved pre-eminence. In order to maintain unity it soon became necessary to hold councils and synods of the bishops at which matters of common concern could be considered. As the bishops were regarded as standing in succession to the apostles, these councils gained binding authority for faith and practice as interpreters of Scripture and the tradition of the church.

Christian beliefs

Central to the development of the church, and crucial in both combating heresy and maintaining unity, was the need to clarify the tenets of the Christian faith. At the heart of this was the need for clarity and consensus on the person of Jesus Christ, his relationship to God, and the nature and meaning of his redemption. Although the debates which took place on these issues were highly intellectual, they arose not out of an interest in philosophy but a practical concern for preaching the gospel in a Hellenistic cultural environment.

A central concept in Hellenistic philosophy, especially in Stoicism, was that of the *Logos*. Literally it meant 'word' or 'reason', but as used in philosophical discourse it also signified the divine source of all existing things, the unifying principle of the universe. In the Greek Old Testament (Septuagint) *Logos* translated the Hebrew word for divine wisdom through which the world was created, and in the New Testament gospel of John, *Logos* refers directly to Jesus Christ (John 1: 1–14). Indeed, it is John who makes the profound declaration that the *Logos* 'was with God from the beginning', and that the *Logos* 'became flesh and dwelt amongst us'. In view of this background it is understandable why *Logos* was used by the Apologists and early Church Fathers, notably Clement (*c.* 150–*c.* 215) and Origen (*c.* 185–254) in Alexandria, to interpret the meaning of Jesus to their Hellenistic culture. Through the *Logos* doctrine they were able to affirm both the unity of Jesus with God, and the full humanity of Jesus 'in the flesh'. This laid the foundation for the developments which led to the classical Christology and trinitarian theology of the creeds.

The *Logos* doctrine is a good example of the way in which theologians attempted to relate Christian faith to contemporary philosophy. Indeed, Justin Martyr (d. 165) saw Hellenistic philosophy as preparing the gentile world for the gospel in the same way as the Old Testament prepared the Jews for the coming of the Messiah. This attempt to positively relate Christian faith and pagan philosophy was a characteristic of Alexandrian theology. This is not surprising, since Alexandria had been the home of the Jewish philosopher Philo who had sought to reinterpret Judaism in terms of Platonic philosophy. But not all orthodox interpreters of Christian faith took such a positive view of Hellenistic philosophy.

The first major theologian in the West, Tertullian (*c.* 160–*c.* 225), who spent a great deal of time combating Gnosticism and Marcionism, regarded the gospel as confronting rather than creatively relating to Hellenism. 'What indeed has Athens to do with Jerusalem?' he asked. 'What has the academy to do with the church? Away with all attempts to produce a Stoic, Platonic and dialectic Christianity!' Philosophy, from Tertullian's point of view, was a source of heresy. Tertullian's attitude, and his conversion to the ascetic and heretical Montanist movement, are understandable, given the fact that the North African church suffered greatly during times of Roman persecution, and had to struggle to keep its faith pure and its commitment to Christ as Lord strong, against the laxity of many church leaders and members. Tertullian, none the less, provided the terminology for the development of orthodox Trinitarian theology in the Latin or Western church.

The successors to Clement and Origen in Alexandria, Athanasius (*c.* 296–373) and Cyril (d. 444), were the great expositors and defenders of Christian orthodoxy. It was in the East, however, especially in Antioch and Alexandria that Christological and Trinitarian theology developed. Indeed, one of the most serious challenges to Christian orthodoxy emerged in Alexandria where a presbyter by the name of Arius (*c.* 250–*c.* 336) accused his bishop of failing to distinguish between God the Father and God the Son (Jesus Christ). Arius argued that God's essence (*ousia*) could not be shared with any other. He therefore declared that the *Logos* was not essentially God but a created being. There was a time, Arius argued, 'when he was not'. Thus while Jesus was in some sense divine and therefore similar to God (*homoiousia*), he was not of the same essence (*homoousia*) as God. Arius had influential friends, and his challenge sent shock waves through the church. His major opponent, and defender of orthodoxy, the bishop Athanasius, was, because of his opposition to Arianism, regularly sent into exile by the emperor. But Athanasius stood firm by his conviction that Arianism meant the undermining of the Christian doctrine of God and redemption in Christ.

In the debates that ensued, two polarising tendencies emerged. Some Alexandrians, in seeking to be faithful to the Logos Christology, took this position to an extreme, which led them to deny the humanity of Jesus. The most famous of these was Apollinarius (*c.* 310–390). In contrast to the theologians of Alexandria, those of Antioch, notably Gregory of Nazianzus (*c.* 329–389), without denying the divinity of Jesus, stressed his full humanity. This, in turn, also led some Antiochenes into heresy. Nestorius (d. *c.* 451), and especially his followers, for example, denied that Jesus was 'fully God'. The struggle to articulate Christian orthodoxy in which Jesus was acknowledged as 'fully God' and 'fully human' was thus a struggle to hold together the emphases of both Alexandria and Antioch without allowing either of them to deny the other.

The challenge of heresy, beginning with that of the Judaisers, the Gnostics, Montanus and Marcion, and then that of Apollinarianism, Nestorianism, Arianism, and several variations of each, eventually led to the clarification of orthodox Christian belief in the doctrine of the Trinity. The process was a long and complicated one that sometimes took on political significance. Indeed, it was the Christian emperor Constantine who convened the bishops together at the Council of Nicaea in 325 in order that they should resolve the issue. Constantine's major concern was the unity of the empire and therefore the unity of the church. But the theological issue which lay behind the debate was the culmination of a process which began the moment Christianity moved beyond the confines of Judaism into the Hellenistic world. Namely, how does one affirm the unity of God and at the same time confess that Jesus Christ is truly God incarnate fully in human form? Moreover, how does one do so, not in the dynamic language and Hebraic thought forms of the Bible but in the more static philosophical categories of Hellenistic thought? Many of the problems of understanding and interpretation which divided theologians then, and continue to do so, have their roots in precisely this problem.

The Council of Nicaea did not fully resolve the problem, but it clarified the issues. Throughout the following decades controversy continued unabated as orthodox theologians countered Apollinarianism on the one hand and Nestorianism on the other, and refinements of both. A major step towards the resolution of the issue was taken at the Council of Constantinople in 381 when the Nicene Creed was adopted and Arianism finally defeated. At the Council of Chalcedon in 451 it was finally resolved, at least from the perspective of orthodox Christianity, and the Nicene Creed became the basis for orthodox belief.

THE NICENE CREED

We believe in one God,
the Father, the Almighty,
Maker of heaven and earth,
of all that is,
seen and unseen.
We believe in one Lord, Jesus Christ,
the only Son of God,
eternally begotten of the Father,
God from God, Light from Light,
true God from true God,
begotten, not made,
of one Being with the Father.
Through him all things were made.
For us men and for our salvation
he came down from heaven;
by the power of the Holy Spirit
he became incarnate of the Virgin Mary
and was made man.
For our sake he was crucified under Pontius Pilate;
he suffered death and was buried.
On the third day he rose again
in accordance with the Scriptures;
he ascended into heaven
and is seated at the right hand of the Father.
He will come again in glory
to judge the living and the dead,
and his kingdom will have no end.
We believe in the Holy Spirit,
the Lord, the giver of life,
who proceeds from the Father [and the Son].[3]
With the Father and the Son he is worshipped and glorified.
He has spoken through the Prophets.
We believe in one holy catholic Church.
We acknowledge one baptism
for the forgiveness of sins.
We look for the resurrection of the dead,
and the life of the world to come.

The Nicene Creed is universally held by most Christians. Despite its terminology and the philosophical and theological debates which produced it, it is regarded by orthodox believers not as a philosophical statement but as a summary of biblical teaching. Nevertheless there were those Christians who refused to accept the Nicene Creed's teaching that Jesus had two natures, one human and the other divine. These Christians argued that Jesus had only a divine nature, hence they were called Monophysites (*mono*, one; *phusis*, nature.) This led to the first major schism within the Christian church in the sixth century with the formation of the Syrian, Egyptian, Armenian, and Ethiopian churches, all of which are monophysite in doctrine and have retained their separate identities until today.

Alongside the Nicene Creed, the so-called Apostles' Creed has been of particular significance for the church in the West, whether Catholic or Protestant. Despite its name and legends about its origin, the Apostles' Creed was not drafted by the original apostles. It is first referred to towards the end of the fourth century, but its developed form dates from the early eighth century. Originating in Spain and southern France, the Apostles' Creed became the accepted baptismal creed within the Roman church and a symbol of unity. Much shorter and less controversial than the Nicene Creed, it also became the basis for catechetical instruction.

Throughout our discussion thus far we have focused on the development of orthodox Christian belief. It should be kept in mind, however, that integral to the Christian understanding of faith was the need to live according to a particular ethical standard of holiness in the world. Baptism meant a turning away from the old way of life characteristic of pagan society, and the beginning of a life of discipleship and obedience to Jesus as Lord. The teaching of Jesus and Paul placed great emphasis on living a life of love towards God, neighbour and even enemy. Many of the Pauline and pastoral letters in the New Testament (such as Ephesians, 1 and 2 Timothy, and Titus) provided so-called 'household tables' for determining Christian conduct. And for the first few centuries of the Christian movement, Christians, in confessing Jesus as Lord, adopted a pacifist position with regard to participation in the Imperial military. Such orthopraxis (right action and behaviour) was of considerable importance in the life of the church, and some of the great theologians were also noted for their holy lives. As Christianity moved from being a persecuted minority sect to becoming an imperial religion, however, the non-conformity to the world characteristic of early Christianity was often replaced by a nominal faith and moral laxity. But even so, throughout the history of the church there have constantly been movements for the renewal of its life in the world according to the example and teaching of Jesus and his call to committed discipleship.

From persecuted sect to imperial religion

While the first Christians were regarded as a sect within Judaism, a lawful religion within the empire, and dealt with accordingly by the Roman authorities, they soon became a source of perplexity to local governors, especially when their separate identity emerged. The focus of this identity, and the source of the conflict, was their confession of Jesus as Lord. By the end of the first century local hostility towards Christians often erupted into persecution and mob violence, sometimes sparked off by Jewish opponents and antagonists. Much depended on the sympathies and convictions of the local authorities and the reigning emperor. But Christians were generally regarded as a disturbing element in society, a charge refuted at great length by the Apologists.

During the second and third centuries there were periods of widespread imperial persecution interspersed with periods of relative peace, once again depending on the whims or dictates of the emperor at the time. It was particularly severe in North Africa, where the church gained a reputation as the church of the martyrs. Several reasons were given for this persecution of Christians by the state. Firstly, they were perceived as a threat to law and order; secondly, they were regarded as a threat to true religion and philosophy; and thirdly, they were charged with creating chaos in the empire and weakening resistance to the barbarian threats on its borders.

The story of the conflict between church and state is a complex one which need not detain us here in detail. However, we can take up the story towards the end of the third century when the empire began to experience the threat of collapse with a new intensity. A particularly severe persecution broke out under the military emperor Decius (249–251), but eventually failed to destroy the church. The next forty years were relatively peaceful for the church, giving it an opportunity to grow strong and even penetrate within the imperial household. But with the accession of Diocletian (284–304), which coincided with the threat of the imminent collapse of the empire, persecution broke out once again. Diocletian regarded the growing influence of the church as a serious threat to his power, and was particularly incensed by the refusal of Christians to serve in the imperial army. In 295 CE several Christians were put to death for such conscientious disobedience, and Diocletian later rid his household and army of Christians. There was also a revival of pagan culture and religion. Between 303 and 304 several imperial edicts were passed. These resulted in Christians losing all civil rights, church buildings being destroyed, the arrest of all clergy, and, in a final act of desperation, the passing of the death sentence against all Christians. There was much suffering and many Christians were martyred for their faith, but Diocletian's persecution failed to achieve its aims.

In 311 Emperor Galerius issued an act of toleration thus preparing the way for the official recognition of Christianity as a legitimate religion within the empire. The rather dramatic conversion of Emperor Constantine to Christianity in 312 took the process a step further. In 313 Constantine promulgated the famous edict of Milan, the first of a series of legislation which not only reinforced toleration but led step by step to the position where Christianity became the official religion of the Roman empire. As a result, the emperor became increasingly involved in the disputes affecting the church, for now they were matters which affected the unity of the empire and his own authority. Hence Constantine's involvement in convening the Council of Nicaea.

The so-called Constantinian settlement was a major turning-point in the development of Christianity and the church, and set the pattern for church–state relations until relatively modern times. It was, however, a mixed blessing. While the emperor was no longer regarded as divine, he now ruled by divine right with the support of the church. While the church could exert considerable influence in society, its prophetic role was neutralised as it became almost a state instrument in preserving law and order. While it now became possible for many more people to join the church, it led to a great deal of superficial and nominal membership; and while it meant that the church was no longer persecuted, it laid the foundations whereby the church became instrumental in the persecution of others, notably the Jews. On top of this, Constantine's Christianity tended to be rather syncretistic, embodying elements of pagan culture along with his Christianity (for example, 25 December, a pagan festival, celebrating the birthday of the sun, became the day for celebrating the birthday of Jesus).

There was one last attempt to turn the clock back. During the reign of Julian 'the Apostate' (361–3) there was a determined effort to restore paganism. Julian, a very upright and moral ruler, blamed Christianity for all the ills in society, and called for a return to a rational and just order based on the ancient customs of Rome and Greece. But Julian failed. Subsequent emperors upheld the Constantinian position and, indeed, extended it further. Theodosius I's edict of Thessaloniki in 380 made the church all-powerful in the life of the state, establishing the bishop of Rome or pope as the supreme authority. Heresy became a crime against the state; the church was given special privileges and protection; discriminatory laws were passed against Jews; and the Christian calendar was adopted. From now on, the birth of Christ became the watershed in imperial and, later, world history.

There were Christians and church leaders who were opposed to the way in which the church was being reduced to a state institution, thereby losing something of its freedom to be the church. A major figure in this regard was Ambrose, bishop of Milan (*c.* 339–397). While he accepted state assistance in fighting heresy, he sought to protect the independence of the church, maintaining that the only true basis for political power was acceptance of God's authority and purpose. Ambrose is also the link to one of the greatest church leaders and theologians in the history of Christianity, for it was under his ministry that a young scholar from North Africa was converted to Christianity. Thus began the important contribution of Augustine, later bishop of Hippo, to the development of Christian thought.

Augustine (354–430) was brought up as a Christian by his devout mother, Monica. During his studies at the university in Carthage he moved away from what was a rather nominal Christian faith and became interested in philosophy. He also joined the sect of the Manichees, a new religious movement which had originated in Persia the century before. Strongly dualistic in nature, Manichaeism stressed the fundamental difference between light and dark, between the evil of matter and the goodness of the spirit. The way of salvation from the body lay through rigorous asceticism. Augustine, though attracted to Manichaeism, was more attracted to his mistress and never became one of the 'elect', the inner core of the movement. Eventually, after ten years he turned away from Manichaeism and went to teach rhetoric, first in Rome and then in Milan. In Milan he was deeply influenced by neo-Platonic philosophy, but even more so by the sermons of Ambrose. After reading a passage in Paul's letter to the Romans which challenged his way of life, Augustine was converted, and in 387 baptised. He returned to North Africa, was ordained a presbyter a few years later, and in 391 became the bishop of Hippo. Augustine's reflections on his spiritual journey are found in his famous book *The Confessions.*

Augustine's theology has been a major influence in the development of Christian thought and practice in the West. He made a major contribution to the development of the doctrine of the Trinity, where, to some extent, we also see the influence of his earlier neo-Platonism. His stress on the belief that the Holy Spirit comes to us not just from the Father but also from the Son was later to be a major reason for the split between the church in the East and the West.

Much of Augustine's theology was worked out in relation to the major controversies in which he was engaged, the dispute with Pelagianism and his opposition to the Donatists. Pelagius, a British monk living in Rome, stressed the role of human free will and personal responsibility in the human quest for salvation. Augustine, on the basis of both his own experience and the doctrine of the human fall portrayed in the story of Adam and Eve in Genesis, was convinced that humans are conceived in sin and were thus quite incapable of participating in any way in their own salvation. Salvation, Augustine taught, was wholly the action of God's grace in Jesus Christ which human beings experienced through the sacraments of baptism and the Eucharist.

Donatism was a movement which arose in the North African church as a consequence of the persecution of the church. The Donatists took a very hard line against those Christians who had denied their faith during persecution, and therefore they also rejected the ministry of presbyters who had done likewise. This meant that the power of the sacraments depended upon the moral worthiness of those who celebrated them, a position which was totally unacceptable to Augustine. God's gift of grace, he argued, was not conditional upon human worthiness, it was a free gift of the Holy Spirit.

Augustine lived during a tumultuous period in the history of the Roman empire. The Goths and Vandals (many of whom were Arian Christians) from the north had several times penetrated deep into the empire, and in 410 the city of Rome itself was sacked. Many pagans of the time believed that Christianity was responsible for this dreadful event, and that it would not have happened if the ancient gods were still honoured. Partly in response to this serious criticism, but also to show how God acts in history and to describe the place of the church and the state within God's providential purposes, Augustine wrote his famous work *The City of God.* Whereas human empires pass away, the city of God, the heavenly kingdom, always endures. Although Augustine never simply equated the church with the city of God, as the empire disintegrated, so the church not only survived but came to fulfil the role of providing at least some security, order and stability to a world in chaos.

The East–West schism

Long before the fall of Rome there had been growing rivalry within the church between the sees (or dioceses) of Constantinople in the East and Rome in the West. One of the major reasons for this was the growing power of the bishop of Rome and the claim that as pope and successor to Peter he had pre-eminence and power over the rest of the church. This claim was strongly resisted in the East, not only by Constantinople but also by the other ancient sees and their patriarchs (the bishops of Alexandria, Antioch, Jerusalem and Athens). There were also theological differences between the churches in the East and the West which were already evident at the councils of Nicaea and Chalcedon. However, as long as the empire held together, the unity of the church remained strong, and the bishop of Rome was acknowledged at least as the first among equals.

The Roman empire had long been under pressure with rival claimants to the imperial throne struggling for power. But it was not until the fall of Rome that its unity really began to crumble resulting in a growing estrangement between the Eastern empire centred on Constantinople, and Rome in the West where the pope increasingly acted as the successor to the emperor. This political cleavage exacerbated the theological and ecclesiastical tensions already existing and laid the foundation for the eventual schism between the Eastern Orthodox churches and the Roman Catholic Church in the eleventh century.

There were several issues which finally led to this schism, though each of them in some way revolved around the question of the authority of the pope. Two issues in particular merit attention. The first was a controversy which had its roots in Augustine's insistence that within the doctrine of the Trinity, the Holy Spirit proceeds not only from the Father but also 'from the Son' (*filioque*). By the end of the sixth century the *filioque* clause was introduced into the Nicene Creed in the West causing great consternation amongst the bishops and theologians of the East. The latter believed that the addition made the Spirit inferior to the Father and the Son and thus undermined their equal identity and unity. Moreover, the fact that the church in Rome could introduce the clause into the Nicene Creed meant that the pope had assumed an authority greater than that of one of the councils of the universal church. Although the schism only officially occurred in 1054, when the pope excommunicated the patriarch of Constantinople, the breach was made much earlier, exacerbated no doubt by a synod held in Constantinople in 876 which declared the pope a heretic because of his espousal of the *filioque* clause!

The other controversy which divided the church, and almost split the Eastern branch itself, was that concerning icons. Christianity, following Judaism, rejected any form of idolatry, obeying the injunction of the Ten Commandments 'not to make any graven images' of God (Exod. 20: 4). Through the centuries, however, Christian art developed, not least in the catacombs in Rome where Christians from early times hid from the authorities during periods of persecution. Gradually the art forms included representations of Christ, the Virgin Mary his mother, and the angels, in the form of icons, a stylised form which flourished in the Eastern church from about the fifth century. In the eighth century, Emperor Leo III, in an endeavour to evangelise both Jews and Muslims, who were equally against any idolatry, embarked on a policy of destroying icons throughout the church. This led to a fierce and lengthy controversy in which the iconoclasts (those who wished to destroy the icons) were finally defeated at a council in 787 at which the use of icons was sanctioned as a means of devotion. Icons have, ever since, played a very important rôle in the devotional and liturgical life of Eastern Orthodoxy, which, unlike the Roman church, has never allowed the use of the crucifix or other sculptured art forms in churches and worship.

Quite apart from these doctrinal and aesthetic differences, the division between Eastern Orthodoxy and Roman Catholicism went much deeper. Over the centuries the two great branches of the church had developed different styles of worship and life arising out of different emphases in theology. The Eastern theologians, for example, stressed the Incarnation as the saving action of God. While human nature was certainly sinful as a result of the fall, the image of God in men and women had not been entirely lost, and through the incarnation human nature was restored. By participation in the true humanity of Christ, human nature was renewed to its original perfection. Such an emphasis also provided the basis for a more mystical approach to Christian spirituality. Of particular significance in this regard were the neo-Platonic writings referred to as those of Pseudo-Dionysius, and the emergence of the monastic way of life.

Monasticism

Already in the third century, as the church was being less persecuted and more tolerated, and especially after the Constantinian settlement when the church began to adapt to the world, numbers of sincere Christians retreated into the deserts of Syria and Egypt to live an ascetic life of prayer and fasting. These Desert Fathers, notably Antony (*c.* 251–356) and Pachomius (*c.* 290–346), as they came to be known, generally lived in small communities, though some withdrew into the solitary life as hermits or anchorites. The original meaning of the word 'monk' (*monachos*, derived from *monos*) meant someone who lived alone. Like Jesus before them, who struggled with the devil in the wilderness, so these hermits saw their vocation as struggling to overcome temptation, and discovering God through the development of a life of prayer and inner silence. Moreover, their role was also one of protest against a church which was growing lax in its commitment, and their retreat into the desert was therefore not seen by them as withdrawal from the church or escape from the world, but as a means of renewal and engagement.

The development of monasticism was not confined to the East. Indeed, the movement soon spread westward and monasteries were already in existence in Italy and Gaul by the fifth century. It was in Italy that Western monasticism was given its decisive character by Benedict of Nursia (*c.* 480–*c.* 547). Benedict lived at a time when society was in a state of disintegration and constant war as northern tribes invaded the Italian peninsula. We do not know much about Benedict's life, but we do have his *Rule* which he developed for life in a monastery. This Rule not only decisively shaped the way in which the monastic movement developed in the West, but it also left an indelible impression on Western Christianity as a whole. Central to the Benedictine way of life was the balance between prayer, study of the Scriptures, and manual work. Also of great importance was the role of the abbot (*abba*, father), or head of the monastery, who, while he was obliged to consult the community, ruled over the monks with the authority of Christ. The daily offices of prayer, beginning with vigil very early in the morning and ending with compline that evening, became the basis for daily worship even beyond the confines of monasteries, eventually being conflated in the services of matins and evensong in the Anglican Church many centuries later.

Christian worship

From the early part of the second century the liturgy (*leitourgia*, service) of Sunday worship took on an increasingly well-defined shape, though the way in which it was celebrated varied considerably from place to place. Christian worship stretching back to the primitive church was a combination of synagogue worship (the singing of psalms and hymns, the reading of Scripture and preaching, and the offering of prayers), and the 'breaking of bread' or sharing in the supper instituted by Jesus. The latter, commonly referred to as the eucharist because of the prayer of thanksgiving (*eucharistein*, to give thanks), was based on the four actions of Jesus at the last supper which he shared with his disciples: Jesus took bread, gave thanks, broke it, and gave to his disciples. These four simple acts, which remain at the heart of the celebration of Holy Communion or the mass, were gradually embellished as the liturgy grew more splendid. This was particularly true in the East where it was named after the great preacher and theologian of Constantinople, John Chrysostom (*c.* 347–407), though its connection with Chrysostom is tenuous. Celebrated in different languages, the liturgy of St John Chrysostom is the basic liturgy of all Eastern Orthodox churches. It is a celebration of great beauty, majesty and spiritual symbolism, in and through which the participant is enabled, as it were, to enter into the 'courts of heaven'.

Whereas Eastern theology stressed the incarnation and the divinisation of humankind in Jesus Christ, the Western theologians placed their emphasis increasingly upon the death of Jesus on the cross and thus on the doctrine of the atonement. This was largely in response to the teaching of Augustine who stressed the radical nature of the human fall and developed the doctrine of original sin. As a result, the Roman mass stressed the sacrificial character of Jesus' death, and it was regarded, in some profound sense, as a repetition of that sacrifice offered up by the church to God. Through baptism, confession of their sins, and participation in the mass, believers received the saving grace of God in Jesus Christ.

The formal schism between Eastern Orthodoxy and the Roman Catholic Church in the eleventh century was thus long in coming, as both churches had gradually grown apart, often for cultural and political reasons over several centuries. Undoubtedly in the end the schism was, on the part of the Eastern church, a rejection of the power of the papacy. For Eastern Orthodoxy each ancient patriarchy (Constantinople, Antioch, Jerusalem and Athens) was autocephalous, that is, having its own spiritual head, and as the church expanded into new areas, such as Russia in the tenth century, so these branches of Orthodoxy likewise became autonomous. Yet Eastern Orthodoxy was united by a common liturgy, a common faith defined by the Nicene Creed and the seven great ecumenical councils of the undivided church prior to the schism, and by its bishops being in communion with each other under the leadership of the patriarchs of the ancient sees.

Whereas Eastern Orthodoxy expanded and flourished in Eastern Europe, the Roman Catholic Church rapidly evangelised Western Europe. Two qualifications are, however, necessary. By the eighth century, Islam had virtually conquered the whole of North Africa, so much so that the once very strong church which had flourished there since the time of Tertullian and Augustine, and which in some ways had been a rival to Rome in the leadership of the Western church, virtually collapsed. The second point to note is that long before Roman missionaries moved north and west, Christianity had already been established by missionaries like Patrick, Columba and Ninian among the Celtic tribes of England, Scotland and Ireland, and Celtic missionaries had evangelised deep into parts of what is now Germany. By the sixth century, however, Celtic Christianity had been seriously weakened by invasions and war, and the evangelisation of Western Europe was now in the hands of Roman missionaries such as Augustine, the first archbishop of Canterbury (died *c.* 605), and Boniface (*c.* 742–814), the great missionary to the Germans. In this way the Roman church, particularly under the leadership of Pope Gregory the Great (*c.* 540–604), laid the foundations for its spiritual and temporal control of Western Europe during the Middle Ages which were about to dawn.

In modern times Eastern Orthodoxy has expanded far beyond its traditional geographical boundaries in the Middle East and Eastern Europe. This has been largely due to the migration of people and the relocation of refugees in countries such as the United States and Australia. The full participation of Eastern Orthodoxy in the life of the World Council of Churches has also enabled the tradition to make a substantial contribution to the ecumenical church. These developments are beyond our present discussion, but it is noteworthy that the celebration in 1988 in Moscow of the millennium of the baptism of Emperor Vladimir in 988, which officially marks the beginning of Russian Orthodoxy, was attended by church leaders of all the major traditions. Despite the divisions and diversity, and even conflict, which have characterised Christianity since its beginnings, this event symbolises the unity which Christians confess in the creeds and which, in the twentieth century, has been reaffirmed through the ecumenical movement. The baptism of Vladimir, a thousand years after the beginning of the Christian movement, is, then, a significant point at which to conclude this discussion of the first thousand years of Christianity.

THE SECOND THOUSAND YEARS: FROM THE MEDIEVAL TO THE MODERN CHURCH

The medieval church

The Medieval Age spans the eighth to the fourteenth centuries. Western European society was in a state of continual ferment and change from the time of the fall of Rome until the eleventh century. Indeed, Christian civilisation was, in many respects, not only in turmoil but also inferior to the much younger but vibrant Muslim civilisation which rapidly spread across North Africa and captured much of Spain, as well as the world of Byzantine Christianity in the East. The city of Rome itself was in a state of decay. Popular historians often refer to this period as the Dark Ages.

Despite the fact that the clergy and even bishops were often ill-trained, the Roman church played a crucial role in holding the fabric of society together. This was largely because of the Benedictine monasteries which began to flourish during this period, spearheading missionary and educational work, maintaining the worship and spiritual life of the church, and providing refuge and stability amidst times of political and social upheaval. At the centre of its life was the sacramental system of the church which had gradually developed through the centuries. Seven sacraments emerged over time which were believed to ensure God's saving grace from birth to death: baptism, confirmation, penance, the mass, marriage, holy orders (ordination to the priesthood), and supreme unction at death.

From about the middle of the eleventh century, however, significant changes occurred which, a century later, slowly but surely began to transform medieval society. Of particular importance were the growth of towns which became centres for the building of massive cathedrals, the establishment of universities, and the formation of merchant guilds. The advance of Islam into Western Europe was halted and Christian civilisation began to flourish in an unprecedented manner. As the monasteries grew in number, acquiring vast tracts of land and endowments, often used for very productive farming, they and their abbots acquired great power. Behind it all lay the authority of the pope on whom even the power of the emperor of the Holy Roman Empire depended.

We cannot trace all the theological and ecclesiastical developments of the Middle Ages, but we shall briefly consider some of the more noteworthy: the crusades, the rise of the mendicant orders, the development of Christian scholastic theology, the rebirth of mysticism, the conciliar movement, the role of early reformers like John Wyclif and John Huss, and the Christian humanism of the Renaissance.

The crusades

It may be difficult for us today to understand the piety which lay behind the calling of the first crusade by Pope Urban II in 1095. Although it was a call to arms, a crusade was regarded as a holy pilgrimage whose purpose was to drive out the Muslims from the Holy Land, restore the ancient Christian sanctuaries to the church, and establish peace and unity with the Eastern Orthodox churches. Thus the Christian knights who led the armies of Christendom into battle did so, at least in the initial crusades, with much prayer, devotion and fasting. Indeed, the crusades were considered holy wars which could lead to the everlasting crown conferred by martyrdom, even if victory in battle remained elusive. The tragedy was that the idea of holy war, whatever its ideals and however noble some of its leaders, was no less war with all its customary violence, greed, and barbarism, quite apart from its being foreign to the gospel of Jesus Christ. Not only did the crusades fail in their aims, but they left death and destruction in their wake. They also evoked a fanatical spirit amongst common people which repeatedly erupted into violent anti-Semitic pogroms, inquisitions against heretics, and witchhunts. The last crusade took place in 1270, and when it was all over, Jerusalem and the holy places remained firmly under Muslim control.

Mendicant orders

Perhaps it was inevitable that the more powerful the church and the monastries grew, the greater the corruption of the higher clergy. By the beginning of the thirteenth century the time was rapidly drawing closer for a reformation and renewal of the church's life. Fortunately two remarkable reformers were at hand, Francis of Assisi in Italy and Dominic of Castile in Spain.

The story of St Francis (1181–1226) is well known. The son of a rich merchant, Francis became a soldier and in one of the many inter-city wars that ravaged Italy at the time, he became desperately ill. During his illness and subsequent convalesence, Francis decided to espouse a life of poverty as a protest against the wealth and corruption of the church and as a means to reform its spiritual life. Soon Francis gathered disciples around him and created a Rule for his community which was, after some effort, approved by Pope Innocent III. Despite this approval Francis and his community were often in conflict with the bishops and clergy. But Francis' evident saintliness was such that by the time of his death in 1226 he had made a decisive contribution to the renewal of the life of the church, and continued to do so through the Franciscan Order which he had established.

St Dominic (1170–1221) founded the Order of Preachers or the Dominican Order in 1220. As its name indicates, it was primarily committed to teaching and preaching. Thus it became largely the Dominicans' responsibility to try and convert so-called infidels and bring back heretics into the embrace of the Catholic church. It was the Dominican Order, for example, which spearheaded the crusade against the Albigenses, a sect in the south of France whose teaching somewhat resembled that of the earlier Manichees to whom Augustine had been attracted. It also became the responsibility of the Dominicans, and some Franciscans, to provide the inquisitors who, during the late Middle Ages, sought by persuasion and, failing all else, torture and execution, to bring heretics back to the true faith.

Christian scholastic theology

The period from Augustine to the beginnings of scholasticism in the twelfth century is not noted for its contribution to Christian thought. But three theologians bridge the gap. The first was Boethius (*c.* 480–*c.* 524), whose commentaries on the Greek philosopher Aristotle provided the basis for the development of scholastic logic and dialectic. The second was Gregory the Great (540–604), who handed on the teachings of Augustine, especially those concerning the church. The third was John Scotus Erigena (*c.* 810–*c.* 877), whose creative neo-Platonic theology, together with his translation of the mystical

Pseudo-Dionysius, contributed to the development of mysticism in the Middle Ages.

Scholasticism, the theology of the 'schoolmen', those medieval scholarly theologians who sought to relate faith to reason and systematically develop the basic principles of Christian doctrine, begins with Anselm (1033–1109), a French abbot who later became Archbishop of Canterbury, and Abelard of Paris (1079–1142), whose romance with Heloise is one of the great love stories of all time. Anselm, following Augustine, insisted that faith in God always precedes our rational understanding of God. In his treatise, the *Proslogion*, Anselm developed his famous ontological proof for the existence of God. When we speak of God, he argued, we conceive a being 'than whom no greater can be conceived to exist'. Thus, while faith precedes reason, reason supports faith. Anselm also made a major contribution to the Christian understanding of the atonement. In *Cur Deus Homo* he argued that through Christ's death on the cross, God's righteous anger towards sin had been satisfied.

Abelard, perhaps the greatest intellectual of his time, opened up basic theological issues to the critical scrutiny of reason, notably in his treatise *Sic et Non*. He did so, not in order to disprove Christian beliefs, but to help people understand them better. In doing so, Abelard laid the foundations for scholastic inquiry, a task taken up by Peter Lombard (*c.* 1100–1160) whose famous *Sentences* provided the first systematic treatment of Christian doctrine based on the Creed. Abelard was a controversial figure, and strongly opposed by the powerful abbot of Clairvaux, Bernard (1090–1153), who argued that the truth about God could never be reached or understood by reason, but only by a life shaped by the supernatural grace of God, a position which could also be traced back to Augustine. Abelard was furthermore at variance with Anselm's view of the atonement as an act of satisfaction, stressing, on the contrary, that through his death on the cross Christ left us rather an example to follow.

Scholasticism took a major step forward as a result of the work of two Spanish Islamic philosophers, Avicenna (ibn Sina; 980–1037) and Averroës (ibn Rushd; 1126–98). Through their translation into Latin of the works of the Greek philosopher Aristotle, and their commentaries, they were largely responsible for the retrieval and dissemination of his philosophical ideas. Aristotle's emphasis on the primacy of reason was, as it had been in ancient Greece, a rejection of Platonic idealism and therefore of the neo-Platonic mysticism which had influenced Augustine and those who followed in his footsteps. While Aristotle's logic had long been known, at least since Boethius, now theology had to come to grips with a reasoned system, the content of which related to the whole of life, including the nature and activity of God in the world. For Aristotle we can only know about God through our knowledge of reality – not the world of ideas (Plato), but the external world in which we actually live.

The greatest of all the scholastic theologians was undoubtedly the Dominican monk, Thomas Aquinas (1225–1274). Thomas, as a professor of theology in Paris and then in Naples, took Aristotle's challenge seriously, and, while not captive to Aristotle's philosophy, he developed his great exposition of Christian doctrine, the *Summa Theologica*, in dialogue with Aristotle. For Thomas there is a clear difference between reason and faith, a position which he adopted from the medieval Jewish philosopher, Moses Maimonides (1135–1204). There are truths about God which only faith can grasp and understand in response to supernatural revelation, such as God's triune nature. At the same time, even if reason cannot tell us who God is, it can and does enable us to know that God exists. Our natural knowledge of God which comes through reason provides the basis upon which we respond to the truth of revelation in Scripture and Jesus Christ. Faith presupposes reason, and builds upon it. Thus, in contrast to the Muslim scholar Averroës, for whom faith and reason were always separate, ultimately for Thomas reason existed in order to serve faith.

Thomas's theological system, now referred to as Thomism, not only provided the church with a systematic account of its faith on the basis of rigorous rational inquiry, it also provided the church with a theology which undergirded the life and place of the church within medieval feudal society. Both church and society were hierarchically structured, that is, there were clearly defined layers of authority and chains of command from pope and emperor through bishop, prince and priest, down to the lowliest serf working on the land. Everyone knew, or was supposed to know, his or her place, and accept it as ordained by God. Thus, just as there was a carefully constructed synthesis between faith and reason, society was likewise a carefully constructed and maintained whole designed by God, ruled over by the church, symbolised in the towering Gothic cathedrals which bridged heaven and earth, and personalised in the sacramental system which graced life from birth to death.

Despite the fact that Thomas Aquinas was the greatest of the medieval scholastics, his system of theology was initially strongly opposed, though his own Dominican Order adopted it towards the end of the thirteenth century. Many centuries later, in 1878, it became the official basis for the theological training of priests within the Catholic Church and remained so until the Second Vatican Council in the 1960s.

The later thirteenth and fourteenth centuries were years of crisis and transition in Western Europe. Indeed, the carefully crafted structure of society was already beginning to crack at the seams. There were many reasons for this, not least the growth of the towns as centres of power and influence and a move away from feudal economies to early forms of capitalism. There was also growing criticism of the affluence and power of the church and the first signs of revolt amongst peasants and nationalist aspirations amongst princes. Symbolic of this gradual break up was the radical critique of Thomism, a critique which rejected the synthesis of faith and reason so carefully constructed by Thomas himself. Several theologians led the attack, beginning with Johannes Duns Scotus (*c.* 1265–1308) and finding its sharpest expression in William of Ockham (*c.* 1285–1347), the last of the great medieval scholastics.

For Duns Scotus reason could not provide a basis for faith simply because God was not bound to creation or the natural order. Indeed, Scotus argued, the truth of God's revelation had to be accepted on the basis of the authority of the church. An unintended consequence which was to have far-reaching effects was that reason was set free from the control and constraints of faith. Ockham went further than Scotus in setting forth a position which was called 'nominalism', and which profoundly affected the development of science and philosophy in the centuries to come. For Ockham and nominalism generally, only individual things are real, not the idea behind them (as taught by Plato, Augustine, Anselm and also in a qualified sense by Aquinas). This meant that there is no such thing as beauty, but there are beautiful things. Thus God cannot be known from rational reflection on the natural world, but only through faith in revelation. Ockham was, on the one hand, a firm believer in God, but on the other, because he stressed even more than Scotus the absolute power of God and God's freedom from creation, he was a sceptic and empiricist with regard to human reason and knowledge.

Medieval mysticism

Periods of social upheaval and transition invariably bring forth new religious movements which seek to meet the human need for security and certainty. The final two centuries of the Middle Ages were no exception. Already in the twelfth century a medieval monk, Joachim of Fiore (*c.* 1132–1202), provided an interpretation of history which claimed that a new era of missionary expansion was about to happen which would result in the coming of the kingdom of God. Joachim's visionary apocalyptic views greatly influenced revolutionary thinkers for the next few centuries, awakening expectations particularly amongst the lower classes.

Joachim's apocalyptic mysticism was, however, very different from the *Devotio Moderna* which flourished in the thirteenth and early fourteenth centuries. This mystical movement, which was particularly strong in the Rhineland and the Netherlands, stressed personal piety rather than revolutionary fervour. Its most significant exponents were the Germans Meister Eckhart (*c.* 1260–1327) and Johann Tauler (*c.* 1300–1361), both Dominican monks, and in the Netherlands the Brethren of the Common Life, of which Thomas à Kempis (*c.* 1380–1471), the author of *The Imitation of Christ*, was the best-known member. There was also a flowering of mysticism in England during the fourteenth century (Richard Rolle and Julian of Norwich are of note), and, in Spain, Catharine of Siena (1347–80) demonstrated how a life of contemplation could also be one of social and even political engagement.

The conciliar movement

Under the leadership of the great medieval popes, Gregory VII (1021–85), Innocent III (1160–1216), and Boniface VIII (1234–1303), the papacy had gained almost absolute power in Western Europe. Several developments led, however, to severe criticism both from territorial rulers and princes and from church leaders and theologians who were concerned about the well-being of the church. Of critical significance was the exile of the papacy from Rome in the southern French city of Avignon from 1309 to 1377. The reasons for this exile were complex, but much of it had to do with the pro-French alignment of the papacy. During this period the whole administrative structure of the church was tightened up, and an oppressive fiscal policy was implemented.

After the death of Gregory XI (1148–1241), who had re-established the papacy in Rome, a controversy arose about the election of a new pope. This resulted in what is known as the Great Schism, a period of forty years during which two popes, one anti-French and the other pro-French, reigned in Rome and Avignon respectively. Before the matter was finally resolved at the Council of Pisa in 1409, there were, for a short while, three claimants to the papal office.

The most significant attempt to reform the papacy took the form of what is known as the conciliar movement. Initiated by theologians such as William of Ockham teaching in Paris, the conciliar movement argued that representative councils of the church had a higher authority than the papacy, and therefore the right to control papal abuses and provide leadership for the church. The intention was by no means to do away with the papacy; the intention was reform. Some conciliarists argued that councils should not only be comprised of bishops or even clergy, but also lay people. Major complaints against the papacy, quite apart from its moral laxity, were its secular and political involvements, and the heavy taxation with which it burdened the common people. The most important council was that of Constance (1414–18), which ended the Great Schism. But the conciliar movement could not withstand the strong opposition of the papacy and the papal court (Curia), or the territorial princes who regarded it as a threat to their own power.

Early reformers

Opposition to the papacy also came from another quarter, namely those prophetic leaders who are sometimes called the pre-Reformation reformers. Three are particularly noteworthy: John Wyclif (*c.* 1330–1384), John Huss (*c.* 1372–1415) and Girolamo Savonarola (1452–1498). Wyclif was an Oxford philosopher who argued amongst other things that the true church was invisible, that the Bible not the papacy or councils was the supreme authority for the church, and that there should be a clear separation of spiritual and temporal power. His followers, known as the Lollards, widely disseminated his views. While he was condemned as a heretic at the Council of Constance, his views found strong support in Bohemia where the well-known preacher and theologian in Prague, John Huss, advocated reform along the same lines. Huss's reforms were closely related to the emerging sense of nationalism which was occurring throughout Europe at that time. He, too, having been excommunicated by the pope, was condemned as a heretic by the Council of Constance and burnt at the stake in 1415. For the people of Prague and what is now Czechoslovakia, Huss became and remains a national hero.

Savonarola, unlike Wyclif and Huss, was basically an orthodox Catholic and Dominican monk. Like the earlier Florentine, Joachim, he was, however, something of a visionary who regarded himself as divinely inspired, proclaiming apocalyptic messages to the church and clergy of Florence, which, he claimed, he had received from God. The fact that he was an outspoken critic of the immorality of the clergy as well as the rest of the people and especially those in power, did not gain him much popularity. After a period of considerable power in Florence, he was declared a schismatic and hanged as a heretic in the market-square.

Christian humanism

Not all those concerned about the need for reformation in the church were radical critics of its doctrine, such as Wyclif and Huss, or visionaries and prophets like Savonarola. Many others were Christian humanists, that is, scholars loyal to the church who had been profoundly influenced by the new learning of the Renaissance. The Renaissance of the fourteenth and fifteenth centuries had many facets, not least in the world of art and natural science. But that which interests us most here was the development of critical historical scholarship with its concern to retrieve the writings of the ancient Greek and Roman philosophers and jurists, and, more especially, the concern for biblical scholarship.

Throughout the Middle Ages, Latin had been the universal language in the West not only of the church but of politics and scholarship as well. But now humanist scholars were no longer content with the Latin translation of the Bible, the Vulgate. The need was felt to return to the original Hebrew and Greek text and translate it afresh into the vernacular languages which were coming into their own in the emergent nation states of Renaissance Europe. This process was greatly helped by the invention of the printing press in Germany by Gutenberg in 1451.

The Christian humanists were not like the secular humanists of our modern world. They were Christian believers and members of the church. But they were humanists in the sense that they believed society could be reformed and the purity of the church achieved through education and human endeavour based on a true knowledge of ancient philosophy, the early Christian Fathers, and especially the Bible. There were many great humanists. Lorenzo Valla (1405–1457), an Italian, for example, showed that the so-called 'Donation of Constantine', upon which the papacy based its territorial claims, was a fraud. Thomas More (1478–1535) applied the new scholarship to political and social issues in England. Johannes Reuchlin (1455–1522), the greatest German humanist of the time, introduced Hebrew scholarship into the church, thus facilitating a more accurate translation of the Old Testament and a new appreciation for Jewish philosophy. But the most renowned Christian humanist was Desiderius Erasmus (1469–1536).

Erasmus, though born and educated in Holland, was equally at home in all the major centres of Western Europe, speaking several languages, advising kings, princes, bishops, and even the pope on occasion, and gaining wide respect amongst the scholars and intellectuals of the day. Although a priest and monk, Erasmus' first love was not the monastic life as such but the opportunity it gave him for reflection and writing. Passionately committed to maintaining the unity of the church in an age when reform threatened to tear it apart, Erasmus stressed moderation, the inwardness of religion, and the virtuous life. Although very critical of the papacy, Erasmus sought to reform it from within. For this reason, after initially supporting Martin Luther, he eventually turned against him, desperately seeking to maintain Christian unity and moderation in all things. He died a disillusioned man in Basle, Switzerland, ironically to be condemned by the Catholic church as a heretic some decades after his death at the Council of Trent.

The Protestant Reformation

The Protestant Reformation of the sixteenth century was a complex movement led by various reformers and assuming different shape in the various nation states in which it took root. But it all began with a German monk, Martin Luther (1483–1546). Perhaps it is inaccurate to say the Reformation began with Luther for it had been coming for a long time and there were, as we have seen, many movements and early reformers who, together with humanist scholarship, prepared the way. But Luther became the catalyst and prophet of a movement which, in the process of reforming the church, also brought about further division

Martin Luther

Born of relatively poor but devout Catholic parents, Luther was well schooled in traditional piety by the time he began his studies in 1501 at the University of Erfurt, a centre of scholastic and especially nominalist thought. Though his father intended that he study law, Luther felt summoned by God to become a monk in order to save his soul. He joined the Augustinian monastery in Wittenberg in 1506 and there began his intense search to find a gracious God, especially through the use of the sacrament of penance. Under the guidance of his superior he began a careful study of the Bible, especially the writings of Paul, and the Church Fathers, especially Augustine. It was in doing so that he began to discover the evangelical truth that men and women are not justified before God by their works of charity but by their trust or faith in God's mercy in Jesus Christ. His study of the Bible also made him increasingly critical of scholastic philosophy and theology.

Luther became a professor of philosophy at the University of Wittenberg in 1508, and assumed increasing pastoral responsibilities in the churches of the district. Sent by his order to Rome to attend to a matter of dispute in 1510 he experienced something of the laxity and corruption of the papacy and the Curia of the time. He returned to Wittenberg a disillusioned man, yet he remained a devout Catholic and still believed in the need for the papacy.

A crisis developed, however, when a Dominican monk, Tetzel, began to sell indulgences in the Wittenberg district. Indulgences grew historically out of the penitential system of the Catholic church, but by this time they had become a source of much abuse. Through the payment of money to the pope (who needed it for the building of St Peter's basilica in Rome amongst other things), people were promised release from the penalties of their sins both for themselves and for those who had already died. Deeply disturbed and angered by this distortion of the gospel and its promise of forgiveness through faith in Jesus Christ, Luther penned his famous ninety-five theses in which he attacked the indulgence system and, implicitly, began to raise serious questions about the papacy itself. Nailed to the door of the Castle church in Wittenberg on 31 October 1517, these theses, intended for scholarly debate, soon circulated throughout Germany and beyond with the aid of the printing press, causing great consternation even in Rome.

In response to the controversy which he had provoked, Luther began to initiate reforms in the church in Wittenberg, and he expressed his views more explicitly in a series of tracts in 1520. In them he called upon the Christian princes to accept their responsibility to help reform the church, arguing that all Christians are priests by virtue of their baptism. Luther went further. While affirming the essential place of the sacraments of baptism, penance and the mass, he rejected the rest of the sacramental system, rejected the doctrine of transubstantiation (the belief that at the mass, through the priestly act of consecration, the bread and wine became the actual body and blood of Christ), and began to call the papacy itself into question. On reading these tracts, Erasmus, who was initially a supporter of Luther, turned against him in the interests of maintaining the unity of the church.

Summonsed by the pope to the Diet of Worms in 1521 to give an account of himself, Luther refused to recant. He was subsequently outlawed and, at the insistence of his friends, he unwillingly went into hiding. During this period he translated the Bible into German. While in hiding the reformation of the church in Wittenberg continued under the guidance of his close companion Philipp Melanchthon (1497–1560), an important figure in the emerging evangelical or Lutheran church. However, very soon the movement became radicalised, especially after the visit of the so-called Zwickau prophets and under the influence of the teachings of a former priest, Thomas Münzer (*c.* 1490–1525). Luther hastily returned from hiding and successfully managed to bring the reformation back to a more moderate position. The imperial edict declaring Luther an outlaw was still in effect, and there was a determined effort by the papacy to get rid of him, but the German princes and people generally rallied behind Luther, regarding him as something of a national hero who embodied their own dislike of having to pay taxes to Rome.

This period in German history was notable for the rising tension between the peasants and the princes supported by the emerging middle class. With the break-up of the feudal system many peasants were forced to leave the relative security of the rural areas where they had previously managed to survive reasonably well, and for a variety of reasons related to urbanisation and early capitalism, they found themselves unemployed and poverty-stricken, living as squatters on the peripheries of the towns. As a result there were several serious peasant revolts during the fifteenth century. None of these compared, however, with the Peasants' War of 1525 which, under the influence of Thomas Münzer, took on a religious character. The only way to end poverty and injustice and bring in the kingdom of God, Münzer argued, was to take up arms against the powerful and fight.

Luther was in two minds about the rights of the peasants. As the son of peasant parents, he had strong sympathies with them. But his understanding of the Christian faith was deeply affected by a sense of obedience to established secular authority. Moreover, he had not only received support from some of the

German princes in his struggles against the papacy and his moves to reform the church, but had been accused by others of being the primary cause of the upheavals taking place in society. He therefore finally came out strongly against the peasant revolt, calling on the princes to crush it and so exercise their divinely given 'power of the sword'. In many respects this lost Luther the support of the lower classes and ensured that the Reformation would be a largely middle-class movement centred in the towns and cities.

By 1524 it was increasingly clear that Germany was, in fact, dividing into two distinct religious groups, the Roman Catholic and the Lutheran. At the Diet of Speyer in 1526 the German princes agreed that there should be toleration towards Lutherans, but at a subsequent diet three years later in Speyer this act of toleration was withdrawn, leading the Lutheran princes to make a historic protest – an act which led to the designation Protestant. By 1530, however, with Emperor Charles V at the height of his power, a diet in the imperial city of Augsburg adopted a more conciliatory attitude. Melanchthon, under Luther's guidance, drafted the *Augsburg Confession*, a statement setting out the fundamental teachings of the Lutherans or *Evangelisch*, as they were known in Germany. The *Augustana*, to use its Latin name, remains the basic confession of Lutherans. But it was soon clear that reconciliation with the Roman Catholics was not possible. After a protracted and often violent struggle between Catholic and Lutheran princes, peace was finally established in 1555 at Augsburg, the Lutheran churches were legalised, and it was agreed that the religious faith of each German territory should be that of its prince. This arrangement determined much of the religious life in Germany until modern times. Martin Luther, by this stage, had been dead for nine years.

The Radical Reformation

In contrast to Luther, the leaders of the Swiss Reformation, notably Ulrich Zwingli (1484–1531) in Zurich, and John Calvin (1523–64) in Geneva, were humanists before they became reformers. Zwingli began his career as a priest in the town of Glarus, becoming an influential preacher and a chaplain to the Swiss mercenaries who comprised much of the papal army. In 1519 he was appointed the senior priest in Zurich and from the beginning of his appointment he began to preach about the need for basic reform in the life and teaching of the church. Although aware of and influenced by Luther's writings, Zwingli came to many of his conclusions from his own careful study of the Bible. Zwingli not only had the support of the people, including the town council, but also the local bishop of Constance. Much to the consternation of the pope and Curia, under his influence Zurich refused to hire out troops to the pope in his war against France in 1521.

Eventually Zwingli's preaching led him to take more radical views with regard to certain doctrines, particularly concerning the mass. At a series of public disputations, attended by priests, theologians and townsfolk, Zwingli defended his views and won the full support of the city and its authorities. Changes rapidly took place as the city fathers put into effect the reforms proposed by Zwingli. These included the destruction of images and statues in the churches, the celebrating of a much simplified form of the mass in the vernacular German, and a rejection of indulgences and papal taxation.

Amongst those who attended Zwingli's public disputations were several priests who, while first supportive of Zwingli's reforms, did not believe that he had gone far enough. Zwingli had some sympathy for their views but felt that reform had to be undertaken at a pace which was acceptable to the people and under the authority of the city council. Very soon, however, they decided to break with Zwingli and to implement the more radical reforms which they believed were taught in the Bible. This meant reconstituting the church itself as a fellowship of believers who were baptised on profession of their faith rather than as infants. Reform of the church could not wait for the authorities to make up their minds; indeed, the church should not depend on secular authority anyway but be free to obey God's will. So to initiate the process, several of the leaders, notably Conrad Grebel, Felix Mantz, and George Blaurock, all of them baptised as infants previously, baptised each other again. This was seen not only as an act of defiance by the city council, but also as a threat to the established social order and life of the church. Calling them Anabaptists (the re-baptised), the city fathers outlawed them, putting many of them to death by drowning.

The story of what is now referred to as the Radical Reformation is complex, as it soon broke into various movements. Thomas Münzer the revolutionary priest, for example, was regarded by some as an Anabaptist, and in some respects he was, but the mainstream of the Anabaptist movement rejected his recourse to violence. Severely punished and persecuted, the Anabaptists had neither time nor opportunity to develop permanent structures. But the movement in its various forms grew and spread widely, having a considerable impact on the future of Christianity as a whole. Eventually some Anabaptists found a secure home in Holland where, a century after the Reformation itself, and under the leadership of Menno Simons (1496–1561), they constituted a more clearly defined structure and laid the foundations for the Mennonite churches of today. The Anabaptists were pioneers of many convictions which have influenced the wider church as a whole, especially the Free Church tradition because of their insistence on the separation of church and state. Other tenets that have been influential are their commitment to pacifism, civil liberties, individual dignity, freedom of conscience, tolerance, and, of course, believers' baptism which is fundamental to Baptist and Pentecostal churches of our day.

John Calvin

John Calvin, who, together with Luther, was the most significant of the Protestant Reformers, was very different from the former German monk Martin Luther, both in temperament and in style. A Frenchman by birth, Calvin was a humanist scholar and lawyer before he became a reformer. Unlike Luther, he did not have a dramatic moment of conversion to evangelical faith, but gradually became committed to the teachings of Luther and the need to give himself fully to reform the church. In 1533 he had clearly broken with Rome and two years later was forced to flee France. Passing through Geneva in 1536 he was persuaded by the Reformed pastor there, Guillaume Farel, to stay and help reform the Genevan church. With reluctance Calvin did so, but after two years both he and Farel were forced to leave because their reforms went further than the city fathers liked.

Calvin settled in Strasburg, a city of great tolerance. There he was strongly influenced by the reformer Martin Bucer. In 1541, aged 32, at the request of the city fathers of Geneva, Calvin was invited to return and establish the Reformation in that city more firmly as it was in a state of disarray. This he did, and over the years until his death in 1564 he sought to establish a model reformed city. His critics regarded his 'rule' as autocratic and legalistic; his admirers, including the many Protestant refugees from other countries, regarded Geneva as a city of freedom and godliness.

Calvin was primarily a pastor, preacher and theologian. His reforms were far-reaching, but always based upon careful biblical study and theological reflection. His most significant writing was *The Institutes of the Christian Religion*, the first edition of which was published in 1536 and the final, much expanded version in 1559. In it, Calvin provides a masterly exposition of the Christian faith. But Calvin also wrote commentaries on virtually all the books of the Bible, preached an enormous number of lengthy biblical sermons, and produced tracts and other material related to a wide range of liturgical and pastoral issues. Whereas for Luther the focus of the gospel was the message of justification by faith alone, for Calvin it was much more God's total claim on human life in all its dimensions. As a result, the Calvinist or Reformed (as distinct from Lutheran) tradition has always had a greater concern to relate the Christian faith to social and political issues.

The Reformation in its different forms rapidly spread throughout Europe, aided by the growing nationalist aspirations of princes and people. In Scandinavia, for example, the Roman Catholic Church virtually changed hands, becoming Lutheran in theology, though its ethos remained much the same. Germany was eventually divided into both Catholic and Protestant (largely Lutheran) territories depending upon the religious convictions of the princes. The story in England is much more complex, for the Reformation there was made more difficult by the marriages and divorces of King Henry VIII. Scotland eventually became Calvinist or Presbyterian under the leadership of the fiery reformer John Knox (1513–72), but the Church of England, despite its break from Rome under Henry VIII, vacillated between being Catholic and Protestant, until finally, after much bitter struggle, a compromise was reached.

The establishment of the Church of England under the authority of the king (or queen) rather than the pope was, however, rejected by those who refused to conform on the grounds that the church should not be under the control of the king or the state. These Nonconformist or Free Churches, notably the Baptist, Congregationalist, and the Society of Friends (Quakers), were influenced by both the Calvinist and Anabaptist traditions, and together with the Presbyterians, provided an alternative to the Church of England, and played a decisive role in the development of English social and church history. Of equal significance, the English Free Churches played a very important role in the colonisation of North America.

The Catholic Reformation

Perhaps the Reformation could have been avoided if Rome had responded more openly and positively to the criticisms that had come its way for centuries, and if the popes of the time had been more sensitive to the genuine concerns of the Reformers. But the papacy and the hierarchy of the Roman church did eventually come to accept the need for reforms, and in the process, gave a much clearer and more comprehensive response to the teachings of the Protestant churches. This was the main reason for calling the Council of Trent by Pope Paul III in 1545, a council which dragged on for almost two decades before concluding in 1563.

Over against the Protestant insistence on the sole authority of Scriptures, Trent affirmed that the Bible and the tradition of the church were equally authoritative, and that the church alone through the office of the papacy, had the right to interpret them. In reaffirming the doctrine of transubstantiation in regard to the mass, Trent rejected the various Protestant doctrines ranging from Luther's, which was similar to the Roman position, to that of Zwingli and the more radical Reformers, which stressed that the Lord's Supper was simply an act of remembering Christ. But quite apart from countering Protestant doctrines, and there were many more that cannot be listed here, Trent, without changing any traditional beliefs, also introduced reforms into the Catholic Church which were long overdue. In all this, and in its follow up, the popes were assisted by the Society of Jesus (Jesuits), a new order founded in 1540 by Ignatius Loyola (1491–1556), a former Spanish soldier and nobleman, who committed the Jesuits to unconditional service of the papacy.

The history of the Reformation demonstrates that it was a highly complex phenomenon with many theological, social, political and ecclesiastical dimensions. The first reformers were, of course, all devout Catholics to begin with who, like many others of their time and the preceding centuries, were concerned about the life and integrity of the church. All the confessions of the Reformers stressed faith in the one, catholic church, and accepted the historic creeds of the early church. Luther had no intention to divide the church, though that was almost an inevitable consequence of his reforms given the situation of the times; Calvin saw his role as reforming the Catholic Church, not starting a new one; and even the Anabaptists, radical as they were, were concerned about the restoration of the purity of the one church of Jesus Christ. But schism occurred, and Protestantism in its different forms, and without a central institutional authority, was to splinter and fragment a great deal in the centuries to come.

Pietism, revival and missions

The decades that followed the Reformation were full of controversy and sometimes violent conflict between Catholic and Protestant princes and rulers as each fought for supremacy in Europe. Eventually an exhausted Europe came to its senses in the seventeenth century amidst the cry for toleration and peace. This cry had its basis in the writings of many intellectuals of the time for whom the dogmas which had torn Europe apart were no longer acceptable or credible. The age of the Enlightenment was, indeed, being born.

By this stage both Protestantism, in its different forms, as well as Catholicism, had developed their own doctrines in clear opposition to each other. In the case of Rome, the emphasis now increasingly lay not simply on the power and authority of the pope, but also on his infallibility in matters of faith and morals. In the case of the Protestants, especially the Lutherans and Calvinists, the emphasis lay on the sole authority of the Bible interpreted by the various confessions or statements of faith that had been written during the Reformation or soon after. Much of the dynamic of the Reformation had been replaced by a Protestant scholasticism or rigid orthodoxy.

Pietism

Alongside the critical attack on dogmatism launched by the intellectuals of the Enlightenment, many of whom rejected Christianity itself and moved outside the church, was the clamour of many Protestants within the established churches who felt the need for a spiritual revitalisation of the church once again. Much Christianity had become formal and nominal, the acceptance of dogmatic formulae rather than a living faith. In Germany this led to a movement within the Lutheran churches commonly referred to as pietism. Two theologians, P. J. Spener (1635–1705) and A. H. Francke (1663–1727), laid the theological foundations of Pietism. But it was a remarkable layman, Count Zinzendorf (1700–60), together with a group of concerned Christians gathered around him, who gave form to the movement. Known as the Moravian Brotherhood, they stressed the need not only for people to be justified by faith (as Luther taught), but also for a genuine spiritual rebirth and holy life. Pietism thus injected into Protestantism a strong emphasis upon spiritual experience, and an understanding of the church as a voluntary association comprised of people who shared that experience and who sought to live a common life together.

Wesley and the Evangelical Revival

The same concern for the revival of spiritual life was felt in England in the eighteenth century by a young Anglican priest John Wesley and his brother Charles. John Wesley (1703–91) had a spiritual awakening or an experience of rebirth as a result of reading the preface of Luther's Commentary on Paul's letter to the Galatians. He was also deeply influenced by Count Zinzendorf and the teaching of the Moravians, visiting their headquarters in Herrnhut, Germany, in 1738. Wesley, though he regarded himself as an Anglican to his dying day, was forced to preach outside the parish churches of England. But his preaching, and the hymns written by his brother Charles, created a spiritual revival in England and beyond, and eventually led to the formation of the Wesleyan (later named the Methodist) Church. The word 'methodist' derived from the fact that Wesley provided a highly structured system of church life and government, with a disciplined core of preachers both lay and ordained.

The Evangelical Revival, initiated by the Wesleys and the Calvinist preacher George Whitefield (1714-70), had a profound effect on the social life of England. England was in the grip of its early industrial revolution, characterised by unplanned urbanisation, exploitative labour practices, massive unemployment and widespread poverty. Somehow Wesley's preaching was able to bring hope and dignity to the poor and at the same time prick the consciences of the rich and powerful. It has been argued, in fact, that the Evangelical Revival prevented a social revolution such as that which happened later in the century in France. While some historians regard this as a positive contribution, others contend that Wesley forestalled a revolution which needed to take place. There can be little doubt, however, that the French Revolution in 1789, which brought the eighteenth century to a dramatic close, radically changed the mood and face of Europe, with far-reaching consequences both for the church and for society more generally.

Christian expansion beyond Europe

The Roman Catholic Church had long since expanded its horizons beyond Europe. In the sixteenth century, Jesuits had reached into southern Africa, India, China and Japan, and under the authority of the kings of Spain and Portugal, Catholic missions had been established throughout Latin America in the wake of colonial conquest. This ensured that Latin America would become virtually a Catholic continent, containing, as it does today, the greatest number of Catholics in the world.

While Catholic missions had also been established in North America at the same time as in the southern continent, the political role of Britain ensured that the planting of Christianity there went hand in hand with and was shaped by Anglo-Saxon colonisation. Thus in the seventeenth century much of the Eastern seaboard of what is now the United States was divided into states in which either the Anglicans, Congregationalists, Presbyterians, Baptists or Quakers predominated and often controlled religious and civic affairs. Moreover, just as England experienced a religious revival under the Wesleys, so the New England states, particularly under the influence of the Congregationalist preacher Jonathan Edwards (1703–58), experienced a time of 'Great Awakening' which would profoundly affect the development of Christianity in the United States. Edwards was undoubtedly the first major theologian to be born and bred in the United States. A powerful preacher, he was also a highly trained philosopher and theologian, and a prolific writer, who sought to respond to the intellectual challenges of the Enlightenment as well as the religious needs of the day. He symbolises the fact that by the middle of the eighteenth century, largely through the foundation of Yale and Harvard universities and their divinity schools, a distinctly North American Protestantism was beginning to emerge with an emphasis on the religious affections and experience.

After the Evangelical Revival in England, the Methodists also became a strong movement in North America, especially on the expanding frontiers of the new world. Indeed, as the colonies began to expand westwards, it was not the rather staid and traditional Christianity of the Congregationalists, Presbyterians and Anglicans which appealed to those who were 'opening up the interior', but the more revivalist Christianity of Methodist and Baptist lay preachers who travelled along with the settlers. Through their 'camp meetings', revivals regularly occurred, creating a distinct type of Christianity, especially amongst the poorer and less-educated classes. In due course this meant that the Baptists and Methodists were to become the largest of all Protestant churches in the United States, with the Baptists particularly strong in the southern and south-western states.

Protestant missions to the 'heathen' as distinct from Protestant religious colonies, owed a great deal to Pietism, the Moravians, the Evangelical Revival and the Great Awakening. The Lutheran and Reformed (Calvinist) churches generally had little interest in missionary outreach beyond the confines of Europe. But Pietism, with its stress on personal faith and the need for conversion, engendered a new sense of concern for the 'heathen' in distant lands who were 'perishing without hearing the gospel of salvation'. Moravian missionaries initiated the era of Protestant missions, and already in the 1730s had established mission stations in various parts of the world, including the Cape of Good Hope.

It was not until the end of the eighteenth century that other Protestants began to take the challenge of foreign missions seriously. In 1795 the London Missionary Society was formed, to be followed shortly by the founding of other societies in Britain and Western Europe. Many of these were denominational societies, and even when they were not specifically controlled by a denomination they were generally closely aligned to one. Even the London Missionary Society, whose charter excluded any commitment to a particular church polity, soon became aligned with the Congregational churches. As a result, through the Protestant missionary societies and the establishment of Roman Catholic missions throughout the world, the confessional and denominational differences which separated Christians in Europe were exported to and took firm root in Africa and Asia. Moreover, as the various denominational missions often concentrated their efforts on different communities in order to avoid unnecessary duplication of effort, ethnic differences were unwittingly accentuated by denominationalism. Thus, instead of Christianity becoming a source of unity it often reinforced division.

A further unfortunate aspect of European missionary endeavour was that it usually went hand in glove with European colonisation. After all, the relationship between the missions and the colonial powers was of mutual benefit, at least in the short term. On the one hand, the missions benefited from colonial power and protection, on the other, the missions provided colonialism with religious legitimation. The aim of evangelising the 'heathen', which was undoubtedly the motivation for the foundation of missionary societies, was invariably modified by this inevitable colonial connection and mutual interests.

At the same time, it cannot be denied that the missionary societies and the missionaries themselves regarded their primary responsibility as that of evangelising the indigenous peoples rather than simply furthering the aims of their governments in Europe. After all, most missionaries had been profoundly influenced by Pietism and a sense of calling to spread the gospel to the ends of the earth. This they did, often at great personal cost. Moreover, missions also played a very important role in introducing medical care and education, and, in certain instances, in combating some of the evils of colonialism such as slavery.

But there can be no doubt that in the process of evangelising and establishing missions, Christianity was often confused with European civilisation, and the cultural traditions and aspirations of the indigenous peoples were more often than not suppressed, sometimes with disastrous effect.

Christian theology in the nineteenth century

The Enlightenment

Pietism and the Evangelical Revival represent one type of Protestant response to the rigid scholasticism and arid spirituality of much of Protestant orthodoxy in the seventeenth and eighteenth centuries. But neither really grappled with the intellectual challenges which the Enlightenment addressed to Christian orthodoxy. For the philosophers of the Enlightenment, such as the eloquent Voltaire (1694–1778), reason was of paramount importance, which meant that only that which could be reasonably argued and maintained could possibly be true. This provoked several responses on the part of those who sought to defend Christianity, the chief of which was to demonstrate that the Christian religion was itself reasonable and could be defended and expressed in rational terms, a position most clearly expressed by the French and British philosophers René Descartes (1596–1650) and John Locke (1632–1704), and by the British theologian John Toland (1670–1722).

The attempt to defend Christianity on purely rational terms had serious consequences. If Christianity can be explained purely in terms of reason, then, it was rightly pointed out, there was no need of revelation. Furthermore, it was inevitable that the attempt to explain supernatural phenomena such as miracles would explain them away, and, in the process, not only deny the Incarnation but also God's providential involvement in the world. This gave rise to what is referred to as Deism, an understanding of God as remote from the world, and an understanding of Christianity which exalted morality but denied both God's redemptive grace and the miraculous. Lord Herbert of Cherbury (1583–1648) gave classic description to this 'natural religion' when he posited that the essence of true religion consisted in the belief that there is a supreme Being who ought to be worshipped; that virtue and piety is the chief part of such worship; that vices and crimes had to be expiated by repentance; and that there were divine rewards and punishments both in this life and in the next.

The Enlightenment was defined by the great German philosopher Immanuel Kant (1724–1804) as 'the emergence of man from immaturity that he is himself responsible for. Immaturity is the incapacity to use one's own intelligence without the guidance of another person.' Figuratively speaking, humanity had 'come of age' and had to stand on its own feet without the benefit of divine intervention. Ironically, however, it was precisely Kant who, together with the philosophers Jean-Jacques Rousseau (1712–78), David Hume (1711–76) and G. E. Lessing (1729–81), undermined the confidence which the Enlightenment had placed in the powers of reason. Finite reason, Kant argued, could neither prove nor disprove the existence of God. The only basis for true religion, he continued, was that of obeying the moral law implanted in each human being.

While the importance of reason was not denied, experience, feeling, intuition, morality and conscience thus became the focus of religion for many who now sought to defend or reinterpret Christianity.

Theological developments

The development of Protestant theology in response to the challenge presented by Kant and the post-Enlightenment philosophers was highly complex and is difficult to compress into a few sentences. However, it would be impossible to appreciate twentieth-century Christianity without some knowledge of the salient features and the major theologians who embarked on the task of reinterpreting Christianity. It should be kept in mind, however, that as we seek to understand the intellectual debates which shaped Christian theology throughout the nineteenth century, a great deal was happening beyond the university faculties of theology, within the churches themselves and within society more generally. Nevertheless, it remains true that much of the stimulus for responding to the challenges of the times, especially theologically, was located in the universities, particularly in Germany.

The first major response to the challenges produced by the Enlightenment and its critics such as Kant or the Romantics such as Rousseau, was that of the German theologian Friedrich Schleiermacher (1768–1834), who may be regarded as the pioneer of modern liberal Christianity. Schleiermacher, who was deeply influenced by the Romanticism of his day, maintained that true religion could not be confused with science or morality. Religion was a distinct reality which had to do with the human affections and especially the sense of being absolutely dependent upon God. It was this which lay behind the emergence of Christianity, a particular and pre-eminent expression of religion in general, and which gave rise to both the church and theological reflection. On this basis, Schleiermacher attempted to recast the whole of Christian doctrine, and, in the process, laid the foundation for what has subsequently been called 'liberal Protestantism'.

Biblical criticism

It would be misleading to assume that, as a result of the work of theologians like Schleiermacher, all Protestants or Protestant churches suddenly became liberal in their theological outlook. On the contrary, traditional confessional and conservative theological views along with evangelical pietism generally continued to rule the day. Such views, however, came under considerable attack not only from philosophers outside Protestantism, but also from biblical scholars within the church. Since the Reformation, Protestantism had regarded the Bible as its sole and final authority, but throughout the eighteenth century and particularly as the nineteenth progressed, more and more biblical scholars questioned the infallibility of the Bible. The Bible, they argued, was not always historically and scientifically accurate, notably in its account of the creation of the world, and there were many instances of contradiction. This did not necessarily imply that the Bible no longer had authority for the church, but it did mean that it could no longer be interpreted in the same way.

Two major issues were of importance in the critical study of the Bible. The first concerned the historicity of the Pentateuch, the first five books of the Hebrew Bible. It was soon demonstrated that they could not possibly have been written by Moses, as was traditionally claimed, but were in fact a compilation based on several strands of oral tradition which were much later written down and edited. The second concerned the heart of the New Testament, namely the four gospels themselves. Schleiermacher had evoked a new interest in trying to discover precisely who Jesus was, especially by examining his own self-consciousness. But it soon became evident that the gospels could not simply be taken at face value, particularly if one compared the synoptic gospels with that of John. Indeed, it was recognised that the gospels were not biographies at all but the testimonies of the early church. In order to hear the authentic voice of Jesus it was thus necessary to penetrate behind the preaching of the first Christians. In attempting to do so the search began to discover the real historical Jesus, a task energetically pursued by biblical scholars throughout the nineteenth century and into the twentieth.

Christianity and science

Alongside the challenge presented by biblical criticism was that of natural science. The development of modern science can be traced back to at least the Renaissance, but it was during the post-Reformation decades and the early Enlightenment that scientists such as Galileo (1564–1642), René Descartes and Isaac Newton (1642–1727) laid the foundations for much of modern science. The Newtonian world-view, in fact, became the basic assumption of all science, namely, that the world is a great machine which, whether originally created by God or not, functions according to mechanical laws of cause and effect. This meant that what religious people call miracles could be explained in scientific terms, and if not, were nonsensical. Indeed, it was precisely this understanding of the world which lay behind Deism and which led to the agnosticism and atheism that so strongly characterise the intellectual life of nineteenth-century Europe. The Newtonian world-view was assumed by all major thinkers, and not only by scientists.

The conflict between Christianity and science, which went back well into the Renaissance, erupted with a passionate vehemence in the nineteenth century with its major focus on the creation of the world. Both critical biblical scholarship and science had already argued that the world could not have been created as indicated in Genesis. But it was only after Charles Darwin (1809–82) published his celebrated *The Origin of Species* in 1859, in which he argued that human life had evolved, that the debate between the advocates of creation and those of evolution almost tore the church apart, particularly in Britain and the United States.

Fortunately there were those who rightly discerned that the debate was based on a fundamental misunderstanding of both religion and science, and that the story of creation in Genesis was not meant to be taken literally. Genesis was a powerful affirmation, rather, of God as creator, not a statement of how God created. The Bible was not after all a scientific textbook, but a witness to what

Jews and Christians believed were the events in history through which God was revealed. Thus, while the conflict between biblical fundamentalists and scientists working within the Newtonian paradigm continued through the century it was increasingly recognised that the debate was misguided. Indeed, the twentieth century has witnessed a remarkable transformation in the relationship between science and Christianity, particularly as a result of the development of the new physics based on the work of Albert Einstein.

Christianity and social issues

We have already noted that while much of the more critical and creative theological discussion of the time was taking place within Protestantism, and especially within the universities and seminaries, the churches were generally more conservative and sometimes reactionary. This was as true in the social and political arena as it was within the theological, and true of, though not confined to, the Roman Catholic Church. The Church of England, which had been seriously affected by the evolutionary debate, was also deeply affected by controversy about its very nature. Theological liberalism and the decline of the influence of the church in society, especially amongst the populace at large, provoked the emergence of the Oxford Movement and its attempt to restore Catholic tradition in the life of the church. The Oxford Movement, led by some outstanding scholars and churchmen of the day, notably John Henry Newman (1801–90), John Keble (1792–1866), and Edward Pusey (1800–82), also sought to awaken a social conscience in the Church of England.

Social concern was not, however, limited to the followers of the Oxford Movement, or Anglo-Catholics as they came to be known. One of the most outspoken advocates of social justice at the time was William Wilberforce (1759–1833), an evangelical in the Church of England and member of parliament who successfully fought for the abolition of the slave trade. A similar concern for social issues was to be found amongst the English Nonconformist churches, above all in the area of civil liberties. It is true, nevertheless, that with the exception of some prophetic voices, the churches were too often silent on many of the serious social problems caused by the industrial revolution.

Other theological developments

The Roman Catholic Church expressed its corporate mind on the theological and social issues of the day at the First Vatican Council convened by Pope Pius IX in 1869–70. This was the first such council since Trent in the sixteenth century, which indicates the extent to which the Roman Catholic Church felt itself threatened by the spirit of the age. The decisions of Vatican I were very traditional and conservative. Anything which smacked of biblical criticism, theological liberalism, or socialism was condemned. But Vatican I is especially memorable for the fact that it gave dogmatic status to the idea of papal infallibility, despite the opposition of some progressive bishops, such as Cardinal Newman, who had converted from the Church of England in 1845. By papal infallibility, Vatican I meant that when the pope speaks *ex cathedra* (that is, only when he defines a doctrine regarding faith and morals) his definitions are 'irreformable of themselves'.

One of the major concerns of conservatives in the churches, whether Roman Catholic or Protestant, was the relativising of doctrine. While all would have agreed that intolerance was not a virtue, it was also agreed that fundamental doctrines and dogmas could not be surrendered. Central to the debate was the growing awareness amongst most scholars that truth is, at least in some measure, historically conditioned. One of the major insights of Schleiermacher, for example, was that truth could not be divorced from its historical context. Indeed, the nineteenth century is characterised by a new sense of historical awareness. This was particularly evident in the work of the German philosopher and theologian G. W. F. Hegel (1770–1831).

Hegel argued that history evolves through a dialectical process in which a thesis evokes an antithesis and leads eventually to a synthesis. While Hegel's interpretation of history was largely in the realm of ideas, it opened up a radically new way for interpreting not only history but also the development of Christianity and its doctrines. It was on the basis of Hegel's dialectical interpretation of history that Karl Marx was later to develop his own doctrine of historical materialism which propounded that out of the revolutionary conflict between capitalism (thesis) and labour (antithesis), a new classless society (synthesis) would be born.

Liberal Protestantism reached its zenith towards the close of the nineteenth century. Of particular note in this regard was the influence of the German theologian Albrecht Ritschl (1822–89) and his 'disciple' Adolf Harnack (1851–1930). Ritschl reacted strongly against both the metaphysical theology of Protestant orthodoxy, the subjective pietism of Schleiermacher, and the dialetical speculation of Hegel. Following Kant, he stressed the ethical core of Christianity, arguing that God is known through the effect of his action on humanity in history. In particular, God is known through Jesus Christ who established the kingdom of God on earth, the extension of which is the task of the church. Following Ritschl, Harnack, whose knowledge of the early church and the patristic theologians was enormous, attempted to liberate Christianity from the metaphysical dogmas of the past and state what he believed to be the 'essence of Christianity'. This he summarised as belief in 'the fatherhood of God, the brotherhood of man, and the infinite value of the human soul'.

Liberal Protestantism was, in many ways, captive to the mood of optimism which characterised Western European bourgeois society in the late nineteenth century. The belief in inevitable human progress related well to the belief that the kingdom of God was gradually being extended across the globe, and that this would lead to the dawning of a new day of human brotherhood. It related well, too, to the awareness that other world religions also had a claim on religious truth, and that no theological system or religion could claim to be absolute, a position articulated by another product of the Ritschlian tradition, Ernst Troeltsch (1865–1923).

The optimistic belief in inevitable human progress was soon to be shattered by the outbreak of the First World War in 1914. But already by then biblical scholars and theologians had themselves begun to question whether Ritschl's interpretation of Jesus and the kingdom of God was, in fact, true to the New Testament. Scholars such as Johannes Weiss (1863–1914) and Albert Schweitzer (1875–1965) argued that the key to interpreting the Gospel was the radical eschatology implicit in Jesus' proclamation of the kingdom of God. By this they meant that the kingdom of God could not be equated with the gradual extension of human brotherhood and morality, as in the secular doctrine of inevitable progress; rather the kingdom of God was something radically new which broke into history from beyond. Certainly the kingdom of God was not something which the church could extend or humans build, it was something which God alone could bring about.

Weiss and Schweitzer believed that although their view was the correct interpretation of the kingdom of God, it was not something that any modern person could accept. Thus the message of Jesus and the kingdom had to be reinterpreted. However, the outbreak of war in 1914 shattered any illusions theologians and others might have had about inevitable progress or human brotherhood, and powerfully suggested that biblical eschatology might be true after all. Eschatology, which traditionally meant the doctrine of 'the last things' (death, heaven, and hell), was now restored to its original, biblical meaning as that which has to do with the coming of God's kingdom, and thus became central to the theological discussion.

The nineteenth century really ended with the First World War, and, as already indicated, so did much of the theological endeavour which characterised Protestant liberalism. The Protestant theologian who most decisively led the break with liberalism was the Swiss Reformed theologian, Karl Barth (1886–1968). Barth's commentary on Paul's letter to the Romans, published in 1919, was a radical rejection of liberal theology and a programmatic tract for the development of what has been described as dialectical theology or neo-orthodoxy. Barth is widely recognised by both Protestants and Catholics as one of the greatest theologians of the twentieth century, and it is certainly true that he has left an enormous legacy. But that legacy and the debates it has stimulated, along with the many other major contributors to the discussion, are beyond the boundaries of what we can describe here.

Christianity in the twentieth century: A concluding interpretation

This chapter began with reference to the fact that Christianity has been shaped not only by its origins as described in the New Testament, but also by its two thousand years of historical development in many different social and cultural contexts. In this final section we shall not attempt to describe twentieth-century Christianity in precisely the same way as we have discussed the first nineteen centuries. Rather, we shall present an overview, which is intended to demonstrate our original thesis that Christianity is an historical movement that is held together by a core of common beliefs but expressed in different and sometimes conflicting ways.

Contemporary Christian diversity

Christianity today is embodied in a variety of institutions and manifests itself in different ways. In the first place, the Christian church remains divided into communions, confessions and denominations which have been the result of historical schisms. The ancient divisions between the churches of the East (Eastern Orthodoxy) and the West (Roman Catholic) remain, as do the divisions which occurred at the time of the Protestant Reformation and resulted in the formation of Lutheran, Reformed (Presbyterian and Congregational) and Anabaptist (Baptist and Mennonite) confessional groups. In many instances the national churches that were established at the time of the Reformation, such as the Church of England (Anglican) and the Church of Sweden (Lutheran), continue to fulfil that role. But as a result of the Protestant missionary movement of the nineteenth century, these churches are now also found in various places throughout the world.

Many other divisions have taken place within Protestantism since the time of the Reformation, particularly in North America, giving rise to the phenomenon of denominationalism. Whereas communions (Roman Catholic, Anglican, Eastern Orthodox) and confessions (Catholic, Lutheran, and Reformed) refer to historic divisions in which the claim to be the true church was asserted, denominationalism is an acceptance of Christian plurality, and an assertion of voluntary association and religious tolerance. While some churches may still claim to be the only true Church, in most secular states all churches are given equal political and social rights. Denominationalism is thus a modern phenomenon, resulting from the Enlightenment and historical developments in North America.

Several reasons may be given for the fragmenting of Protestantism, and its continued division into different groups in the modern world. Chief amongst these must be the fact that unlike the Roman Catholic Church with its strong hierarchical structure and focus of unity in the papacy, Protestantism, with its insistence on the authority of Scripture alone, has, since the time of the Reformation, stimulated almost inevitably a variety of interpretations of Christianity. But note must also be taken of the effect which cultural factors, as well as social and political forces, have had in creating and reinforcing division. The theological issues which divide Christians today are often integrally related to different socio-political perceptions, interests and commitments. Such divisions do not necessarily result in schism and the formation of new denominations.

One of the characteristics of Christianity today is that in so many denominations there are polarised groups, some more conservative, evangelical or fundamentalist, and others more liberal or radical, both in their interpretation of Christianity and in their political convictions. Fundamentalism is a movement which originated in the United States in the 1920s in protest against liberal Christianity, biblical criticism, an increasing emphasis on what was called 'the social gospel', and the espousal of the theory of evolution. 'Evangelical' broadly speaking is an equivalent of Protestant, especially in Europe (*Evangelisch* as distinct from Catholic). But it has come to mean those Christians who affirm the verbal inerrancy and infallibility of Scripture, and who seek to remain faithful to the doctrinal convictions of Protestant orthodoxy. In the popular media it is generally associated with the pietistic teaching on being 'born again', a special spiritual experience of conversion which all true Christians are meant to have, and, because fundamentalism originated amongst evangelicals, they are often equated. But many contemporary evangelicals have distanced themselves from fundamentalism because of what they see as its obscurantist views, and there are increasing variations within evangelicalism itself.

The fragmenting of Protestantism, and the resultant rise of new denominations, have had repercussions throughout the world. For example, many of the denominations which emerged in North America during the nineteenth and twentieth centuries, have engaged in missionary work, especially in the so-called third world. In consequence there is now a plethora of Christian denominations found in most countries. A significant factor in this development has been the rapid growth of evangelical and fundamentalist missions, many of which have their origin in the United States, during the second half of the twentieth century. The vast majority of Christian missionaries today are either Roman Catholic or members of some evangelical or fundamentalist denomination. One reason for the gradual demise of the more historic and liberal missions is that the latter have consciously developed self-supporting partner churches in their own right, and, in some cases have united with other denominations.

The ecumenical movement

Indeed, the modern ecumenical movement (*oikumene*, literally meaning 'the whole inhabited universe') came about largely as a result of the nineteenth-century Protestant missionary movement, when denominationalism was seen as a barrier to mission. The first great ecumenical gathering of the twentieth century was held in Edinburgh in 1910, and subsequently the International Missionary Council was formed. Related developments saw the establishment of other ecumenical forums, notably the Council on Life and Work (1925), and the Commission on Faith and Order (1927). Gradually these three instruments of Christian unity and witness moved together.

After the interruption of the Second World War, Life and Work and Faith and Order united to form the World Council of Churches at Amsterdam in 1948. The International Missionary Council also became part of the World Council in 1961. Another noteworthy development took place at the 1961 Third Assembly of the World Council, held in New Delhi, when the Eastern Orthodox churches joined the Council. These churches, which were traditionally confined to the Middle East, Greece and Eastern Europe, have made a significant contribution to the life of the modern church, not least through their diaspora in Western Europe and North America as a consequence of persecution and immigration.

One of the most important events which has shaped contemporary Christianity was the Second Vatican Council (1962–5), called into being by Pope John XXIII. This council of Roman Catholic bishops, the first for almost a century and the first attended by official Protestant observers, not only brought about far-reaching changes within the Catholic Church, but also brought the Catholic Church into a more creative relationship with other churches and the ecumenical movement generally. Since Vatican II the Catholic Church has been deeply involved in dialogue with other churches, and has contributed to the growth of an ecumenical consensus on many aspects of faith and practice. Catholic theologians have been particularly active in the work of the Faith and Order Commission of the World Council of Churches, and participated in the drafting of the important consensus document on 'Baptism, Eucharist and Ministry' adopted by the Faith and Order Commission in 1982. This document, which has been affirmed by many different churches, opens up new possibilities in the search for church union and indicates the extent to which Christians are agreed on matters that have hitherto divided them.

While the ecumenical movement has not fulfilled all of its early promise it has undoubtedly had a profound impact on contemporary Christianity. It has facilitated the formation of united churches in many different countries, thus reversing historic divisions. But the ecumenical movement has had a much wider impact, enabling Christians from many traditions and cultural backgrounds to understand each other better, share their resources, and combine in the service of the needs of the world. This has been of particular importance in meeting various crises that have threatened the church, such as during the church struggle in Germany under the Nazi regime, and in current struggles against racism and oppression. It has also enabled the world-wide church to respond more ably to the many critical disaster situations which have arisen in our time.

Recent developments

Despite the fact that the twentieth century has been marked by considerable efforts towards church unity and co-operation, divisions have continued to mark the development of Christianity in our time. Two such developments are noteworthy. The first is the emergence of the Pentecostal movement at the turn of the century, and the subsequent formation of many Pentecostal denominations such as the Apostolic Faith Mission and Assemblies of God. Pentecostalism, which stresses the need for all Christians to have a special 'baptism in the Holy Spirit' accompanied by 'speaking in tongues', is the fastest-growing form of Christianity in the modern world. It has also had an impact on the more traditional churches through the emergence of the charismatic movement in the 1960s.

Secondly, in many third world countries, where Protestant missions were established in the nineteenth century, indigenous churches have evolved, such as the Kibanguist Church in Zaire and the Zionist Christian Church in South Africa. Indeed, in South Africa, the many African indigenous churches have more than six million members, which makes them the largest church group in the country. These, and many others like them in other parts of the world, have grown rapidly and contributed a vibrant new dimension to Christianity today.

Alongside the emergence of denominations and new movements, the twentieth century has also seen the development of many para-church groups.

These groups have arisen to meet particular needs as perceived by their founders. Some of them, like the Bible Societies, YMCA, or the Sunday School movement, have their origins in the nineteenth century, but continue to fulfil a role today. Others are of more recent origin and represent in certain respects an alternative form of ecumenism to that embodied in the World Council of Churches and in the many national and regional councils which are to be found throughout the world. Of particular note is the work of the organisation founded by the evangelist Billy Graham (1918–), which has played a decisive role in the revitalisation of conservative evangelical Christianity in the latter half of the twentieth century. This evangelical renaissance, which found international expression at the Lausanne Congress of Evangelicals in 1976, has seen the formation of several important new initiatives in Christian witness and service, such as a renewed attempt to evangelise the world, but also a rediscovery of evangelical social concern and commitment.

Despite the ecumenical movement, divisions have continued to occur amongst Christians and churches. Often these divisions are the result of social and political developments, but theological differences also play an important role. Notable amongst the theological differences are those which separate Protestants into liberal, evangelical, and fundamentalist groups. At issue between them is primarily the nature of the Bible, its authority and interpretation for the church today. These issues have become more complex and divisive because of the emergence of contextual theologies which seek to relate the Bible and Christian faith to the socio-political and cultural situations in which Christians find themselves. Of significance has been the development of liberation theology in Latin America, black theology in the United States and South Africa, feminist theology in North America and elsewhere, and, most recently various forms of 'people's theologies' in Asia.

The emergence of such contextual theologies is not a modern phenomenon. All theologies, from the period of the early church through to our own time, have been contextual. But what characterises contextual theologies today is the extent to which they relate to the needs of the poor and oppressed. This reflects the extent to which the church has penetrated deeply into the third world. Indeed, one of the most remarkable aspects of Christianity today is the fact that the vast majority of Christians are no longer found in those countries which formerly constituted European Christendom, but in Africa, Asia, and Latin America. An illustration of this is the strength of the church in South Korea, the new vibrancy of the church in Latin America, and the forecast that Africa will become the Christian continent in the twenty-first century.

The demise of European Christendom, due largely to the inroads of secularism since the Enlightenment and the devastation of two world wars, has resulted in what some scholars refer to as the neo-paganism of Europe. Western Europe is now regarded as a new missionary field that has to be re-evangelised. Partly for this reason, Christian theology in Europe has sought to address a different set of issues from that facing it in the third world. Chief amongst these is the problem of faith in God in a post-Enlightenment age, a problem which raises questions about the interpretation of the Bible and Christian faith for today, or, to use the technical term, hermeneutical issues.

But the shrinking of the world, together with the emergence of an ecumenical awareness, has increasingly forced churches and theologians, whether in the 'first' or 'third' worlds, to relate their faith and reflection to similar issues. The struggle for justice and peace in the world; the challenge of other religious faiths, as well as the challenge of Marxism; and the ongoing task to give a reasonable account of the Christian faith in a sceptical world, are tasks which engage and unite all Christians. Christianity is an historical religion, and this inevitably means change, even decay, renewal and transformation. Undoubtedly Christianity in the twenty-first century will be different from that of today, but some of the developments of our time have undoubtedly set the agenda for the next generation of Christians.

NOTES

1. See C. D. Dodd, *The Apostolic Preaching and its Developments*. London, Hodder & Stoughton, 1936

2. James D. G. Dunn, *Unity and Diversity in the New Testament: An Inquiry into the Character of Earliest Christianity*. Philadelphia, Westminster Press, 1977, p. 32

3. The phrase 'and the Son' (*filioque*) was added later in the sixth century.

SELECT BIBLIOGRAPHY

Dunn, James D. G. *Unity and Diversity in the New Testament*. Philadelphia: Westminster Press, 1977

Frend, W. H. C. *The Rise of Christianity*. Philadelphia: Fortress Press, 1984

Walker, W., Norris, Richard, Lotz, David W. & Handy, Robert T. *A History of the Christian Church*, 4th edition. New York: Charles Scribner's Sons, 1985

Chadwick, Henry. *The Early Church*. Harmondsworth: Penguin Books, 1971

Kelly, H. N. D. *Early Christian Doctrines*, 5th revised edition. London: A & C Black, 1985

Cunliffe-Jones, H. (ed). *A History of Christian Doctrine*. Edinburgh: T & T Clark Ltd., 1978

Neuner, J. & Dupuis, J. (eds). *The Christian Faith in the Doctrinal Documents of the Catholic Church*, revised edition. London: Collins, 1983

Southern, R. W. *Western Society and the Church in the Middle Ages*. Harmondsworth: Penguin Books, 1972

Knowles, David. *The Evolution of Medieval Thought*. London: Longman, 1962

Leff, Gordon. *Medieval Thought: St Augustine to Ockham*. Harmondsworth: Penguin Books, 1970

Chadwick, O. *The Reformation*. Harmondsworth: Penguin Books, 1972

Grimm, Harold J. *The Reformation Era 1500–1650*, 2nd edition. New York: Macmillan, 1965

Williams, George H. *The Radical Reformation*. Philadelphia: The Westminster Press, 1952

Edwards, David L. *Christian England: Its Story to the Reformation, Volume 1*. Grand Rapids: Michigan, 1983

Edwards, David L. *Christian England from the Reformation to the 18th Century, Volume 2*. Grand Rapids: William B. Eerdmans Publishing Co., 1983

Edwards, David L. *Christian England from the 18th Century to the First World War, Volume 3*. Grand Rapids: William B. Eerdmans Publishing Co., 1984

Ahlstrom, Sydney E. *A Religious History of the American People, Vols. 1 and 2*. New York: Doubleday and Company, 1975

Dussel, Enrique. *A History of the Church in Latin America – Colonialism to Liberation (1492–1979)*. Grand Rapids: William B. Eerdmans Publishing Co., 1981
Rouse, R. & Neill, S. C. (eds). *A History of the Ecumenical Movement 1517–1948*. London: SPCK, 1970
Fey, Harold E. (ed). *The Ecumenical Advance: A History of the Ecumenical Movement, Vol. Two 1948–1968*. London: S.P.C.K., 1970
Neill, S. *A History of Christian Missions*. Harmondsworth: Penguin Books, 1964
Livingston, James C. *Modern Christian Thought From the Enlightenment to Vatican II*. New York: Macmillan Publishing Co., 1971
Abbott, Walter M. *The Documents of Vatican II*. London: Geoffrey Chapman, 1966
Fern, Deane William (ed). *Third World Liberation Theologies: A Reader*. New York: Orbis, 1986
Hodgson, Peter C. & King, Robert H. (eds). *Christian Theology: An Introduction to its Tasks and Traditions*. Philadelphia: Fortress Press, 1985
Hodgson, Peter C. & King, Robert H. (eds) *Readings in Christian Theology*. Philadelphia: Fortress Press, 1985
Hastings, A. *A History of African Christianity 1950–1975*. Cambridge: University Press, 1979
De Gruchy, J. W. *Church Struggle in South Africa,* 2nd edition. London: Collins, 1986
Villa-Vicencio, Charles. *Trapped in Apartheid*. New York: Orbis, 1988

9

Islam

EBRAHIM MOOSA

has roots in Judaism + Xtianity as well. Stories like Noah's Ark + the creation are in the Qur'an.

God is one – everything is dependant on God. If he stops, everything will fall away.

Near the end of the sixth century CE, an epoch-making religious figure, Muhammad the Prophet of Islam, was born. The life and teachings of this man herald the advent of Islam in history.

Muslims do not regard Islam as a new religion. For them it is rather the purification and reconstitution of the unique monotheistic religion which the Creator had provided for humankind from the beginning. Islam is the eternal religion, the culmination of a series of divine communications to humanity. Countless prophets in history, Muslims believe, have shared a common objective to preach the divinity of a transcendent creator to their own peoples. In Islamic thought this line of prophecy culminated in the Arabian prophet Muhammad.

Literally, the word 'Islam' originates from the Arabic root *s-l-m*, which means 'to be safe and free'. The infinitive *islam* means 'to surrender' and 'to be unfettered'. For this reason a person who 'surrenders' is called a Muslim (the active participle of *islam*) for submitting to the will of God. On the universality of *islam*, the Islamic tradition declares that throughout history all the prophets, sages and persons of wisdom have taught humanity the essential message to 'surrender' to God. It is in this sense that Muhammad's prophecy is a confirmation of the teachings of previous prophets. It is from the same root *s-l-m* that the familiar Islamic greeting, *salam* (peace) is derived. Implicit in it is the truth that peace in the world can only occur if humans 'surrender' themselves to God.

THE CONTEXT OF ISLAM

Arabia is the crucible of Islam and also forms part of a larger religious context, Mesopotamia, sometimes called the Near East. This was the region in which the Judaeo-Christian family of religions first flourished. From this perspective the origins and content of Islam cannot be viewed in isolation from the religious history of Zoroastrianism, Judaism and Christianity, which also have their roots in the Near East. Though different in orientation, the three religions share

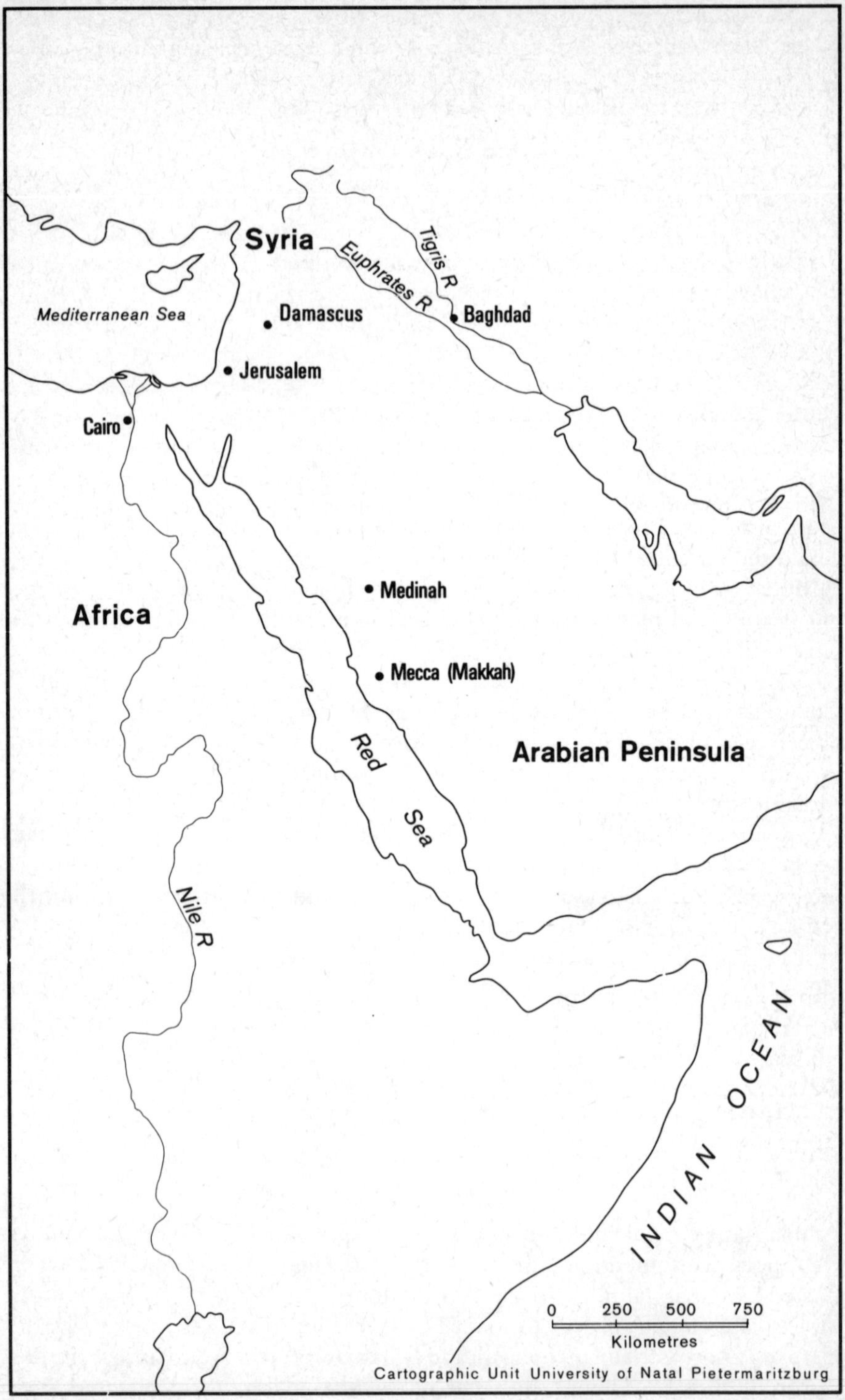
Syria
Tigris R
Euphrates R
Mediterranean Sea
Damascus
Baghdad
Jerusalem
Cairo
Medinah
Africa
Mecca (Makkah)
Arabian Peninsula
Red
Sea
Nile R
INDIAN OCEAN
0
250
500
750
Kilometres
Cartographic Unit University of Natal Pietermaritzburg

certain basic features. All are transcendental, holding that beyond this life there is a higher world, the realm of the divine, which can be attained through ethical action and faith in God; each one claims God exclusively, as a monotheistic deity; and they are all universal, believing that God created and continues to govern the whole universe and all people.

Makkah (Mecca)

The centre of the new religion that arose in seventh-century Arabia was Makkah – sometimes called Mecca. It was both a commercial centre and capital of the pre-Islamic religion and its pagan cults. The *Ka'bah* (literally, 'the cube'), a rectangular stone building surrounded by a holy space associated with Abraham, formed the point of annual pilgrimage for the whole of Arabia. Makkah had the added attraction of hosting the Fair of Ukaz, which coincided with the annual pilgrimage to the Makkan shrine. These activities were of immense political, economic and cultural importance to the prestige of the city.

At the time that Islam emerged, major changes were taking place in the political economy of Arabia. Under the impact of commercial development and commodity trade, the nomadic way of life based on kinship and a barter economy was giving way to a more settled society, characterised by increasing stratification and division. Towns grew in importance, notably the two centres associated with Muhammad – Makkah and Madinah – and came under the power of a merchant oligarchy which also controlled the new money economy.

At the same time religious practices were also becoming more centralised. Smaller tribes abandoned their local shrines and increasingly venerated those patronised by larger groups. While household gods and other religious symbols denoting kinship ties of the older society continued to exist until the advent of Islam, there was an increasing tendency in Arabia to worship one god above others.

Muhammad at Makkah

Muhammad was born about 570 CE into an impoverished branch of the main merchant family in the trading city of Makkah, an important junction of caravan routes along which products of the Arabian peninsula were carried to the Mediterranean. In terms of kinship and lineage, Muhammad was well placed, but he was orphaned at an early age and grew up in straitened circumstances. While many chroniclers have attempted to paint a picture of an unusual, even fantastic childhood, he seems to have been according to authentic accounts a serious, intelligent and normal young man. From a very early age he impressed his fellow citizens as an individual of integrity and enjoyed widespread respect and admiration. In his teens he earned the title of the Trustworthy among the citizens of Makkah.

Muhammad's personality is inseparable from any discussion of Islam, for he is seen by Muslims as the messenger of God to the world. In addition to the Qur'an, his prophetic example, known as the *sunnah*, also forms part of the central teaching of Islam. Muslims view the Muhammad as the 'seal of prophets', in that he both confirmed previous revelations and was the last in the line of prophets, after whom there will be no other. Although he is considered a mere mortal in one sense, he is also the religious symbol of God in another. Dogma defines him as infallible. On mentioning his name in ordinary speech, Muslims offer a prayer and salute him by saying silently or audibly – depending on the circumstances – May God's peace and blessings be upon him.

Biographers record that from an early age Muhammad showed concern for the injustices of his society. The main features of Arab society at the time were the oppression of the poor and the weak, fratricidal tribal wars, gender discrimination, slavery and commercial exploitation. Muhammad often retired in isolation to a cave called Hira, near Makkah, in order to reflect and contemplate. On one such occasion, around his fortieth birthday in the year 610, he had a vision, in which appeared the archangel Gabriel (*Jibril*), who declared:

> Recite: In the Name of thy Lord who created,
> created the Human of a blood-clot.
> Recite: And thy Lord is the Most Generous,
> who taught by the Pen,
> taught Man, that he knew not. (Qur'an 96:1–5)

This supernatural event – as Muslims regard it – marked the beginning of thirteen years of prophetic mission in Makkah. Muhammad's central message stressed the supremacy of Allah, as the only deity worthy of worship, rejecting at the same time the multitude of gods which the majority of people in the Arabian Peninsula worshipped.

Towards Madinah

As the Prophet's faith-movement and ideas gained a small but significant number of converts, there was increasing opposition from Makkah's mercantile aristocracy, whose materialist greed Muhammad censured. The hostility this aroused led to his *hijrah* (exodus or emigration) with his family and a few followers in 622 to the town of Yathrib, some 300 miles to the north of Makkah. This migration forms the turning-point in the development of Islam. In subsequent Muslim history, the *hijrah* marks the start of the Islamic calendar, signifying the beginning of a new community.

When the exiled prophet arrived in Yathrib, or Madinah (the City of the prophet, as it came to be known), conditions there were favourable for the new faith. The existing socio-religious order was riven by internecine strife between the two main tribes. Like Makkah, Madinah was undergoing social change. Here, Muhammad increasingly assumed the dual role of spiritual and temporal leader. And within a decade he had united the greater part of Arabia under his authority.

Soon after his arrival in Yathrib, it became necessary to defend the new Muslim community against attack. At the same time Muhammad's primary objective was to spread his message as widely as possible with the greatest degree of success. To this end he employed the Arab military traditions of raiding and plundering, which he infused with the notion of *jihad*, or moral struggle. One of his first moves was to strike at the commercial trade-routes which were vital to the Makkan economy. The Makkan caravans had to pass by Madinah on their way to the prosperous markets of Syria. Muhammad's plan was to weaken Makkah so that he might establish Islam there, in what was already the religious capital of Arabia. The journey back to Makkah – a symbolic return after the *hijrah* – would thus be crucial.

The last years

After several encounters between Muhammad's forces and the Makkan army, the Prophet marched into Makkah in 630 in a surprise but bloodless take-over of the city. This momentous victory marked the fulfilment of the Prophet's wish to make Makkah the spiritual home of Islam.

In 632, the last year of his life, Muhammad led the first Islamic pilgrimage to Makkah, where he delivered his historic Farewell Pilgrimage speech. The speech covered a wide range of moral and social issues, and enunciated some of the central beliefs of Islam – humanitarianism, egalitarianism, social and economic justice, righteousness and solidarity. A summary of the principal ideas is contained in the following edited version of this famous address.

> O men, listen to my words. I do not know whether I shall ever meet you in this place after this year. Your blood and your property are sacrosanct until you meet your Lord, as this day and this month is holy . . . He who has a pledge let him return it to him who entrusted him with it; all usury is abolished, but you have your capital. Wrong not and you shall not be wronged . . . You have your rights over your wives and they have rights over you . . . I have left with you something if you hold fast to it you will never fall into error – a plain indication, the book of God and the practice of His prophet, so give heed to what I say. Know that every Muslim is a Muslim's brother, and that the Muslims are brethren. It is only lawful to take from your brother what he gives you willingly, so wrong not yourselves. O God, have I not told you? [Those who were present said] "O God, yes," and the apostle said, "O God bear witness."[1]

THE BELIEFS OF ISLAM

Formal entry into Islam is achieved by proclaiming the *Shahadah*, which means 'to witness'. It is probably the simplest and tidiest credal statement in the Abrahamic religious tradition, and it declares: 'There is no other god but God, and Muhammad is God's Messenger.' When this formula – known as the 'two-witnesses', or 'the word' – is consciously uttered, one becomes a Muslim. In other words, surrender to God's will has taken place. Islam stresses the universality of monotheism as the primal creed of all humanity, which finds expression in the doctrine of unity – *tawhid*.

God

The Qur'an emphasises that within the Near Eastern tradition monotheism was the fundamental creed of faith. This is evident in the Qur'an's account of

Abraham, the patriarch of the Judaeo-Christian tradition. The doctrine of *tawhid* maintains the indivisible nature and oneness of God. Because Arabic is the liturgical language of Islam, Muslims from Jakarta to Boston describe God as 'Allah'.[2]

The term 'Allah' refers to a 'high god' in pre-Islamic religion. But Muhammad's revelatory inspiration changed this notion. In Islam, 'Allah' signifies a transcendent, omnipotent, omnipresent and sovereign deity, who is beyond human perception. The character and attributes of Allah are clearly described in both metaphorical expressions and unequivocal descriptive statements.

God has no intermediaries and has created everything by the command 'Be'. Although the Divine is believed to be present everywhere, it does not inhere in anything. The picture of God in the Qur'an does not categorically resolve the question of divine immanence or transcendence. 'We are closer to a human being than his jugular vein', says one verse, while another says: 'There is nothing like Him.' Above all, the Divine is the God who guides one along the 'straight path'. Compassion, mercy and power tempered with justice are the salient features of the God of the Qur'an. And, unlike the pre-Islamic concept of belief in a blind and inexorable fate over which humans had no control, Islam proposes a powerful but provident and merciful God.

Tawhid

The doctrine of *tawhid* or monotheism is the essence of Islamic faith. For outsiders, *tawhid* may appear to be a statement of the obvious, but for a Muslim it represents the alpha and omega of the faith.

> [It is] in addition to a metaphysical assertion about the nature of the Absolute, a method of integration, a means of becoming whole and realizing the profound oneness of all existence. Every aspect of Islam rotates about the doctrine of Unity which Islam seeks to realize first of all in the human being in his inner and outward life.[3]

A world-view based on *tawhid* considers God as the normative criterion of religious experience. In other words, God is the Being who commands. Every command of God becomes an ought-to-be, or an ought-to-do; in short, a value.

This emphasis on the oneness of God, or *tawhid*, recognises that nature is well knit and operates on the basis of laws of natural causation. But this does not render God a *deus otiosus*. Nor does it mean that God and nature are rivals which function at the expense of one another; or that God operates in addition to the activities of man and nature.

According to Fazlur Rahman, 'things and humans are, indeed, directly related to God just as they are related to each other'. In other words, God is 'with' everything in so far as the Divine constitutes the integrity of everything. Since everything is related directly to the Divine, 'so is everything, through and in relation to other things, related to God as well. God, then, is the very meaning of reality, a meaning manifested, clarified, and brought home by the universe.'[4] Without God's activity, both nature and humanity become delinquent, purposeless and self-wasting. The role of human beings is to further God's meaningful and purposeful activity through creative moral action.

Muslim theologians thus replaced the philosopher's explanation of causality with the doctrine of 'occasionalism'. This means that at every moment, God recreates the world and is directly responsible for what takes place. The upshot of this theory was the establishment of a causality of divine presence. This is what is meant by the expression that God is with everything, which is different from the immanentist belief that God is everything or is in everything.

The Muslim theologian perceives God as a 'core of normativeness'. Being normative means that God is that sought-after end which is an end-in-itself. In Islam the Creator is the Final End, which implies the uniqueness of the Other. This precludes the dependence of the Ultimate upon another entity. In this sense God is self-sufficient. God's self-sufficiency does not preclude human beings from knowing God's imperatives and obeying these commands. In the Islamic tradition it is possible for human beings to come to know God's will by means of reason. However, Muslims believe, certainty can only be arrived at by revelation. It is revelation that enables human beings to fulfil their ethical vocation with intellectual certainty.

Significance of tawhid

Al-Faruqi, one of the leading Islamic scholars of the twentieth century, has described the core principles of *tawhid* as five self-evident truths: duality, ideationality, teleology, human capacity/the malleability of nature, and responsibility/judgement.

Duality insists that reality is of two generic kinds – God and non-God, or Creator and creature. These are separate realms, both in terms of being (ontology) and of existence. One is infinite and the other is finite. Hence, it is impossible for the finite to transcend its finitude and pass into infinity, or for these two orders of reality to be united, confused or diffused into each other.

This relationship between the Creator and creature is ideational in nature, for it is human understanding that mediates between the infinite and the finite. The ideational faculties such as the intellect, reason, imagination, intuition and observation enable humankind to understand the will of God when it is expressed through revelation or the laws of nature or both.

Because of *tawhid* human endeavour is purposive, with a *telos* (goal) in sight. While human actions do have a utilitarian aspect, it is the teleological character of actions that provides them with the distinctive quality of being moral.

Human beings also possess the capacity and potentiality to realise the divine raison d'être of creation. Without potentialities *per se*, human beings would be unable to further the divine Will. The actualisation of these potentialities results in moral action. Nature and the entire universe is *'muslim'* (that which submits or surrenders). It conforms to the laws of nature ingrained in it; in other words it is automatically *'muslim'*.

Human beings are designated as the Creator's vice-regents on earth and are therefore required to 'surrender' to God's law by choice; in other words, to be *'muslim'* by choice. This indicates the uniqueness of humans in that they possess a free will. By following divine commands, in terms of which they ought to act, they fulfil a responsibility placed on them by God. Effective responsibility requires that one has the ability to make a judgement and be decisive in such decision-making.

SOURCES OF DOCTRINE AND LAW

Islamic doctrine and law (in short, the social views of Islam) are based on four primary sources of knowledge. They are: (1) the Qur'an, (2) the *sunnah* (tradition), (3) *ijma'* (consensus), and (4) *qiyas* (analogy). The first two – the Qur'an and *sunnah* – are called the transmitted sources; *ijma'* and *qiyas* are rational sources. When these sources are employed to explicate theology they are known as the sources of theology; when used to elaborate the moral and social law, they are termed the science of jurisprudence.

The Qur'an

Literally, the Qur'an means a 'recitation' or 'reading', a reference to its oral character. Muslim tradition regards it as the Word or Speech of God, as the *ipsissima verba* of God revealed to Muhammad over a period of 23 years. Using a familiar Christian idiom one could say that for Muslims it is the 'incarnated word of God'. The text is divided into 114 chapters, called *surah*. Each *surah* consists of a varying number of verses. A *surah* may derive its title from the overall theme discussed in it, or by virtue of an idea or item mentioned in it, such as 'the Cow', 'Women', 'the Bee', 'Daybreak' and so forth. For devotional purposes the text is divided into 30 divisions so that one division may be read for each day of the month.

For practical and exegetical purposes, the chapters of the Qur'an are distinguished between those revealed in Makkah and those in Madinah. The two phases should not be seen as separate careers in the life of the Prophet, though they are discrete periods. They reflect the history of the Prophet's mission as spiritual teacher and statesman. The Makkan chapters deal primarily with such concerns as belief in a monotheistic God, eschatology (with specific reference to the Day of Judgement), and socio-economic justice. The style and tenor of the Makkan verses is short, abrupt and staccato – like volcanic eruptions. The early Makkan verses symbolise the spiritual struggle of the Prophet and give it a deep and powerful 'psychological moment'. This tone gradually gives way to a more fluent and easy style in the Madinan phase. Here the themes are of a theological and legal nature prescriptive of moral and ritual behaviour.

Collection and commitment to writing

As soon as the Prophet received the divine revelation he immediately dictated it to scribes. The earliest copies of the Qur'an were written on pieces of parchment, skins, bones and leaves. The Prophet also permitted people to recite the Qur'an in their various local dialects. However, after his death the Qur'an was standardised into the dominant Qurayshi dialect. Variant readings came to be regarded as unacceptable and the standard version became known as the 'Uthmanic codice, after the third caliph, who successfully completed this task.

Abrogation of Qur'anic verses

A document revealed over a period of 23 years in the life of a community is bound to reflect the various stages of change such a people experience. In the Qur'an (2: 106) mention is made of verses being abrogated, which are either replaced by a similar revelation or a better version. An example would be the verses which reportedly prescribed stoning to death as the penalty for adultery. Although no longer part of the Qur'anic text, these verses are believed to have been repealed by those which prescribe corporal punishment for sexual offences. Similarly, verses which propose that the inheritance of a dead person be distributed on the basis of kinship are still part of the written text, but have been superseded by others which suggest inheritance on the basis of agnate and cognate relations.

Controversy surrounds the exact number of abrogated verses, the figures varying between a dozen and close to a hundred. A small group of scholars denies that textual abrogation ever took place and interprets 2: 106 to mean the supersession of the Hebrew and Christian biblical dispensation by the Qur'an.

Inimitability of the Qur'an

Those who know Arabic well and who appreciate the genius of the language acknowledge that the Qur'an is both graceful and numinous. The inability of Muhammad's contemporaries to match the literary eloquence and beauty of the Qur'an is viewed as a triumph over those who disputed its divine origin, and gave rise to the dogma of the 'inimitability' or 'matchlessness' of the Qur'an. This claim has limited value for the non-Arabic speaker who is unable to appreciate the literary genius of the Qur'an at first hand. The dogma of inimitability has to a large extent contributed to the belief that the Qur'an is untranslatable. Some orthodox practitioners have in fact resolutely prohibited the publication of translations unaccompanied by the Arabic text.

The process of revelation

The Qur'an is regarded by Muslims as a revelation or inspiration from God. Its cosmic 'descent' is said to have taken place between the 26th and 27th night of the month of Ramadan. Revelation unfolds gradually and intermittently, after the initial 'descent'. Gabriel, who is frequently referred to as the 'spirit', was also instrumental in the gradual revelation. Early traditions record the appearance of Gabriel impersonating a man, but many of these traditions are no longer uncritically accepted.

Revelation is said to have been accompanied by periods of heavy sweating, which signifies the extraordinary 'weight' of the message. The Qur'an itself testifies to the crushing burden and power of its message. 'If We had sent this Qur'an down upon a mountain, you would have seen it humbled and split asunder through fear of God' (59: 21).

Interpretation

The Qur'an is traditionally interpreted by considering the chronology of revelation and the context or background against which revelation took place.

This genre of literature is called the 'occasions of revelation'. The primary source of this genre is the explanations given by the Prophet and his Companions. But the bulk of commentaries and interpretations can be traced back to the post-prophetic era. During the first two centuries of Islam (seventh and eighth centuries CE) certain principles were formulated to enable scholars to arrive at the correct literal interpretation (*tafsir*) of the Qur'an.

Interpreters were required to be skilled in the Arabic language, in grammar and rhetoric, knowledgeable in the 'occasions of revelation' and the theories of abrogation, and capable of classifying verses of a general or specific nature or differentiating between clear and unclear verses. Another form of interpretation was to resort to an esoteric interpretation, *ta'wil*, based on a personal reading of the text.

Commentaries on the Qur'an

There are a large number of classical and modern commentaries. Some of the more famous commentaries are those of al-Tabari (839–923), an encyclopaedic compendium of exegesis or *tafsir*; al-Zamakhshari (1075–1143), who despite his rational theological views, has been acclaimed for his commentary; and Fakhr al-Din al-Razi (d. 1209), known for his valuable insights on *tafsir*. In modern times a plethora of commentaries is available in virtually every major Muslim language. In major European languages there have also been several translations or commentaries. In English, the most popular are *The Holy Qur'an* by 'Abdullah Yusuf 'Ali, *The Koran Interpreted* by A. J. Arberry, *The Glorious Koran* by Marmaduke Pickthall and *The Message of the Qur'an* by Muhammad Asad. The incomplete Arabic commentary *Tafsir al-Manar* ('The Light-house'), a series of lectures by the modern Egyptian scholar Muhammad Abduh (1849–1905), which was edited by his Syrian disciple, Rashid Rida (1865–1935), deserves mention. The Urdu commentary *Tarjuman al-Qur'an* ('Interpreter of the Qur'an') by the Indian scholar and politician Abu al-Kalam Azad (1888–1958), and that of the revivalist scholar, Abu-l-A'la Mawdudi (1904–79), called *Tafhim al-Qur'an* ('Understanding the Qur'an'), are also of note. Both have been translated into English.

Symbolism and beauty

Our encounter with the Qur'an must include a grasp of its significance in the symbolic and semiotic universe of Muslims. As previously mentioned, the Qur'an is primarily an oral work. For this reason Muslims have developed an elaborate science of the art of recitation or *tajwid* which prescribes the proper recitation of the holy scripture. The Qur'an is most often read for liturgical purposes in the daily ritual prayers. It is also read at social events, celebrations and festivals. The melodious recitation (*qirat*) of the Qur'an is highly appreciated in devout circles.

The sunnah (tradition)

For Muslims, revelation ceased at the death of Muhammad. With the conclusion of scriptural mediation and the absence of a prophetic presence, the normative practice of Muhammad, the *sunnah*, came to gain increasing importance. Literally, *sunnah* means 'the well-trodden path'. Within the broader cultural context of pre-Islamic Arabia the term carried the wider meaning of an organic social practice accepted as the community norm. But early Islam baptised the term into the Islamic discourse. The Islamised *sunnah* has evolved into a precise and definitive understanding of the model practice of the Prophet as a religious norm. It needs to be stressed that this norm has undergone various stages of conceptual development. A grasp of these changes is therefore crucial in order to avoid a mechanical understanding of the *sunnah*.

The term *hadith* derives from the Arabic root *h-d-th*, which means 'to happen', 'to tell a happening' or 'to report', and refers to the verbal transmission of the *sunnah*. The corpus of *ahadith* is of titanic inclusiveness, ranging from instructions on how to cut toe-nails to the running of a government. A *hadith* is defined as a statement or action of the Prophet or those approved by him. In other words, it is the literary attestation of the *sunnah*. However, a great deal of discussion and debate has taken place, and still continues today, whether of necessity every *hadith* can be attributed verbally to the Prophet.

While the *sunnah* means the normative behaviour of the Prophet one must remember that the Prophet's society was primarily oral. During the growth and formative period of the original Muslim community the religious norms or *sunnan* were less of a verbal nature and more of a silent exemplification in action. It was this non-verbal 'living tradition' that in practice always aspired towards reproducing and fulfilling the example of the Prophet, which Muslims speak of as the Apostolic model. Knowledge of how the first generation of scholars after Muhammad's death accepted the tradition is the key to understanding the *sunnah* or the Apostolic model. Thus when speaking about the formative period of Islam we can say that the *sunnah* and the *hadith* were consubstantial and coeval.

The early community, especially during the time of the Companions or close followers of the Prophet and their Successors, deduced the living *sunnah* from an understanding of the ideal *sunnah* of the Prophet. In a sense the understanding of *sunnah* was organic to the community to the extent that the deeds and sayings of the Companions also became known as the *sunnah*. This means that the Companions interpreted the Prophet's conduct. For the first generation this was a relatively easy exercise since they reported what they witnessed the Prophet of God do. These eyewitnesses in turn became the actual sources of transmission.

After that early period, especially after the rapid expansion of the first two centuries, the difficulty of assessing *hadith* grew. What further complicated matters was the host of interpretations of the variety of living *sunnah*. Technical terms were invented to systematise this complex process of tradition and soon became a field for specialists. For instance, the chain of witnesses and transmitters who conveyed a specific tradition came to be known as the *isnad*. The content or 'text' of the transmission was called the *matn*. The *isnad* which introduces a *hadith* would read as follows: 'It was related to me by A, on the authority of B, on the authority of C, on the authority of D, from E (who may be a Companion of the Prophet) that the Prophet said: "My community will never agree on an error".'

Science of hadith

The *hadith* literature laid stress on the authenticity and credibility of the transmitters. In pursuit of authenticity a sophisticated science developed to sift *hadith*, known as the 'science of disparaging and declaring trustworthy'. This science was only fully articulated in the tenth century CE, after the major compilations came into existence.

With the emphasis on the chain of transmission (*isnad*), traditions can be divided into four broad categories: (1) the number of transmitters in the chain; (2) the soundness of the *isnad* itself; (3) some special features in the *isnad* (chain) or the *matn* (text); and (4) in terms of accepted and rejected traditions. We shall discuss each of these in turn.

1. When an overwhelming number of reliable transmitters narrate a *hadith* it attains the highest quality of *mutawatir* or *tawatur* – meaning consecutive testimony. It relies on the large number of narrators at every stage of the chain of transmission, which makes the *hadith* inductively so certain that doubt is logically excluded. Traditionists would say it is 'impossible to accuse all the narrators of colluding or being compelled to lie'.

All those *ahadith* which cannot make the category of *tawatur* are called *'ahad* (isolated). That means the number of transmitters are few. In between the *mutawatir* and *'ahad* categories are a number of sub-categories, such as a *mashur* (popular) tradition narrated by more than two persons, and *'aziz*, a tradition supported by at least one person.

2. In terms of the nature of the *isnad*, a tradition that has an unbroken or uninterrupted transmission from the source is known as a *muttasil* (continuous) *hadith*. When this unbroken chain cites the Prophet as the source it is known as *muttasil marfu'* or just *marfu'* (unbroken and elevated). If the source is a Companion it would be called a *muttasil mawquf* tradition (unbroken but discontinued at the source). Other categories are *mursal*, where a Companion quotes the Prophet directly and possibly skips the person he heard it from; and *munfasil*, a transmission with several breaks in the *isnad*.

3. As regards the special features of the chain or text, the most popular transmission is the *mu'an'an* (on the authority of), where successive transmitters report on the authority of a previous transmitter without indicating how the transmission was received; *tadlis* (hiding defects) in the transmission; *muharraf* (altered), when words are changed in a text; or *musahhaf* (mistaken) when a slight error takes place in the text or chain.

4. Rejected traditions which are fictitious are called *mawdu'*, which is the worst type; others are *munkar* (ignored), when one transmitter narrates something contrary to or different from what more reliable transmitters had stated.

The collection of hadith

Conflicting reports abound about the recording and collection of *hadith* during the Prophetic period and in the formative period of Islam. The Prophet is said to have discouraged the writing down of his own sayings, fearing that people would confuse his sayings with that of the Holy Book, the Qur'an. Other evidence indicates however that he allowed and even instructed people to record his statements.

Whatever the reasons for the prohibition of writing *hadith*, it is fairly certain that some persons made notes for their own guidance and these formed the basis of later works.

The earliest extant collection of *hadith* is the *Muwatta'* of Malik ibn Anas (d. 795) and the narratives of the biographer, Ibn Ishaq (d. 767). Neither of these scholars always provided the full chain of narrators. Later, it was al-Shafi'i (d. 819), whose insistence on correlating tradition with the law resulted in the rigorous pursuit of *hadith* as the second authoritative source in Islam.

The six canons of hadith

From the ninth century CE onwards, six authoritative canons of *hadith* were recognised by the Sunni tradition (the numerically larger of the two main branches of Islam), and these are known as the Six Genuine Ones. These books were named after their editors or compilers. Materials were included and excluded on the basis of criteria adopted by each compiler. The most authentic and revered collection is the *Authentic Collection* of al-Bukhari (810–70 CE), which is acclaimed as next only to the Qur'an in authority. The other highly rated collection is that of Muslim ibn al-Hajjaj (817–75 CE). These are the most important collections, with scholarly preferences shifting between the two. They are also known as the *Jawami* (sing. *Jami*), namely collections embracing all fields of reported prophetic knowledge. Another collection in the *Jami* category is that of al-Tirmidhi (d. 892).

Three other works are called the *Sunan* (Traditions) collections. Each is known as the *Kitab al-Sunan* of such an author. They are classified as *Sunan* because they cover specialised areas of *hadith*. Abu Da'ud al-Sijistani (817–889 CE) produced the *Kitab al-Sunan* ('Book of Traditions'), which contains only matters of jurisprudence. His student, Ibn Majah (824–86 CE) also compiled a collection with the same title, and they are popularly known as the *Sunan* of Abu Da'ud and *Sunan* of Ibn Majah. Al-Nasa'i (830–915 CE) likewise titled his work the *Kitab al-Sunan*, which contains materials on religious law relating to ritual acts.

The 'Genuine Six' are also known as the *musannafat* (classified) works since their materials are arranged according to subject matter. Some collections are labelled as the *masanid* (chains) since their content is arranged according to the name of the Companion from whom the *isnad* starts.

The minority Shi'i tradition (the smaller of Islam's two main sections) developed its own corpus of traditions, although some *ahadith* appear in both Sunni and Shi'i branches. Unlike the Sunnis, the Shi'ahs only accept traditions that are reported by the people of the House of the Prophet. The basic belief of all Shi'ism is that the legitimate successor of Muhammad as *imam* (spiritual leader) was his cousin and son-in-law, 'Ali. He was followed by a number of successors who provided spiritual and worldly guidance. The traditions of the Prophet and the imams are documented in special collections known as *Kitab al Kafi fi-'Ilm al-Din* ('What is Sufficient for Knowledge of Religion') by al-Kulayni

(d. 939); *Kitab man la Yahduruhu al-faqih* ('Everyone His Own Lawyer') by Ibn 'Ali Babawayh al-Qummi (d. 991); and *Tahdhib al-Ahkam* ('Refining Judgements') and *al-Istibsar fi ma ukhtulifa min al-akhbar* ('Examination of What is In Dispute among the Reporters') by al-Tusi (d. 1067). In the Shi'i tradition these 'Four Books' enjoy the same status as the 'Genuine Six' in the Sunni tradition.

Ijtihad

Ijtihad (literally, 'to exert') means in legal philosophy to engage in systematic and creative original thinking. The intention of this creative process is to understand the purposes and intentions of God the Law-giver in the revealed sources. It also means to derive rules and principles from the Qur'an, the *sunnah* and the legal precedents of previous jurists. The aim is either to alter, modify, restrict or extend those rules in order that they might subsume a new situation. Over the centuries *ijtihad* has laid the groundwork for an intricate interpretive process or hermeneutics within Islamic thought.

In the post-Shafi period, original thinking gradually gave way to a greater reliance on two very formal methods of *ijtihad*, namely *ijma'* (consensus) and the limited use of *qiyas* (analogical reasoning). As the architect of the science of jurisprudence, al-Shafi'i introduced these two forms of *ijtihad* with the view of safeguarding the *sunnah*. Later jurists restricted the scope of *ijtihad* to a very rigid and formalistic procedure and in effect it became a dead letter. Thus, by the tenth century in Sunni thought 'the doors of *ijtihad* were closed'. However, in Shi'i thought this door must of necessity always remain open.

The end of *ijtihad* can partly be explained by the political upheavals during the formative period of Islam. As soon as relative stability was established around the tenth century it certainly suited some political leaders to discourage original thinking in the hope that political instability would end. With the co-operation of the religious authorities this became possible and the corpus of Islamic thought was assumed 'closed'. From then onwards it was sufficient to 'follow precedents' and acknowledge the prescriptions of the past authorities. Two methods of interpretation (sometimes called 'sources'), namely *ijma'* and *qiyas* were allowed, because they were widely approved and were also less threatening to the stability of the Muslim community.

In recent times several Muslims, notable among them the modern Egyptian thinker Muhammad 'Abduh and the Indian philosopher Muhammad Iqbal (1875–1938), have advocated the reintroduction of creative thinking and an end to the uncritical following of past authorities.

Consensus

In the usage of Islamic jurists *ijma'* (literally, 'to be resolute') means the agreement or unanimity of competent thinkers on a religious matter for which there is no explicit previous textual evidence. For example, it is agreed by *ijma'* that when polluted water changes one of its features (colour, taste or smell), it becomes unsuitable for the purpose of ritual purification. Similarly, the five daily prayers and the five pillars of Islam are all validated by consensus.

The definition of *ijma*ʻ has been a source of disagreement among scholars. According to the classical definition, the disagreement of even a single competent scholar proves invalidating. This seems to be the result of al-Shafiʻi's influence on religious thought. But many classical scholars held that a 'majority view' constitutes an *ijma*ʻ. Unanimity, in their view, applies to the few essentials of religion only.

Shah Wali Allah (d. 1176), an outstanding Indian mystic and scholar, criticised the classical definition of *ijma*ʻ. Total unanimity, he said, was impossible, if not impractical. He favoured the consensus of those in authority. This consensus should then be enforced by the caliph in order that it may gain greater communal recognition. The well-known tradition of the Prophet which says that 'my community will not agree on error' does not imply *ijma*ʻ, according to Wali Allah. This tradition is often construed in such a way as to impute infallibility to the process of *ijma*ʻ. In Wali Allah's opinion, it can be explained by another tradition in the *hadith* collection of Muslim ibn al-Hajjaj, which states: 'A section of my community will continue to obey God's command, and those who desert or oppose them shall not be able to do them any harm. They will be dominating the people until God's command is executed.' According to Wali Allah, if both traditions are read in context they refer to a defined group of people who will not deviate from the *sunnah* and who fulfil their obligatory religious duties. This interpretation is very different from the view which holds consensus to be infallible.

*Ijma*ʻ can be construed to mean 'soundness of opinion'. It demonstrates that consensus lends an amount of relative certainty and exactitude to the content itself. It is in a sense a collective *ijtihad* or legislation. In Fazlur Rahman's view, *ijma*ʻ provides an idea of authority which is not absolute. It is a method and principle to provide 'working security from error'. As a method and organic process it grows. At any given moment it has 'supreme functional validity and power and in that sense is 'final' but at the same moment it creates, assimilates, modifies and rejects.' As such it guarantees no absolute truth-value. In the post-Shafiʻ period, however, *ijma*ʻ imposed an absolute authority not only on the present and future, but also on the past. It determined what was *sunnah* and what was not. It also determined the correct interpretation of the Qur'an. As a method it shaped the complex beliefs and practices of Muslims, but cut off from genuine *ijtihad* it became a 'static tool of oppression'. For example, if a husband utters the triple divorce formula to his wife in one sitting even in anger, then according to the dominant interpretation of the law she becomes irrevocably divorced from him. This ruling is even today enforced by many jurists on the grounds that it is supported by consensus, despite the painful consequences it has on people's lives.

In the Shiʻi view *ijma*ʻ means the unanimity of all the jurists in this branch of Islam. It is assumed that since consensus is the unanimity of 'all' the jurists, it would include the views of the imams of the past, because the views of the ancient imams are of paramount importance in the Shiʻi tradition.

Analogical reasoning

Analogical reasoning or *qiyas* literally means 'to approximate one thing with another' or 'to equate two things'. Muslim jurists understand it to mean the application of a known ruling to a case where no ruling exists, simply because the two cases at hand share a common cause (*'illah*) or *ratio legis*. Simply put, it means to solve the unknown with the known because they share a common legal cause.

Of the two rational methods, *qiyas* is the more disputed. Leading scholars, including Ahmad ibn Hanbal (780–855 CE) and Ibn Hazm (994–1063 CE), have rejected it as a method of ascertaining and resolving religious questions. However, the majority of Islamic scholars and jurists accept it as an authoritative method of discovering the law in areas where there is no statute.

At best analogical reasoning is a linguistic device. It should not be confused with analogy as understood in logic. Analogy in logic requires two premises with a concluding middle. It further requires philosophical demonstration on the basis of universals to solve particulars. Analogy in Sunni jurisprudence differs significantly from its counterpart in the science of logic. In *qiyas* one premiss suffices and conclusions may be reached by way of particulars and not universals. *Qiyas* is flexible and admits of interpretation whereas logic has rigid and formal rules. An example of *qiyas* is the prohibition on the use of intoxicating drugs (for non-medicinal purposes) which is derived from the ruling on alcohol. Both drugs and alcohol share a common *'illah* (causative factor), which is intoxication. For this reason drugs, like alcohol, are unlawful.

According to the Shi'i school, reason (*'aql*) and not *qiyas* is the fourth source. By reason is meant the categorical judgements of pure and practical reason. Here reason implies its formal status in logic and philosophy. In Shi'i thought there is a principle which states that 'whatever is ordered by reason, is also ordered by religion'. Therefore, the judgement of practical reason deems that justice is good and injustice is evil. The modern Shi'i scholar, Muhammad Baqir al-Sadr (1931–80), believes that reason is a potential rather than an actual source in Shi'i law. He holds that while reason can discover a religious injunction on its own, in actual practice the categorical verdicts in Shi'i jurisprudence have always been derived from the Qur'an and the tradition.

ORIGINS OF THE LAW

The Shari'ah

The *Shari'ah* or the ethical and religious law looms large in the religious discourse of Islam. Literally, *Shari'ah* means the 'path' or 'road' leading to water. Like water, it is a life-giving source on the road to moral and ethical felicity. This path is ordained and revealed by God himself. For Muslims the *Shari'ah* embodies the will of God since it is God who is the author of the law. One may call the law of Islam the totality of ordinances laid down by the Prophet of God in matters of religion. According to one definition the *Shari'ah* comprises the unequivocal ordinances of the Qur'an and the *sunnah* as understood literally.

Contingencies not catered for by the revealed *Shari'ah* are met by legal ordinances formulated by lawyer-theologians or jurists. Through meticulous research, jurists arrive at new formulations by means of *ijtihad*. This gave rise to the science of *fiqh* (jurisprudence), a word which literally means 'to understand'. In time the principles and methods on the basis of which jurisprudence was practised also became formalised into a science called *usul al-fiqh* (literally, 'roots' of understanding). While there is a theoretical and qualitative difference between *fiqh* derived by human beings and the original revealed *Shari'ah*, such subtleties are not always observed in practice. All juristic formulations and deductions are ordinarily described as the *Shari'ah*.

Schools of law

During the second and third centuries of Islam major intellectual movements in both law and theology emerged. In various centres in Arabia, as well as Egypt, Syria and Iraq, religious thought flourished. Students formed study circles around certain well-known scholars, and in the process a variety of schools of thought developed whose concern lay with elaborating and interpreting the Qur'an and *hadith* materials.

Although there was an early proliferation of schools for nearly three centuries, four have managed to survive to this day. In Kufah (Iraq) but of Persian extract was Nu'man bin Thabit (d. 767), better known by his agnomen Abu Hanifah. His school was characterised by the exercise of free opinion and stood in good favour with the Abbasid dynasty. In Madinah, Malik ibn Anas (d. 795), formed a school relying on the 'living tradition' of the city as the key feature of his thinking. The third school is known as the Shafi' school, founded by al-Shafi'i (d. 819). He was a pupil of Malik, and played a great role in the development of Islamic thought. The feature of this school is that it bases its opinion on 'the most sound *hadith* to be found on a subject'. In the third century, a pupil of al-Shafi'i, Ibn Hanbal (d. 855), gained a substantial following in Baghdad. He was well known for his rigid traditionalism and staunchly opposed the rationalist currents of his day.

Legal reform

From the earliest days of Islam the disparities in the interpretations and rules of the law were a cause for concern. Ibn al-Muqaffa' (d. 756), a capable Persian writer, counselled the Abbasid caliph, Abu Ja'far al-Mansur, to codify the law. One of the reasons why this attempt was unsuccessful was the suspicion the early jurists had for state patronage. Hence, the *Shari'ah* remained officially uncodified until the nineteenth century. Prior to this, in the seventeenth century, the Indian sultan Awrangzeb instructed a committee of his country's leading academic jurists to compile the most distinguished verdicts in one compendium. This semi-official compilation called the *Verdicts of Alamgiri* reflected only the views of the Hanafi school. In the later nineteenth century, the Ottoman state charged a seven-man committee to prepare a civil code. The Committee of the Majallah, as it came to be known, enacted several pieces of legislation in modern form which applied in the territories of the Ottoman empire until its demise in 1924.

In the twentieth century the pioneers of the *salafiyah* movement, al-Afghani (1839–97), Muhammad 'Abduh and his disciple Rashid Rida, all advocated legal reform in line with the spirit of the Qur'an. In addition, they emphasised that use be made of the authentic *hadith* of the *salaf*, early pious ancestors, from which the movement takes its name. Modern scholars like Muhammad Asad (b. 1900), Fazlur Rahman (1919–88), and the late 'Abd al-Razzaq al-Sanhuri, have actively campaigned for legal reform.

ORIGINS OF ISLAMIC THEOLOGY AND PHILOSOPHY

In order to understand Islamic theology and philosophy it is useful to explain their intellectual and political history. The beginnings of what is today known as Islamic theology and philosophy are intricately interwoven with the conflicts of the early political history of Islam. Two distinct periods feature in the discussion below. The period after the death of Muhammad (632–61 CE) is seen as an extension of the 'golden age' of the Prophet. This is followed by the era of dynasties – the Umayyad (661–750) and the Abbasid (750–1258), which for many people also represent the 'golden age' when the Islamic imperium controlled large parts of the globe.

Civil strife and sectarianism: The rise of ideology

The period after the Prophet's death was followed by some three decades of rule (632–61) by four of his senior companions, known as the caliphs, 'Abu Bakr, 'Umar, 'Uthman and 'Ali. Their rule is famed as the period of the 'Righteous Successors'. An indication of the political climate in post-Muhammadan Arabia is the fact that three of the four caliphs died at the hands of assassins.

During the reigns of 'Uthman and 'Ali political upheaval reached a high point, producing a large number of schisms and sects. The origins of these sects are invariably related to some practical and political issues. Eventually these struggles coalesced into the schools of dogma and theology which were to be found in early Islam.

It must be borne in mind that in the Arabian Peninsula of the seventh century, Islam was both the faith and patriotism of individuals and of society. Islam was the official credo of the state-community, known as the *ummah*. The rules of government, religious ritual and dogma were all derived from the same religious source and authority – God and the Prophet. Where politics and religion were so inextricably interwoven, dissent from the state-community was adjudged an act of disloyalty and heresy. Deviation in politics implied being unfaithful to religion, and vice versa.

The early sects

Shi'ism

Dissatisfaction within the rapidly expanding Muslim empire was fuelled by a dispute over the succession to the caliphate between the followers of 'Ali and of Mu'awiyah, who later became the first caliph of the Umayyad dynasty. Those who pressed for 'Ali's special right to the leadership based their claim on 'Ali's closeness to the Prophet through both family and marital ties, and on the grounds that he had been the first Muslim converted as a child, and had been designated the Prophet's successor, the supreme spiritual leader or imam of the Muslim community. The 'divine light' from Muhammad had been passed on to 'Ali, it was claimed. Propagating these claims was a group whose members called themselves the party of 'Ali – *Shi'at 'Ali*, and eventually became known as the 'Partisans' or *Shi'ah*.

As this movement expanded it pressed 'Ali's claim as the Prophet's spiritual heir. Shi'ahs believe that on returning from the Farewell Pilgrimage the Prophet delivered a sermon at a place called Ghadir Khumm, where he said: 'For whomsoever I am his master and authority, 'Ali will be his master. O God! Befriend the friends of 'Ali and be hostile to his enemies.' According to the Shi'ahs, the spiritual heirs of Muhammad must be as pure and sinless as the Prophet was. Only 'Ali and his patrilineal descendants inherited this quality. Each successor is an imam who is a source of divine grace and inspiration, and together they form the Shi'i spiritual hierarchy.

The Shi'ahs can be divided into three major groups. The majority who follow a line of twelve imams are called the 'Twelvers'. Twelver Shi'ism is also the official tradition of Iran. Adherents of this branch are to be found in Iraq, India, Pakistan and Afghanistan. The second group are the seven-imam Shi'ahs – the 'Seveners', who are also called the Isma'ilis. They are a diffuse group in India, Africa, parts of Syria and Iran, whose current spiritual head is the Agha Khan. The five-imam Shi'ahs are also called the Zaydis, who are found in the Yemen. In many respects the last group closely resembles the Sunnis.

Hostility between the orthodox Sunnis and the more mystical and philosophical Shi'ahs has continued through the centuries, except for rare occasions of mutual tolerance. Under the Umayyad dynasty (661–750) the persecution of the Shi'ahs reached its height. In the early years of Abbasid rule (750–1258) Shi'ism enjoyed some amount of freedom. The Shi'ahs also established their own dynasty in Egypt, known as the Fatimid dynasty which lasted for 202 years (969–1171 CE), until Egypt was re-conquered for Sunnism by Salah al-Din Ayyubi (Saladdin) in 1171.

One modern Shi'i scholar views the emergence of Sunnism and Shi'ism as providential, enabling Islam to satisfy different psychological and spiritual temperaments. However, despite the conciliatory overtures of modern scholars, the mainstream traditions of Sunnism and Shi'ism each view themselves as exclusively orthodox.

The Khawarij

The divisions among Arabs caused by the dispute over the succession to the caliphate polarised doctrinal issues. At the height of the conflict between the factions, 'Ali accepted Mu'awiyah's offer of arbitration 'according to the will of God'. While the outcome of the arbitration was confusing and unclear, what is certain is that it failed to resolve the dispute and in fact gave rise to the formation of further political parties.

'Ali's acceptance of human arbitration infuriated a group of Bedouin tribesmen who took exception on theological grounds. They denounced him for submitting to arbitration when his claim to succession was in their belief in the right. Theirs was a fanatical and literal adherence to the axiom, 'there is no rule but the rulership of God'. Anyone who did not accept their doctrines or committed a major sin was viewed as committing infidelity (*kufr*).

The Khawarij, or Seceders as they were called, introduced a radical egalitarian doctrine of political justice into the religious discourse of Islam. They were quick to recognise the implications of the power struggles among the Arab aristocracy and mobilised the rural people in uprisings. They were the first, moreover, to raise the question of human rights in Islam and opposed the tyranny of the state. While the Shi'ahs claimed that only a patrilineal descendant of 'Ali could be an imam, the Khawarij argued that any virtuous Muslim, even a slave, could be the imam. Ultimately, they believed that in pursuing justice by enforcing the Law 'there would be no need for the Imamate and the state, both logically and doctrinally will "wither away" – only the rule of Law would prevail'.[5]

Doctrines of qadar (free will) and jabr (predestination)

Denouncing all acts of injustice, the Khawarij were perhaps the first group of Muslims to advocate the doctrine of *qadar* (free will). They held that individuals were personally responsible for their acts and not God. These arguments were fuelled after Islam's contact with Syrian Christianity, where the debate on free will and predestination was already in progress. The doctrine of *jabr*, which literally means 'compulsion', is based on the assumption that both man and his acts were created by God and therefore the question of human responsibility is irrelevant. The Umayyads, who were opposed to the Khawarij and Shi'ahs, found in *jabr* a useful doctrinal ally. Their legitimacy rested on the view that it was an act of God – *jabr* (predeterminism) – that entitled them to rule.

Within political circles exponents of *qadar* and *jabr* found willing followers. Two Qadarites (Voluntarists) of note were Ma'bad al-Juhani (d. 699) and Ghaylan al-Dimashqi (d. 743). While Ma'bad held moderate views, Ghaylan was an extremist. Contrary to the Shi'ahs and in agreement with the Khawarij, he held that any person, not only members of the Quraysh tribe, to which Muhammad had belonged, can qualify to be an imam. Both Ghaylan and Ma'bad were executed after being accused of conspiring against the Umayyads.

Among the Jabarites (Predestinarians), Jahm bin Safwan (d. 746) was the most prominent. His views were similar to those of the Mu'tazilah (Rationalists), holding that the Qur'an was created and not uncreated as the majority of people believed.

The Murji'ah

Following a middle path between these two extreme groups were the Murji'ah (Suspenders of Judgement). They tried to avoid passing judgement on those with whom they differed. Judgement was the prerogative of God, they argued. Their opinions on the issue of justice were of a theological and philosophical kind. The Murji'ah claimed the support of leading scholars, especially Hasan al-Basri (642–728 CE) and the jurist Abu Hanifah. Though neither of them seem to have been members, some of their views strikingly resembled those of the Murji'ah.

Hasan especially, who had good relations with the Umayyads, held views which were neither strictly Qadarite or Jabarite. Several scholars suspect him of being overtly supportive of the political regime. This is largely because he distinguished between political and ethical justice. He favoured order and solitude to disorder and chaos. Invoking the Qur'an (4: 62) he argued in support of the authority of the rulers but also cautioned them against injustice and oppression. Asked whether humans were the authors of their own actions, Hassan replied: 'Guidance comes from God but wrong-doing comes from humans.' He spoke of human actions being dependent on the volition (*qadar*) of God but insisted that specific acts involved the moral and religious responsibility of the individual.

The Mu'tazilah

Concern for political justice characterises the sectarian milieu of the second and third centuries of Islam. Hasan al-Basri's student, Wasil bin 'Ata' (699–749 CE) once asked his teacher what the status of a grave sinner would be. Al-Basri's reluctance to give a ruling on the question caused Wasil to leave the master's study circle. The break-away group came to be known as the Mu'tazilah, literally meaning the 'Separatists'. For Wasil and his followers, political justice was of primary concern. He contended that in failing to pronounce on a grave sinner, Hasan had relieved such a person from responsibility. This meant setting aside the political principle of justice, and thus undermined the spirit and purpose of the revelation and the *Shari'ah*.

Like the Khawarij and the Qadarites, the Mu'tazilah placed great emphasis on justice and called themselves the 'Partisans of Justice and Unity of God'. Humans were the authors of their own actions – both just and unjust deeds, good as well as bad. This notion was soon overshadowed by an understanding of the justice of God in the wider theological advance of Mu'tazilism. The Mu'tazilah believed that God can only do justice and good for man. Failing to do so, such a deity would be neither just nor God. In other words, God is obligated to the Mu'tazilites' own ratiocinations. There were undoubtedly Hellenistic and Stoic influences on their doctrines which later influenced Muslim theology.

In order to safeguard the utter transcendence of God, the Mu'tazilah maintained that the Divine attributes should be interpreted in a rational spirit. Anthropomorphism – likening God to a human being – was anathema to them. But in the process of denying anthropomorphism they virtually negated all the Divine attributes. For this reason they were labelled the *mu'attila*, the deniers of all Divine attributes. Reason, they believed, had parity with revelation. Consistent with their views about the Divine attributes was their denial that the Speech of God was a divine attribute. The consequence of this line of reasoning was that they described the Qur'an, the Word of God, as created.

This belief caused serious controversy in the ninth century CE when the Mu'tazilite creed was adopted as the state tradition by the Caliph al-Ma'mun (d. 833). Those who opposed this doctrine were severely persecuted, especially Ibn Hanbal (d. 855), who tirelessly resisted its imposition. While Mu'tazilism introduced some creative elements into the systematic study of theology, it also caused more orthodox practitioners to go to the other extreme in stressing divine power, will, grace and determinism.

Islam and Hellenism

It is evident from a study of the theological divisions within Islam that Hellenistic and Stoic culture and philosophy were important influences on the development of Islamic religious ideas. While they were a source of enrichment to Islam's own cultural ethos, they also posed a severe challenge to traditional Islamic thought.

Arabic translations of Greek and Syriac texts made during the reign of the Abbasid caliph al-Ma'mun were among the first fruits of Islam's contact with Hellenism and Greek philosophy. Al-Ma'mun founded an academy, called the *Bayt al-Hikmah* (House of Wisdom), where scholarly work and philosophical reflection were encouraged by state patronage. Interestingly, it was the Syrian Christians, especially the Nestorians and the Jacobites, who were responsible for passing on the Greek legacy to the Muslims.

Islamic philosophy

Some scholars deny that philosophy in Islam started with the translation of Greek texts, and argue that certain verses in the Qur'an reveal a reflective attitude towards life. According to this argument, Greek thought only provided a spur to an existing philosophical current within Islam, which later developed into a systematic mode of thought.

The emergence of legal reasoning in early Islam provides further evidence of an original Muslim contribution to philosophical thought. In order to explicate the law, Muslim jurists developed appropriate rules and methods of legal reasoning which were of a philosophical nature.[6] These juristic modes of interpretation – analogy, deduction and the classification of knowledge – were produced in a milieu largely insulated from the intellectual influences of Hellenism. A plausible explanation may be that the Muslim thinkers responded favourably to Greek thought since they shared a similar intellectual interest in philosophy.

Muslim philosophers came to be known as the *falasifah*, a term likely to have been derived from Greek. Theologians who used dialectical methods of argument were known as the *mutakallimun*. Their works, though not exclusively so, were more of a polemical and defensive nature directed against some of the theologically unacceptable premisses and ideas of the philosophers. The *mutakallimun* argued from premisses originating from religious doctrine, which were rejected by the philosophers on the grounds that they could not be proved logically. This method of the *mutakallimun* is called dialectical reasoning. The philosophers in turn argued from premisses which were established as logically certain and unchallengeable, known as demonstrative reasoning.

The theologians dealt with the speculative content of Islamic beliefs. They employed both the authority of religious texts and acceptable philosophical methods. The philosophers were not obliged to invoke the authority of religious texts in support of their arguments. Although some did, others held reason to be equal to revelation. It goes without saying that given their respective approaches, there was little love lost between the philosophers and the dialectical theologians.

Among the leading Muslim philosophers were al-Kindi (801–73 CE), 'Abu Bakr al-Razi (865–925), al-Farabi (870–950), Ibn Miskaway (933–1030), Ibn Sina (or Avicenna; 980–1037), Ibn Bajjah (or Avempace; d. 1138) and Ibn Rushd (Averroës; 1126–98). A number of philosophical ideas were unacceptable to the theologians. These included the dominant Aristotelian dualism in philosophical thought as to the eternity of matter which stood in opposition to God; and also deism, in terms of which God is recognised but has no will. God is not the efficient cause of things, according to this argument, but pure energy and the final cause of things. Later Muslim philosophers renounced Aristotelian metaphysics and turned to neo-Platonism.

Theological schools

'Abu'l Hassan al-'Ash'ari (d. *c.* 936 CE) is perhaps the most famous exponent of theological dialectics (*'ilm al-kalam*). Having been under Mu'tazilite tutelage before converting to more traditional views, his theological dialectics was largely influenced by the intellectual tools of his early career. His fame as a theologian is based mainly upon his discovery of an intellectual middle ground for orthodoxy. It was in his hands that *kalam*, until then largely suspect, became an acceptable method for the theologians.

Sunni orthodoxy: The middle ground

As one of the chief defenders of the Sunni tradition, an example of Al-'Ash'ari's definition of the creed is appropriate:

> The substance of our belief is that we confess God, His angels, His apostles, the revelation of God, and what the trustworthy have handed down on the authority of God's Apostle, rejecting none of them. We confess that God is one God – there is no god but He – unique, eternal, possessing neither consort nor child; and that Muhammad is His

> Servant and Apostle, whom He sent with the guidance and the real Religion; and that Paradise is real and Hell is real; and that there is no doubt regarding the coming Hour; and that God will raise up those who are in the graves; and that God is seated on His throne . . . and that he has a face . . . and that He has two hands *bila kayfa* . . . and that there is no good or evil on earth, save what God wishes; and that things exist by God's wish; and that not a single person has the capacity to do anything until God causes him to act, and we are not independent of God, nor can we pass beyond the range of God's knowledge; and that there is no creator save God, and the works of human beings are things created and decreed by God . . . and that human beings have not the power to create anything, but are themselves created. . . .[7]

The 'science of dialectics' systematically explained Islamic beliefs in relation to revelation and prophetic tradition. The emergence of controversial doctrinal divisions only reinforced the need to develop a formal and official credal statement. The product of this effort was the orthodox middle-ground, known as the 'Followers of the Tradition and the United Community' (*ahl al-sunnah wa'l jama'ah*). The Sunnis (as they came to be known) made the *sunnah* and consensus their principal legitimising techniques. If something was deemed to be the *sunnah* and verified by consensus it qualified for acceptance in the Sunni fold.

This middle group considered its methods to be correct and disqualified all other groups as 'sects', *firaq*. Given the political and historical conditions which gave rise to sectarianism, ideology played a major role in the legitimation of schisms. Al-'Ash'ari's credal formulae are designed to refute the views of the Mu'tazilah, the Qadarites, the Jabarites, Khawarij and the philosophers.

Al-'Ash'ari reaffirmed the doctrine of occasionalism or atomism in order to prove that God recreates the world at every moment in time. Causation and potentialities in bodies as a theory was denied in favour of the direct efficacy of God in the production of events. He insisted on using the literal expressions of God's hands, face, and so forth as true expressions of the Divine attributes, adding that these should be accepted 'without asking how' – *bila kayfa*. The reason given is that God's attributes can be neither figuratively explained nor regarded as similar to human forms. On the question of human voluntarism or will-power he introduced the doctrine of acquisition, whereby all acts are created and produced by God but are attached to the will of the human being concerned who 'acquires' those acts.

Contemporaneous with al-'Ash'ari, in Samarkand (presently part of the Soviet Union) there was another theologian, 'Abu Mansur al-Maturidi, who died in 944 CE. Despite the common purpose between 'Ash'arism and Maturidism, they were not in agreement on all issues. Later reconciliation between the two schools certainly did take place, but al-'Ash'ari himself was never of the same mind as his contemporary. Al-Maturidi also believed in determinism like al-'Ash'ari, but maintained that evil acts did not occur with the good pleasure of God. He also allowed greater room for human efficacy; in later developments within this school the absolute efficacy of the human will was emphatically stated.

Sufism

Historical background

Legalism, political schisms and dissension of both a theological and a philosophical kind not only created a great deal of instability within the Muslim lands, but also contributed to growing cynicism and scepticism among more serious-minded people. As a result some of them sought refuge in more intense meditative and esoteric practices, which came to be known as Sufism.

The proponents of Sufism argue that Muhammad's religious and social consciousness was underpinned and informed by an acute mystical experience. They obviously refer to his earliest visions of the Holy Spirit and his mystical sojourn, known as the *Mi'raj*, which are alluded to in the Qur'an. The practice of the art of the esoteric (*tasawwuf*) or following the spiritual path (*tariqah*) is thus seen as the 'inner' dimension of the 'outer' practice of the *Shari'ah*.

The word *tasawwuf* literally means 'to dress in wool', a reference to the ascetic mode of dress adopted by the early practitioners of mysticism. Another explanation traces its origin from the word *safa*', meaning 'to be pure'. In the West *tasawwuf* is known as Sufism.

The spiritual path or *tariqah* is rooted in both the Qur'an and the prophetic practice, and it gained great momentum in the eighth to ninth centuries CE. The increasing worldliness and secularism of the Umayyad dynasty, as well as the tumultuous political controversies of the age, created in many a desire to practise greater abstinence and personal piety. This impulse towards ascetic piety also served to correct the impersonal development of Islamic law, by providing that authentic ethos which appeared to have suffered at the hands of legalism and theology.

What is Sufism?

The Sufis' ideal model is the Prophet, from whom they receive divine grace. Some of the Companions are also viewed as models of renunciation, like 'Abu Bakr and 'Ali. Sufism or *tasawwuf* attempts to instil within the novice the ability to go beyond a purely mechanical obedience to God. Another Companion of the Prophet, 'Abu Dharr al-Ghiffari, who deeply interiorised the moral motive, became one of the leading figures of the early ascetism of Islam.

The Sufi discourse seeks to combine the *Shari'ah* and the spiritual path (*tariqah*). It focuses on the literal meaning of things (*tafsir*) as the entry point to their inner meaning, which tends towards allegory and symbolism (*ta'wil*). Some Sufis provide as an illustration the symbol of a geometric circle. From the centre a number of radii connect with the circumference of the circle. The circumference represents the *Shari'ah*, which comprises the 'totality of the Muslim community'. Each radius symbolises the various spiritual paths or *tariqahs* that emanate from the centre, which in turn represents the *Haqiqah* or Truth. It is the centre which is the source of both the *Shari'ah* and the *Haqiqah*.

Several theories have been proposed to account for the syncretic nature of Sufism. According to some, it is adapted from elements of neo-Platonism, Christianity, Judaism, Zoroastrianism, Hinduism and Buddhism. However, more earnest practitioners deny these claims. It is plausible to say that while Sufism was located within the prophetic and Qur'anic framework, many practices adopted later share features of mysticism found in other, non-Islamic traditions.

Sufi practices

The emphasis in Sufi practice is on remembrance of God in order to attain a close relationship with the Divine. These practices include repeating the names of God and singing hymns to his glory and greatness. A number of mystics concentrated their efforts on awakening absolute trust in God, which later became an important theme in Sufism. When the faith of the novice is perfected he or she attains an inner illumination, known as interior knowledge. In contrast to learnedness, this is an intuitive knowledge, which mystics describe as knowing 'by' God.

There are also various levels of proximity to God. Sufi orders define the higher stages of union with God as *fana'* (extinction) and *baqa'* (survival). These are indicative of the experience the mystic undergoes by obeying the law and engaging in meditative practices or *muraqabah*. '*Fana'* and *baqa'* are two sides of the same experience',[8] where total self-effacement (*fana'*) is achieved and union with the Divine is accomplished and subsistence continues in him (*baqa'*).

The novice in the Sufi path selects a teacher who is called a *shaykh*, *pir* or *murad*. Under the supervision of this teacher the novice is guided along the mystical path. There are various spiritual brotherhoods with their own distinguishing characteristics. Early brotherhoods had an established retreat (*ribat*) where novices came to spend time with their mentors. After a novitiate or period of early training, the 'seeker' would be invested on graduation with the *khirqah* or mantle, when the teacher was confident that the novice is capable of inducting others into the Sufi path.

Some of the famous Sufi brotherhoods are the Qadiriyyah order, named after 'Abd al-Qadir Jilani (1078–1166 CE), one of the greatest saints in Sufism, and the Suhrawardiyyah order, founded by al-Suhrawardi (1144–1234); another major order was founded by al-Shadhili (1196–1258).

The Sufi view of ultimate reality

The way in which Sufis view ultimate reality is perhaps the most important part of the mystical path. The doctrine relating to ultimate reality is known as the doctrine of *wahdat al-wujud* (unity of being), which has had a controversial career in Islamic intellectual history. S. H. Nasr maintains that this doctrine stems from the Muslim 'witness' (*shahadah*) in which God's sovereignty is proclaimed:

> It asserts that there cannot be two completely independent orders of reality or being which would be sheer polytheism or *shirk* . . . The

> relation between God and the order of existence is not just a logical one in which if one thing is equal to another the other is equal to the first. Through that mystery which lies in the heart of creation itself, everything is, in essence, identified with God while God infinitely transcends everything. To understand this doctrine intellectually is to possess contemplative intelligence; to realise it fully is to be a saint who alone sees "God everywhere".

Although criticised from various quarters, the doctrine of the unity of being remains central to Sufi discourse. The Indian mystic, Ahmad Sirhindi (1564–1624), better known as 'the Renewer of the second thousand years', reinterpreted the doctrine, and it reached its fullest expression in the writings of the Spanish mystic, Ibn 'Arabi (1165–1240 CE), who settled in Egypt and died in Damascus. Sirhindi declared that the experience of *fana'* (extinction) and *baqa'* (survival) can be compared to a dream and has no independent reality. Similarly, the doctrine of the 'unity of being' is only a matter of subjective perception or *shuhud*. The concept of *Wahdat as-shuhud* (unity of being in vision), which is a reinterpretation of the mystical idea of unity of being, insists that God is completely and absolutely 'other' and is not one with the world. 'God is one being, and the world is another, and the two beings have nothing in common.'

For Sirhindi reality is dual and not unitary. His basic thesis is that this dualism is not ultimate; 'for although the world is not one with God it does proceed from God'. He also believed that while the existence of God is real that of the world is imaginary and unreal. In reality only God exists, in his Oneness. Sirhindi held that God excludes the world since there is in reality only One Being. The world being imaginary 'the presence of an unreal image by no means threatens the unity of the Real Being'.

This view differs marginally from that of Ibn 'Arabi. Identity, according to the latter, is one being and indivisible. For Ibn 'Arabi reality is one all-inclusive Existence which can be seen from different angles. Seen from the one, it is God and from the other, it is the world. He considered all created things to be manifestations of God, which does not mean he equated creation with God. The universe was linked to God by archetypes in the divine mind. In other words, 'things exist because they have been perceived by God'.[9] According to Ibn 'Arabi, the unity of being was consistent with *tawhid*, the fundamental principle of belief in Islam.

Ibn 'Arabi also advocated that the purpose of creation is to become the perfect human. Humanity is the microcosm which reflects the glory of God – the macrocosm. All prophets reflected this glory of God and became 'the friends of God', *awliya* (sing. *wali*). He himself claimed to be a *wali* and the 'seal of the friends of God'. Ibn 'Arabi was charged with claiming that the quality of being 'a friend of God' is higher than prophecy, a contention which led to great controversy.

Decades prior to Ibn 'Arabi, the Persian theologian and Sufi, al-Ghazali (1058–1111), tried to realign mysticism with theology. But Ibn 'Arabi's theories of 'friends of God' and his identification of the world with God gave him notoriety among the theologians. It ran counter to al-Ghazali's sobering effects on *tasawwuf*.

Types of Sufism

Denny uses three useful categories to classify the various trends of Sufism – sober Sufism, antinomian Sufism and intoxicated Sufism.

Sober Sufism is practised by *Shari'ah*-minded disciples. Practitioners do not allow Sufi practices to violate the religious law and in fact constantly strive to seek realignment between *tasawwuf* and the *Shari'ah*. The majority of Sufis fall in this category, including al Basri (d. 728 CE), the celebrated woman mystic Rabi'ah al-'Adawiyah (d. 801), Junayd al-Baghdadi (d. 910), al-Ghazali and al-Rumi (d. 1273).

Antinomian Sufism, the second of Denny's categories, rejects the *Shari'ah* or the letter of it. They favour pure dependence on God alone. The most famous group in this category is the ninth-century Malamatiyah branch. As the name indicates, the group hoped to earn the reproach of people. They refused to gain approval of people and were concerned with purely obeying God in a sincere manner without ostentation of any kind.

Intoxicating Sufism seeks to reach union with God at all costs. Love and passion seem to be the central elements of this category. Some of the utterances of Sufis in a state of intoxication offended the theologians and ordinary people. Abu Yazid al-Bistami, who died in 875, once exclaimed: 'Glory to Me! How Great is My Majesty!' While ordinary folk interpreted this to be either madness or self-praise, the Sufi saw this as acknowledging an intense proximity to God. Another mystic, al-Hallaj (d. 922), ended up as a martyr for his beliefs. He uttered *ana al-Haqq*, 'I am God' (literally, 'I am the Truth'), and made claims to miraculous powers. In the end he was crucified in Baghdad when the religious establishment and authorities found his views intolerable.

THE FIVE PILLARS OF ISLAM

Common to all Muslims are the 'Five Pillars of Islam', the fundamental religious practices or rites by which faith is expressed. These are the confession of faith (*Shahadah*); prayer (*salah*); fasting (*saum*); alms (*zakah*); and pilgrimage (*hajj*).

The confession of faith

The formal expression of faith in Islam is the utterance of the *kalimah*, 'There is no god but God and Muhammad is the Messenger of God'. According to Islamic doctrine, this formula should be uttered at least once in a person's lifetime in a loud and clear manner. To understand and believe the truth of this credal formula is a prerequisite of faith. As consequence of this belief a number of other beliefs are derived. They are belief in angels, books, messengers, decrees of good and evil, and in resurrection after death.

Angels

According to Muslim tradition angels are created out of light and are sexless. The religious sources are not definite about their true nature. What is known is that they act as functionaries of the Divine Will and execute God's commands. Famous among the angels is Gabriel (Jibril) who is the agent of revelation to all the prophets in history. Two other high angels are Israfil who will sound the trumpet on the day of resurrection and Michael (Mika'il) who is in charge of general planning in the cosmic world. Then there are also angels assigned to each person who record all his or her activities. Among those angels who have fallen is Satan (Iblis or Shaytan) who lost his status for his refusal to salute Adam on God's instruction.

Books and messengers

Both these elements are connected. Muslims are required to affirm the revelatory and heavenly nature of all holy books. Special emphasis is placed on the following books (*kutub*, sing. *kitab*): the Torah (*Tawrah*) of Moses, the Psalms (*Zabur*) of David, the Bible (*Injil*) of Jesus and the Qur'an of Muhammad. Scriptures given to Abraham and other prophets are called sheets (*suhuf*). No count has been kept of how many scriptures, major or minor, have been circulated in the world.

Similarly, Muslims are also required to believe that all the prophets in history, especially those in the Judaeo-Christian tradition mentioned in the Qur'an, preached the same message of God's lordship in different circumstances. Tradition has it that approximately 124 000 prophets were sent to the world, an indication of the pervasiveness of the prophetic communication in the Islamic world-view. The significance of these two beliefs underlines the deference Muslims accord to the faith and belief-systems of others, especially when the Qur'an emphasises that all people in history have been the recipients of divine teachings.

Decrees of good and evil

This is perhaps the most controversial article of faith. In the mainstream doctrine of al-'Ash'ari's theological school it is widely accepted that good and evil are decreed by God. This doctrine is known as *qada' wa 'l-qadar*, divine decree and predestination. However, in more revisionist interpretations of Sunnism this doctrine is not widely accepted. Modern scholars are inclined to interpret it to mean that human beings have responsibility for their deeds.

Resurrection

The belief in resurrection after death, accountability to God and judgement forms part of the Qur'an's eschatology. The 'Final Day', or 'the Hour' as the Qur'an terms it, signals the end of the world and the beginning of a new eternal life. This doctrine is emphasised in view of the pagan Arab rejection of any meaningful purpose of life and the after-life. When the trumpeter signals the end of time, all people shall be presented to God for judgement. The sinners shall be doomed in Hell and the righteous shall attain the enjoyment of Paradise. On that day, the righteous shall have the opportunity to see God, in the same way that the full moon is seen on a clear night. This will be the supreme reward of the faithful, an experience that will lead to ultimate bliss.

Worship

Literally *salah* means 'to supplicate'. In the ritual practice of Islam it refers to the five daily prayers. These prayers are named after the various times of the day at which they are performed. The earliest appointed time for prayers is before sunrise is the morning (*fajr*). This is followed by the midday (*zuhr*) and afternoon ('*asr*) prayers. Shortly after sunset (*maghrib*) and an hour later ('*isha*') are the occasions for the evening and night prayers.

Each prayer has a specific set of postures, called *rak'ah* (pl. *raka'at*). Each set involves a period of standing, bending and two prostrations. Prayers generally consist of units of two or four *rak'ah* but at times solitary units are also prayed. Prior to worshipping, worshippers are required to perform a ceremonial wash, called *wudu'*.

Congregational prayer is strongly encouraged. For this reason the *mu'adhdhin* (the caller to prayer) calls the worshippers to the mosque at every prayer-hour. In pre-modern times the *mu'adhdhin* would ascend to the minaret of the mosque in order to be heard effectively. Nowadays modern electronic amplification is used.

In terms of significance, the *salah* is perhaps the most important act of worship in the life of a Muslim after the confession of faith. It is viewed as the central pillar that upholds the canopy of spirituality. The Prophet of Islam had stressed prayer, and even held it to be the distinguishing mark between belief and unbelief.

Prayer is expected to produce a specific spiritual effect in the soul of the believer. The consciousness of God and the awareness of divine presence and majesty are the most important effects desired from worship. Talking is prohibited during *salah*. Postures and prostrations are made in a disciplined manner in order to maintain decorum. Sprawling on the ground, speedy prostration like a cock pecking or crouching like a camel are viewed as incompatible with the dignity characteristic of humans. *Salah* is one of the main symbols of Islam and therefore it is held in public. According to Shah Wali Allah, the purpose of Friday congregational prayer is to stress this symbol.

Fasting

Abstaining from food, drink and sex from dawn to dusk is the discipline of fasting during the month of Ramadan, the tenth month of the lunar calendar. According to the Qur'an fasting is a spiritual practice, whose effect is to inculcate a sense of God-consciousness (*taqwa*).

The physical restrictions of fasting combined with the remembrance of God, giving charity, recitation of the Qur'an and the performance of voluntary prayers are said to be therapeutic to the individual psyche. This spiritual practice is meant to convert the individual from practices which are injurious to spiritual and moral well-being. Through fasting the faithful demonstrate their desire to sacrifice personal comfort and pleasure and show restraint in order to win the pleasure of the Creator. The end of the month of fasting is celebrated with the Feast of Ending the Fast ('*Id al-Fitr*).

Alms-giving

This is the compulsory tax in Islam. All people owning wealth above a specified taxable amount must pay towards the social upliftment of the underprivileged. On cash and metals (gold and silver) there is a 2,5 per cent tax. On agricultural produce the tax differs between 5 and 10 per cent, depending on the nature of farming. The prime function of *zakah* is to create an egalitarian Muslim society.

In spiritual terms the tax is viewed as an act which invokes God's mercy and benevolence. When a person spends in order to meet the need of others it is as if the giver had responded to a divine inspiration and served God's creation. It is an act which brings about an intimacy between Creator and creature.

Pilgrimage

This pillar is obligatory for those who can afford to visit the holy mosque in Makkah during the pilgrimage season, which takes place in the twelth month of the lunar calendar, Dhu al-Hijjah. It is the ritual of honouring the symbols of God, especially the shrine in Makkah, the *Ka'bah* (literally the cube), which is believed to have been built by the prophet Abraham and his son Ishmael as a place of monotheistic worship. The pilgrimage rites extend over a number of days. Pilgrims wear a seamless white ritual garb called the *ihram*, which symbolises their purity and other-worldly orientation. Entry points to the holy precincts are known as the *miqats* from where the pilgrims must be ritually prepared for the sacred pilgrimage.

Pilgrims walk around the *Ka'bah* seven times, which is called the ritual of *tawaf.* They also take a brisk walk between the two adjacent hills in imitation of the rituals performed by Abraham's wife Hagar. In the last three days of *hajj* the pilgrims travel to the little town of Mina, a few miles from Makkah. On the ninth day of the month of Dhu al-Hijjah they are required to stand in penance for some time on the plains of Arafat, the meeting place of Adam and Eve after they were expelled from the Garden of Eden. This is called the *wuquf* or standing ceremony, and is the most important part of the ritual, without which the *hajj* is incomplete. On their return from Arafat the pilgrims stop at a place called Muzdalifa where they pray and collect pebbles with which to pelt the symbol of the devil the next day.

The pelting of the symbol of the devil is once again a replay of the story of Abraham and Ishmael. The latter was tempted by the devil to refuse to be his father's sacrifice as God had commanded. Ishmael then rebuked the devil by pelting him with stones. This ritual symbolises each person's struggle with his or her temptations.

Finally, the pilgrims slaughter a sacrificial animal and have their hair cut or trimmed in order to symbolise the end of the restrictions of the seamless pilgrimage robe or *ihram.* This takes place on the tenth day, which is known as the Festivity of Sacrifice. The *hajj* is completed by a farewell *tawaf,* after which the pilgrims return to their homes. Those who have not been to Madinah would do so after the pilgrimage to Makkah in order to visit the grave of Muhammad and pray in his mosque. After Makkah, the Prophet's mosque in Madinah is the second most holy place of Islam, followed by the Masjid al-Aqsa in Jerusalem.

A lesser pilgrimage can be performed at any time of the year, called the '*umrah*. The *hajj*, however, can only be performed during a fixed period.

(6)? Hajj → Holy War → must be prepared to go into ~~gow~~ war for Isl faith

ISLAMIC ART

Islamic civilisation over the centuries has become a rich repository of art which is as varied as that of any other tradition. Recently there has been renewed interest in Islamic art as the Western world seeks aesthetic inspiration from other cultures of the Far and Near East. Art allows us to understand what type of world shaped the artist and how the artist viewed the world when communicating through one or other medium. Islamic art forms range from the visual mediums to music and architecture.

The philosophy of art

Specialists believe that Islamic art aesthetically expresses the fundamental concept of *tawhid*, the oneness of God. The dominant forms in Muslim art are a ceaseless symphony of lines and patterns. The patterns are mainly non-representational. When living things are represented they are normally subjected to denaturalisation in order to suppress the effect of the natural forms. Islam's aversion to representational art is attributed to its commitment to monotheism. Natural forms of art would compromise this commitment in an aesthetic sense because God completely transcends nature. Another reason for prohibition is the fear that the artist may create images of living things. In Islam the creative act is strictly reserved for God and thus it comes into conflict with doctrine. But the ban against representational art was not total. In the past some jurists permitted the artistic representation of living objects provided that the art forms did not cast a shadow.

Visual arts

One of the main visual art forms is the arabesque. It is an abstract design which may have recognisable patterns and designs. It is said that the purpose of this design is to generate within the viewer an intuition of infinity. The viewer is aesthetically released from the material world into the abstract and unseen world. Thus, through contemplation and reflection on the patterns, the observer is reminded of the Divine.

Calligraphy is another important dimension of the visual arts. This art form represents the divine word, the religious communication God made to the Prophet Muhammad. Here the artistic modes of the Qur'anic verses also become abstract, resembling the arabesque, which enhances its symbolic quality.

Architecture

Mosques are perhaps the architectural form par excellence in Islam. While they are designed to meet the needs of worshippers they are often ornately embellished with designs and patterns. In different parts of the world mosques have different shapes. In remote areas of Africa, a mosque would be a basic shelter made of wood and mud. In more prosperous surroundings they reflect the material advancement of the people. Mosques are often rectangular or round in shape. The front wall is directed towards Makkah, known as the *qiblah*. Along the centre of the wall a small niche would be cut, known as the *mihrab*. Calligraphy is often used to decorate the inside walls. Mosques have courtyards with adjacent ablution blocks. In Eastern countries large pools are used for ablution purposes. The characteristic mark of the mosque is the minaret. In pre-modern times the minaret served as a platform to call the worshippers to prayer. Today it has an aesthetic function as part of the decoration of the mosque.

Music

Music, though frowned upon by conservatives, is an integral part of Muslim culture. Folk music, military music, popular and religious music span a wide variety. To the Western ear, Islamic music has a monotonous rhythm and melodic structure. The musician constantly improvises his or her musical skills, which once again provides the intuitive quality of infinity. Vocal music is not totally absent. The recitation of the Qur'an, while not exactly musical, is certainly one of the most popular vocal art practices.

Belles lettres

Poetry (*sh'ir*) and literature (*'adab*) are two forms in which Islamic culture has made a major contribution. Poetry had been the major pastime of the pre-Islamic Arabs, a skill that continued to flourish in the Islamic era as well. Prose writing also developed, especially as literacy increased. It was primarily used to disseminate religious ideas. One of the famous productions of this kind is the *Conference of the Birds* of Al-Attar (d. 1230). In this work, through the character of birds, the mystic sets out in his journey for the search of God.

CONTEMPORARY DEVELOPMENTS IN ISLAM

The post-colonial phase of modern history has witnessed significant developments in the Muslim world. Islam's contact with Europe has to some extent irreversibly changed certain traditional features of Muslim society. The effect of this has been a growing tension between modern and traditional trends of thinking. These categories of modern and traditional should in no way be seen as watertight. People can and do subscribe to both modern and traditional ideas at the same time. The traditional or orthodox view generally maintains that Islam's self-image is unchanging, and if it does change it should not be determined by external influences. Hence a great deal of resistance to modernisation has been forthcoming from the orthodox and conservative '*ulama*' (literally, 'those who have knowledge').

From the nineteenth century onwards, modern thinkers have increasingly made an impact on Muslim society. Many of these thinkers have had a major concern for Islam and its civilisation. Some of them were educated in the West or were familiar with Western ideas. These include people like Muhammad

Abduh (d. 1905), Rashid Rida (d. 1935), Ahmad Amin (d. 1954) and Taha Husayn (d. 1973) in Egypt; Zia Gökalp (d. 1924) in Turkey; and Muhammad Iqbal (d. 1938) in India. Influenced by Western modes of thinking, these thinkers have attempted to bring about reforms in the Muslim world.

Although many Muslim countries gained political independence from the West, they were unable to rid themselves of neo-colonialism and Westernisation. In order to counter this, a revivalist tendency espousing an Islamic political and economic order emerged in many Muslim countries at the beginning of the twentieth century. These tendencies found expression in organisations like the Egyptian-based Muslim Brotherhood and the *Jama'at-i Islami* in Pakistan. For nearly five decades such revivalist activity has been dominant in Muslim countries, dubbed by the Western media as 'Islamic fundamentalism', which is a misleading term derived from developments in Christianity. Revivalists were responsible for the most eventful political development of the 1970s, the 1979 Islamic revolution in Iran. This revolution was spearheaded by the Ayatollah Khomeini (1902–89) after alliances between the major opposition forces ousted the ruling monarch, Muhammad Reza Shah Pahlavi (1919–80).

CONCLUSION

A study of Islam extends to virtually every dimension of human life. This is because Islam today is a living civilisation, in one form or another, for nearly one billion people on the globe. For many centuries prior to the rise of the West, it exerted great influence over large parts of the world. Islam, like all religions, is itself experiencing fascinating changes in its own heartland – the Middle East, Asia, large parts of Africa, Europe and North America. As a social process the multiple dimensions of this civilisation cannot be ignored by serious students of religion and society. Towards that end, this chapter forms merely an introduction.

NOTES

I gratefully acknowledge the assistance of a UCT Research Grant which made this contribution possible. I would also like to thank my friend and colleague A. K. Tayob for reading through an earlier draft of this chapter.

1. Ibn Ishaq, *The Life of Muhammad: A Translation of Ishaq's Sirat Rasul Allah*, (trans.) Alfred Guillaume (Karachi: Oxford University Press, 1970), pp. 651–652.

2. Because the notion of God is also linked to a theological complexity in Christianity, which involves the status of Jesus in terms of the Trinity, some Muslims may argue that the semantic fields of 'God' and 'Allah' are discursively different. Mindful of these considerations, I have chosen to use the word 'God' in this essay for practical reasons. The reader should consider my use of the word God to assume the standard Muslim understanding of Allah.

3. Seyyid Hossein Nasr, *Ideals and Realities of Islam* (London: George Allen & Unwin, 1971), p. 29.

4. Fazlur Rahman, *Major Themes of the Qur'an* (Minneapolis: Bibleotheca Islamica, 1980), pp. 4–5.

5. Majid Khadduri, *The Islamic Conception of Justice* (Baltimore: The Johns Hopkins University Press, 1984), p. 22.

6. Oliver Leaman, *An Introduction to Medieval Islamic Philosophy* (Cambridge: Cambridge University Press, 1985), p. 6.

7. Abu'l-Hassan al-'Ash'ari, *Al-Ibanah 'an Usul ad-Diyanah (The Elucidation of Islam's Foundation)*, (trans.) Walter Conrad Klein (New Haven, Connecticut: American Oriental Series, 1940), vol. 19, reprint, p. 50.

8. Muhammad Abdul Haq Ansari, *Sufism and Shari'ah* (Leicester: The Islamic Foundation, 1986), p. 36.

9. Frederick Mathewson Denny, *An Introduction to Islam* (New York: Macmillan Publishing Company, 1985), p. 290.

SELECT BIBLIOGRAPHY

al-Faruqi, I. *The Cultural Atlas of Islam*. New York: Macmillan, 1986

al-Faruqi, I. *Tawhid: Its Implications for Thought and Life*. Kuala Lumpur: The International Institute of Islamic Thought, 1982

Denny, F. M. *An Introduction to Islam*. New York: Macmillan Publishing Company, 1985

Nasr, S. H. *Ideals and Realities of Islam*. London: George Allen & Unwin, 1971

Rahman, F. *Islam*. Chicago: University of Chicago Press, 1966

Rahman, F. *Major Themes of the Qur'an*. Minneapolis: Bibleotheca Islamica, 1980

MAJOR LIVING AND DEAD RELIGIONS

	Near East & Europe	*India*	*China & Japan*	*Americas*	*Africa*	*Australia*
DEAD	Mesopotamian Egyptian Canaanite Hittite Greek Roman Hellenistic Germanic Celtic Persian Gnosticism Manichaeism	Pre-Vedic religion (Indus Valley religion)	Ancient Chinese & Japanese religion	Mayan Aztec Inca	Ancient Egyptian religion	
LIVING	Abrahamic: 1. Judaism 2. Christianity 3. Islam Parsees (Zoroastrianism Bahai	Hinduism: 1. Vedic 2. Upanishadic 3. Bhakti Jainism Buddhism Sikhism	Confucianism Taoism Chinese folk religion Shinto (in Japan)	Primal (e.g. Native American religions)	Primal (e.g. traditional Zulu, Xhosa, Yoruba, Nuer, Dinka)	Primal (e.g. Australian Aborigine, Maori, other Polynesian)
	New religious movements, arising in all of these regions of the world					

WORLD RELIGIONS

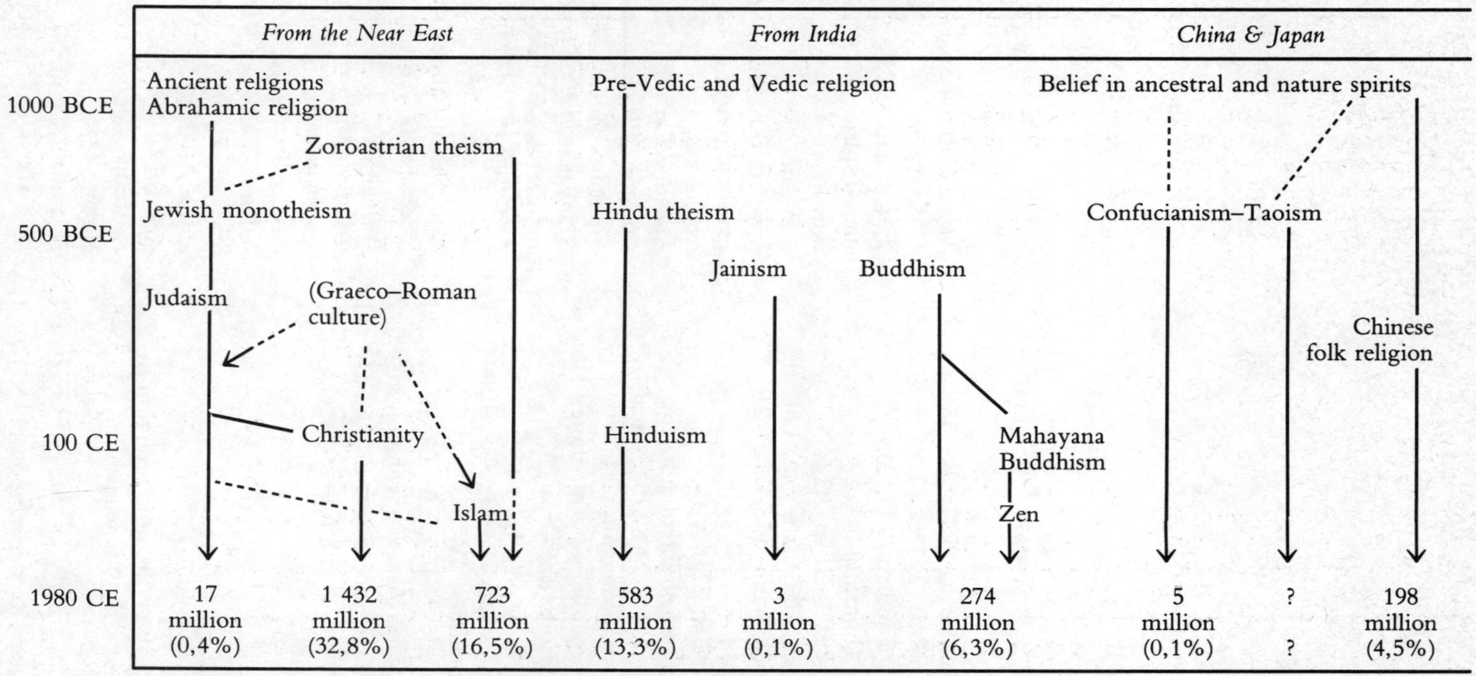

(Statistics: D. Barrett (ed), *World Christian Encyclopaedia* (Nairobi: OUP, 1982))

Index

Trompe le monde
Bossanova
Doolittle

R30 - Amanda
R40 - buy Woolf + Faulkner
R19 - sugar, tea, creamer
R13 - candles
R40 - jersey 4 Mom.
- soap + exf

Matthew
Mark
Luke
John
Acts
Romans
Corinthians I
" II
Galatians
Ephesians
Hebrews
James
Peter I
Peter II
John I
" II
" III
Jude
Revelations